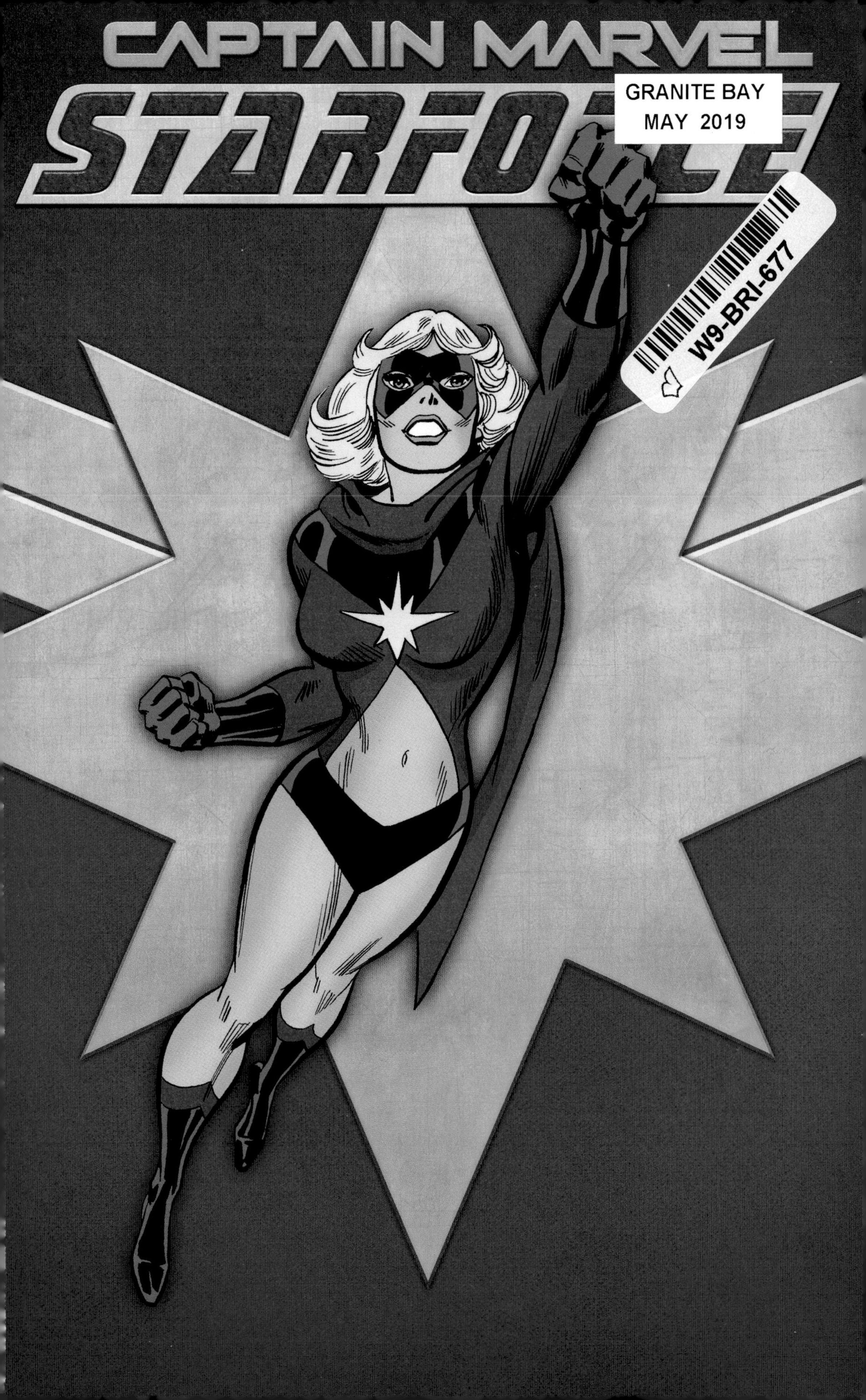
CAPTAIN MARVEL
STARFORCE

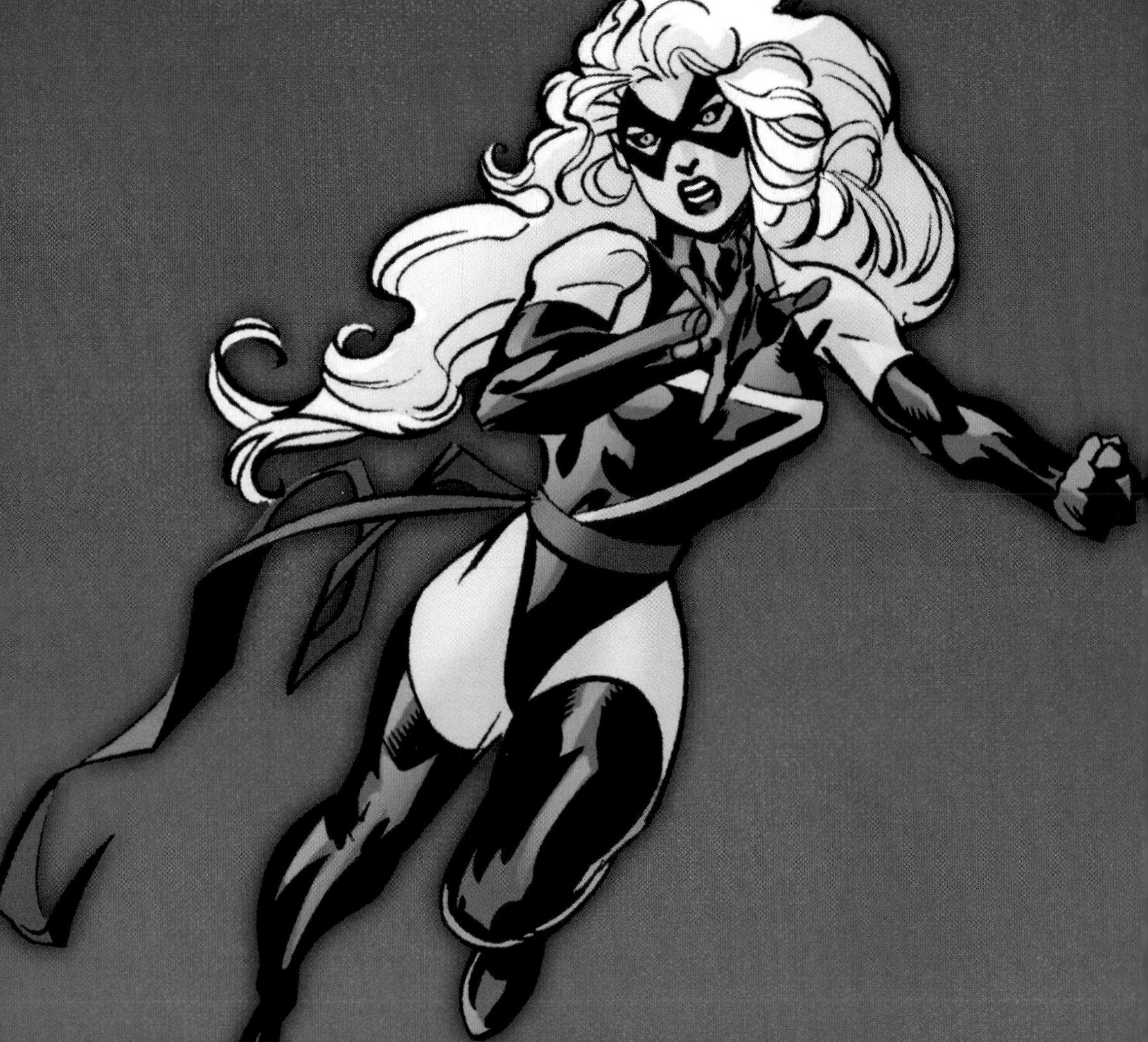

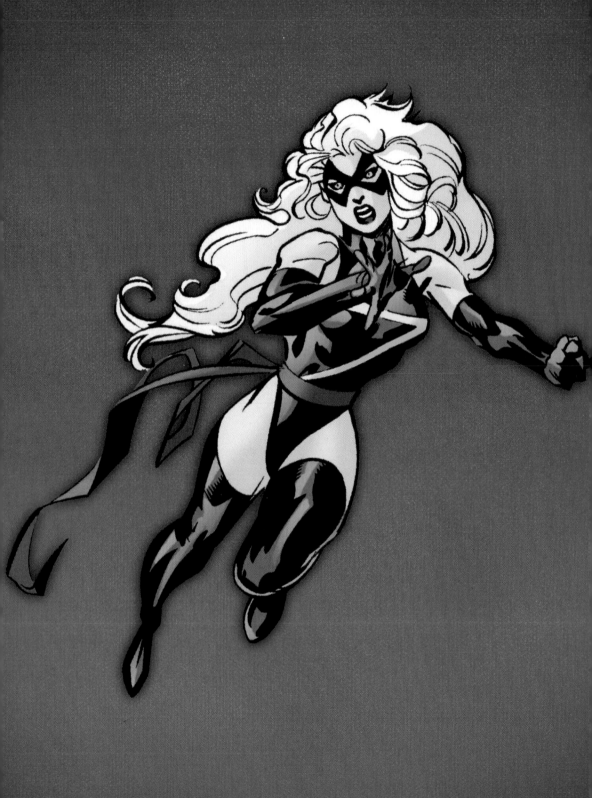

CAPTAIN MARVEL
STARFORCE

STAN LEE, GERRY CONWAY, SCOTT EDELMAN,
MARK GRUENWALD, BOB HARRAS & MARK WAID
WRITERS

JACK KIRBY, GENE COLAN, JOHN BUSCEMA, AL MILGROM,
MIKE MANLEY, RIK LEVINS, STEVE EPTING & ANDY KUBERT
PENCILERS

JOE SINNOTT, FRANK GIACOIA, TERRY AUSTIN,
DANNY BULANADI, TOM PALMER &
JESSE DELPERDANG WITH TOM MORGAN
INKERS

STAN GOLDBERG, MARIE SEVERIN, IRENE VARTANOFF,
PAUL BECTON, CHRISTIE SCHEELE, TOM PALMER,
JASON WRIGHT & DIGITAL CHAMELEON
COLORISTS

ARTIE SIMEK, JOHN COSTANZA, JANICE CHIANG,
JOE ROSEN, BILL OAKLEY & TODD KLEIN
LETTERERS

GARY FRIEDRICH, ROY THOMAS, LEN KAMINSKI, PAT GARRAHY & PAUL TUTRONE
ASSISTANT EDITORS

STAN LEE, GERRY CONWAY, ARCHIE GOODWIN,
HOWARD MACKIE, RALPH MACCHIO & MATT IDELSON
EDITORS

STEVE EPTING, TOM PALMER &
VERONICA GANDINI WITH ADAM DEL RE
FRONT COVER ARTISTS

JACK KIRBY & JOE SINNOTT
BACK COVER ARTISTS

COLLECTION EDITOR **MARK D. BEAZLEY**
ASSISTANT EDITOR **CAITLIN O'CONNELL**
ASSOCIATE MANAGING EDITOR **KATERI WOODY**
ASSOCIATE MANAGER, DIGITAL ASSETS **JOE HOCHSTEIN**
MASTERWORKS EDITOR **CORY SEDLMEIER**
SENIOR EDITOR, SPECIAL PROJECTS **JENNIFER GRÜNWALD**

VP PRODUCTION & SPECIAL PROJECTS **JEFF YOUNGQUIST**
RESEARCH & LAYOUT **JEPH YORK**
PRODUCTION **JOE FRONTIRRE**
BOOK DESIGNER **ADAM DEL RE**
SVP PRINT, SALES & MARKETING **DAVID GABRIEL**
DIRECTOR, LICENSED PUBLISHING **SVEN LARSEN**

EDITOR IN CHIEF **C.B. CEBULSKI**
CHIEF CREATIVE OFFICER **JOE QUESADA**
PRESIDENT **DAN BUCKLEY**
EXECUTIVE PRODUCER **ALAN FINE**

CAPTAIN MARVEL: STARFORCE. Contains material originally published in magazine form as FANTASTIC FOUR #65, MARVEL SUPER-HEROES #12, MS. MARVEL #1, CAPTAIN MARVEL #52, QUASAR #10, AVENGERS #346, CAPTAIN AMERICA #8 and CAPTAIN AMERICA #399. First printing 2019. ISBN 978-1-302-91797-5. Published by MARVEL WORLDWIDE, INC., a subsidiary of MARVEL ENTERTAINMENT, LLC. OFFICE OF PUBLICATION: 135 West 50th Street, New York, NY 10020. **Printed in the U.S.A.** DAN BUCKLEY, President, Marvel Entertainment; JOHN NEE, Publisher; JOE QUESADA, Chief Creative Officer; TOM BREVOORT, SVP of Publishing; DAVID BOGART, Associate Publisher & SVP of Talent Affairs; DAVID GABRIEL, SVP of Sales & Marketing, Publishing; JEFF YOUNGQUIST, VP of Production & Special Projects; DAN CARR, Executive Director of Publishing Technology; ALEX MORALES, Director of Publishing Operations; DAN EDINGTON, Managing Editor; SUSAN CRESPI, Production Manager; STAN LEE, Chairman Emeritus. For information regarding advertising in Marvel Comics or on Marvel.com, please contact Vit DeBellis, Custom Solutions & Integrated Advertising Manager, at vdebellis@marvel.com. For Marvel subscription inquiries, please call 888-511-5480. **Manufactured between 3/22/2019 and 4/23/2019 by LSC COMMUNICATIONS INC., KENDALLVILLE, IN, USA.**

10 9 8 7 6 5 4 3 2 1

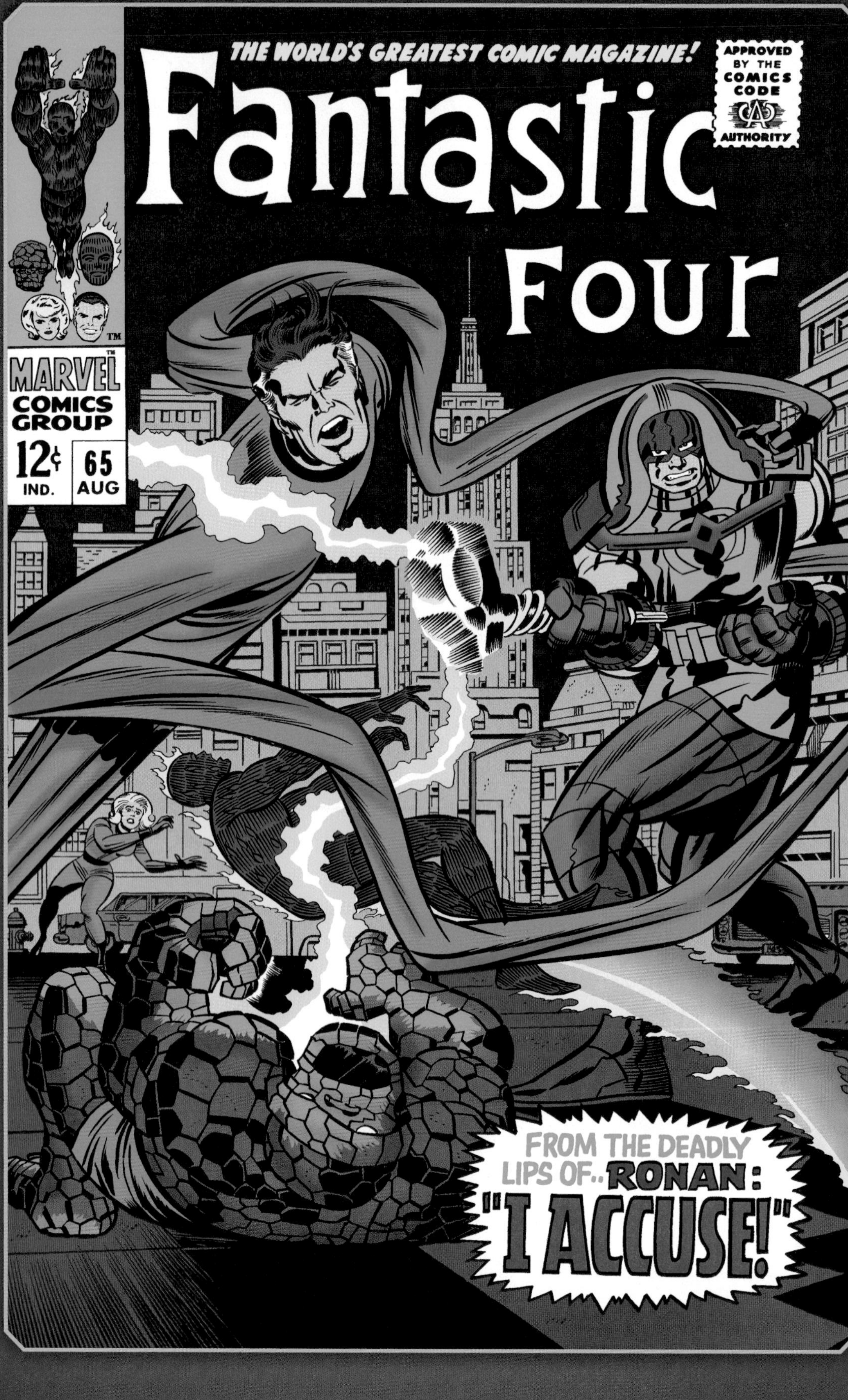
THE WORLD'S GREATEST COMIC MAGAZINE!
Fantastic Four
APPROVED BY THE COMICS CODE AUTHORITY
MARVEL COMICS GROUP
12¢ IND.
65 AUG
FROM THE DEADLY LIPS OF.. RONAN:
"I ACCUSE!"

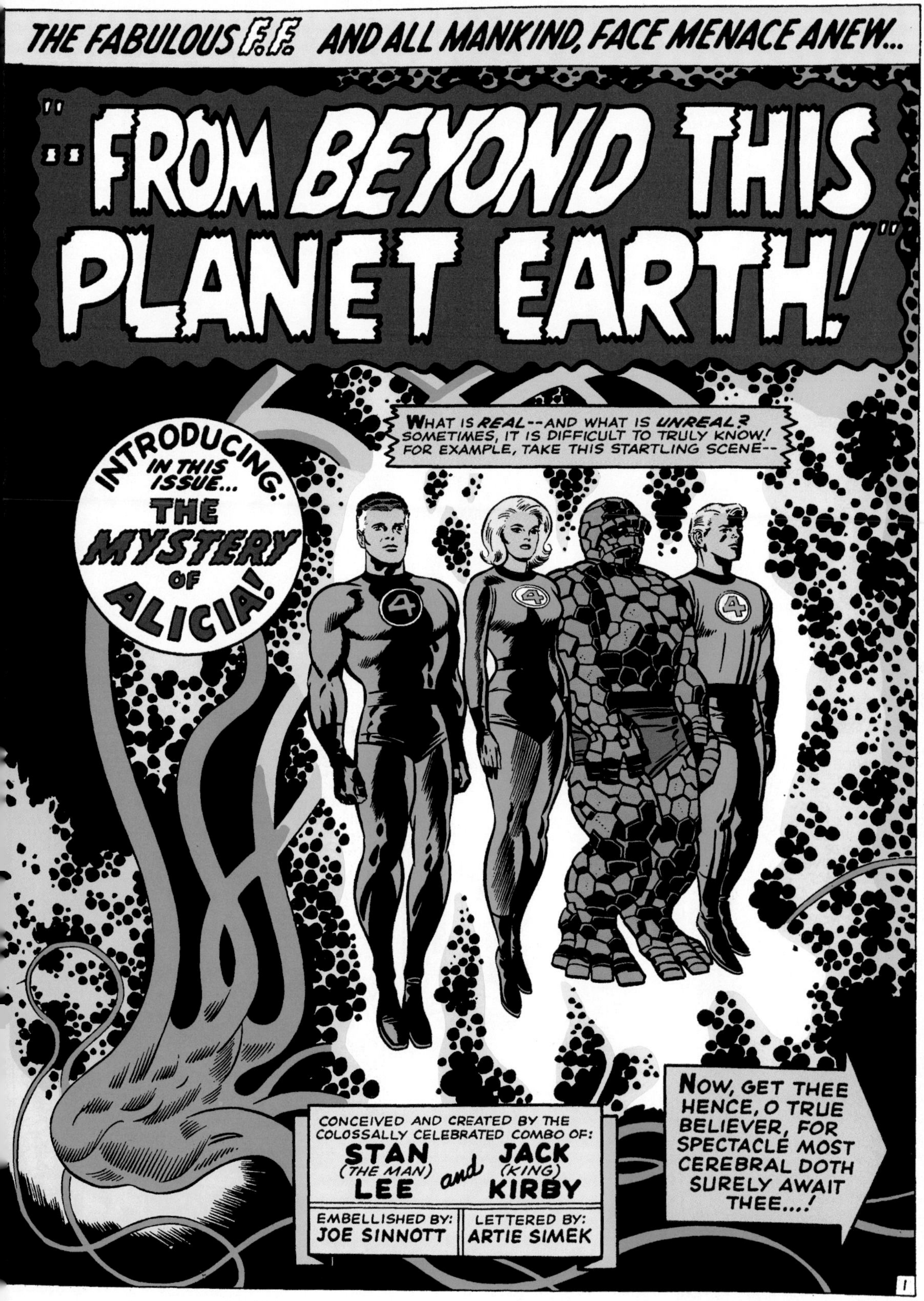
THE FABULOUS F.F. AND ALL MANKIND, FACE MENACE ANEW...
"--FROM BEYOND THIS PLANET EARTH!"
INTRODUCING IN THIS ISSUE... THE MYSTERY OF ALICIA!
WHAT IS REAL--AND WHAT IS UNREAL? SOMETIMES, IT IS DIFFICULT TO TRULY KNOW! FOR EXAMPLE, TAKE THIS STARTLING SCENE--
CONCEIVED AND CREATED BY THE COLOSSALLY CELEBRATED COMBO OF:
STAN (THE MAN) LEE and JACK (KING) KIRBY
EMBELLISHED BY: JOE SINNOTT
LETTERED BY: ARTIE SIMEK
NOW, GET THEE HENCE, O TRUE BELIEVER, FOR SPECTACLE MOST CEREBRAL DOTH SURELY AWAIT THEE...!
1

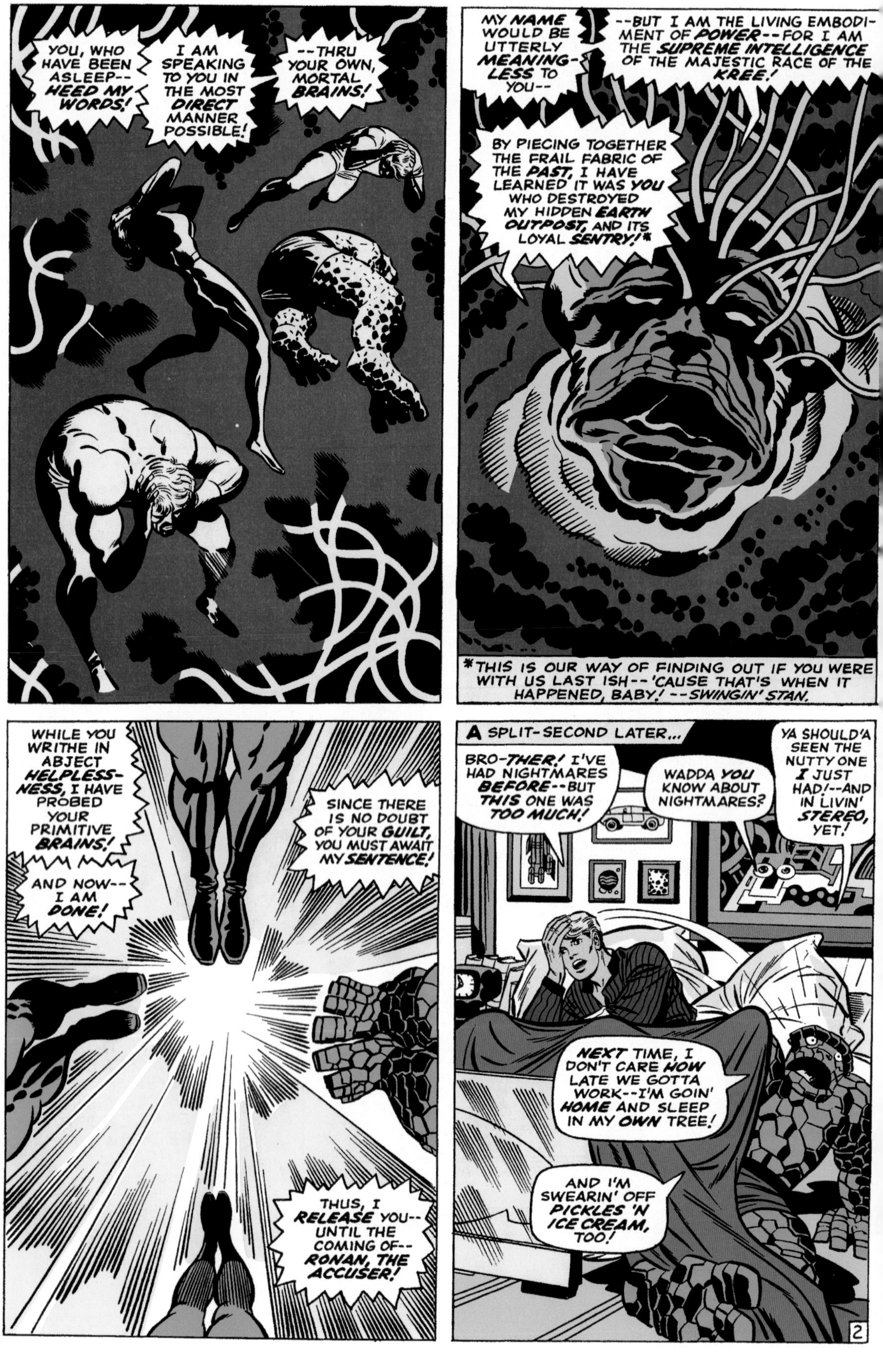
YOU, WHO HAVE BEEN ASLEEP-- HEED MY WORDS!
I AM SPEAKING TO YOU IN THE MOST DIRECT MANNER POSSIBLE!
--THRU YOUR OWN, MORTAL BRAINS!
MY NAME WOULD BE UTTERLY MEANINGLESS TO YOU--
--BUT I AM THE LIVING EMBODIMENT OF POWER--FOR I AM THE SUPREME INTELLIGENCE OF THE MAJESTIC RACE OF THE KREE!
BY PIECING TOGETHER THE FRAIL FABRIC OF THE PAST, I HAVE LEARNED IT WAS YOU WHO DESTROYED MY HIDDEN EARTH OUTPOST, AND ITS LOYAL SENTRY!*
*THIS IS OUR WAY OF FINDING OUT IF YOU WERE WITH US LAST ISH--'CAUSE THAT'S WHEN IT HAPPENED, BABY! --SWINGIN' STAN.
WHILE YOU WRITHE IN ABJECT HELPLESSNESS, I HAVE PROBED YOUR PRIMITIVE BRAINS!
AND NOW-- I AM DONE!
SINCE THERE IS NO DOUBT OF YOUR GUILT, YOU MUST AWAIT MY SENTENCE!
THUS, I RELEASE YOU-- UNTIL THE COMING OF-- RONAN, THE ACCUSER!
A SPLIT-SECOND LATER...
BRO-THER! I'VE HAD NIGHTMARES BEFORE--BUT THIS ONE WAS TOO MUCH!
WADDA YOU KNOW ABOUT NIGHTMARES?
YA SHOULD'A SEEN THE NUTTY ONE I JUST HAD!--AND IN LIVIN' STEREO, YET!
NEXT TIME, I DON'T CARE HOW LATE WE GOTTA WORK--I'M GOIN' HOME AND SLEEP IN MY OWN TREE!
AND I'M SWEARIN' OFF PICKLES 'N ICE CREAM, TOO!
2

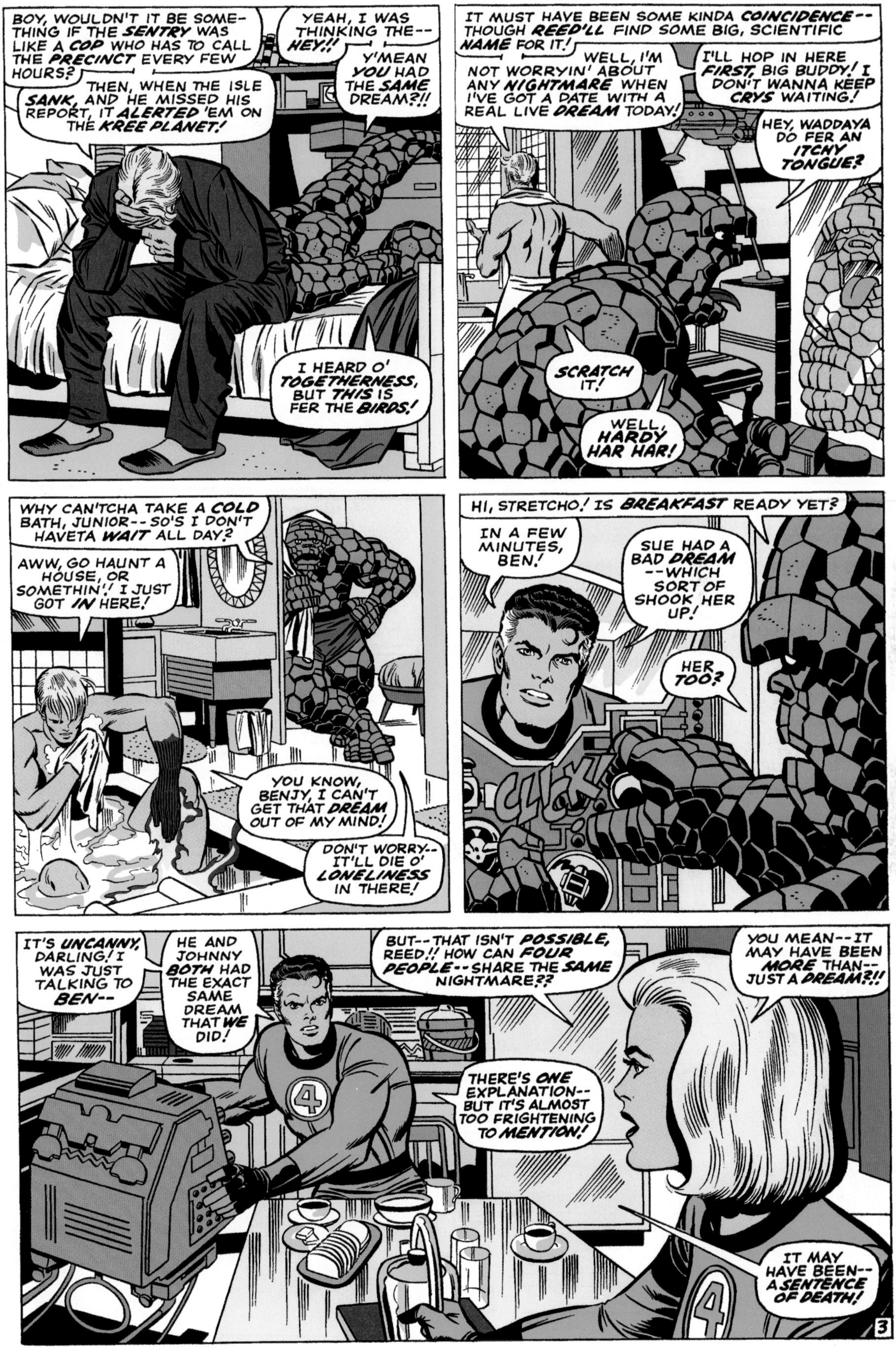

BOY, WOULDN'T IT BE SOMETHING IF THE SENTRY WAS LIKE A COP WHO HAS TO CALL THE PRECINCT EVERY FEW HOURS?
THEN, WHEN THE ISLE SANK, AND HE MISSED HIS REPORT, IT ALERTED 'EM ON THE KREE PLANET!
YEAH, I WAS THINKING THE-- HEY!!
Y'MEAN YOU HAD THE SAME DREAM?!!
I HEARD O' TOGETHERNESS, BUT THIS IS FER THE BIRDS!
IT MUST HAVE BEEN SOME KINDA COINCIDENCE-- THOUGH REED'LL FIND SOME BIG, SCIENTIFIC NAME FOR IT!
WELL, I'M NOT WORRYIN' ABOUT ANY NIGHTMARE WHEN I'VE GOT A DATE WITH A REAL LIVE DREAM TODAY!
I'LL HOP IN HERE FIRST, BIG BUDDY! I DON'T WANNA KEEP CRYS WAITING!
HEY, WADDAYA DO FER AN ITCHY TONGUE?
SCRATCH IT!
WELL, HARDY HAR HAR!
WHY CAN'TCHA TAKE A COLD BATH, JUNIOR--SO'S I DON'T HAVETA WAIT ALL DAY?
AWW, GO HAUNT A HOUSE, OR SOMETHIN'! I JUST GOT IN HERE!
YOU KNOW, BENJY, I CAN'T GET THAT DREAM OUT OF MY MIND!
DON'T WORRY-- IT'LL DIE O' LONELINESS IN THERE!
HI, STRETCHO! IS BREAKFAST READY YET?
IN A FEW MINUTES, BEN!
SUE HAD A BAD DREAM --WHICH SORT OF SHOOK HER UP!
HER TOO?
CLICK!
IT'S UNCANNY, DARLING! I WAS JUST TALKING TO BEN--
HE AND JOHNNY BOTH HAD THE EXACT SAME DREAM THAT WE DID!
BUT--THAT ISN'T POSSIBLE, REED!! HOW CAN FOUR PEOPLE--SHARE THE SAME NIGHTMARE??
YOU MEAN--IT MAY HAVE BEEN MORE THAN--JUST A DREAM?!!
THERE'S ONE EXPLANATION-- BUT IT'S ALMOST TOO FRIGHTENING TO MENTION!
IT MAY HAVE BEEN-- A SENTENCE OF DEATH!
3

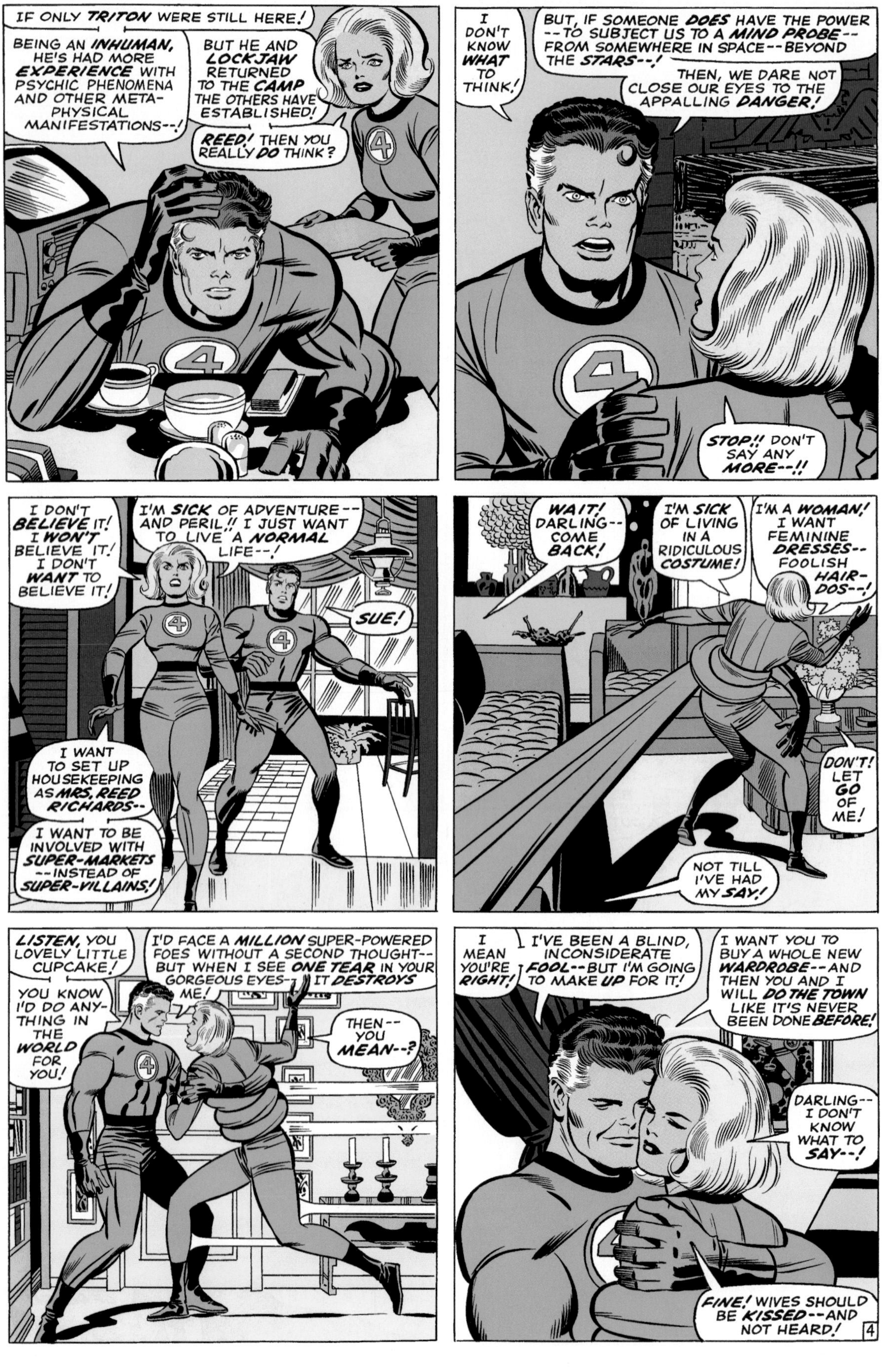
IF ONLY TRITON WERE STILL HERE!
BEING AN INHUMAN, HE'S HAD MORE EXPERIENCE WITH PSYCHIC PHENOMENA AND OTHER META-PHYSICAL MANIFESTATIONS--!
BUT HE AND LOCKJAW RETURNED TO THE CAMP THE OTHERS HAVE ESTABLISHED!
REED! THEN YOU REALLY DO THINK?
I DON'T KNOW WHAT TO THINK!
BUT, IF SOMEONE DOES HAVE THE POWER --TO SUBJECT US TO A MIND PROBE-- FROM SOMEWHERE IN SPACE--BEYOND THE STARS--!
THEN, WE DARE NOT CLOSE OUR EYES TO THE APPALLING DANGER!
STOP!! DON'T SAY ANY MORE--!!
I DON'T BELIEVE IT! I WON'T BELIEVE IT! I DON'T WANT TO BELIEVE IT!
I'M SICK OF ADVENTURE--AND PERIL!! I JUST WANT TO LIVE A NORMAL LIFE--!
SUE!
I WANT TO SET UP HOUSEKEEPING AS MRS. REED RICHARDS--
I WANT TO BE INVOLVED WITH SUPER-MARKETS --INSTEAD OF SUPER-VILLAINS!
WAIT! DARLING--COME BACK!
I'M SICK OF LIVING IN A RIDICULOUS COSTUME!
I'M A WOMAN! I WANT FEMININE DRESSES--FOOLISH HAIR-DOS--!
DON'T! LET GO OF ME!
NOT TILL I'VE HAD MY SAY!
LISTEN, YOU LOVELY LITTLE CUPCAKE!
YOU KNOW I'D DO ANY-THING IN THE WORLD FOR YOU!
I'D FACE A MILLION SUPER-POWERED FOES WITHOUT A SECOND THOUGHT--BUT WHEN I SEE ONE TEAR IN YOUR GORGEOUS EYES--IT DESTROYS ME!
THEN--YOU MEAN--?
I MEAN YOU'RE RIGHT!
I'VE BEEN A BLIND, INCONSIDERATE FOOL--BUT I'M GOING TO MAKE UP FOR IT!
I WANT YOU TO BUY A WHOLE NEW WARDROBE--AND THEN YOU AND I WILL DO THE TOWN LIKE IT'S NEVER BEEN DONE BEFORE!
DARLING--I DON'T KNOW WHAT TO SAY--!
FINE! WIVES SHOULD BE KISSED--AND NOT HEARD!
4

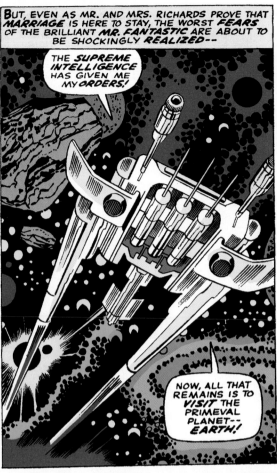

BUT, EVEN AS MR. AND MRS. RICHARDS PROVE THAT *MARRIAGE* IS HERE TO STAY, THE WORST *FEARS* OF THE BRILLIANT *MR. FANTASTIC* ARE ABOUT TO BE SHOCKINGLY *REALIZED*--

THE *SUPREME INTELLIGENCE* HAS GIVEN ME MY *ORDERS!*

NOW, ALL THAT REMAINS IS TO *VISIT* THE PRIMEVAL PLANET-- *EARTH!*

ONCE THERE, I SHALL EASILY *LOCATE* THE SO-CALLED *FANTASTIC FOUR!*

THEY SHALL BE FORCED TO ANSWER TO *RONAN, THE PUBLIC ACCUSER*-- AND TO MY *UNIVERSAL WEAPON!*

ALL WHO INHABIT THIS PRIMITIVE GALAXY MUST BE TAUGHT THAT *NONE* MAY DESTROY A *SENTRY* OF THE SUPREME *KREE RACE*--

I HAVE *REACHED* MY DESTI-NATION!

NOW, HAVING ESTABLISHED MY PREARRANGED *ORBIT* AROUND EARTH, I SHALL ENTER THE BASIC *MATTER TRANSMITTER*--

--SO THAT I MAY STEP FORTH, WITHIN ONE *MICRO-SECOND*, UPON THE ALIEN SOIL OF THE PLANET BELOW!

HAD I THE *RIGHT* TO QUESTION A COMMAND OF THE *SUPREME INTELLIGENCE*, I WOULD HAVE QUESTIONED THE *NECESSITY* OF THIS MISSION--!

FOR, *EARTH* IS OF NO IMPORTANCE TO THE KREE!

IT LIES FAR BEYOND THE FAINTEST *BACKWASH* OF OUR MOST REMOTE SHIPPING LANES!

INDEED, THE *SENTRY* WHO HAD BEEN STATIONED HERE MANY MILLENNIA BEFORE HAD BEEN ALL BUT *FORGOTTEN*--

UNTIL HIS *DEFEAT* WAS RECORDED UPON OUR AUTOMATIC *SCANNING DETECTORS!*

STILL, MY *ORDERS* ARE CLEAR-- AND THEY *MUST* BE EXECUTED!

5

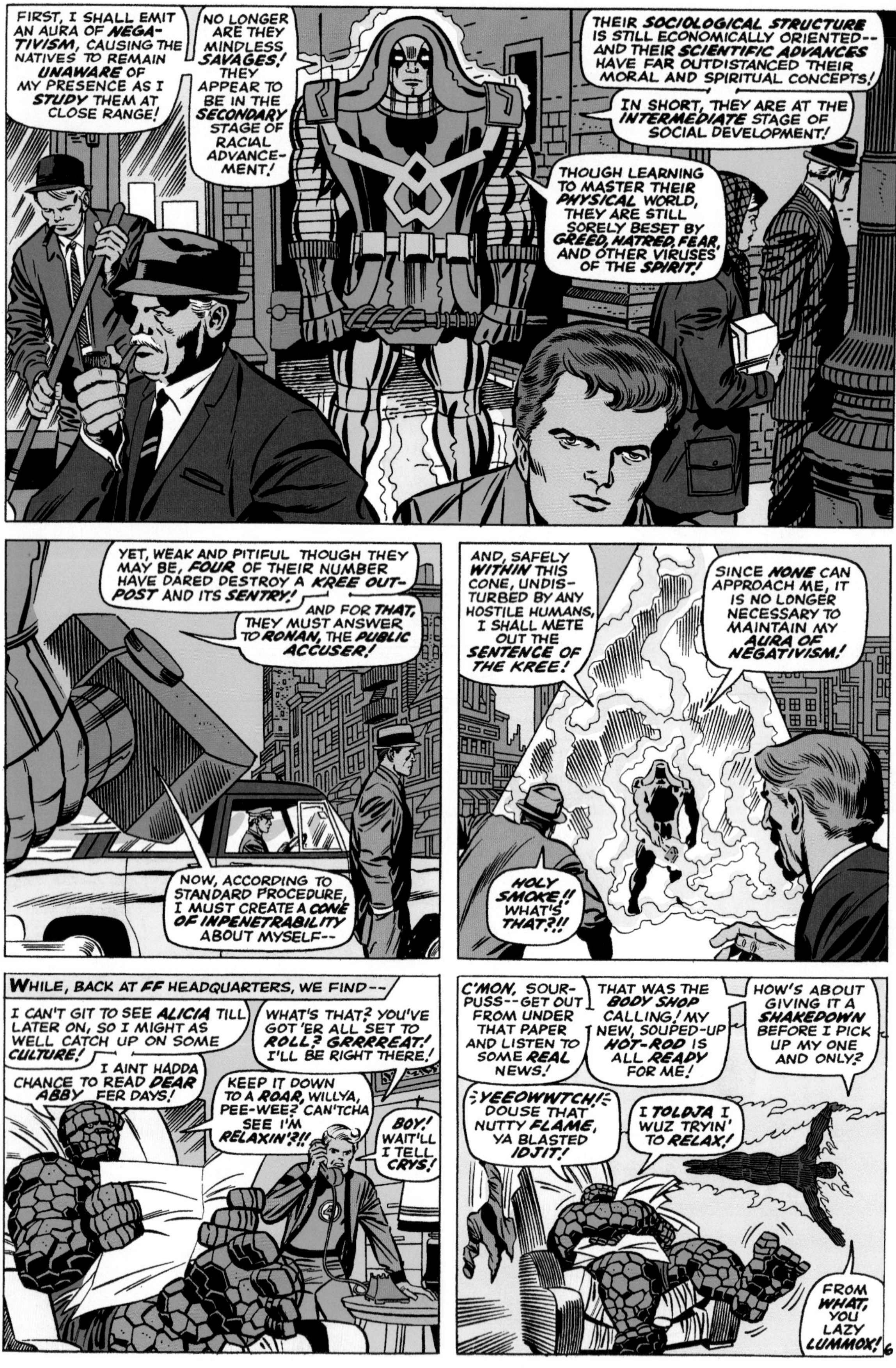
FIRST, I SHALL EMIT AN AURA OF NEGATIVISM, CAUSING THE NATIVES TO REMAIN UNAWARE OF MY PRESENCE AS I STUDY THEM AT CLOSE RANGE!
NO LONGER ARE THEY MINDLESS SAVAGES! THEY APPEAR TO BE IN THE SECONDARY STAGE OF RACIAL ADVANCEMENT!
THEIR SOCIOLOGICAL STRUCTURE IS STILL ECONOMICALLY ORIENTED-- AND THEIR SCIENTIFIC ADVANCES HAVE FAR OUTDISTANCED THEIR MORAL AND SPIRITUAL CONCEPTS!
IN SHORT, THEY ARE AT THE INTERMEDIATE STAGE OF SOCIAL DEVELOPMENT!
THOUGH LEARNING TO MASTER THEIR PHYSICAL WORLD, THEY ARE STILL SORELY BESET BY GREED, HATRED, FEAR, AND OTHER VIRUSES OF THE SPIRIT!
YET, WEAK AND PITIFUL THOUGH THEY MAY BE, FOUR OF THEIR NUMBER HAVE DARED DESTROY A KREE OUTPOST AND ITS SENTRY!
AND FOR THAT, THEY MUST ANSWER TO RONAN, THE PUBLIC ACCUSER!
NOW, ACCORDING TO STANDARD PROCEDURE, I MUST CREATE A CONE OF INPENETRABILITY ABOUT MYSELF--
AND, SAFELY WITHIN THIS CONE, UNDISTURBED BY ANY HOSTILE HUMANS, I SHALL METE OUT THE SENTENCE OF THE KREE!
SINCE NONE CAN APPROACH ME, IT IS NO LONGER NECESSARY TO MAINTAIN MY AURA OF NEGATIVISM!
HOLY SMOKE!! WHAT'S THAT?!!
WHILE, BACK AT FF HEADQUARTERS, WE FIND--
I CAN'T GIT TO SEE ALICIA TILL LATER ON, SO I MIGHT AS WELL CATCH UP ON SOME CULTURE!
I AINT HADDA CHANCE TO READ DEAR ABBY FER DAYS!
WHAT'S THAT? YOU'VE GOT 'ER ALL SET TO ROLL? GRRRREAT! I'LL BE RIGHT THERE!
KEEP IT DOWN TO A ROAR, WILLYA, PEE-WEE? CAN'TCHA SEE I'M RELAXIN'?!!
BOY! WAIT'LL I TELL CRYS!
C'MON, SOUR-PUSS--GET OUT FROM UNDER THAT PAPER AND LISTEN TO SOME REAL NEWS!
THAT WAS THE BODY SHOP CALLING! MY NEW, SOUPED-UP HOT-ROD IS ALL READY FOR ME!
HOW'S ABOUT GIVING IT A SHAKEDOWN BEFORE I PICK UP MY ONE AND ONLY?
YEEOWWTCH! DOUSE THAT NUTTY FLAME, YA BLASTED IDJIT!
I TOLDJA I WUZ TRYIN' TO RELAX!
FROM WHAT, YOU LAZY LUMMOX!
6

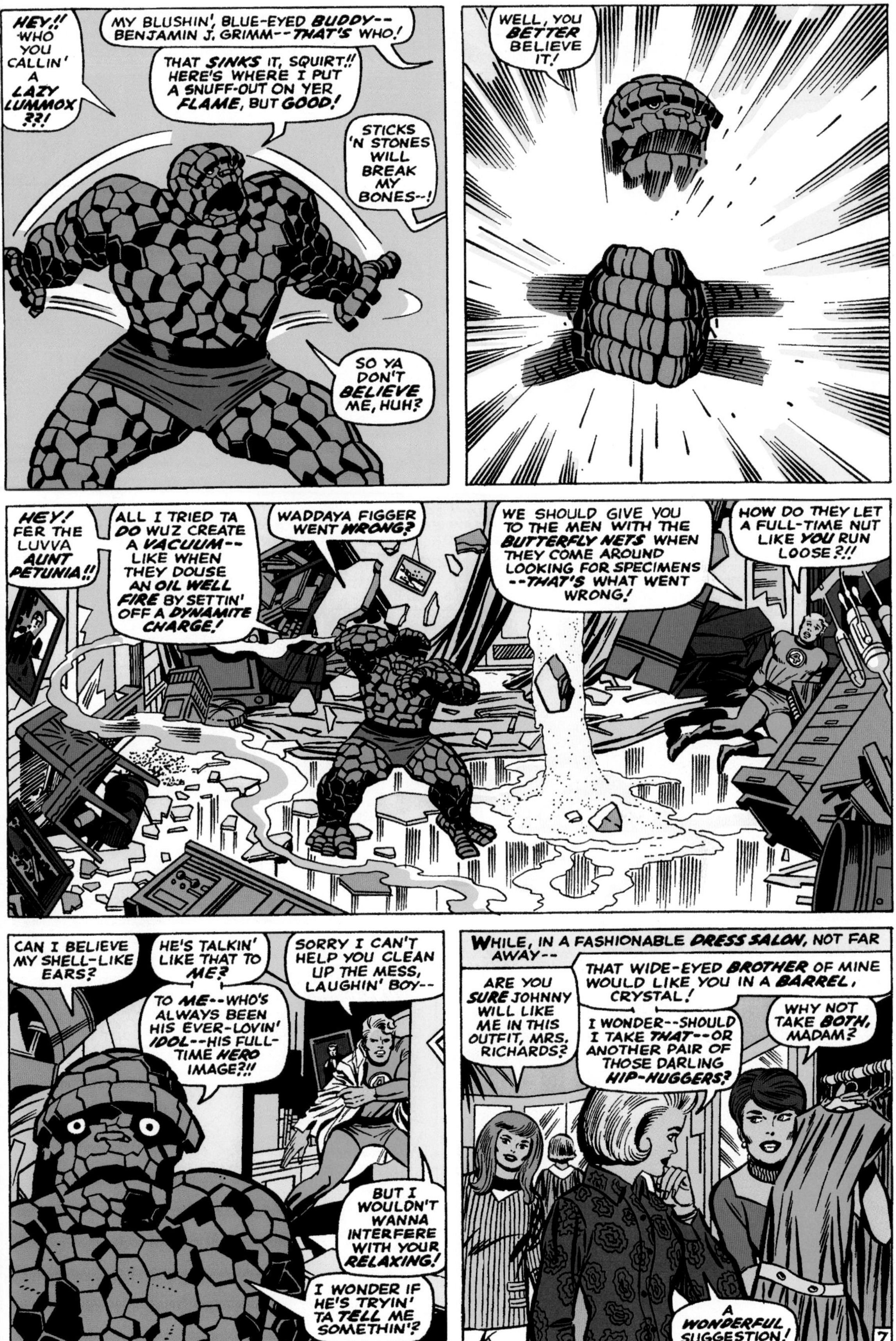
HEY!! WHO YOU CALLIN' A LAZY LUMMOX ??!
MY BLUSHIN', BLUE-EYED BUDDY-- BENJAMIN J. GRIMM--THAT'S WHO!
THAT SINKS IT, SQUIRT!! HERE'S WHERE I PUT A SNUFF-OUT ON YER FLAME, BUT GOOD!
STICKS 'N STONES WILL BREAK MY BONES--!
SO YA DON'T BELIEVE ME, HUH?
WELL, YOU BETTER BELIEVE IT!
HEY! FER THE LUVVA AUNT PETUNIA!!
ALL I TRIED TA DO WUZ CREATE A VACUUM-- LIKE WHEN THEY DOUSE AN OIL WELL FIRE BY SETTIN' OFF A DYNAMITE CHARGE!
WADDAYA FIGGER WENT WRONG?
WE SHOULD GIVE YOU TO THE MEN WITH THE BUTTERFLY NETS WHEN THEY COME AROUND LOOKING FOR SPECIMENS --THAT'S WHAT WENT WRONG!
HOW DO THEY LET A FULL-TIME NUT LIKE YOU RUN LOOSE?!!
CAN I BELIEVE MY SHELL-LIKE EARS?
HE'S TALKIN' LIKE THAT TO ME?
TO ME--WHO'S ALWAYS BEEN HIS EVER-LOVIN' IDOL--HIS FULL-TIME HERO IMAGE?!!
SORRY I CAN'T HELP YOU CLEAN UP THE MESS, LAUGHIN' BOY--
BUT I WOULDN'T WANNA INTERFERE WITH YOUR RELAXING!
I WONDER IF HE'S TRYIN' TA TELL ME SOMETHIN'?
WHILE, IN A FASHIONABLE DRESS SALON, NOT FAR AWAY--
ARE YOU SURE JOHNNY WILL LIKE ME IN THIS OUTFIT, MRS. RICHARDS?
THAT WIDE-EYED BROTHER OF MINE WOULD LIKE YOU IN A BARREL, CRYSTAL!
I WONDER--SHOULD I TAKE THAT--OR ANOTHER PAIR OF THOSE DARLING HIP-HUGGERS?
WHY NOT TAKE BOTH, MADAM?
A WONDERFUL SUGGESTION!
7

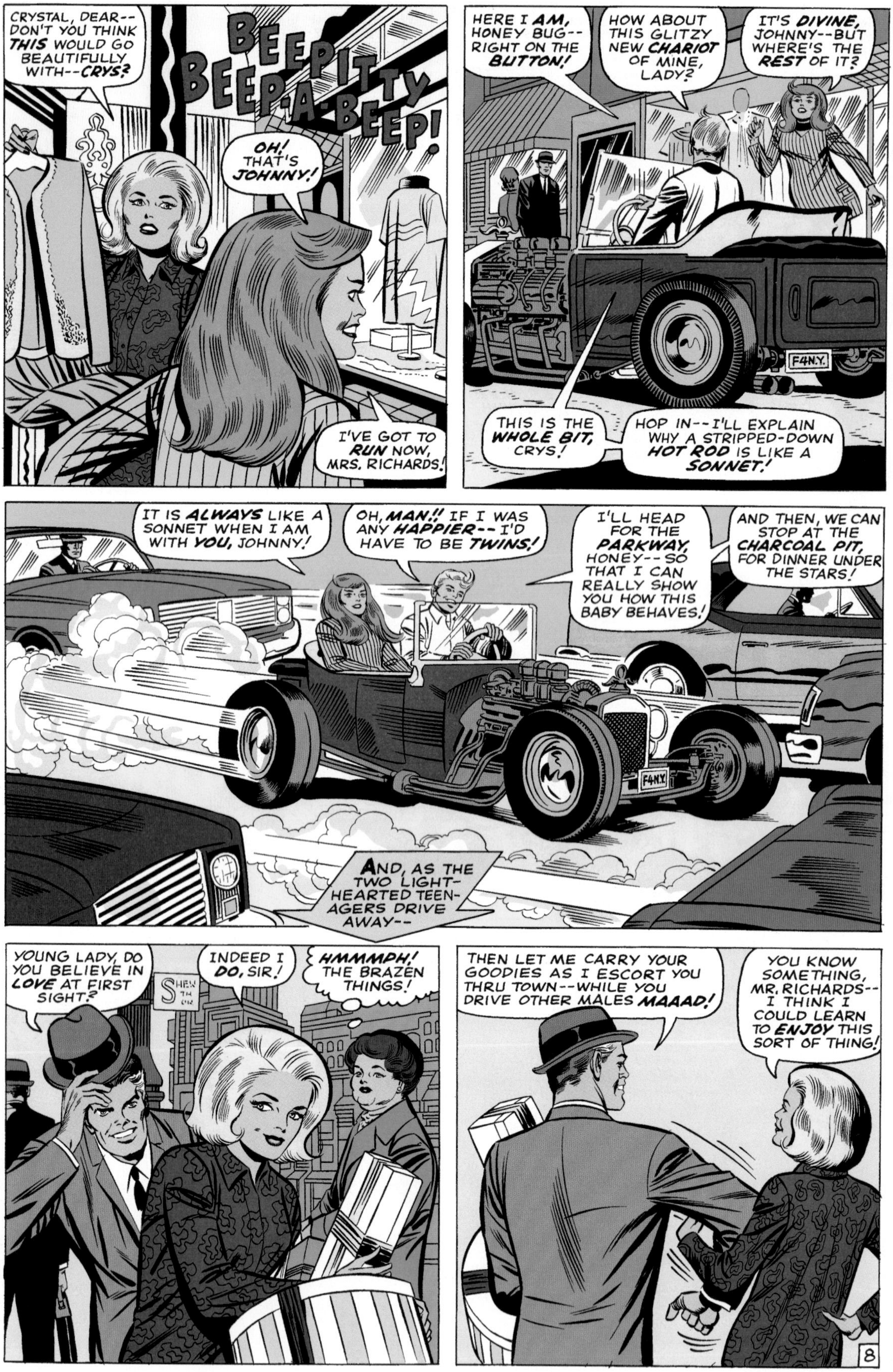
CRYSTAL, DEAR-- DON'T YOU THINK THIS WOULD GO BEAUTIFULLY WITH--CRYS?
BEEP BEEP-A-BEEPITTY BEEP!
OH! THAT'S JOHNNY!
I'VE GOT TO RUN NOW, MRS. RICHARDS!
HERE I AM, HONEY BUG-- RIGHT ON THE BUTTON!
HOW ABOUT THIS GLITZY NEW CHARIOT OF MINE, LADY?
IT'S DIVINE, JOHNNY--BUT WHERE'S THE REST OF IT?
F4N.Y.
THIS IS THE WHOLE BIT, CRYS!
HOP IN--I'LL EXPLAIN WHY A STRIPPED-DOWN HOT ROD IS LIKE A SONNET!
IT IS ALWAYS LIKE A SONNET WHEN I AM WITH YOU, JOHNNY!
OH, MAN!! IF I WAS ANY HAPPIER-- I'D HAVE TO BE TWINS!
I'LL HEAD FOR THE PARKWAY, HONEY-- SO THAT I CAN REALLY SHOW YOU HOW THIS BABY BEHAVES!
AND THEN, WE CAN STOP AT THE CHARCOAL PIT, FOR DINNER UNDER THE STARS!
F4N.Y.
AND, AS THE TWO LIGHT-HEARTED TEEN-AGERS DRIVE AWAY--
YOUNG LADY, DO YOU BELIEVE IN LOVE AT FIRST SIGHT?
INDEED I DO, SIR!
HMMMPH! THE BRAZEN THINGS!
THEN LET ME CARRY YOUR GOODIES AS I ESCORT YOU THRU TOWN--WHILE YOU DRIVE OTHER MALES MAAAD!
YOU KNOW SOMETHING, MR. RICHARDS-- I THINK I COULD LEARN TO ENJOY THIS SORT OF THING!
8

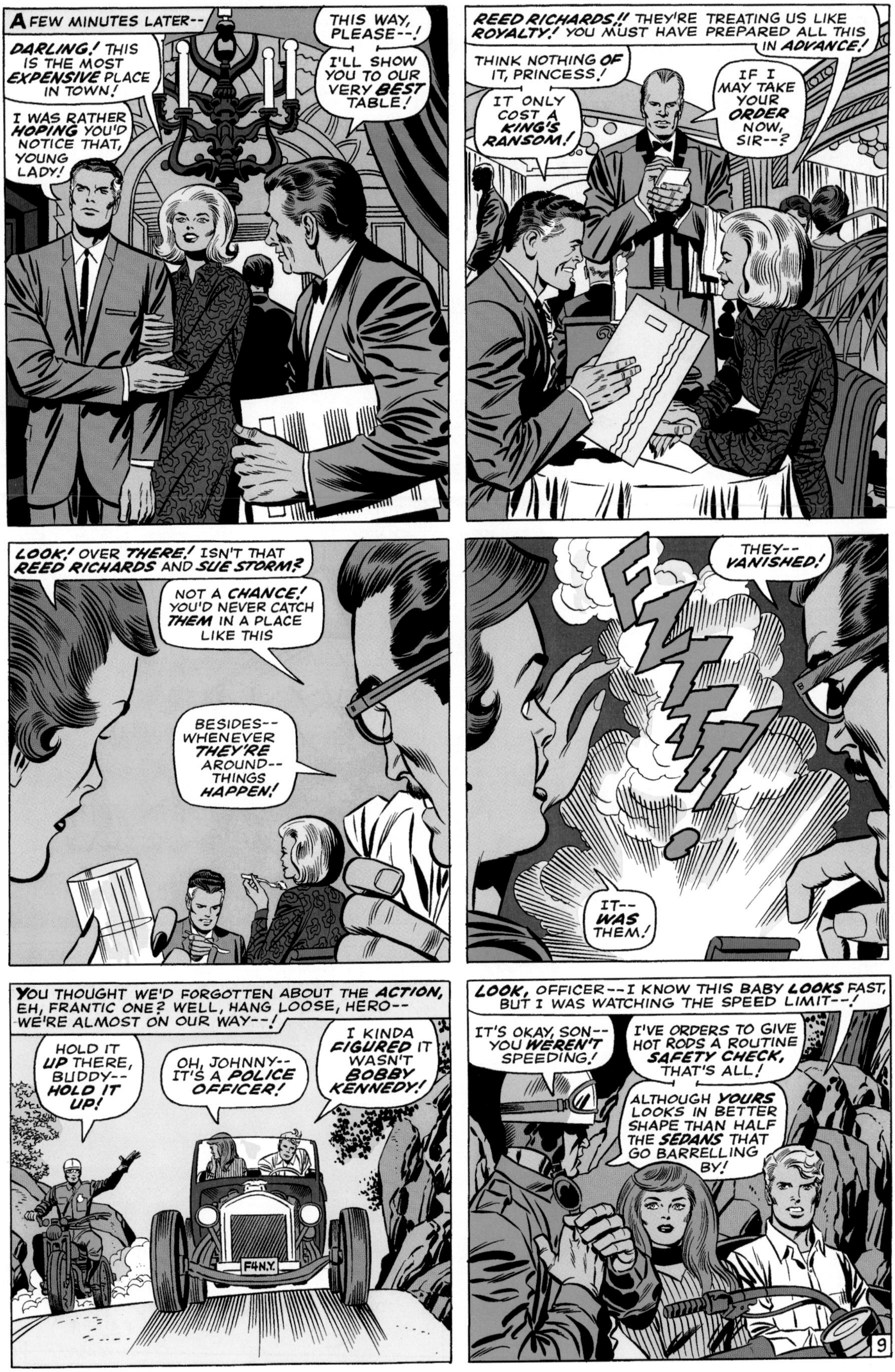

A FEW MINUTES LATER--
DARLING! THIS IS THE MOST EXPENSIVE PLACE IN TOWN!
I WAS RATHER HOPING YOU'D NOTICE THAT, YOUNG LADY!
THIS WAY, PLEASE--!
I'LL SHOW YOU TO OUR VERY BEST TABLE!
REED RICHARDS!! THEY'RE TREATING US LIKE ROYALTY! YOU MUST HAVE PREPARED ALL THIS IN ADVANCE!
THINK NOTHING OF IT, PRINCESS!
IT ONLY COST A KING'S RANSOM!
IF I MAY TAKE YOUR ORDER NOW, SIR--?
LOOK! OVER THERE! ISN'T THAT REED RICHARDS AND SUE STORM?
NOT A CHANCE! YOU'D NEVER CATCH THEM IN A PLACE LIKE THIS
BESIDES-- WHENEVER THEY'RE AROUND-- THINGS HAPPEN!
FZTTT!
THEY-- VANISHED!
IT-- WAS THEM!
YOU THOUGHT WE'D FORGOTTEN ABOUT THE ACTION, EH, FRANTIC ONE? WELL, HANG LOOSE, HERO-- WE'RE ALMOST ON OUR WAY--!
HOLD IT UP THERE, BUDDY-- HOLD IT UP!
OH, JOHNNY-- IT'S A POLICE OFFICER!
I KINDA FIGURED IT WASN'T BOBBY KENNEDY!
F4N.Y.
LOOK, OFFICER--I KNOW THIS BABY LOOKS FAST, BUT I WAS WATCHING THE SPEED LIMIT--!
IT'S OKAY, SON-- YOU WEREN'T SPEEDING!
I'VE ORDERS TO GIVE HOT RODS A ROUTINE SAFETY CHECK, THAT'S ALL!
ALTHOUGH YOURS LOOKS IN BETTER SHAPE THAN HALF THE SEDANS THAT GO BARRELLING BY!
9

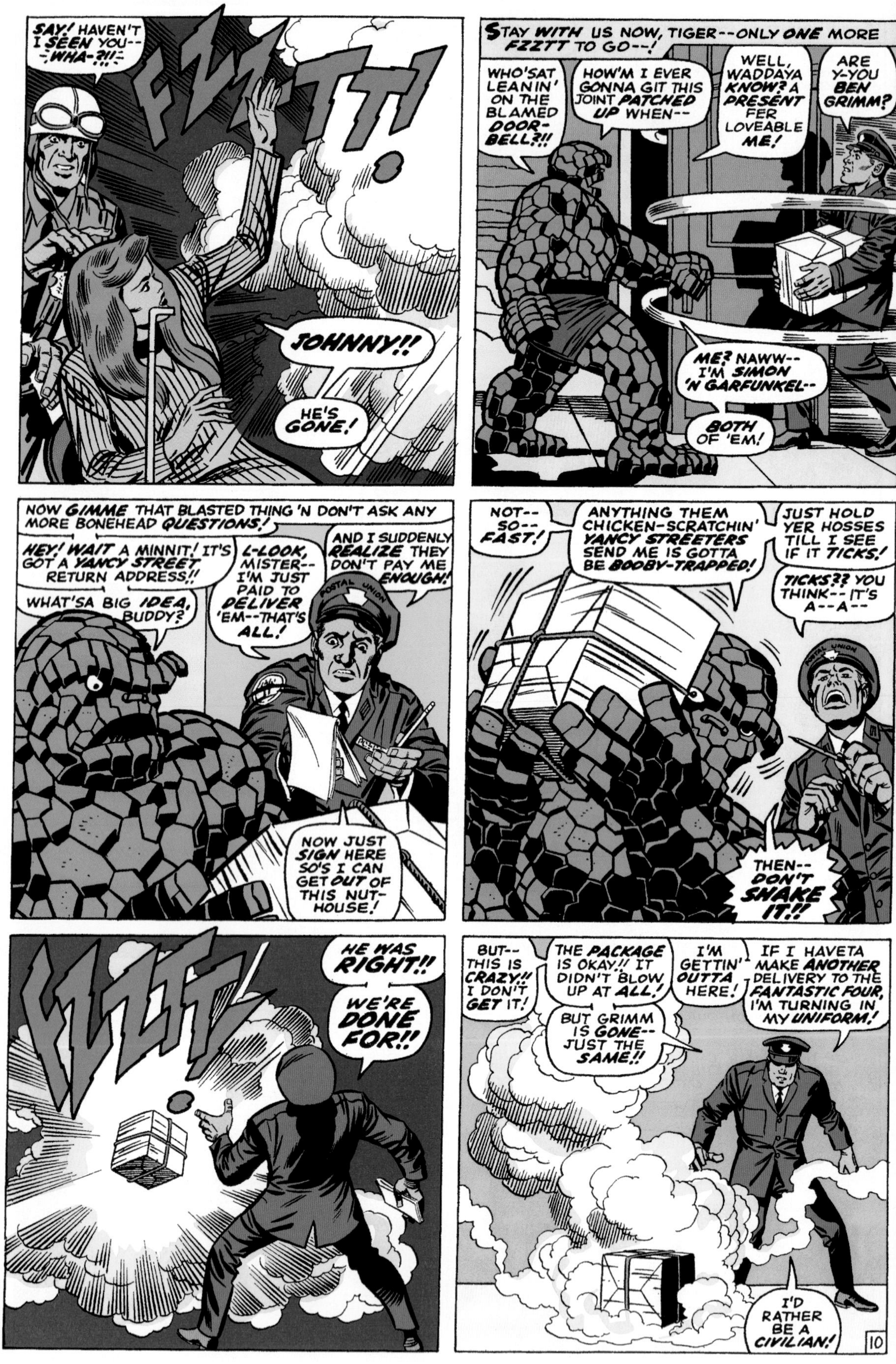
SAY! HAVEN'T I SEEN YOU-- -WHA-?!!-
FZZ-TTT!
JOHNNY!!
HE'S GONE!
STAY WITH US NOW, TIGER--ONLY ONE MORE FZZTT TO GO--!
WHO'SAT LEANIN' ON THE BLAMED DOOR-BELL?!!
HOW'M I EVER GONNA GIT THIS JOINT PATCHED UP WHEN--
WELL, WADDAYA KNOW? A PRESENT FER LOVEABLE ME!
ARE Y-YOU BEN GRIMM?
ME? NAWW-- I'M SIMON 'N GARFUNKEL--
BOTH OF 'EM!
NOW GIMME THAT BLASTED THING 'N DON'T ASK ANY MORE BONEHEAD QUESTIONS!
HEY! WAIT A MINNIT! IT'S GOT A YANCY STREET RETURN ADDRESS!!
WHAT'SA BIG IDEA, BUDDY?
L-LOOK, MISTER-- I'M JUST PAID TO DELIVER 'EM--THAT'S ALL!
AND I SUDDENLY REALIZE THEY DON'T PAY ME ENOUGH!
NOW JUST SIGN HERE SO'S I CAN GET OUT OF THIS NUT-HOUSE!
NOT-- SO-- FAST!
ANYTHING THEM CHICKEN-SCRATCHIN' YANCY STREETERS SEND ME IS GOTTA BE BOOBY-TRAPPED!
JUST HOLD YER HOSSES TILL I SEE IF IT TICKS!
TICKS?? YOU THINK-- IT'S A--A--
THEN-- DON'T SHAKE IT!!
HE WAS RIGHT!!
WE'RE DONE FOR!!
BUT-- THIS IS CRAZY!! I DON'T GET IT!
THE PACKAGE IS OKAY!! IT DIDN'T BLOW UP AT ALL!
BUT GRIMM IS GONE-- JUST THE SAME!!
I'M GETTIN' OUTTA HERE!
IF I HAVETA MAKE ANOTHER DELIVERY TO THE FANTASTIC FOUR, I'M TURNING IN MY UNIFORM!
I'D RATHER BE A CIVILIAN!
10

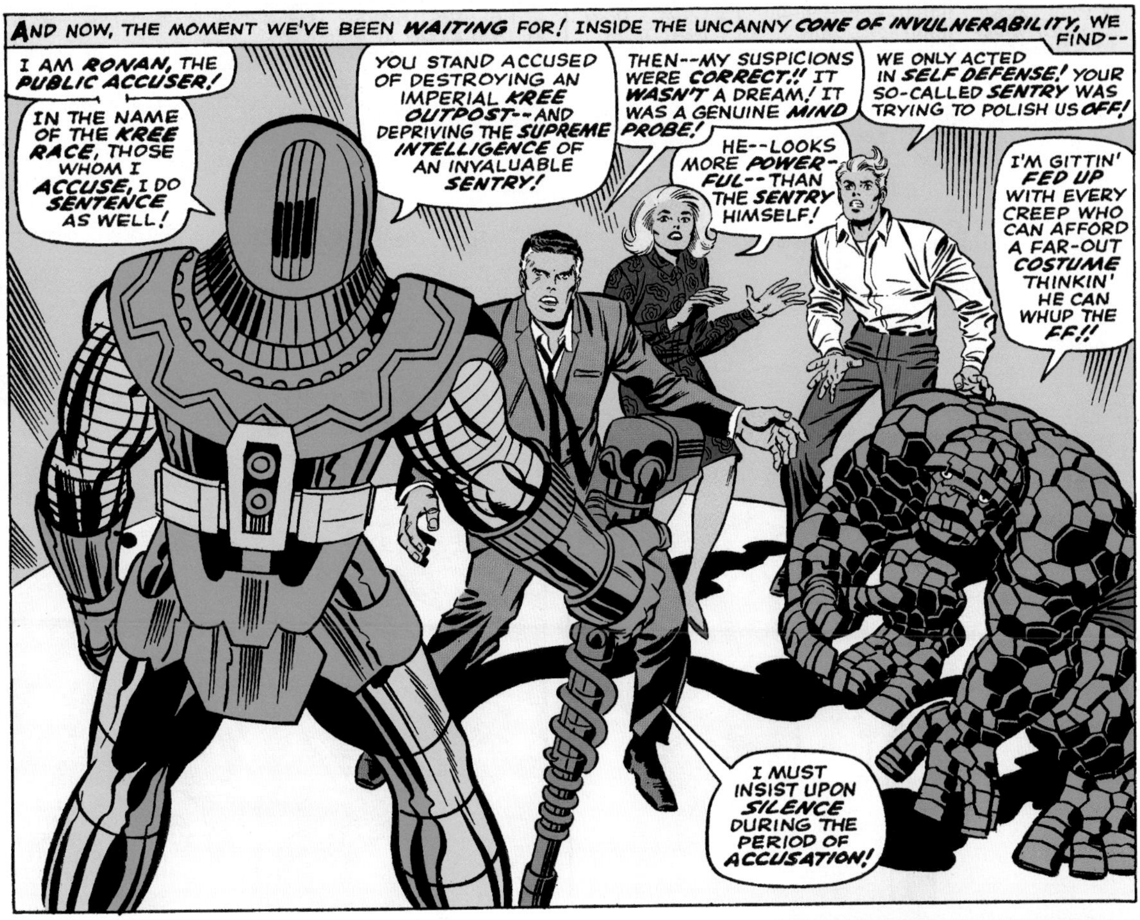
AND NOW, THE MOMENT WE'VE BEEN WAITING FOR! INSIDE THE UNCANNY CONE OF INVULNERABILITY, WE FIND--
I AM RONAN, THE PUBLIC ACCUSER!
IN THE NAME OF THE KREE RACE, THOSE WHOM I ACCUSE, I DO SENTENCE AS WELL!
YOU STAND ACCUSED OF DESTROYING AN IMPERIAL KREE OUTPOST--AND DEPRIVING THE SUPREME INTELLIGENCE OF AN INVALUABLE SENTRY!
THEN--MY SUSPICIONS WERE CORRECT!! IT WASN'T A DREAM! IT WAS A GENUINE MIND PROBE!
HE--LOOKS MORE POWER-FUL--THAN THE SENTRY HIMSELF!
WE ONLY ACTED IN SELF DEFENSE! YOUR SO-CALLED SENTRY WAS TRYING TO POLISH US OFF!
I'M GITTIN' FED UP WITH EVERY CREEP WHO CAN AFFORD A FAR-OUT COSTUME THINKIN' HE CAN WHUP THE FF!!
I MUST INSIST UPON SILENCE DURING THE PERIOD OF ACCUSATION!

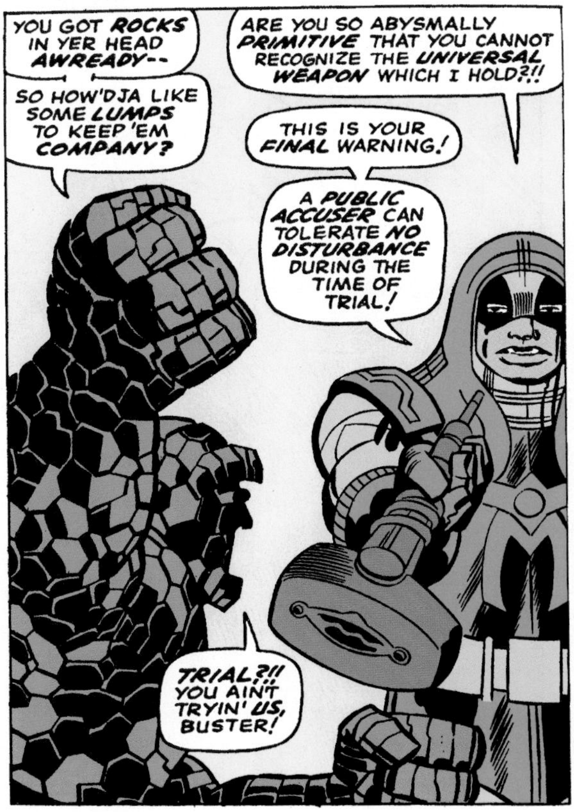
YOU GOT ROCKS IN YER HEAD AWREADY--
SO HOW'DJA LIKE SOME LUMPS TO KEEP 'EM COMPANY?
ARE YOU SO ABYSMALLY PRIMITIVE THAT YOU CANNOT RECOGNIZE THE UNIVERSAL WEAPON WHICH I HOLD?!!
THIS IS YOUR FINAL WARNING!
A PUBLIC ACCUSER CAN TOLERATE NO DISTURBANCE DURING THE TIME OF TRIAL!
TRIAL?!! YOU AIN'T TRYIN' US, BUSTER!

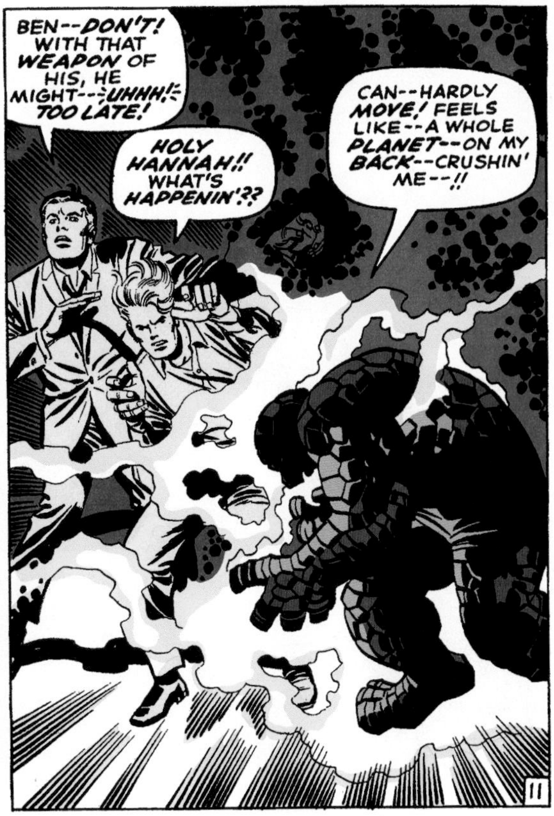
BEN--DON'T! WITH THAT WEAPON OF HIS, HE MIGHT--UHHH!--TOO LATE!
HOLY HANNAH!! WHAT'S HAPPENIN'??
CAN--HARDLY MOVE! FEELS LIKE--A WHOLE PLANET--ON MY BACK--CRUSHIN' ME--!!
11

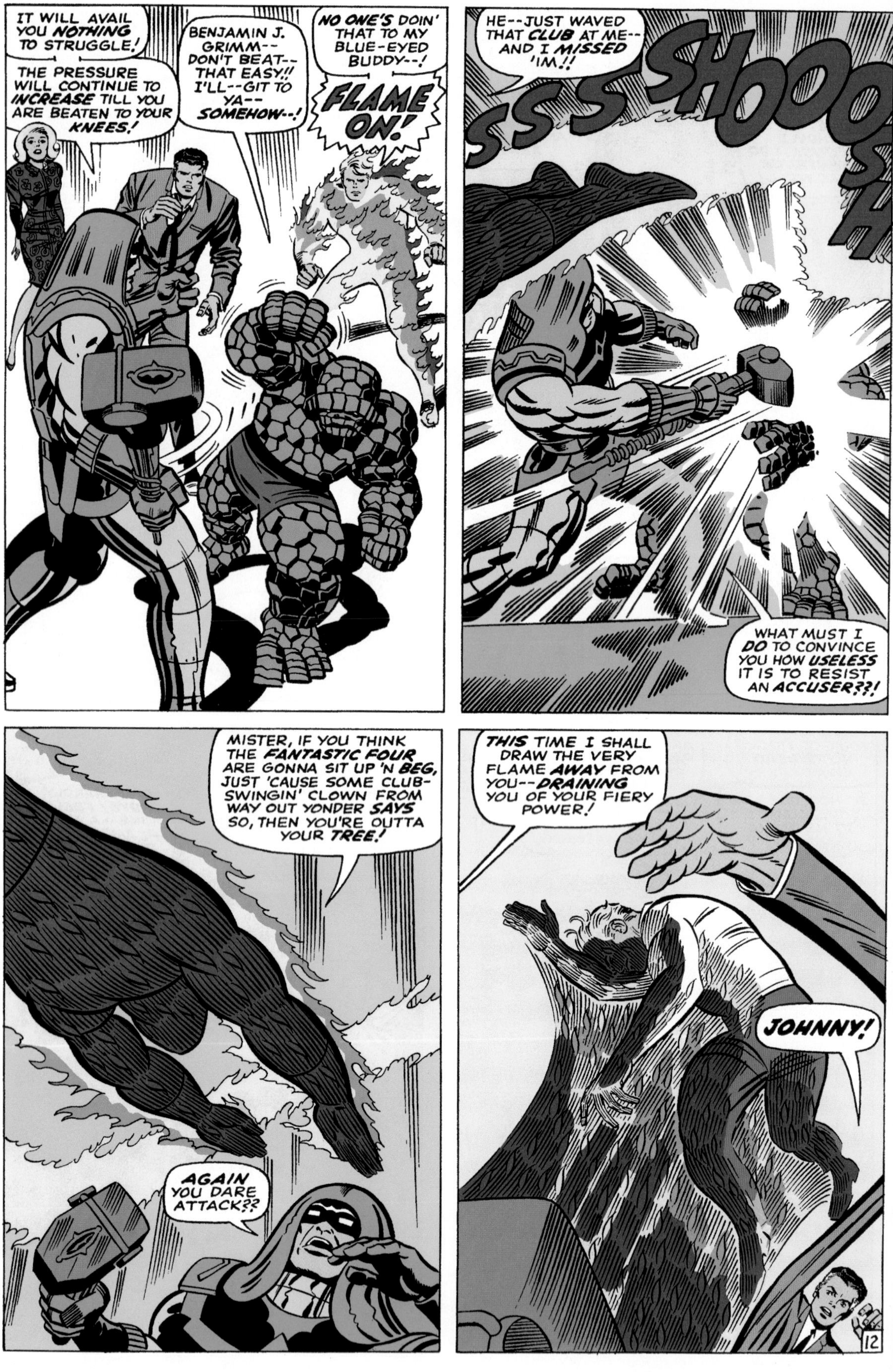
IT WILL AVAIL YOU NOTHING TO STRUGGLE!
THE PRESSURE WILL CONTINUE TO INCREASE TILL YOU ARE BEATEN TO YOUR KNEES!
BENJAMIN J. GRIMM-- DON'T BEAT-- THAT EASY!! I'LL--GIT TO YA-- SOMEHOW--!
NO ONE'S DOIN' THAT TO MY BLUE-EYED BUDDY--!
FLAME ON!
HE--JUST WAVED THAT CLUB AT ME-- AND I MISSED 'IM!!
SSSSHOOOOSH
WHAT MUST I DO TO CONVINCE YOU HOW USELESS IT IS TO RESIST AN ACCUSER??!
MISTER, IF YOU THINK THE FANTASTIC FOUR ARE GONNA SIT UP 'N BEG, JUST 'CAUSE SOME CLUB-SWINGIN' CLOWN FROM WAY OUT YONDER SAYS SO, THEN YOU'RE OUTTA YOUR TREE!
AGAIN YOU DARE ATTACK??
THIS TIME I SHALL DRAW THE VERY FLAME AWAY FROM YOU--DRAINING YOU OF YOUR FIERY POWER!
JOHNNY!
12

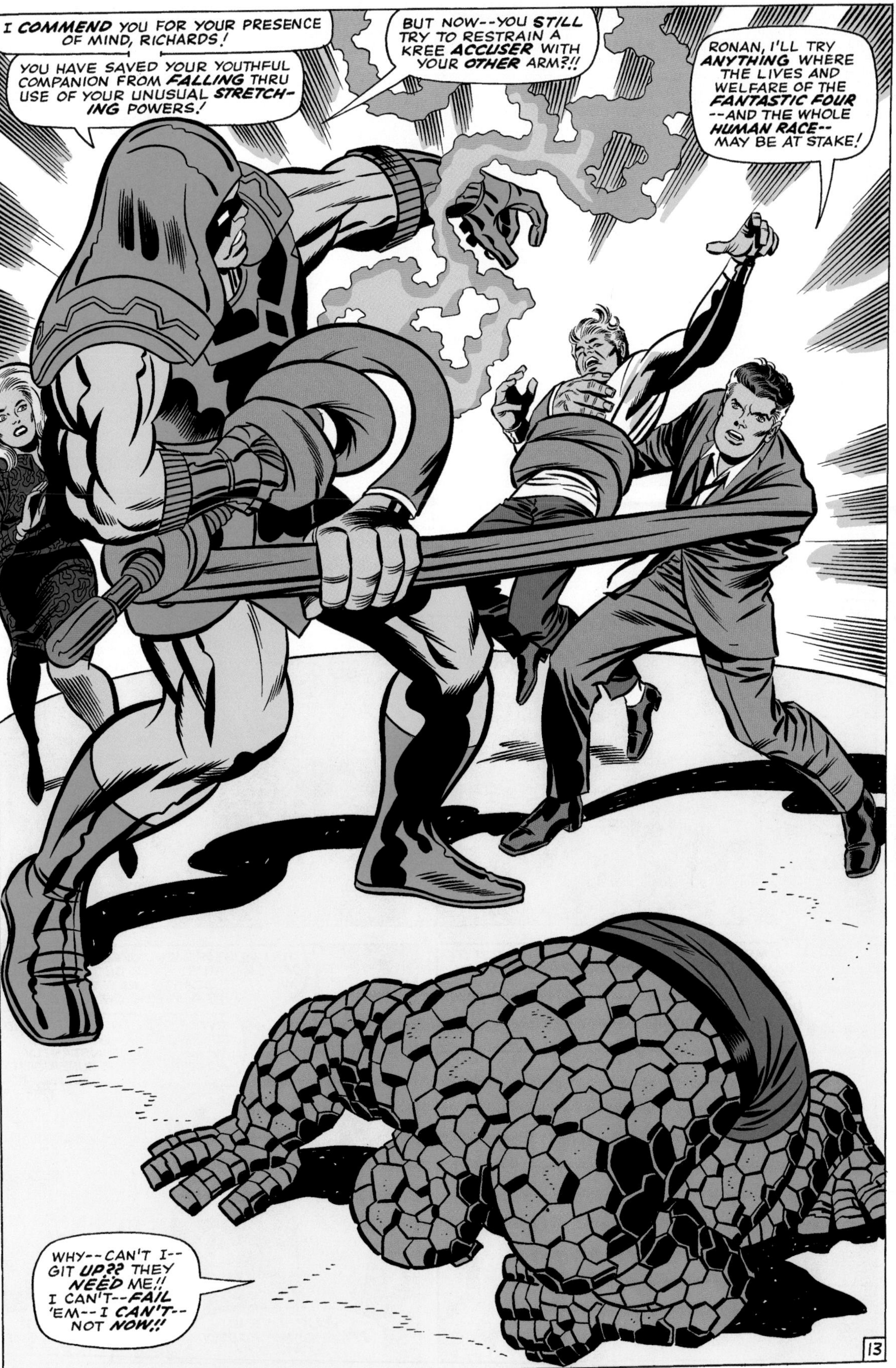
I COMMEND YOU FOR YOUR PRESENCE OF MIND, RICHARDS!
YOU HAVE SAVED YOUR YOUTHFUL COMPANION FROM FALLING THRU USE OF YOUR UNUSUAL STRETCHING POWERS!
BUT NOW--YOU STILL TRY TO RESTRAIN A KREE ACCUSER WITH YOUR OTHER ARM?!!
RONAN, I'LL TRY ANYTHING WHERE THE LIVES AND WELFARE OF THE FANTASTIC FOUR --AND THE WHOLE HUMAN RACE-- MAY BE AT STAKE!
WHY--CAN'T I--GIT UP?? THEY NEED ME!! I CAN'T--FAIL 'EM--I CAN'T--NOT NOW!!
13

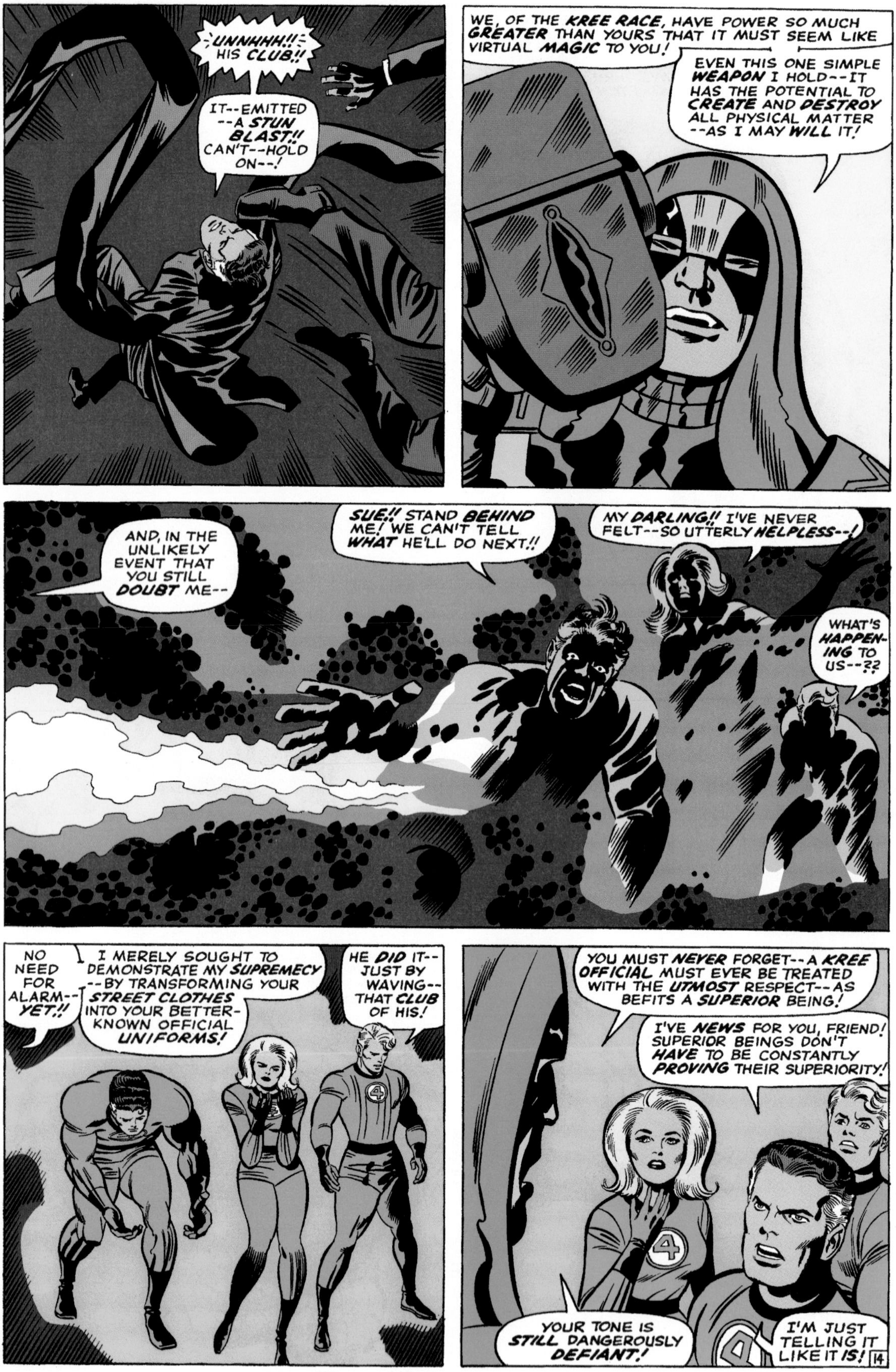
UNNHHH!! HIS CLUB!!
IT--EMITTED --A STUN BLAST!! CAN'T--HOLD ON--!
WE, OF THE KREE RACE, HAVE POWER SO MUCH GREATER THAN YOURS THAT IT MUST SEEM LIKE VIRTUAL MAGIC TO YOU!
EVEN THIS ONE SIMPLE WEAPON I HOLD--IT HAS THE POTENTIAL TO CREATE AND DESTROY ALL PHYSICAL MATTER --AS I MAY WILL IT!
AND, IN THE UNLIKELY EVENT THAT YOU STILL DOUBT ME--
SUE!! STAND BEHIND ME! WE CAN'T TELL WHAT HE'LL DO NEXT!!
MY DARLING!! I'VE NEVER FELT--SO UTTERLY HELPLESS--!
WHAT'S HAPPENING TO US--??
NO NEED FOR ALARM--YET!!
I MERELY SOUGHT TO DEMONSTRATE MY SUPREMECY --BY TRANSFORMING YOUR STREET CLOTHES INTO YOUR BETTER-KNOWN OFFICIAL UNIFORMS!
HE DID IT--JUST BY WAVING--THAT CLUB OF HIS!
YOU MUST NEVER FORGET--A KREE OFFICIAL MUST EVER BE TREATED WITH THE UTMOST RESPECT--AS BEFITS A SUPERIOR BEING!
I'VE NEWS FOR YOU, FRIEND! SUPERIOR BEINGS DON'T HAVE TO BE CONSTANTLY PROVING THEIR SUPERIORITY!
YOUR TONE IS STILL DANGEROUSLY DEFIANT!
I'M JUST TELLING IT LIKE IT IS!
14

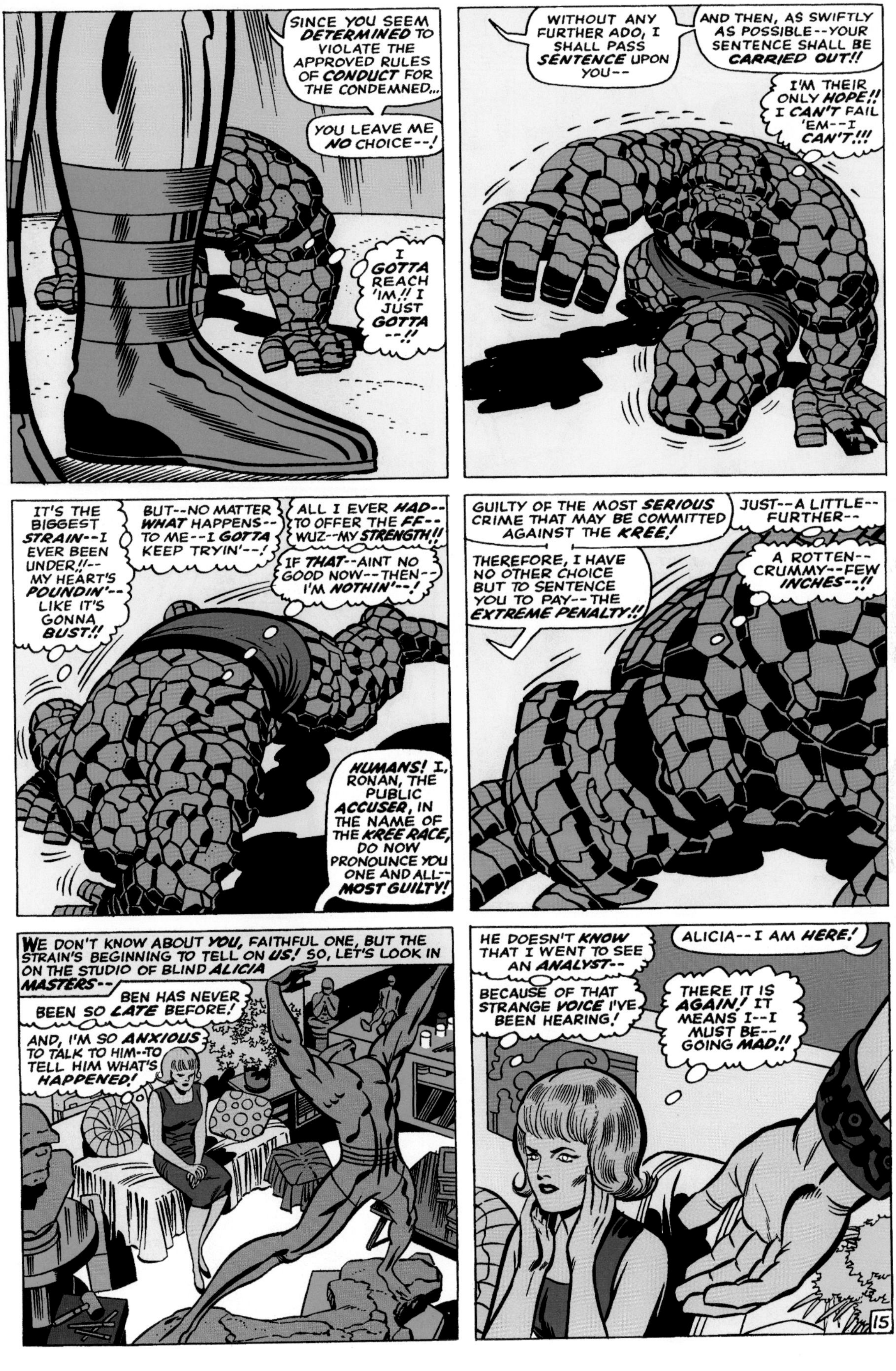
SINCE YOU SEEM DETERMINED TO VIOLATE THE APPROVED RULES OF CONDUCT FOR THE CONDEMNED...
YOU LEAVE ME NO CHOICE--!
I GOTTA REACH 'IM!! I JUST GOTTA--!!
WITHOUT ANY FURTHER ADO, I SHALL PASS SENTENCE UPON YOU--
AND THEN, AS SWIFTLY AS POSSIBLE--YOUR SENTENCE SHALL BE CARRIED OUT!!
I'M THEIR ONLY HOPE!! I CAN'T FAIL 'EM--I CAN'T!!!
IT'S THE BIGGEST STRAIN--I EVER BEEN UNDER!!--MY HEART'S POUNDIN'--LIKE IT'S GONNA BUST!!
BUT--NO MATTER WHAT HAPPENS--TO ME--I GOTTA KEEP TRYIN'--!
ALL I EVER HAD--TO OFFER THE FF--WUZ--MY STRENGTH!!
IF THAT--AINT NO GOOD NOW--THEN--I'M NOTHIN'--!
HUMANS! I, RONAN, THE PUBLIC ACCUSER, IN THE NAME OF THE KREE RACE, DO NOW PRONOUNCE YOU ONE AND ALL--MOST GUILTY!
GUILTY OF THE MOST SERIOUS CRIME THAT MAY BE COMMITTED AGAINST THE KREE!
THEREFORE, I HAVE NO OTHER CHOICE BUT TO SENTENCE YOU TO PAY--THE EXTREME PENALTY!!
JUST--A LITTLE--FURTHER--
A ROTTEN--CRUMMY--FEW INCHES--!!
WE DON'T KNOW ABOUT YOU, FAITHFUL ONE, BUT THE STRAIN'S BEGINNING TO TELL ON US! SO, LET'S LOOK IN ON THE STUDIO OF BLIND ALICIA MASTERS--
BEN HAS NEVER BEEN SO LATE BEFORE!
AND, I'M SO ANXIOUS TO TALK TO HIM--TO TELL HIM WHAT'S HAPPENED!
HE DOESN'T KNOW THAT I WENT TO SEE AN ANALYST--
BECAUSE OF THAT STRANGE VOICE I'VE BEEN HEARING!
ALICIA--I AM HERE!
THERE IT IS AGAIN! IT MEANS I--I MUST BE--GOING MAD!!
15

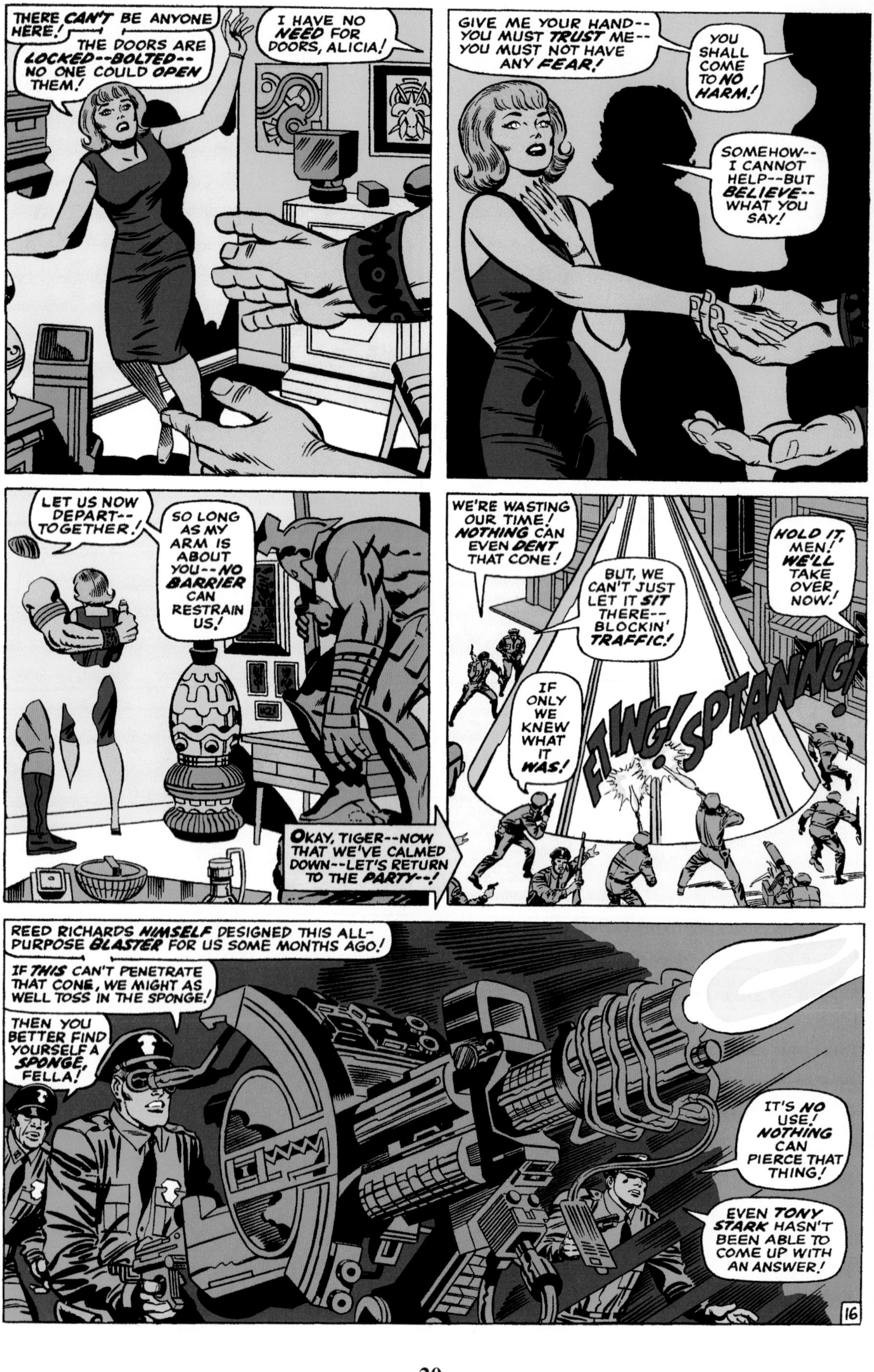
THERE CAN'T BE ANYONE HERE!
THE DOORS ARE LOCKED--BOLTED--NO ONE COULD OPEN THEM!
I HAVE NO NEED FOR DOORS, ALICIA!
GIVE ME YOUR HAND--YOU MUST TRUST ME--YOU MUST NOT HAVE ANY FEAR!
YOU SHALL COME TO NO HARM!
SOMEHOW--I CANNOT HELP--BUT BELIEVE--WHAT YOU SAY!
LET US NOW DEPART--TOGETHER!
SO LONG AS MY ARM IS ABOUT YOU--NO BARRIER CAN RESTRAIN US!
OKAY, TIGER--NOW THAT WE'VE CALMED DOWN--LET'S RETURN TO THE PARTY--!
WE'RE WASTING OUR TIME! NOTHING CAN EVEN DENT THAT CONE!
BUT, WE CAN'T JUST LET IT SIT THERE--BLOCKIN' TRAFFIC!
HOLD IT, MEN! WE'LL TAKE OVER NOW!
IF ONLY WE KNEW WHAT IT WAS!
FTING! SPTANNG!
REED RICHARDS HIMSELF DESIGNED THIS ALL-PURPOSE BLASTER FOR US SOME MONTHS AGO!
IF THIS CAN'T PENETRATE THAT CONE, WE MIGHT AS WELL TOSS IN THE SPONGE!
THEN YOU BETTER FIND YOURSELF A SPONGE, FELLA!
IT'S NO USE! NOTHING CAN PIERCE THAT THING!
EVEN TONY STARK HASN'T BEEN ABLE TO COME UP WITH AN ANSWER!
16

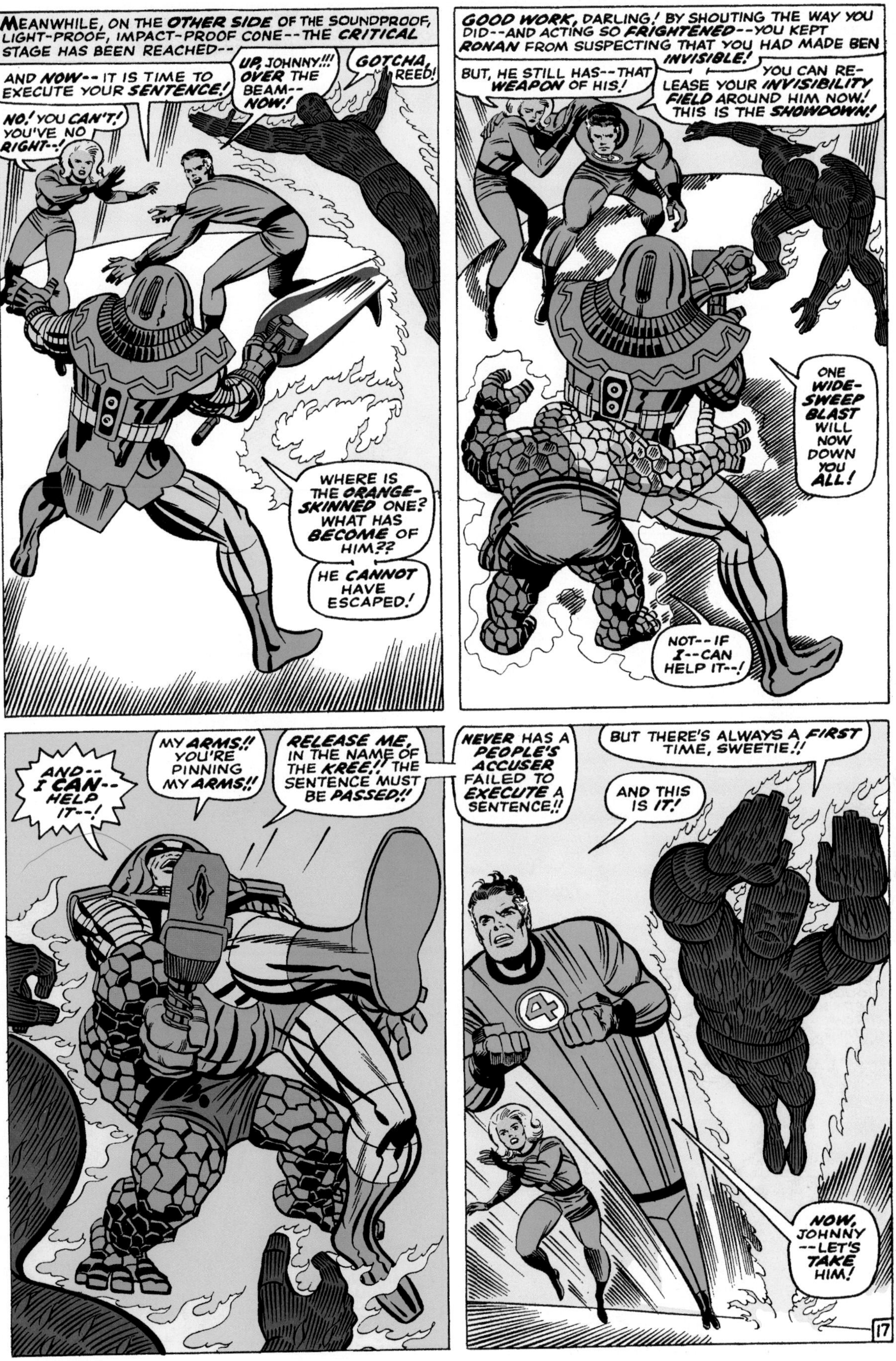

MEANWHILE, ON THE OTHER SIDE OF THE SOUNDPROOF, LIGHT-PROOF, IMPACT-PROOF CONE--THE CRITICAL STAGE HAS BEEN REACHED--
AND NOW--IT IS TIME TO EXECUTE YOUR SENTENCE!
UP, JOHNNY!!! OVER THE BEAM--NOW!
GOTCHA, REED!
NO! YOU CAN'T! YOU'VE NO RIGHT--!
WHERE IS THE ORANGE-SKINNED ONE? WHAT HAS BECOME OF HIM??
HE CANNOT HAVE ESCAPED!
GOOD WORK, DARLING! BY SHOUTING THE WAY YOU DID--AND ACTING SO FRIGHTENED--YOU KEPT RONAN FROM SUSPECTING THAT YOU HAD MADE BEN INVISIBLE!
YOU CAN RE-LEASE YOUR INVISIBILITY FIELD AROUND HIM NOW! THIS IS THE SHOWDOWN!
BUT, HE STILL HAS--THAT WEAPON OF HIS!
ONE WIDE-SWEEP BLAST WILL NOW DOWN YOU ALL!
NOT--IF I--CAN HELP IT--!
AND--I CAN--HELP IT--!
MY ARMS!! YOU'RE PINNING MY ARMS!!
RELEASE ME, IN THE NAME OF THE KREE!! THE SENTENCE MUST BE PASSED!!
NEVER HAS A PEOPLE'S ACCUSER FAILED TO EXECUTE A SENTENCE!!
BUT THERE'S ALWAYS A FIRST TIME, SWEETIE!!
AND THIS IS IT!
NOW, JOHNNY--LET'S TAKE HIM!
17

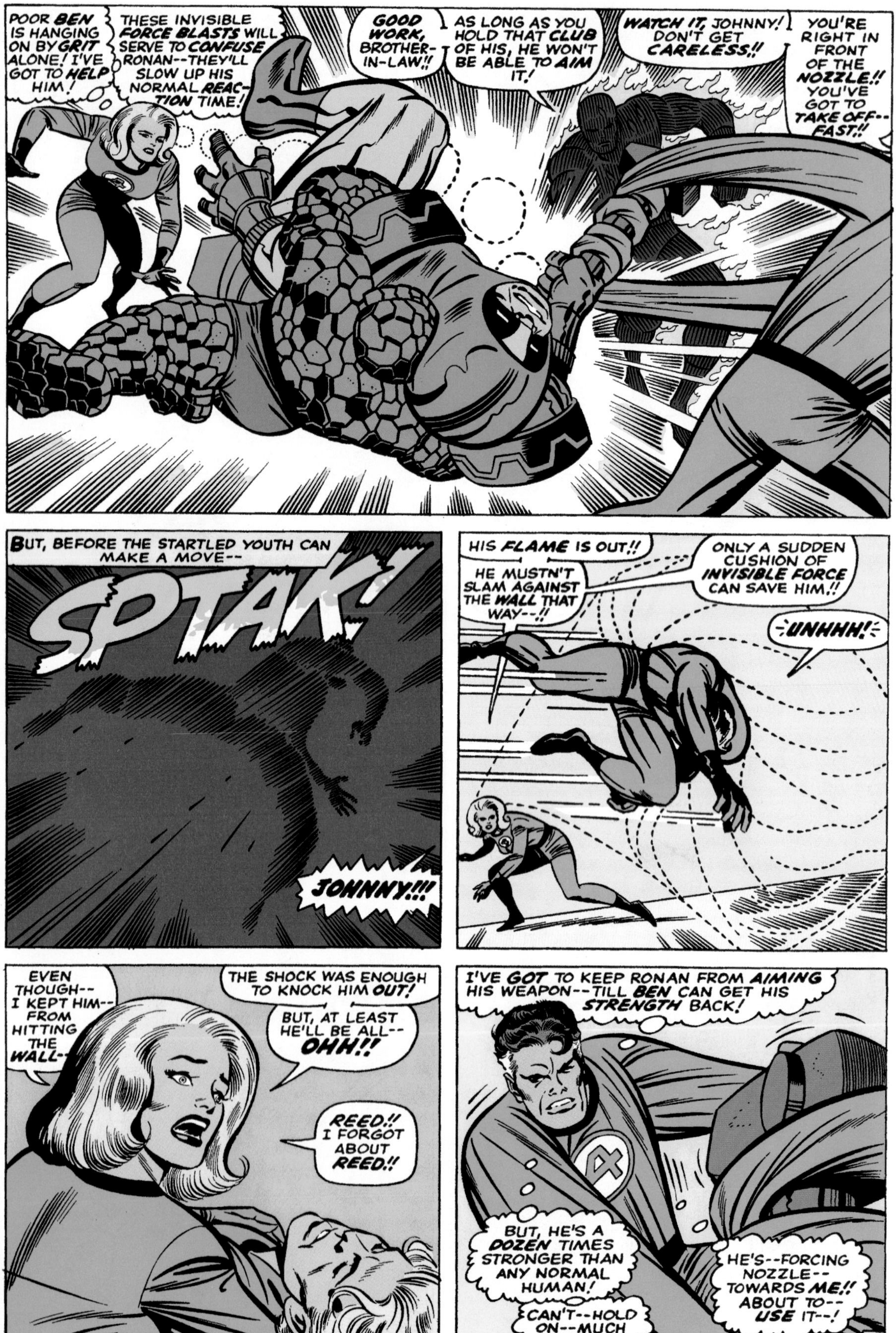
POOR BEN IS HANGING ON BY GRIT ALONE! I'VE GOT TO HELP HIM!
THESE INVISIBLE FORCE BLASTS WILL SERVE TO CONFUSE RONAN--THEY'LL SLOW UP HIS NORMAL REACTION TIME!
GOOD WORK, BROTHER-IN-LAW!!
AS LONG AS YOU HOLD THAT CLUB OF HIS, HE WON'T BE ABLE TO AIM IT!
WATCH IT, JOHNNY! DON'T GET CARELESS!!
YOU'RE RIGHT IN FRONT OF THE NOZZLE!! YOU'VE GOT TO TAKE OFF--FAST!!
BUT, BEFORE THE STARTLED YOUTH CAN MAKE A MOVE--
SPTAK!
JOHNNY!!!
HIS FLAME IS OUT!!
HE MUSTN'T SLAM AGAINST THE WALL THAT WAY--!!
ONLY A SUDDEN CUSHION OF INVISIBLE FORCE CAN SAVE HIM!!
UNHHH!
EVEN THOUGH--I KEPT HIM--FROM HITTING THE WALL--
THE SHOCK WAS ENOUGH TO KNOCK HIM OUT!
BUT, AT LEAST HE'LL BE ALL--OHH!!
REED!! I FORGOT ABOUT REED!!
I'VE GOT TO KEEP RONAN FROM AIMING HIS WEAPON--TILL BEN CAN GET HIS STRENGTH BACK!
BUT, HE'S A DOZEN TIMES STRONGER THAN ANY NORMAL HUMAN!
CAN'T--HOLD ON--MUCH LONGER--!
HE'S--FORCING NOZZLE--TOWARDS ME!! ABOUT TO--USE IT--!
18

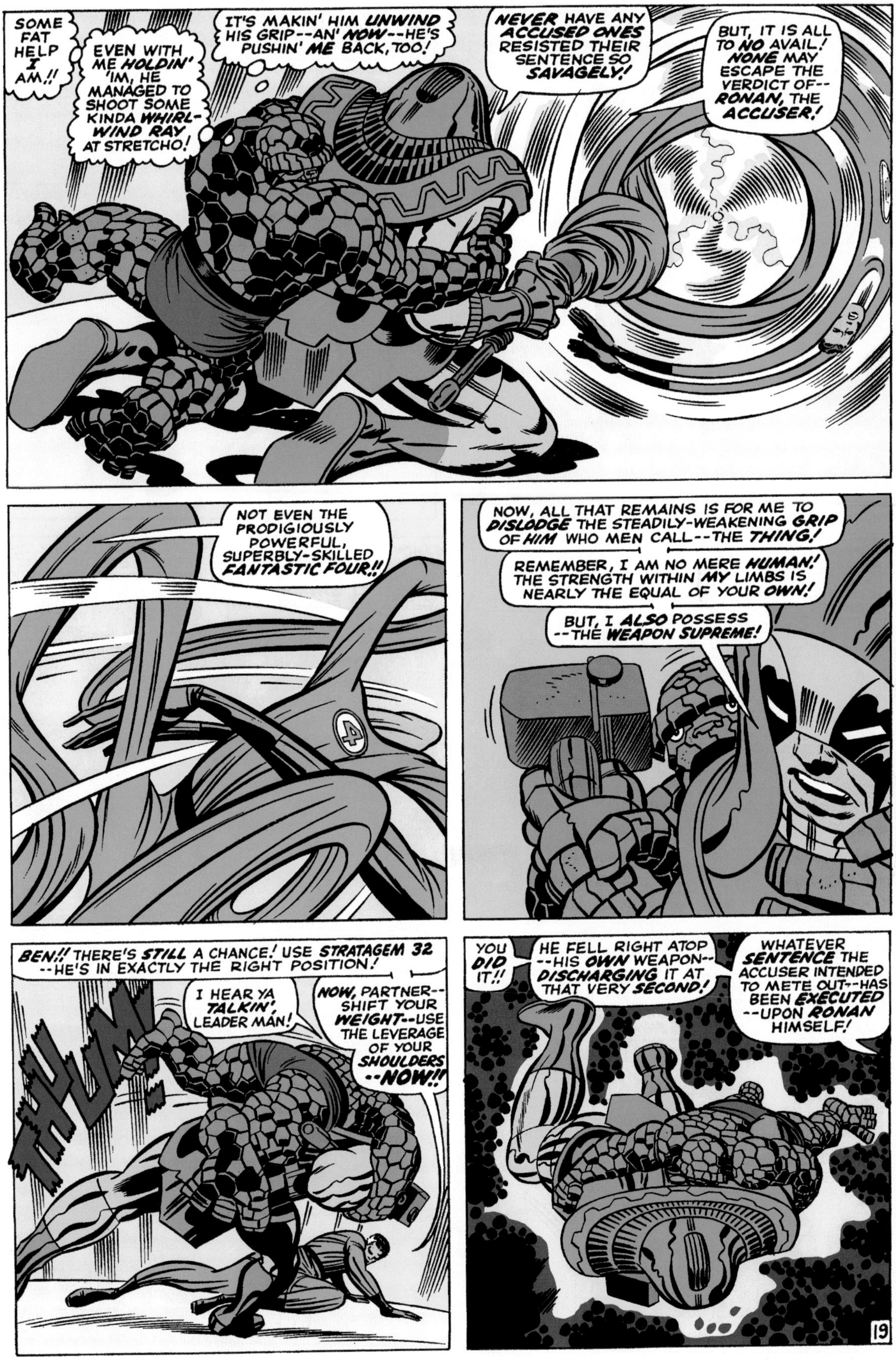
SOME FAT HELP I AM.!!
EVEN WITH ME HOLDIN' 'IM, HE MANAGED TO SHOOT SOME KINDA WHIRL-WIND RAY AT STRETCHO!
IT'S MAKIN' HIM UNWIND HIS GRIP--AN' NOW--HE'S PUSHIN' ME BACK, TOO!
NEVER HAVE ANY ACCUSED ONES RESISTED THEIR SENTENCE SO SAVAGELY!
BUT, IT IS ALL TO NO AVAIL! NONE MAY ESCAPE THE VERDICT OF--RONAN, THE ACCUSER!
NOT EVEN THE PRODIGIOUSLY POWERFUL, SUPERBLY-SKILLED FANTASTIC FOUR!!
NOW, ALL THAT REMAINS IS FOR ME TO DISLODGE THE STEADILY-WEAKENING GRIP OF HIM WHO MEN CALL--THE THING!
REMEMBER, I AM NO MERE HUMAN! THE STRENGTH WITHIN MY LIMBS IS NEARLY THE EQUAL OF YOUR OWN!
BUT, I ALSO POSSESS --THE WEAPON SUPREME!
BEN!! THERE'S STILL A CHANCE! USE STRATAGEM 32 --HE'S IN EXACTLY THE RIGHT POSITION!
I HEAR YA TALKIN', LEADER MAN!
NOW, PARTNER--SHIFT YOUR WEIGHT--USE THE LEVERAGE OF YOUR SHOULDERS --NOW!!
THUM!
YOU DID IT!!
HE FELL RIGHT ATOP --HIS OWN WEAPON--DISCHARGING IT AT THAT VERY SECOND!
WHATEVER SENTENCE THE ACCUSER INTENDED TO METE OUT--HAS BEEN EXECUTED --UPON RONAN HIMSELF!
19

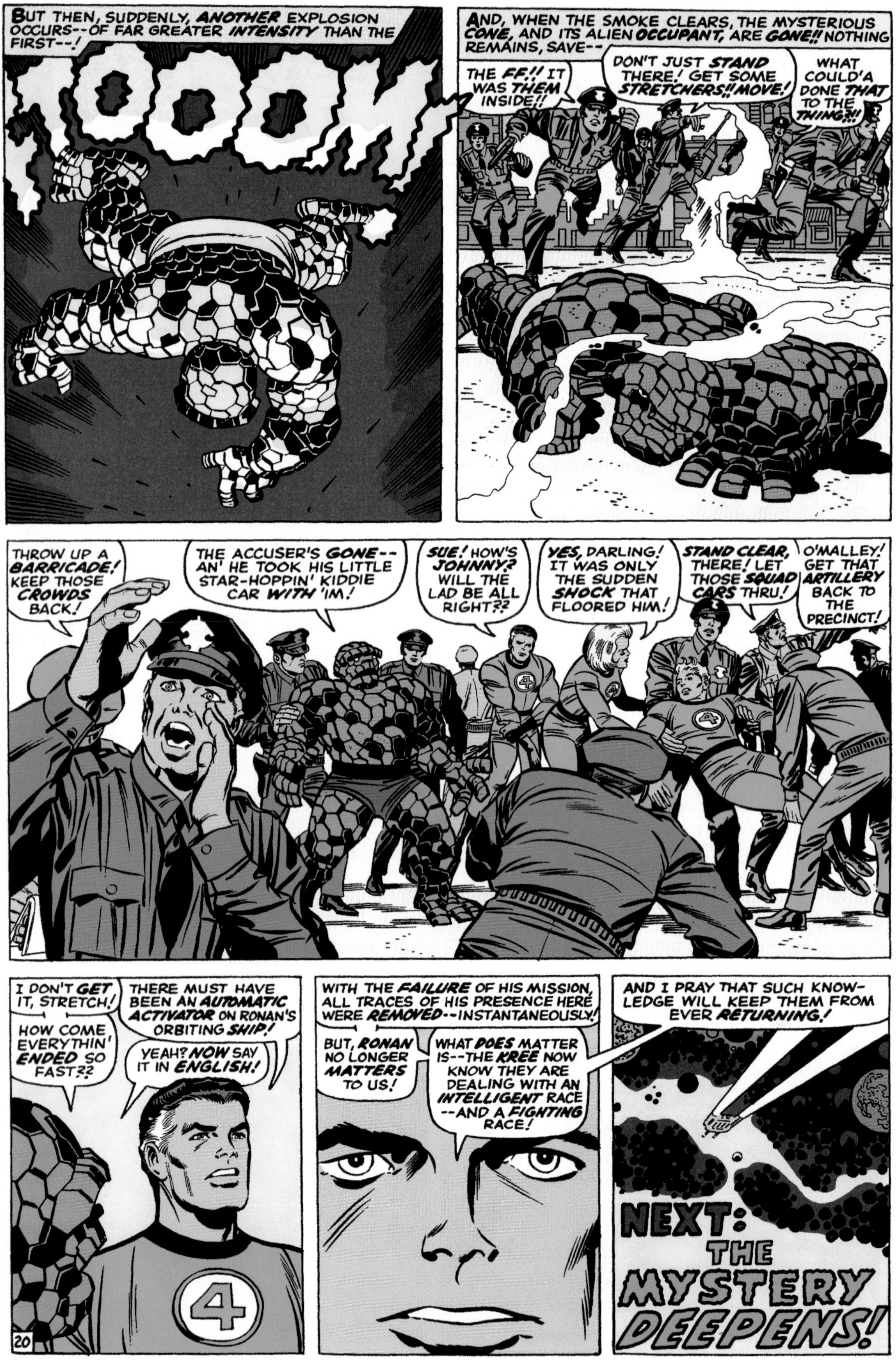
BUT THEN, SUDDENLY, ANOTHER EXPLOSION OCCURS--OF FAR GREATER INTENSITY THAN THE FIRST--!
TOOOM
AND, WHEN THE SMOKE CLEARS, THE MYSTERIOUS CONE, AND ITS ALIEN OCCUPANT, ARE GONE!! NOTHING REMAINS, SAVE--
THE FF!! IT WAS THEM INSIDE!!
DON'T JUST STAND THERE! GET SOME STRETCHERS!! MOVE!
WHAT COULD'A DONE THAT TO THE THING?!!
THROW UP A BARRICADE! KEEP THOSE CROWDS BACK!
THE ACCUSER'S GONE-- AN' HE TOOK HIS LITTLE STAR-HOPPIN' KIDDIE CAR WITH 'IM!
SUE! HOW'S JOHNNY? WILL THE LAD BE ALL RIGHT??
YES, DARLING! IT WAS ONLY THE SUDDEN SHOCK THAT FLOORED HIM!
STAND CLEAR, THERE! LET THOSE SQUAD CARS THRU!
O'MALLEY! GET THAT ARTILLERY BACK TO THE PRECINCT!
I DON'T GET IT, STRETCH!
HOW COME EVERYTHIN' ENDED SO FAST??
THERE MUST HAVE BEEN AN AUTOMATIC ACTIVATOR ON RONAN'S ORBITING SHIP!
YEAH? NOW SAY IT IN ENGLISH!
20
WITH THE FAILURE OF HIS MISSION, ALL TRACES OF HIS PRESENCE HERE WERE REMOVED--INSTANTANEOUSLY!
BUT, RONAN NO LONGER MATTERS TO US!
WHAT DOES MATTER IS--THE KREE NOW KNOW THEY ARE DEALING WITH AN INTELLIGENT RACE --AND A FIGHTING RACE!
AND I PRAY THAT SUCH KNOW-LEDGE WILL KEEP THEM FROM EVER RETURNING!
NEXT: THE MYSTERY DEEPENS!

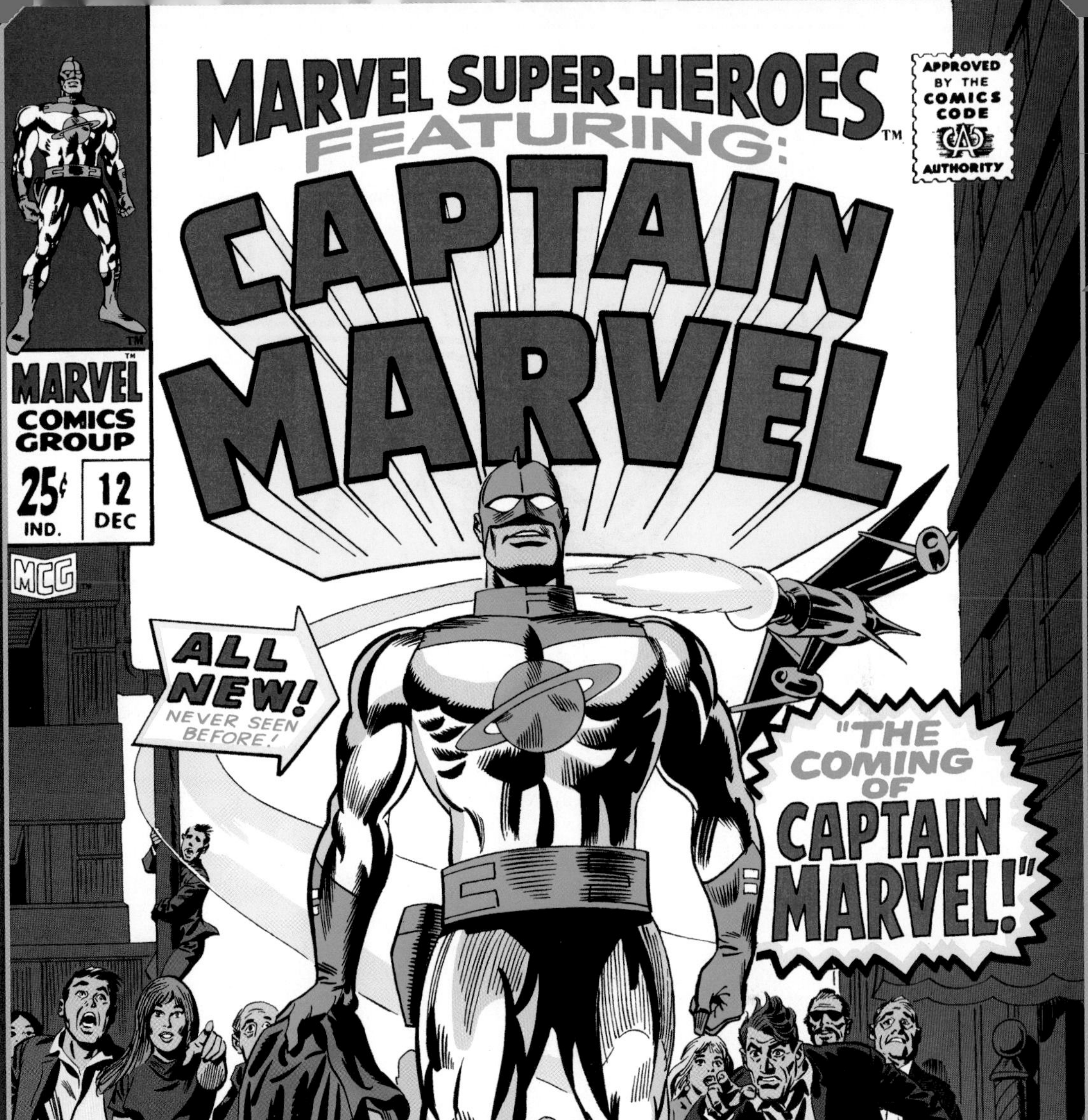
MARVEL SUPER-HEROES FEATURING: CAPTAIN MARVEL
APPROVED BY THE COMICS CODE AUTHORITY
MARVEL COMICS GROUP
25¢ IND.
12 DEC
MCG
ALL NEW! NEVER SEEN BEFORE!
"THE COMING OF CAPTAIN MARVEL!"
PLUS: FIVE ALL-TIME GREATS FROM THE GOLDEN AGE!
THE BLACK KNIGHT!
THE DESTROYER!
CAPTAIN AMERICA!
THE HUMAN TORCH!
THE SUB-MARINER!
FACE IT, TIGER! THIS IS THE BIGGEST ONE YET FROM THE HOUSE OF IDEAS!

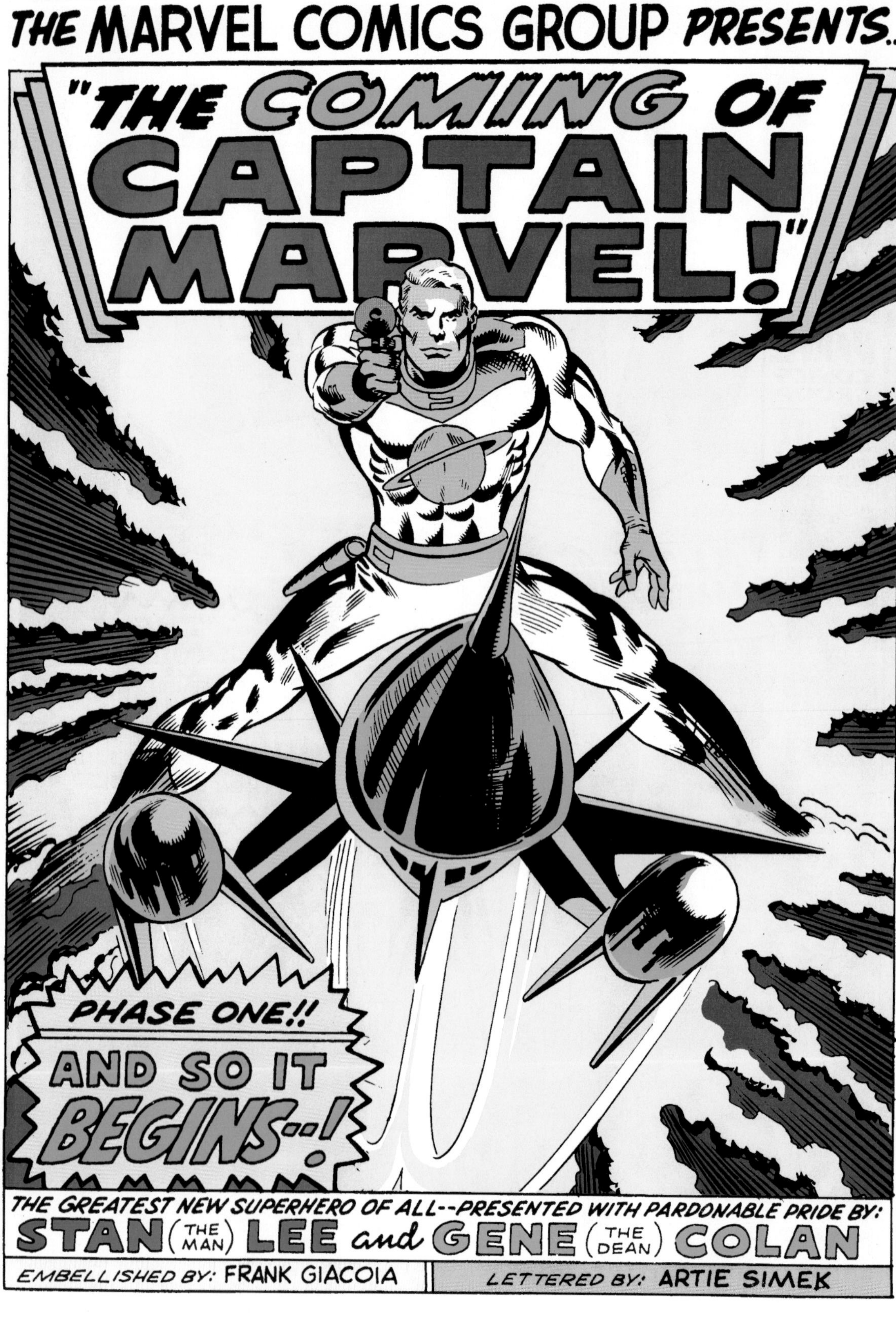
THE MARVEL COMICS GROUP PRESENTS...
"THE COMING OF CAPTAIN MARVEL!"
PHASE ONE!!
AND SO IT BEGINS..!
THE GREATEST NEW SUPERHERO OF ALL--PRESENTED WITH PARDONABLE PRIDE BY:
STAN (THE MAN) LEE and GENE (THE DEAN) COLAN
EMBELLISHED BY: FRANK GIACOIA
LETTERED BY: ARTIE SIMEK

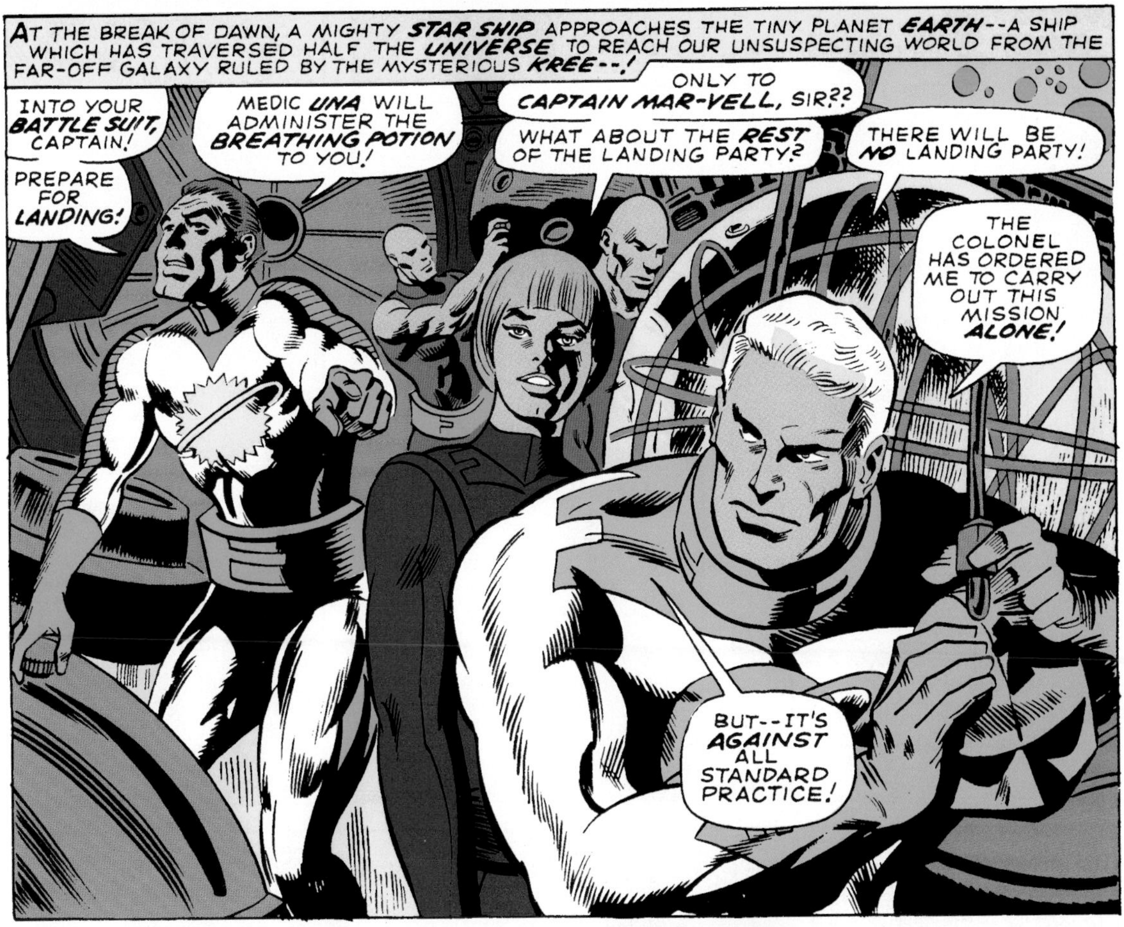
AT THE BREAK OF DAWN, A MIGHTY STAR SHIP APPROACHES THE TINY PLANET EARTH--A SHIP WHICH HAS TRAVERSED HALF THE UNIVERSE TO REACH OUR UNSUSPECTING WORLD FROM THE FAR-OFF GALAXY RULED BY THE MYSTERIOUS KREE--!
INTO YOUR BATTLE SUIT, CAPTAIN!
PREPARE FOR LANDING!
MEDIC UNA WILL ADMINISTER THE BREATHING POTION TO YOU!
ONLY TO CAPTAIN MAR-VELL, SIR??
WHAT ABOUT THE REST OF THE LANDING PARTY?
THERE WILL BE NO LANDING PARTY!
THE COLONEL HAS ORDERED ME TO CARRY OUT THIS MISSION ALONE!
BUT--IT'S AGAINST ALL STANDARD PRACTICE!

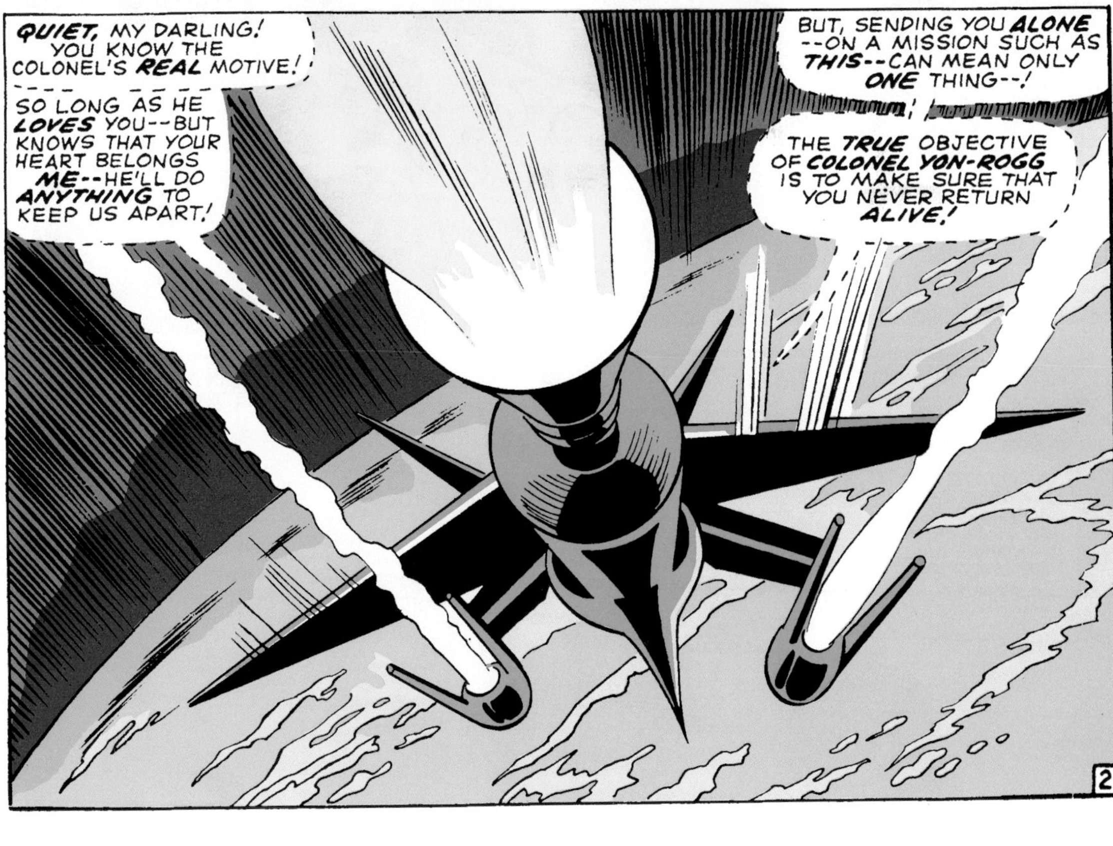
QUIET, MY DARLING! YOU KNOW THE COLONEL'S REAL MOTIVE!
SO LONG AS HE LOVES YOU--BUT KNOWS THAT YOUR HEART BELONGS TO ME--HE'LL DO ANYTHING TO KEEP US APART!
BUT, SENDING YOU ALONE --ON A MISSION SUCH AS THIS--CAN MEAN ONLY ONE THING--!
THE TRUE OBJECTIVE OF COLONEL YON-ROGG IS TO MAKE SURE THAT YOU NEVER RETURN ALIVE!
2

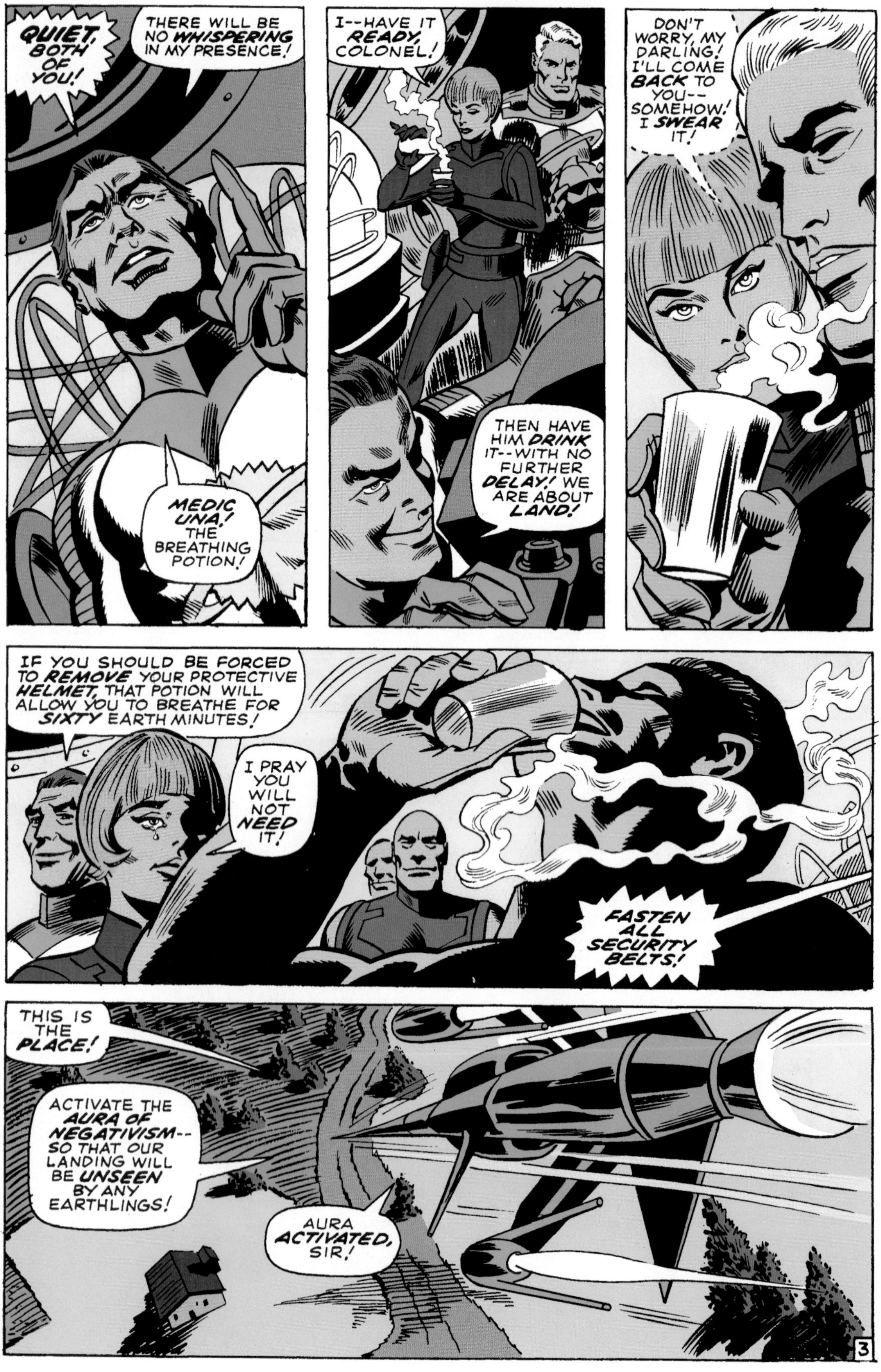
QUIET, BOTH OF YOU!
THERE WILL BE NO WHISPERING IN MY PRESENCE!
MEDIC UNA! THE BREATHING POTION!
I--HAVE IT READY, COLONEL!
THEN HAVE HIM DRINK IT--WITH NO FURTHER DELAY! WE ARE ABOUT LAND!
DON'T WORRY, MY DARLING! I'LL COME BACK TO YOU--SOMEHOW! I SWEAR IT!
IF YOU SHOULD BE FORCED TO REMOVE YOUR PROTECTIVE HELMET, THAT POTION WILL ALLOW YOU TO BREATHE FOR SIXTY EARTH MINUTES!
I PRAY YOU WILL NOT NEED IT!
FASTEN ALL SECURITY BELTS!
THIS IS THE PLACE!
ACTIVATE THE AURA OF NEGATIVISM--SO THAT OUR LANDING WILL BE UNSEEN BY ANY EARTHLINGS!
AURA ACTIVATED, SIR!
3

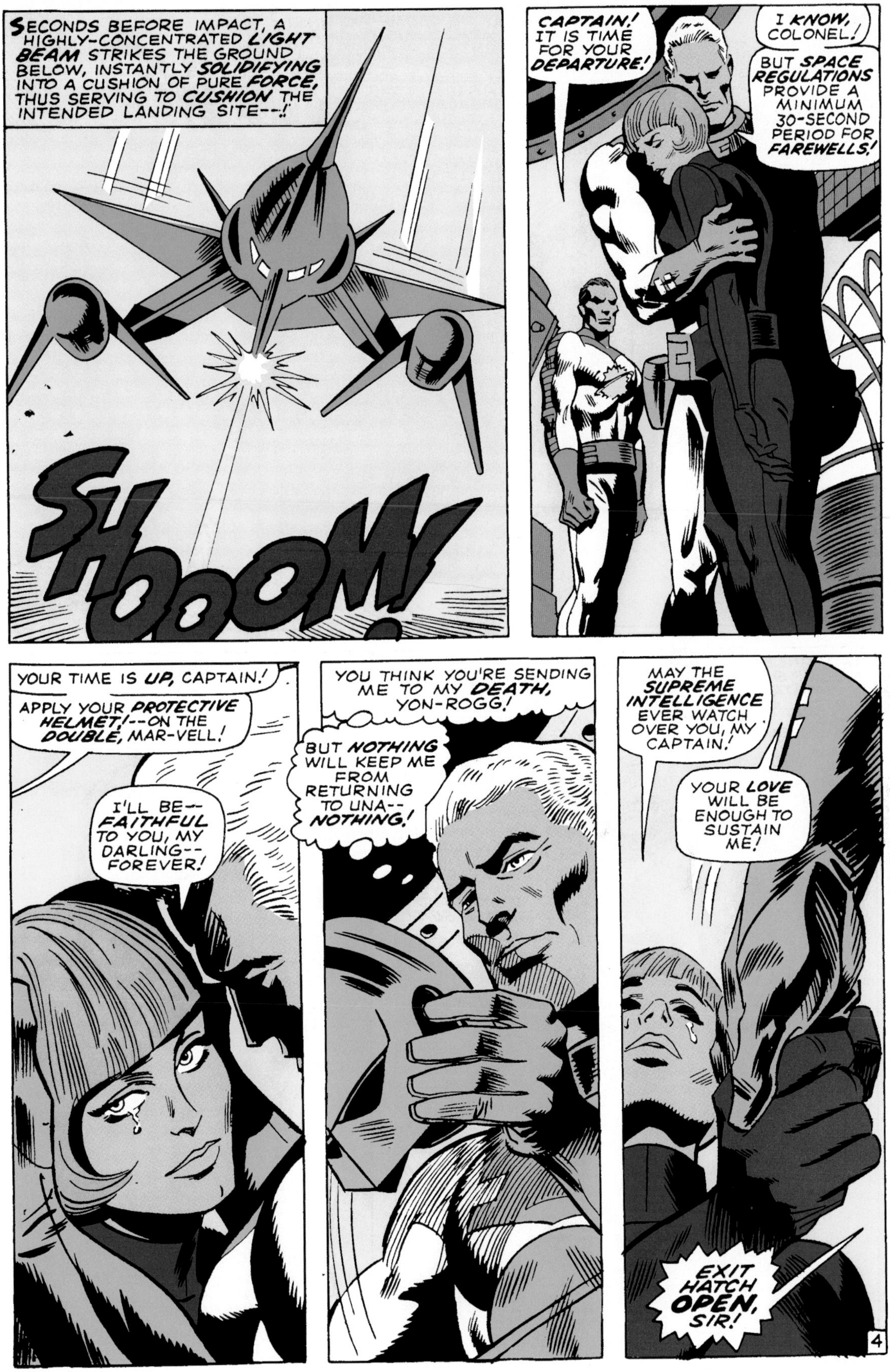
SECONDS BEFORE IMPACT, A HIGHLY-CONCENTRATED LIGHT BEAM STRIKES THE GROUND BELOW, INSTANTLY SOLIDIFYING INTO A CUSHION OF PURE FORCE, THUS SERVING TO CUSHION THE INTENDED LANDING SITE--!
SHOOOOM!
CAPTAIN! IT IS TIME FOR YOUR DEPARTURE!
I KNOW, COLONEL!
BUT SPACE REGULATIONS PROVIDE A MINIMUM 30-SECOND PERIOD FOR FAREWELLS!
YOUR TIME IS UP, CAPTAIN!
APPLY YOUR PROTECTIVE HELMET!--ON THE DOUBLE, MAR-VELL!
I'LL BE--FAITHFUL TO YOU, MY DARLING--FOREVER!
YOU THINK YOU'RE SENDING ME TO MY DEATH, YON-ROGG!
BUT NOTHING WILL KEEP ME FROM RETURNING TO UNA--NOTHING!
MAY THE SUPREME INTELLIGENCE EVER WATCH OVER YOU, MY CAPTAIN!
YOUR LOVE WILL BE ENOUGH TO SUSTAIN ME!
EXIT HATCH OPEN, SIR!
4

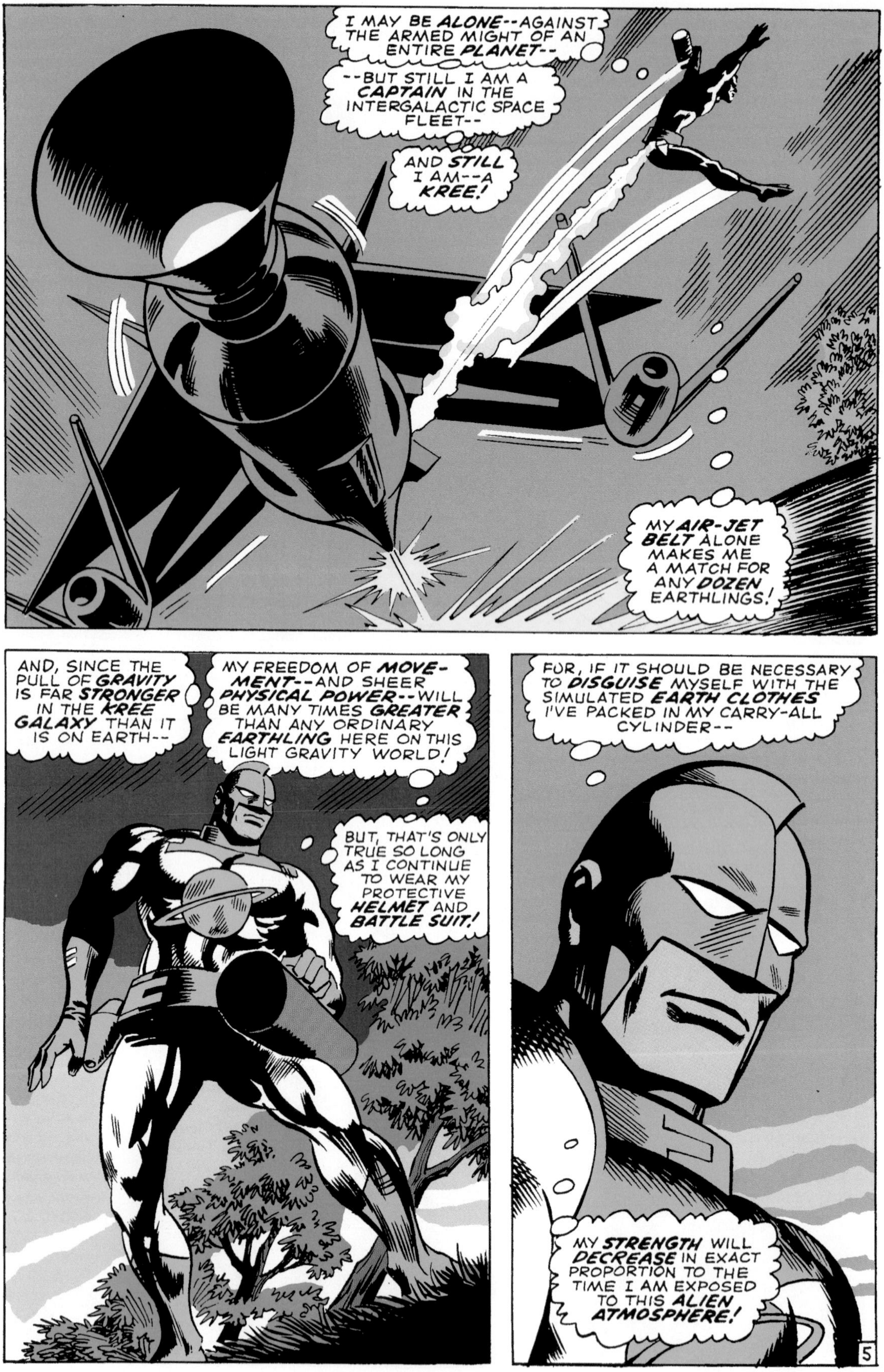
I MAY BE ALONE--AGAINST THE ARMED MIGHT OF AN ENTIRE PLANET--
--BUT STILL I AM A CAPTAIN IN THE INTERGALACTIC SPACE FLEET--
AND STILL I AM--A KREE!
MY AIR-JET BELT ALONE MAKES ME A MATCH FOR ANY DOZEN EARTHLINGS!
AND, SINCE THE PULL OF GRAVITY IS FAR STRONGER IN THE KREE GALAXY THAN IT IS ON EARTH--
MY FREEDOM OF MOVE-MENT--AND SHEER PHYSICAL POWER--WILL BE MANY TIMES GREATER THAN ANY ORDINARY EARTHLING HERE ON THIS LIGHT GRAVITY WORLD!
BUT, THAT'S ONLY TRUE SO LONG AS I CONTINUE TO WEAR MY PROTECTIVE HELMET AND BATTLE SUIT!
FOR, IF IT SHOULD BE NECESSARY TO DISGUISE MYSELF WITH THE SIMULATED EARTH CLOTHES I'VE PACKED IN MY CARRY-ALL CYLINDER--
MY STRENGTH WILL DECREASE IN EXACT PROPORTION TO THE TIME I AM EXPOSED TO THIS ALIEN ATMOSPHERE!
5

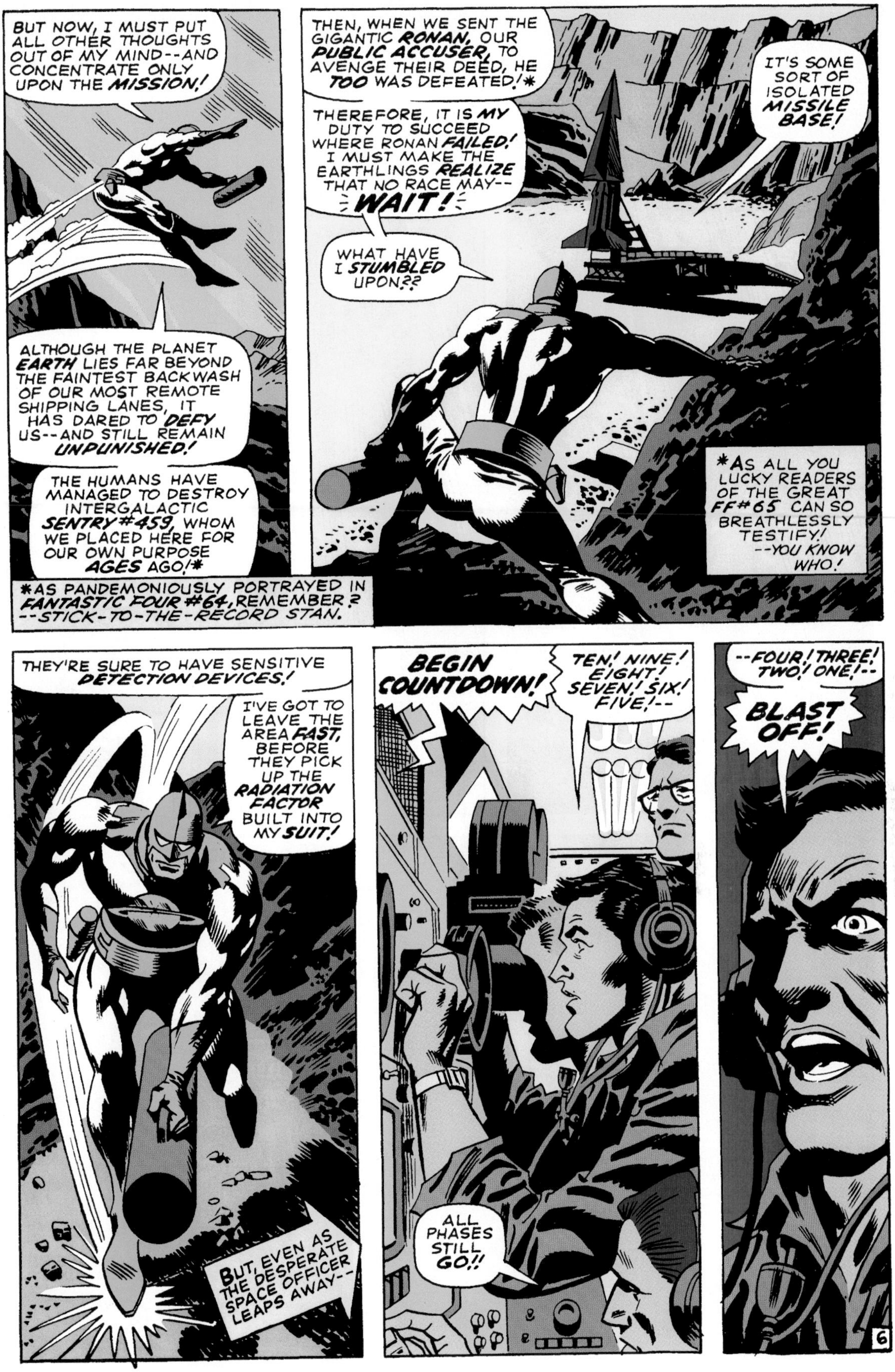
BUT NOW, I MUST PUT ALL OTHER THOUGHTS OUT OF MY MIND--AND CONCENTRATE ONLY UPON THE MISSION!
ALTHOUGH THE PLANET EARTH LIES FAR BEYOND THE FAINTEST BACKWASH OF OUR MOST REMOTE SHIPPING LANES, IT HAS DARED TO DEFY US--AND STILL REMAIN UNPUNISHED!
THE HUMANS HAVE MANAGED TO DESTROY INTERGALACTIC SENTRY #459, WHOM WE PLACED HERE FOR OUR OWN PURPOSE AGES AGO!*
*AS PANDEMONIOUSLY PORTRAYED IN FANTASTIC FOUR #64, REMEMBER? --STICK-TO-THE-RECORD STAN.
THEN, WHEN WE SENT THE GIGANTIC RONAN, OUR PUBLIC ACCUSER, TO AVENGE THEIR DEED, HE TOO WAS DEFEATED!*
THEREFORE, IT IS MY DUTY TO SUCCEED WHERE RONAN FAILED! I MUST MAKE THE EARTHLINGS REALIZE THAT NO RACE MAY--
WAIT!
WHAT HAVE I STUMBLED UPON??
IT'S SOME SORT OF ISOLATED MISSILE BASE!
*AS ALL YOU LUCKY READERS OF THE GREAT FF#65 CAN SO BREATHLESSLY TESTIFY! --YOU KNOW WHO!
THEY'RE SURE TO HAVE SENSITIVE DETECTION DEVICES!
I'VE GOT TO LEAVE THE AREA FAST, BEFORE THEY PICK UP THE RADIATION FACTOR BUILT INTO MY SUIT!
BUT, EVEN AS THE DESPERATE SPACE OFFICER LEAPS AWAY--
BEGIN COUNTDOWN!
TEN! NINE! EIGHT! SEVEN! SIX! FIVE!--
ALL PHASES STILL GO!!
--FOUR! THREE! TWO! ONE!--
BLAST OFF!
6

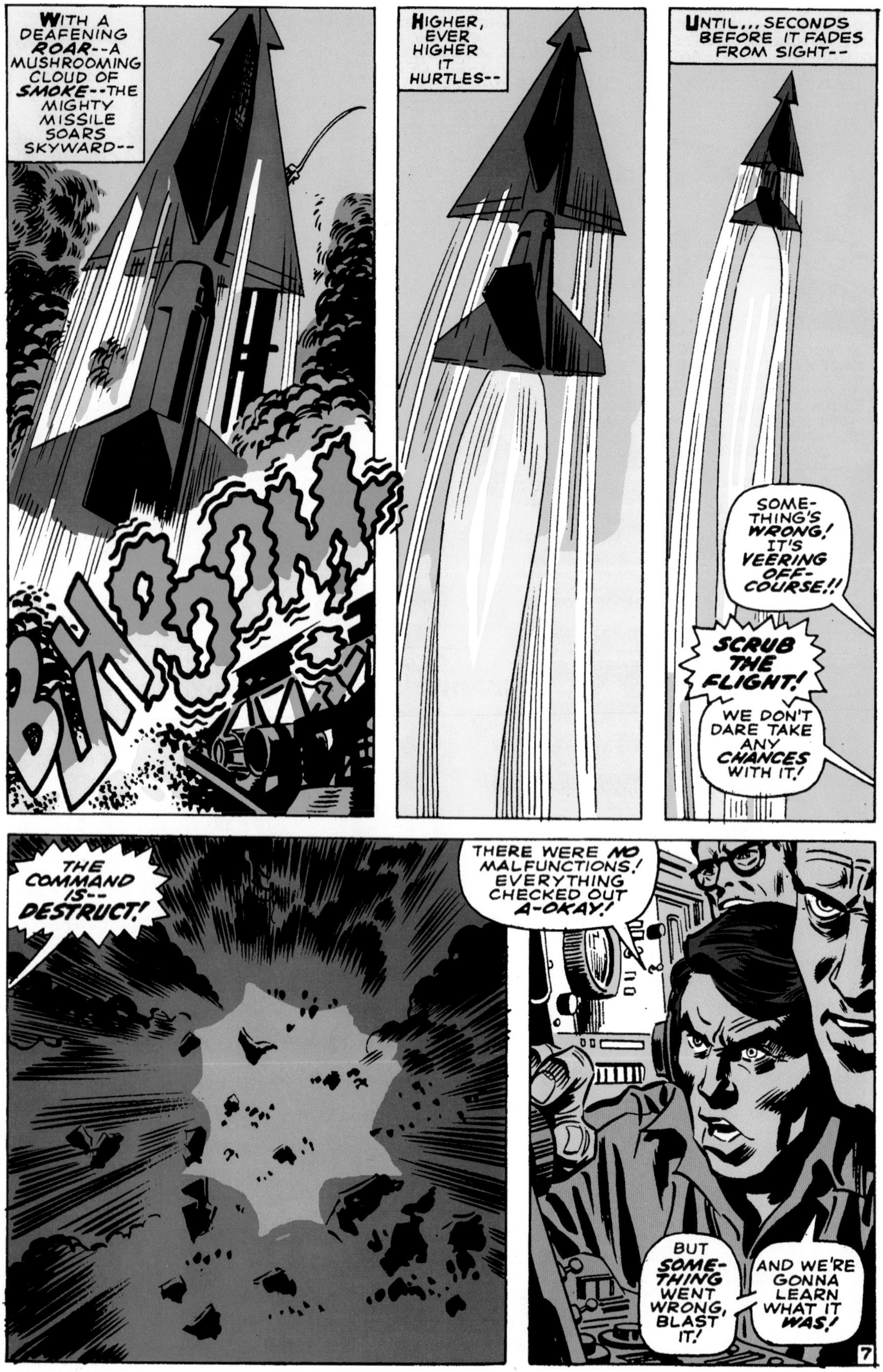

WITH A DEAFENING ROAR--A MUSHROOMING CLOUD OF SMOKE--THE MIGHTY MISSILE SOARS SKYWARD--
BHOOM!
HIGHER, EVER HIGHER IT HURTLES--
UNTIL... SECONDS BEFORE IT FADES FROM SIGHT--
SOME-THING'S WRONG! IT'S VEERING OFF-COURSE!!
SCRUB THE FLIGHT!
WE DON'T DARE TAKE ANY CHANCES WITH IT!
THE COMMAND IS--DESTRUCT!
THERE WERE NO MALFUNCTIONS! EVERYTHING CHECKED OUT A-OKAY!
BUT SOME-THING WENT WRONG, BLAST IT!
AND WE'RE GONNA LEARN WHAT IT WAS!
7

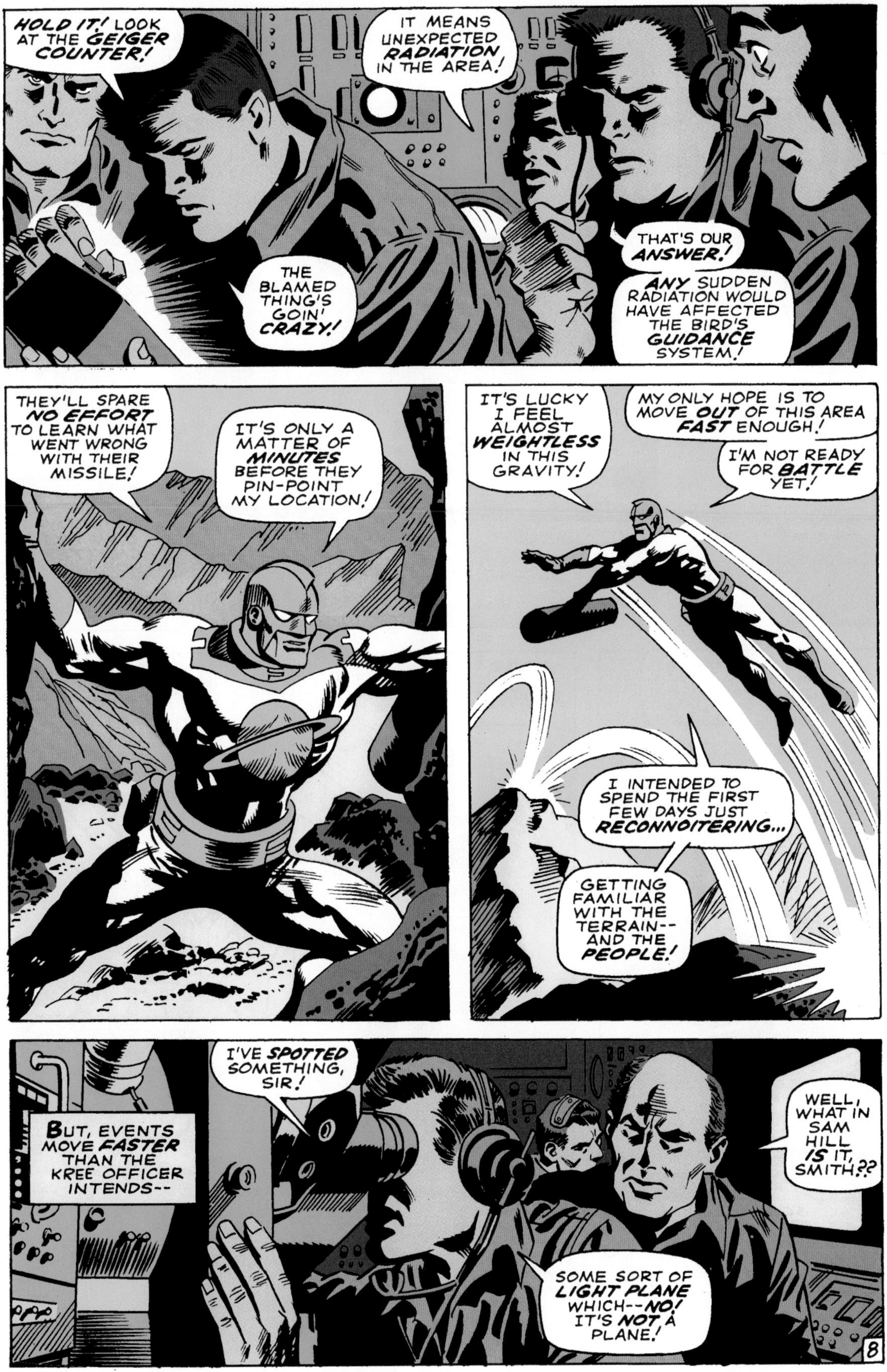
HOLD IT! LOOK AT THE GEIGER COUNTER!
IT MEANS UNEXPECTED RADIATION IN THE AREA!
THE BLAMED THING'S GOIN' CRAZY!
THAT'S OUR ANSWER!
ANY SUDDEN RADIATION WOULD HAVE AFFECTED THE BIRD'S GUIDANCE SYSTEM!
THEY'LL SPARE NO EFFORT TO LEARN WHAT WENT WRONG WITH THEIR MISSILE!
IT'S ONLY A MATTER OF MINUTES BEFORE THEY PIN-POINT MY LOCATION!
IT'S LUCKY I FEEL ALMOST WEIGHTLESS IN THIS GRAVITY!
MY ONLY HOPE IS TO MOVE OUT OF THIS AREA FAST ENOUGH!
I'M NOT READY FOR BATTLE YET!
I INTENDED TO SPEND THE FIRST FEW DAYS JUST RECONNOITERING...
GETTING FAMILIAR WITH THE TERRAIN-- AND THE PEOPLE!
BUT, EVENTS MOVE FASTER THAN THE KREE OFFICER INTENDS--
I'VE SPOTTED SOMETHING, SIR!
WELL, WHAT IN SAM HILL IS IT, SMITH??
SOME SORT OF LIGHT PLANE WHICH--NO! IT'S NOT A PLANE!
8

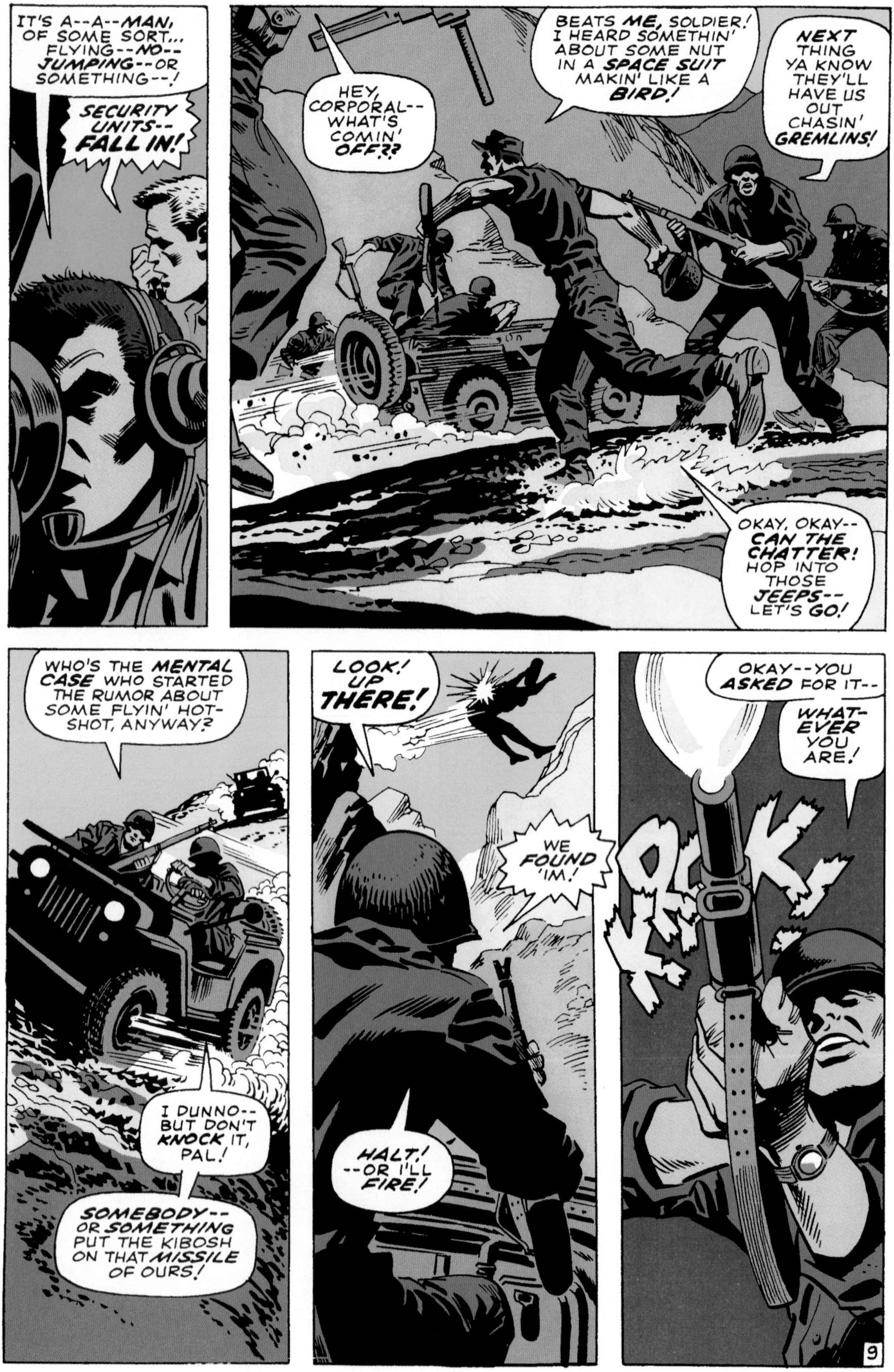
IT'S A--A--MAN, OF SOME SORT... FLYING--NO--JUMPING--OR SOMETHING--!
SECURITY UNITS--FALL IN!
HEY, CORPORAL--WHAT'S COMIN' OFF??
BEATS ME, SOLDIER! I HEARD SOMETHIN' ABOUT SOME NUT IN A SPACE SUIT MAKIN' LIKE A BIRD!
NEXT THING YA KNOW THEY'LL HAVE US OUT CHASIN' GREMLINS!
OKAY, OKAY--CAN THE CHATTER! HOP INTO THOSE JEEPS--LET'S GO!
WHO'S THE MENTAL CASE WHO STARTED THE RUMOR ABOUT SOME FLYIN' HOT-SHOT, ANYWAY?
I DUNNO--BUT DON'T KNOCK IT, PAL!
SOMEBODY--OR SOMETHING PUT THE KIBOSH ON THAT MISSILE OF OURS!
LOOK! UP THERE!
WE FOUND 'IM!
HALT! --OR I'LL FIRE!
OKAY--YOU ASKED FOR IT--
WHAT-EVER YOU ARE!
9

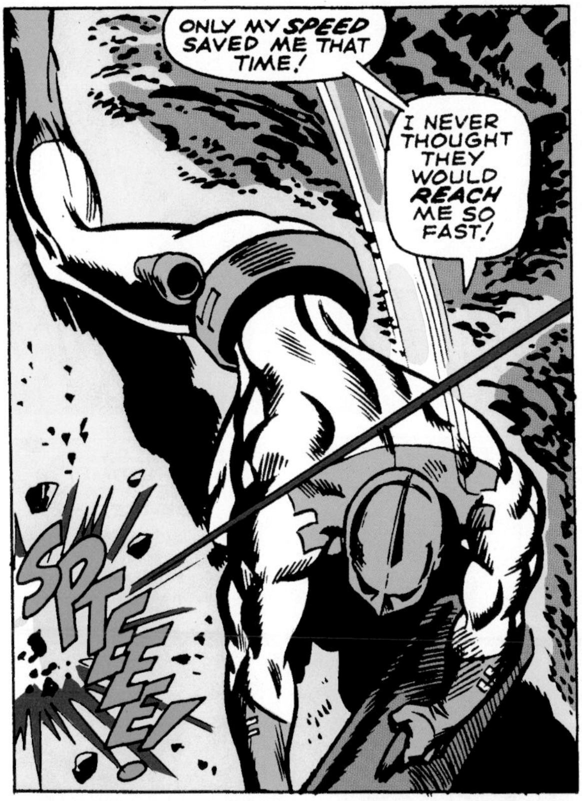
ONLY MY SPEED SAVED ME THAT TIME!
I NEVER THOUGHT THEY WOULD REACH ME SO FAST!
SPTEEEE!

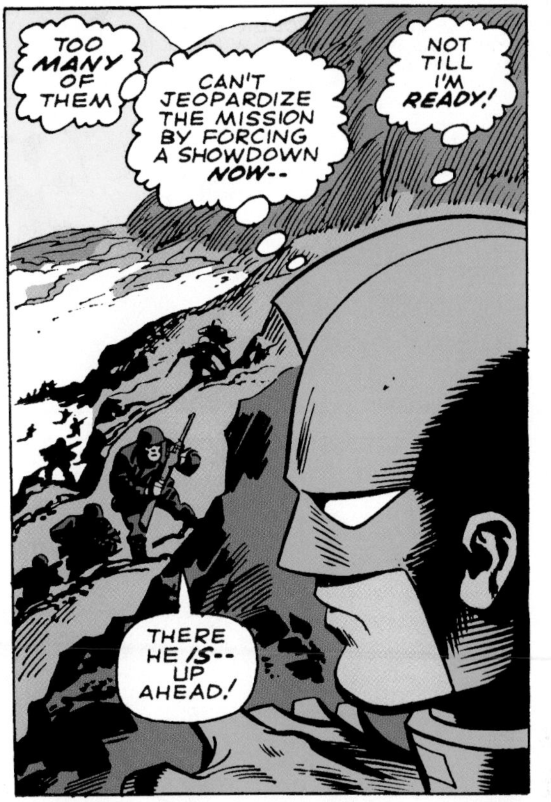
TOO MANY OF THEM
CAN'T JEOPARDIZE THE MISSION BY FORCING A SHOWDOWN NOW--
NOT TILL I'M READY!
THERE HE IS-- UP AHEAD!

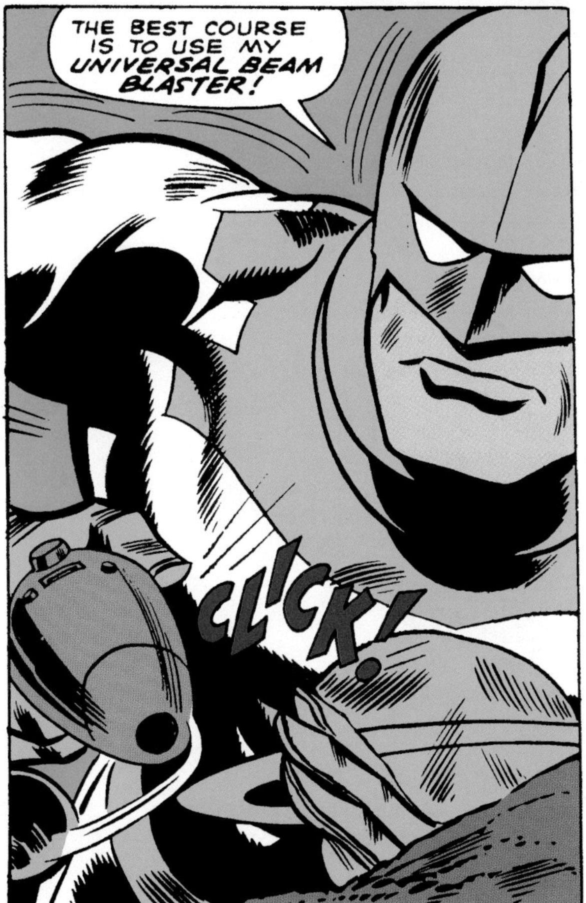
THE BEST COURSE IS TO USE MY UNIVERSAL BEAM BLASTER!
CLICK!

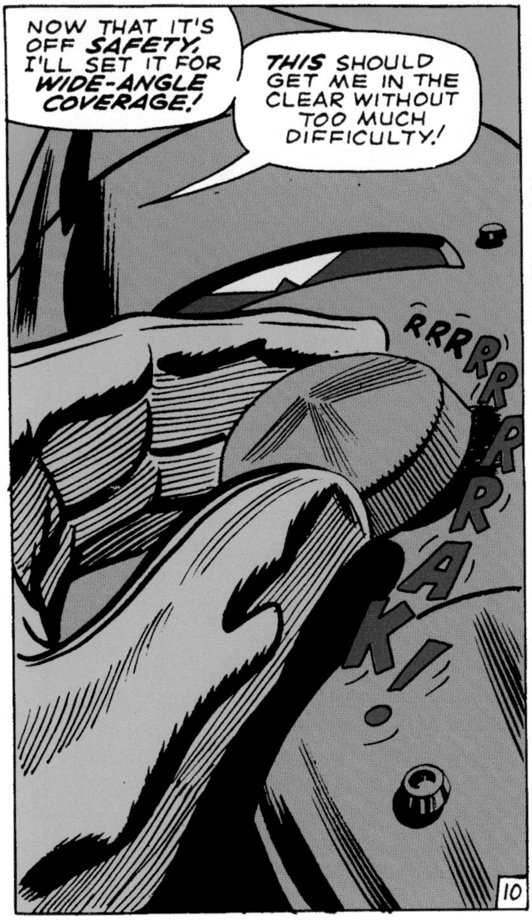
NOW THAT IT'S OFF SAFETY, I'LL SET IT FOR WIDE-ANGLE COVERAGE!
THIS SHOULD GET ME IN THE CLEAR WITHOUT TOO MUCH DIFFICULTY!
RRRRRRRAK!
10

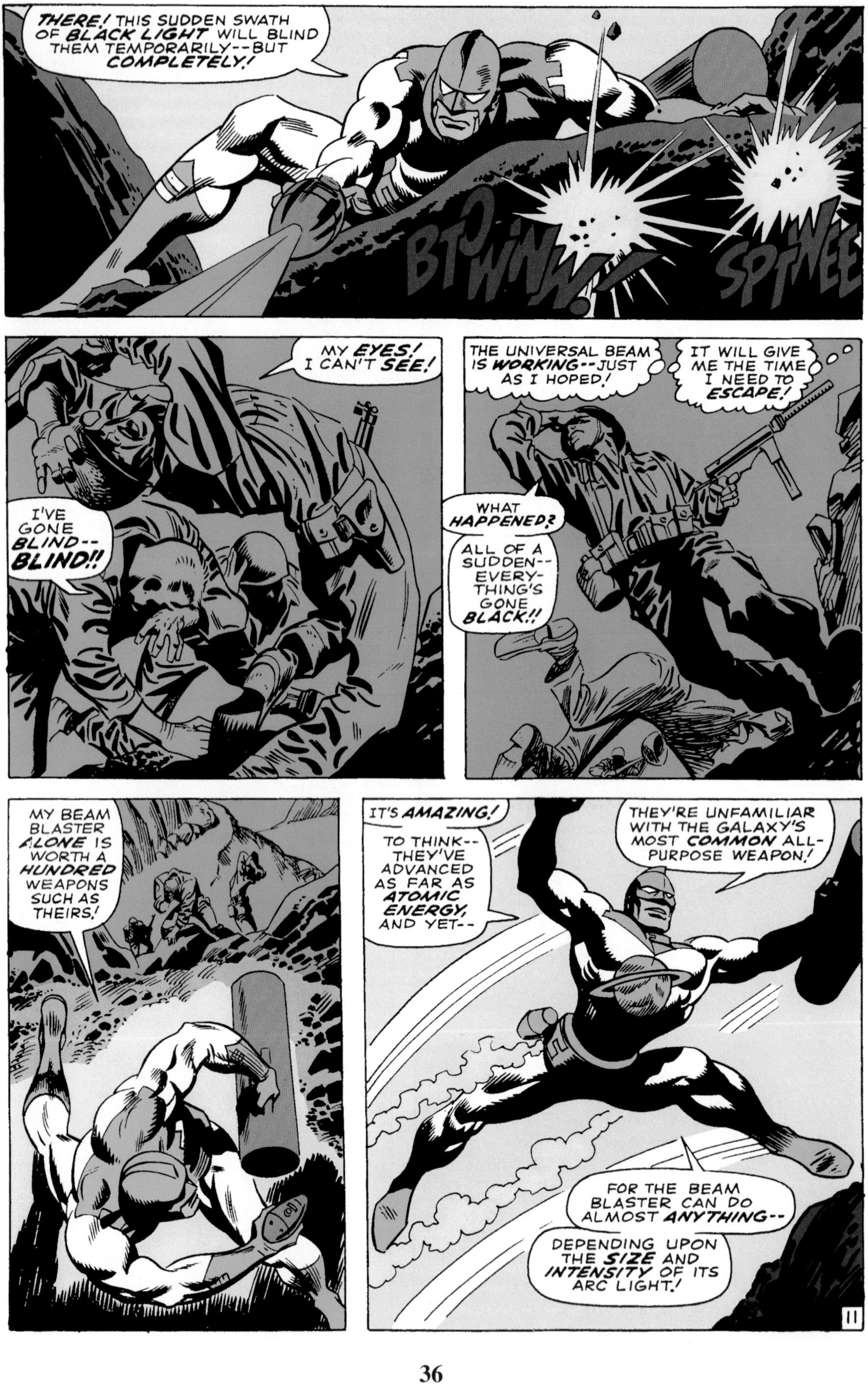
THERE! THIS SUDDEN SWATH OF BLACK LIGHT WILL BLIND THEM TEMPORARILY--BUT COMPLETELY!
BTOWINW!
SPTWEE
MY EYES! I CAN'T SEE!
I'VE GONE BLIND--BLIND!!
THE UNIVERSAL BEAM IS WORKING--JUST AS I HOPED!
IT WILL GIVE ME THE TIME I NEED TO ESCAPE!
WHAT HAPPENED?
ALL OF A SUDDEN--EVERYTHING'S GONE BLACK!!
MY BEAM BLASTER ALONE IS WORTH A HUNDRED WEAPONS SUCH AS THEIRS!
IT'S AMAZING!
TO THINK--THEY'VE ADVANCED AS FAR AS ATOMIC ENERGY, AND YET--
THEY'RE UNFAMILIAR WITH THE GALAXY'S MOST COMMON ALL-PURPOSE WEAPON!
FOR THE BEAM BLASTER CAN DO ALMOST ANYTHING--
DEPENDING UPON THE SIZE AND INTENSITY OF ITS ARC LIGHT!
11

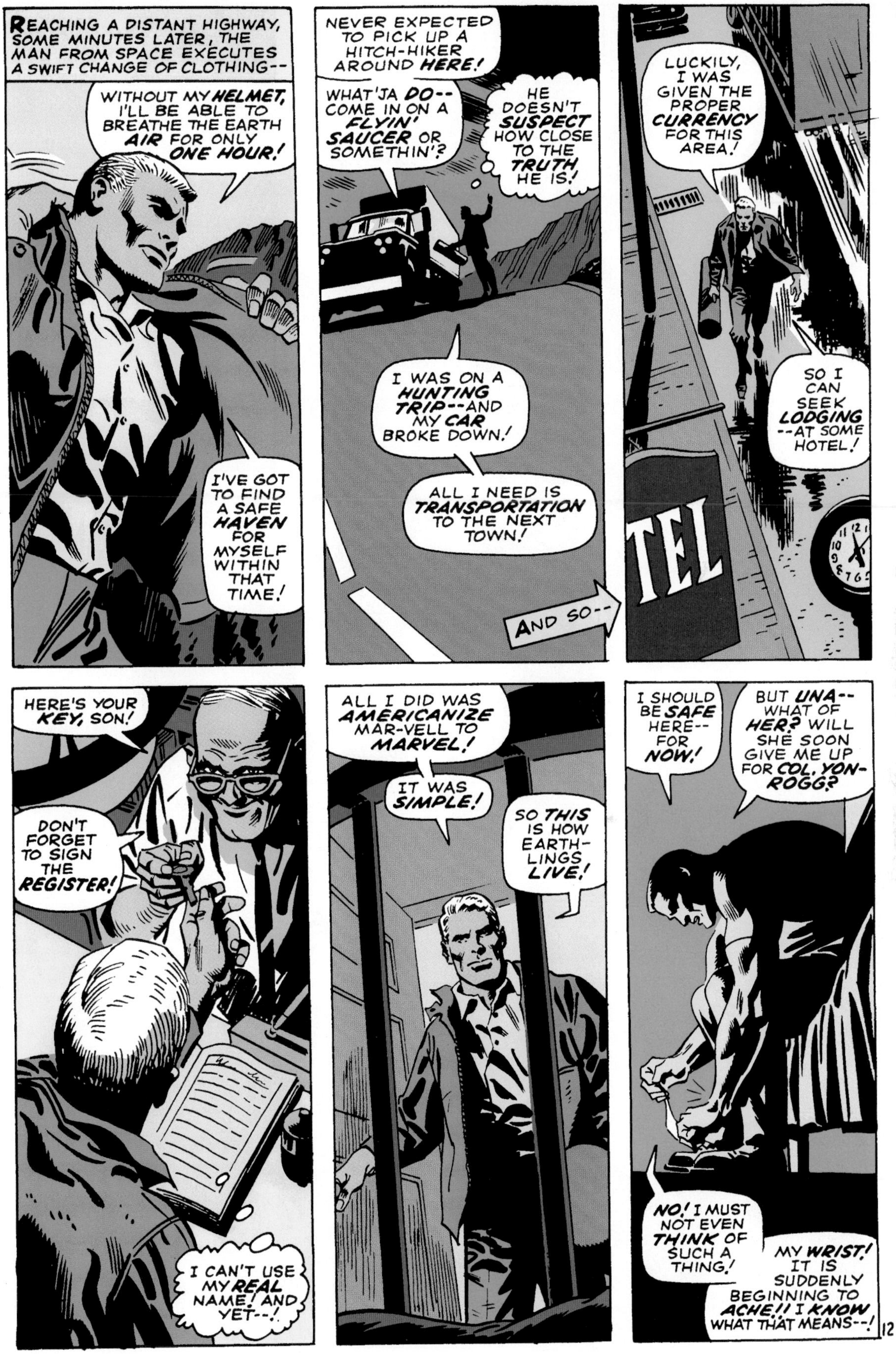
REACHING A DISTANT HIGHWAY, SOME MINUTES LATER, THE MAN FROM SPACE EXECUTES A SWIFT CHANGE OF CLOTHING--
WITHOUT MY HELMET, I'LL BE ABLE TO BREATHE THE EARTH AIR FOR ONLY ONE HOUR!
I'VE GOT TO FIND A SAFE HAVEN FOR MYSELF WITHIN THAT TIME!
NEVER EXPECTED TO PICK UP A HITCH-HIKER AROUND HERE!
WHAT'JA DO--COME IN ON A FLYIN' SAUCER OR SOMETHIN'?
HE DOESN'T SUSPECT HOW CLOSE TO THE TRUTH HE IS!
I WAS ON A HUNTING TRIP--AND MY CAR BROKE DOWN!
ALL I NEED IS TRANSPORTATION TO THE NEXT TOWN!
AND SO--
LUCKILY, I WAS GIVEN THE PROPER CURRENCY FOR THIS AREA!
SO I CAN SEEK LODGING--AT SOME HOTEL!
TEL
HERE'S YOUR KEY, SON!
DON'T FORGET TO SIGN THE REGISTER!
I CAN'T USE MY REAL NAME! AND YET--!
ALL I DID WAS AMERICANIZE MAR-VELL TO MARVEL!
IT WAS SIMPLE!
SO THIS IS HOW EARTH-LINGS LIVE!
I SHOULD BE SAFE HERE--FOR NOW!
BUT UNA--WHAT OF HER? WILL SHE SOON GIVE ME UP FOR COL. YON-ROGG?
NO! I MUST NOT EVEN THINK OF SUCH A THING!
MY WRIST! IT IS SUDDENLY BEGINNING TO ACHE!! I KNOW WHAT THAT MEANS--!
12

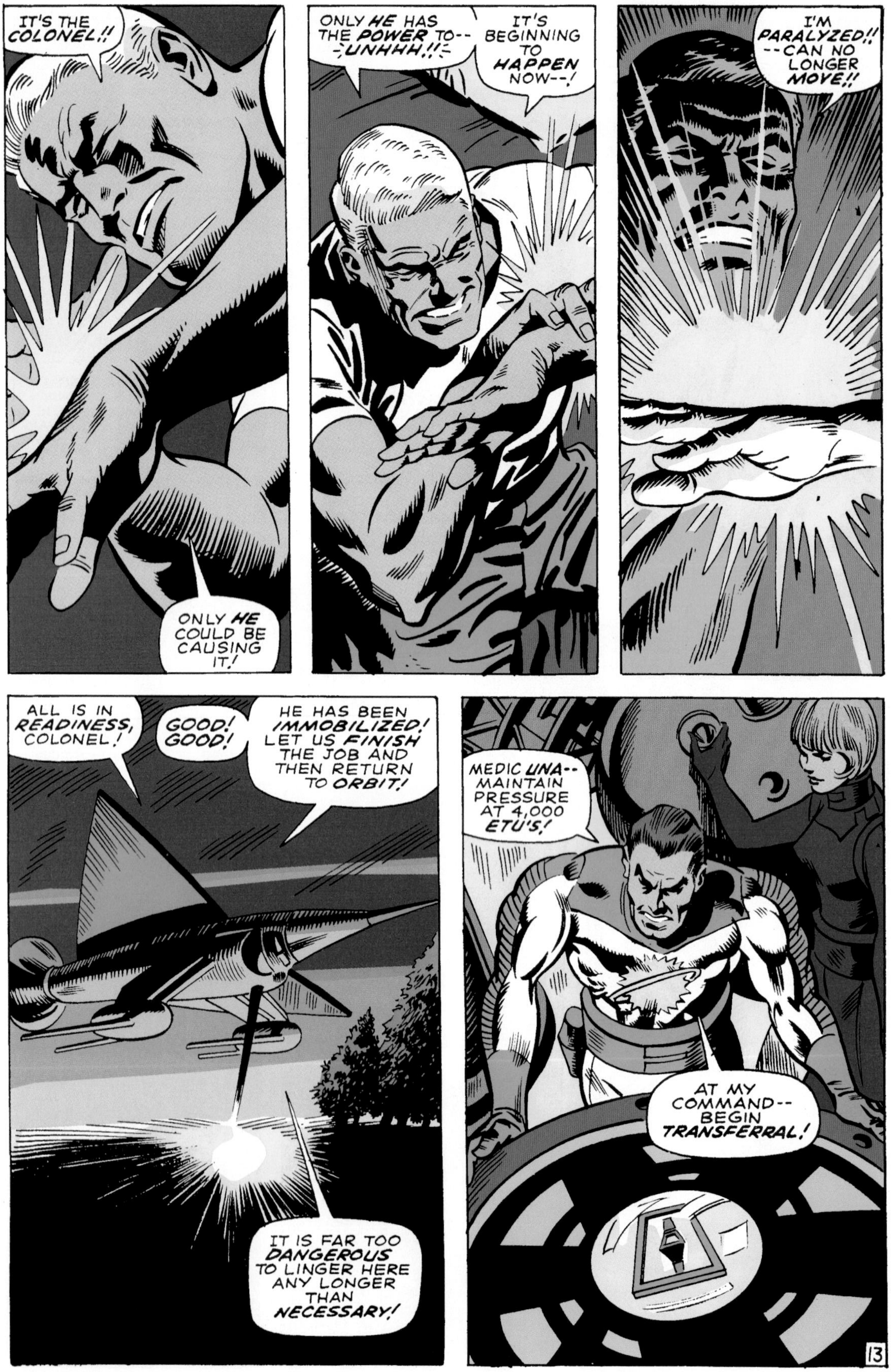
IT'S THE COLONEL!!
ONLY HE COULD BE CAUSING IT!
ONLY HE HAS THE POWER TO-- -UNHHH!!-
IT'S BEGINNING TO HAPPEN NOW--!
I'M PARALYZED!! --CAN NO LONGER MOVE!!
ALL IS IN READINESS, COLONEL!
GOOD! GOOD!
HE HAS BEEN IMMOBILIZED! LET US FINISH THE JOB AND THEN RETURN TO ORBIT!
IT IS FAR TOO DANGEROUS TO LINGER HERE ANY LONGER THAN NECESSARY!
MEDIC UNA-- MAINTAIN PRESSURE AT 4,000 ETU'S!
AT MY COMMAND-- BEGIN TRANSFERRAL!
13

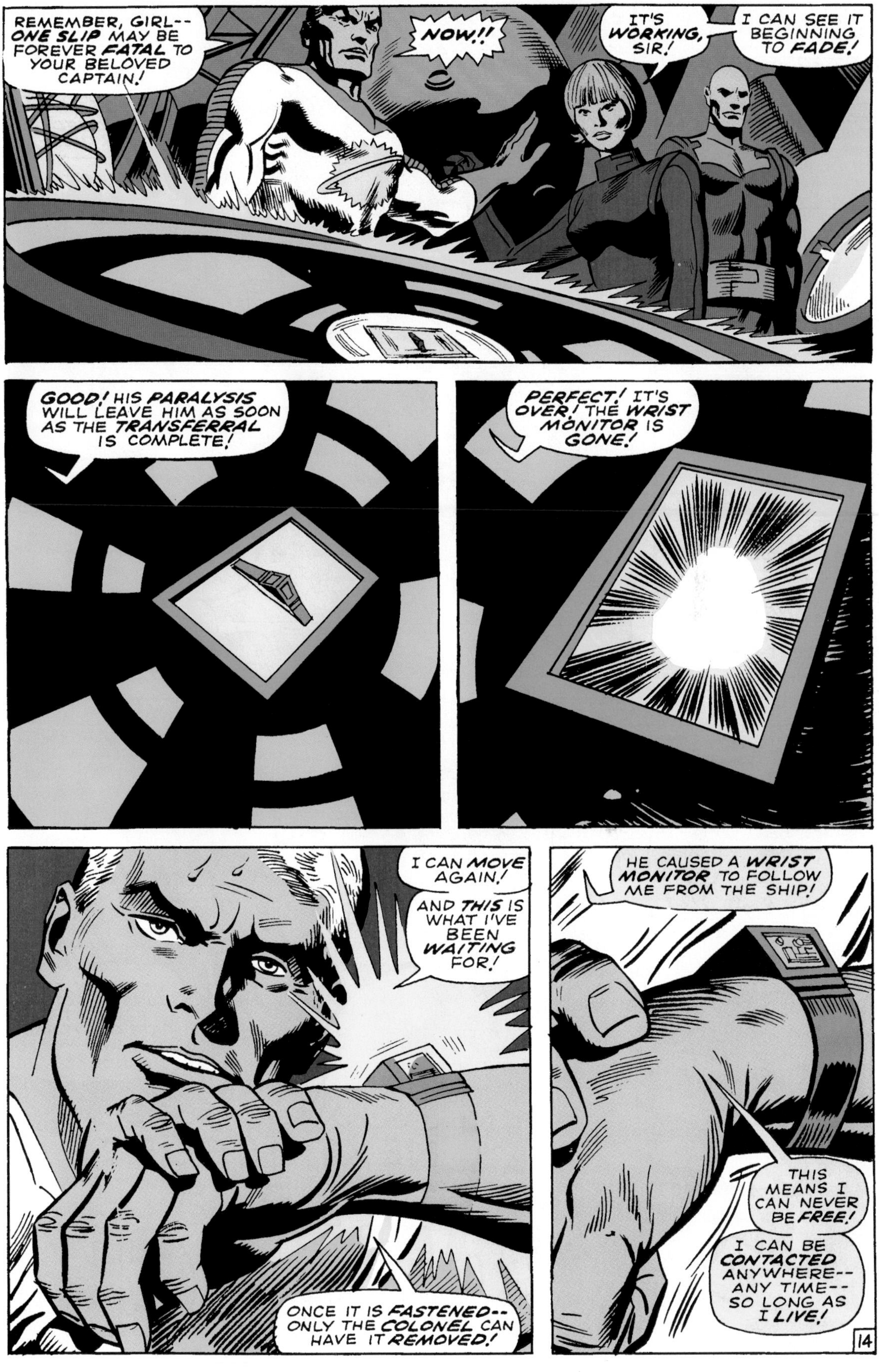
REMEMBER, GIRL-- ONE SLIP MAY BE FOREVER FATAL TO YOUR BELOVED CAPTAIN!
NOW!!
IT'S WORKING, SIR!
I CAN SEE IT BEGINNING TO FADE!
GOOD! HIS PARALYSIS WILL LEAVE HIM AS SOON AS THE TRANSFERRAL IS COMPLETE!
PERFECT! IT'S OVER! THE WRIST MONITOR IS GONE!
I CAN MOVE AGAIN!
AND THIS IS WHAT I'VE BEEN WAITING FOR!
ONCE IT IS FASTENED-- ONLY THE COLONEL CAN HAVE IT REMOVED!
HE CAUSED A WRIST MONITOR TO FOLLOW ME FROM THE SHIP!
THIS MEANS I CAN NEVER BE FREE!
I CAN BE CONTACTED ANYWHERE-- ANY TIME-- SO LONG AS I LIVE!
14

IT'S SIGNALLING *ALREADY!*

YON-ROGG MUST BE TRYING TO *SUMMON* ME!

NO! IT *ISN'T* THE *COLONEL--*

BEEP BEEEE BEEE

THE SIGNAL IS TOO *POWERFUL!*

IT'S--THE *HOME PLANET,* ITSELF!!

CAPTAIN MAR-VELL!! HEED THE WORDS OF THE *IMPERIAL MINISTER* OF THE *SUPREME INTELLIGENCE!*

OUR INTERGALACTIC *SENTRY* HAS *FAILED* IN HIS MISSION ON *EARTH--*AS HAS *RONAN,* THE *ACCUSER!*

KNOW YOU *THIS* THEN, SPACE WARRIOR--

YOU MUST *SUCCEED--* OR *DIE!*

NOW IT IS *YOU* WHO HAVE BEEN *CHOSEN* FOR THE *TASK!*

IN THE NAME OF THE *EVER-LASTING KREE--*

I NOW *BREAK CONTACT!*

AND, AT THAT VERY SECOND-- MY HOUR IS *UP--*CAN'T *BREATHE!*

HAVE TO--PUT ON--MY *HELMET--!*

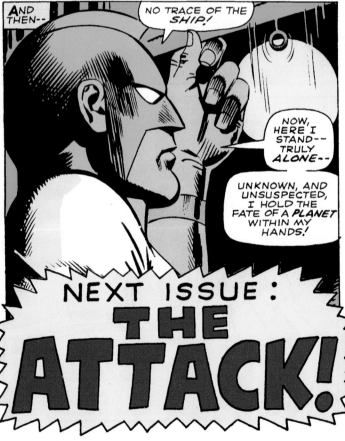

AND THEN--

NO TRACE OF THE *SHIP!*

NOW, HERE I STAND-- TRULY *ALONE--*

UNKNOWN, AND UNSUSPECTED, I HOLD THE FATE OF A *PLANET* WITHIN MY HANDS!

NEXT ISSUE:

THE ATTACK!

15

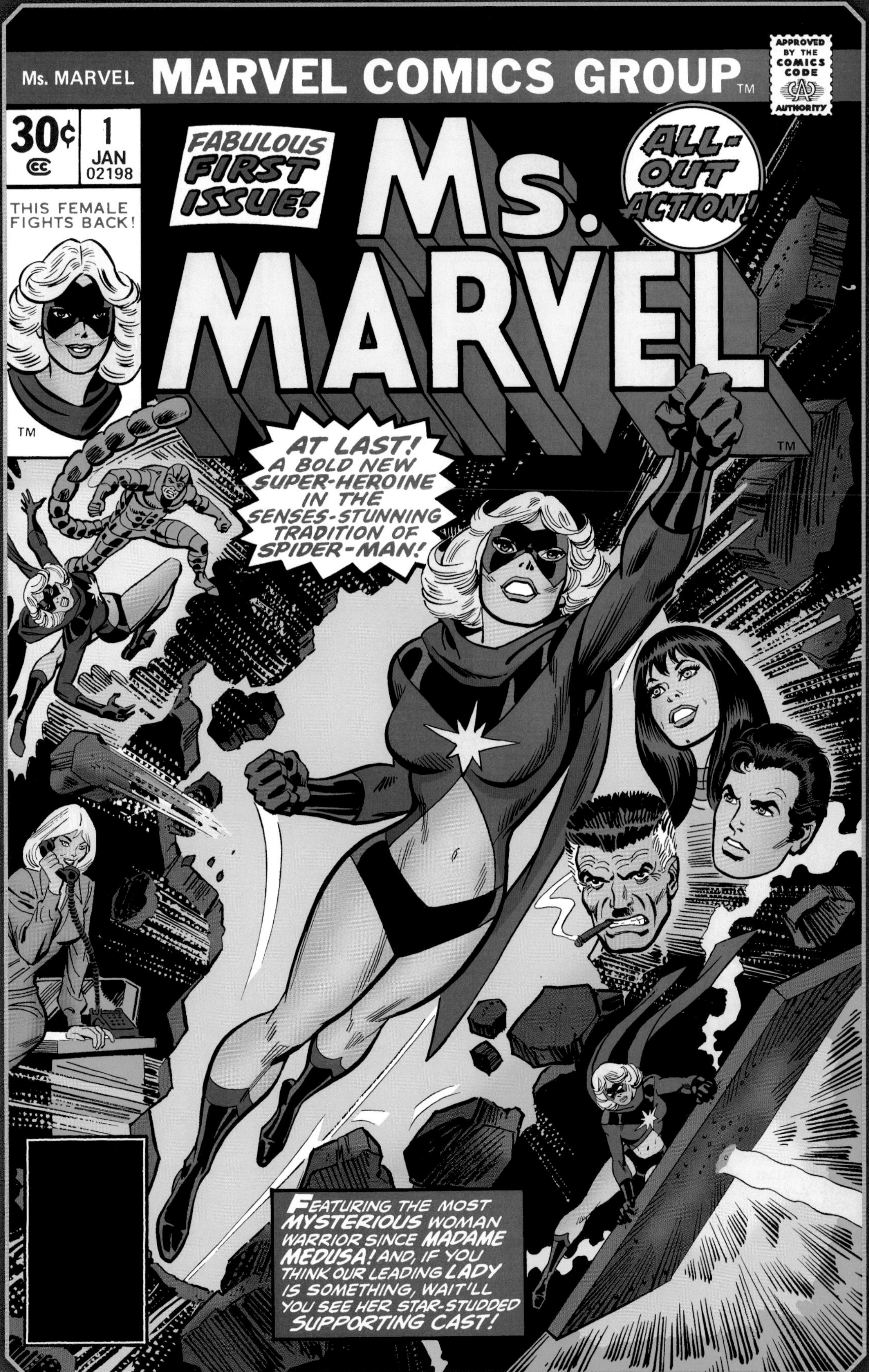
Ms. MARVEL
MARVEL COMICS GROUP
APPROVED BY THE COMICS CODE AUTHORITY
30¢
1
JAN
02198
THIS FEMALE FIGHTS BACK!
FABULOUS FIRST ISSUE!
Ms. MARVEL
ALL-OUT ACTION!
AT LAST! A BOLD NEW SUPER-HEROINE IN THE SENSES-STUNNING TRADITION OF SPIDER-MAN!
FEATURING THE MOST MYSTERIOUS WOMAN WARRIOR SINCE MADAME MEDUSA! AND, IF YOU THINK OUR LEADING LADY IS SOMETHING, WAIT'LL YOU SEE HER STAR-STUDDED SUPPORTING CAST!

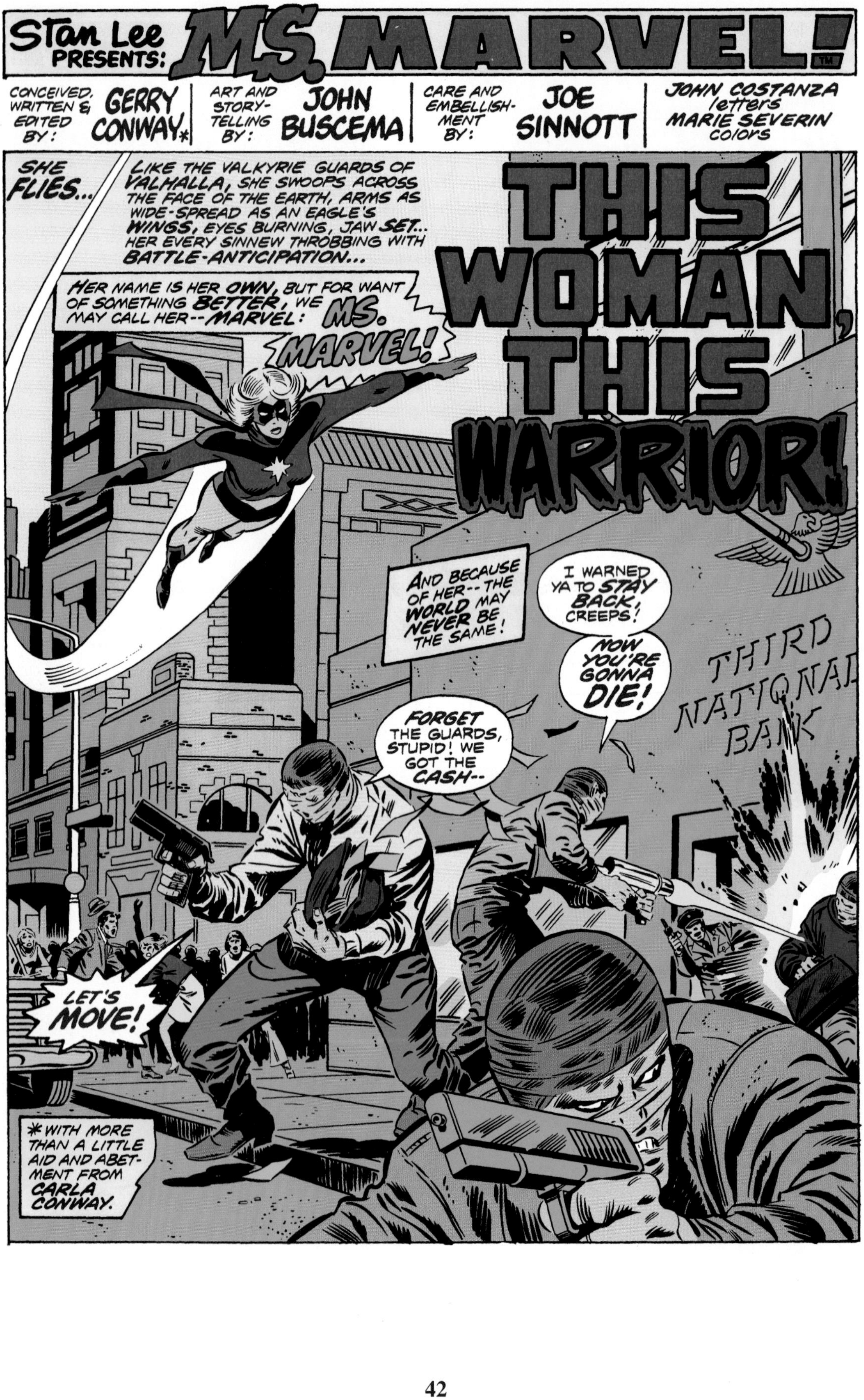
Stan Lee PRESENTS: MS. MARVEL!™
CONCEIVED, WRITTEN & EDITED BY: GERRY CONWAY*
ART AND STORY-TELLING BY: JOHN BUSCEMA
CARE AND EMBELLISH-MENT BY: JOE SINNOTT
JOHN COSTANZA letters
MARIE SEVERIN colors
SHE FLIES...
LIKE THE VALKYRIE GUARDS OF VALHALLA, SHE SWOOPS ACROSS THE FACE OF THE EARTH, ARMS AS WIDE-SPREAD AS AN EAGLE'S WINGS, EYES BURNING, JAW SET... HER EVERY SINNEW THROBBING WITH BATTLE-ANTICIPATION...
THIS WOMAN, THIS WARRIOR!
HER NAME IS HER OWN, BUT FOR WANT OF SOMETHING BETTER, WE MAY CALL HER--MARVEL: MS. MARVEL!
AND BECAUSE OF HER--THE WORLD MAY NEVER BE THE SAME!
I WARNED YA TO STAY BACK, CREEPS!
NOW YOU'RE GONNA DIE!
THIRD NATIONAL BANK
FORGET THE GUARDS, STUPID! WE GOT THE CASH--
LET'S MOVE!
*WITH MORE THAN A LITTLE AID AND ABETMENT FROM CARLA CONWAY.

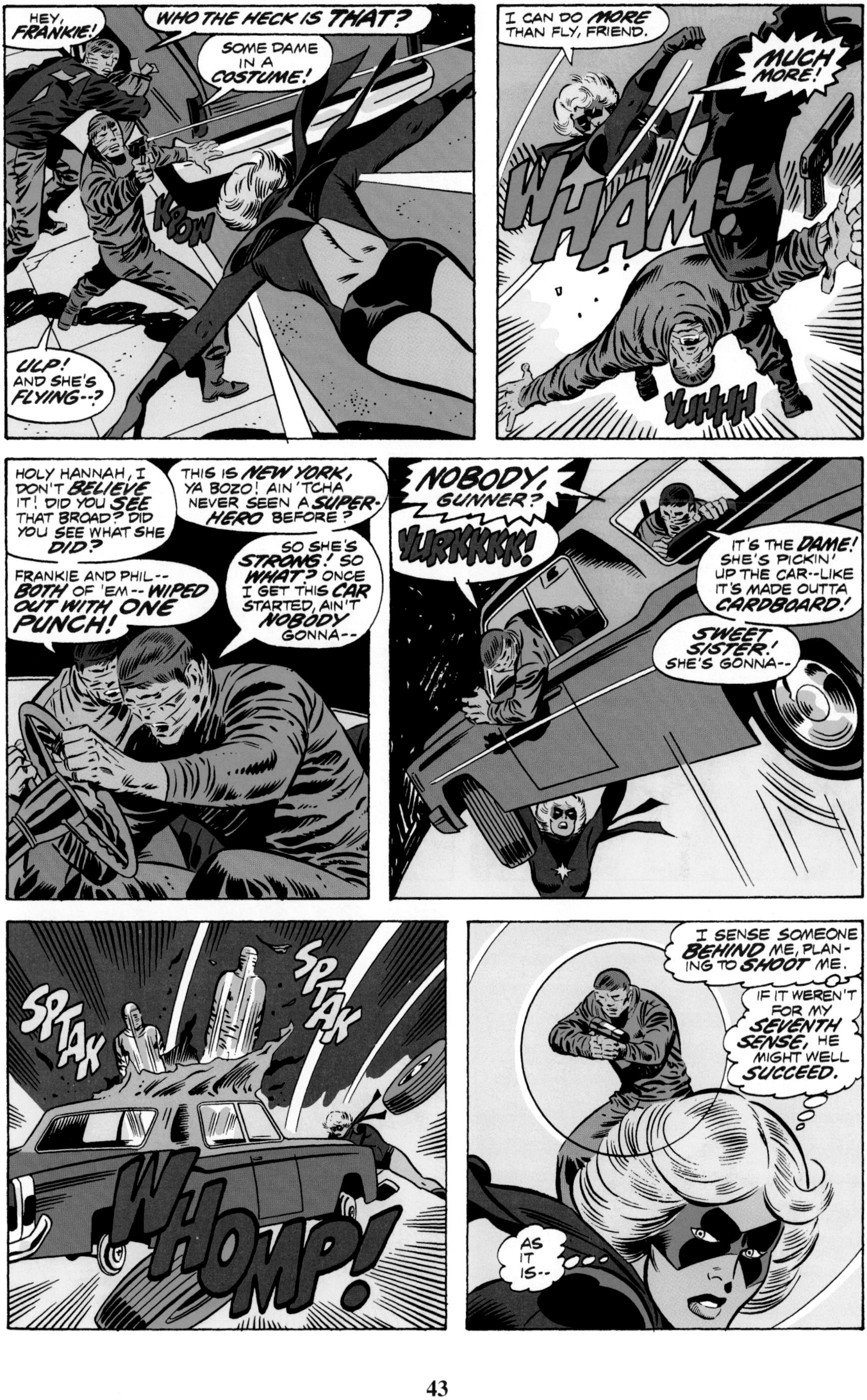
HEY, FRANKIE!
WHO THE HECK IS THAT?
SOME DAME IN A COSTUME!
KPOW
ULP! AND SHE'S FLYING--?
I CAN DO MORE THAN FLY, FRIEND.
MUCH MORE!
WHAM!
YUHHH
HOLY HANNAH, I DON'T BELIEVE IT! DID YOU SEE THAT BROAD? DID YOU SEE WHAT SHE DID?
THIS IS NEW YORK, YA BOZO! AIN'TCHA NEVER SEEN A SUPER-HERO BEFORE?
FRANKIE AND PHIL-- BOTH OF 'EM--WIPED OUT WITH ONE PUNCH!
SO SHE'S STRONG! SO WHAT? ONCE I GET THIS CAR STARTED, AIN'T NOBODY GONNA--
NOBODY, GUNNER?
YURKKKK!
IT'S THE DAME! SHE'S PICKIN' UP THE CAR--LIKE IT'S MADE OUTTA CARDBOARD!
SWEET SISTER! SHE'S GONNA--
SPTAK
SPTAK
WHOMP!
I SENSE SOMEONE BEHIND ME, PLANING TO SHOOT ME.
IF IT WEREN'T FOR MY SEVENTH SENSE, HE MIGHT WELL SUCCEED.
AS IT IS--

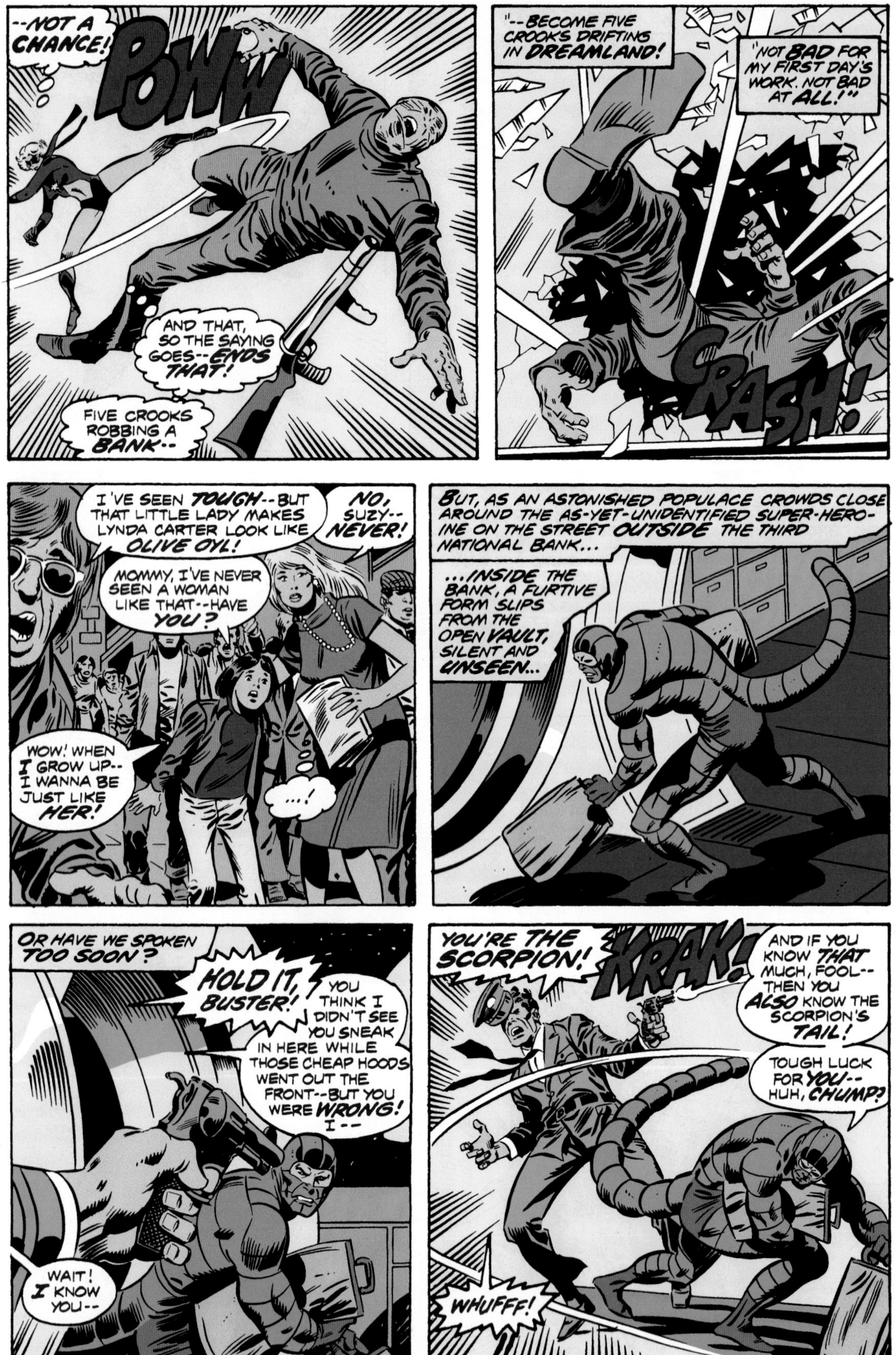
--NOT A CHANCE!
POWW
FIVE CROOKS ROBBING A BANK--
AND THAT, SO THE SAYING GOES--ENDS THAT!
"--BECOME FIVE CROOKS DRIFTING IN DREAMLAND!
"NOT BAD FOR MY FIRST DAY'S WORK. NOT BAD AT ALL!"
CRASH!
I'VE SEEN TOUGH--BUT THAT LITTLE LADY MAKES LYNDA CARTER LOOK LIKE OLIVE OYL!
NO, SUZY--NEVER!
MOMMY, I'VE NEVER SEEN A WOMAN LIKE THAT--HAVE YOU?
WOW! WHEN I GROW UP--I WANNA BE JUST LIKE HER!
...!
BUT, AS AN ASTONISHED POPULACE CROWDS CLOSE AROUND THE AS-YET-UNIDENTIFIED SUPER-HEROINE ON THE STREET OUTSIDE THE THIRD NATIONAL BANK...
...INSIDE THE BANK, A FURTIVE FORM SLIPS FROM THE OPEN VAULT, SILENT AND UNSEEN...
OR HAVE WE SPOKEN TOO SOON?
HOLD IT, BUSTER!
YOU THINK I DIDN'T SEE YOU SNEAK IN HERE WHILE THOSE CHEAP HOODS WENT OUT THE FRONT--BUT YOU WERE WRONG! I--
WAIT! I KNOW YOU--
YOU'RE THE SCORPION!
KRAK!
AND IF YOU KNOW THAT MUCH, FOOL--THEN YOU ALSO KNOW THE SCORPION'S TAIL!
TOUGH LUCK FOR YOU--HUH, CHUMP?
WHUFFF!

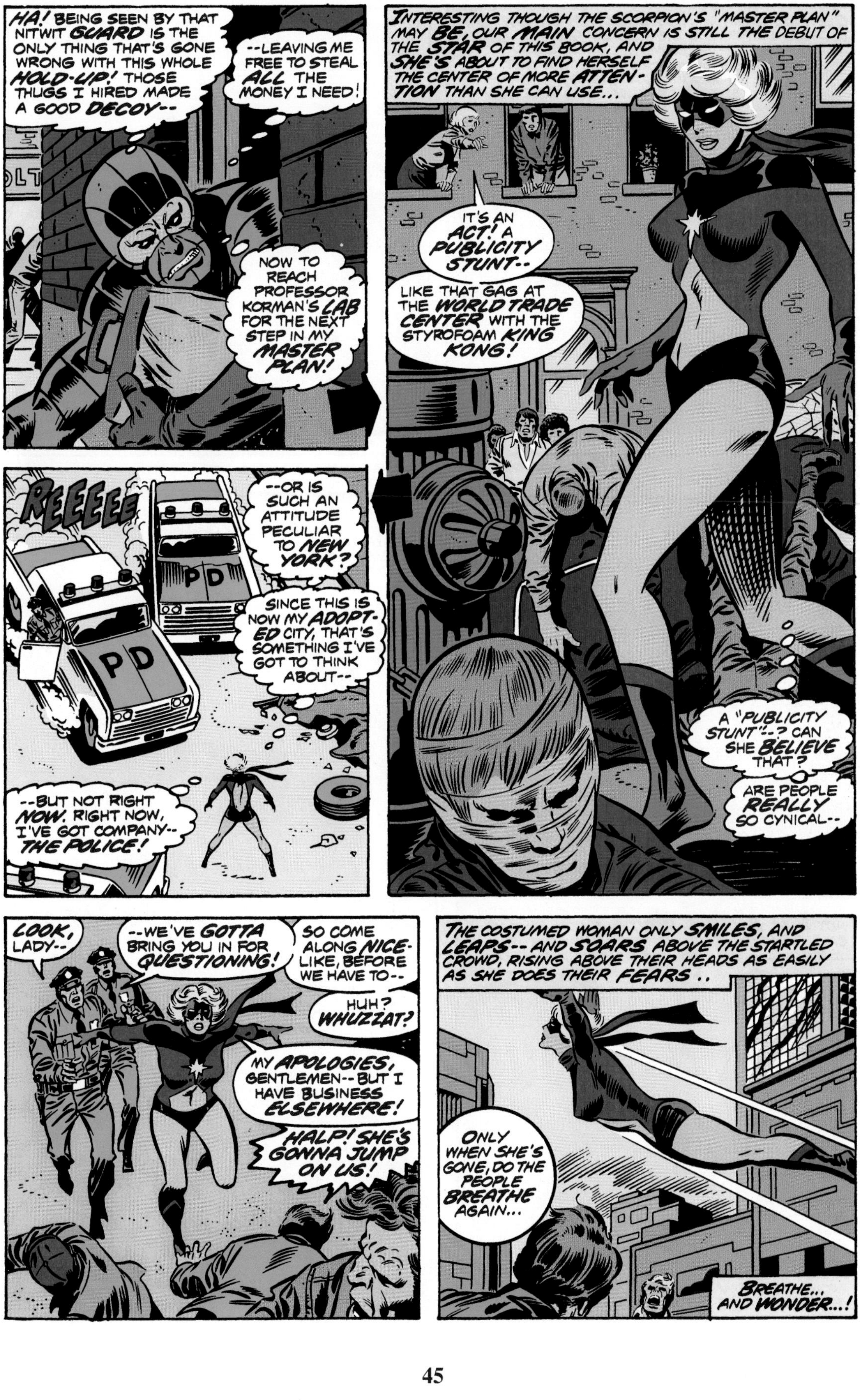
HA! BEING SEEN BY THAT NITWIT GUARD IS THE ONLY THING THAT'S GONE WRONG WITH THIS WHOLE HOLD-UP! THOSE THUGS I HIRED MADE A GOOD DECOY--
--LEAVING ME FREE TO STEAL ALL THE MONEY I NEED!
NOW TO REACH PROFESSOR KORMAN'S LAB FOR THE NEXT STEP IN MY MASTER PLAN!
INTERESTING THOUGH THE SCORPION'S "MASTER PLAN" MAY BE, OUR MAIN CONCERN IS STILL THE DEBUT OF THE STAR OF THIS BOOK, AND SHE'S ABOUT TO FIND HERSELF THE CENTER OF MORE ATTENTION THAN SHE CAN USE...
IT'S AN ACT! A PUBLICITY STUNT--
LIKE THAT GAG AT THE WORLD TRADE CENTER WITH THE STYROFOAM KING KONG!
A "PUBLICITY STUNT"--? CAN SHE BELIEVE THAT?
ARE PEOPLE REALLY SO CYNICAL--
--OR IS SUCH AN ATTITUDE PECULIAR TO NEW YORK?
SINCE THIS IS NOW MY ADOPTED CITY, THAT'S SOMETHING I'VE GOT TO THINK ABOUT--
REEEEEE
PD
PD
--BUT NOT RIGHT NOW. RIGHT NOW, I'VE GOT COMPANY-- THE POLICE!
LOOK, LADY--
--WE'VE GOTTA BRING YOU IN FOR QUESTIONING!
SO COME ALONG NICE-LIKE, BEFORE WE HAVE TO--
HUH? WHUZZAT?
MY APOLOGIES, GENTLEMEN-- BUT I HAVE BUSINESS ELSEWHERE!
HALP! SHE'S GONNA JUMP ON US!
THE COSTUMED WOMAN ONLY SMILES, AND LEAPS-- AND SOARS ABOVE THE STARTLED CROWD, RISING ABOVE THEIR HEADS AS EASILY AS SHE DOES THEIR FEARS ..
ONLY WHEN SHE'S GONE, DO THE PEOPLE BREATHE AGAIN...
BREATHE... AND WONDER...!

ONE HOUR LATER, IN A *PROJECTION ROOM* LOCATED WITHIN THE OFFICES OF THE *DAILY BUGLE* BUILDING...

LET ME GET THIS *STRAIGHT,* MR. JAMESON: YOU WANT TO HIRE ME AS AN *EDITOR* FOR A NEW MAGAZINE CALLED *"WOMAN"--*

--AND YOU WANT MY FIRST ISSUE TO BE AN EXPOSE OF-- *HER?*

RIGHT.

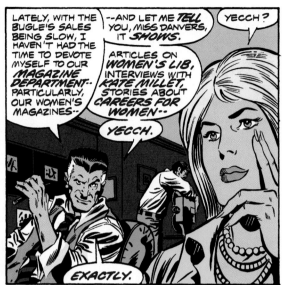

LATELY, WITH THE BUGLE'S SALES BEING SLOW, I HAVEN'T HAD THE TIME TO DEVOTE MYSELF TO OUR *MAGAZINE DEPARTMENT*-- PARTICULARLY, OUR WOMEN'S MAGAZINES--

--AND LET ME *TELL* YOU, MISS DANVERS, IT *SHOWS.*

ARTICLES ON *WOMEN'S LIB,* INTERVIEWS WITH *KATE MILLET,* STORIES ABOUT *CAREERS FOR WOMEN--*

YECCH.

YECCH?

EXACTLY.

THE WAY *I* SEE IT, A WOMAN'S MAGAZINE SHOULD HAVE ARTICLES THAT ARE *USEFUL--*

--LIKE *NEW DIETS,* AND FASHIONS, AND RECIPES. THINGS LIKE THAT.

SO HOW DOES THIS NEW *SUPER-HEROINE* FIT IN? UNDER *FASHION?*

NAW, THIS IS SOME-THING *ELSE.* SOMETHING *MORE IMPORTANT.*

I *HATE* SUPER-HEROES, MISS DANVERS. *HATE* THEM!

SO YOU WANT TO HIRE ME. AND YOU WANT ME TO EDIT A WOMAN'S MAGAZINE *YOUR* WAY-- INCLUDING A FEATURE ON THIS *SUPER-WOMAN.*

OKAY, MR. JAMESON-- WHAT ABOUT MY *SALARY?*

SALARY?

SURE-- AS IN *WEEKLY PAYCHECK?*

HMMMM...

I REALIZE I'M NOT WHAT YOU CALL *PRIME* MATERIAL--

--SINCE I'VE ONLY BEEN *WRITING* FOR A YEAR, AFTER LEAVING THE *SECURITY FIELD.**

BUT I *DO* HAVE SOME-THING OF A *REPUTA-TION* NOW--

AND REPS COST MONEY.

MONEY? EH...?

*EVERYONE REMEMBER CAROL DANVERS, CAPE KENNEDY SECURITY CHIEF FROM *CAPTAIN MARVEL* #1-18? --GER.*

TWENTY THOUSAND?

TWENTY-TWO?

TWENTY-FIVE?

THIRTY.

THIRTY!

THIRTY!

BLAST IT! HOW CAN I ARGUE MONEY WITH A *WOMAN?*

ALL RIGHT, ALL RIGHT-- *THIRTY!*

AND ONE THING *MORE,* JONAH... MY NAME IS *MS.* CAROL DANVERS.

AND AS FAR AS *DIETS* AND *RECIPES* GO--

FORGET IT.

HURRUMPH!

46

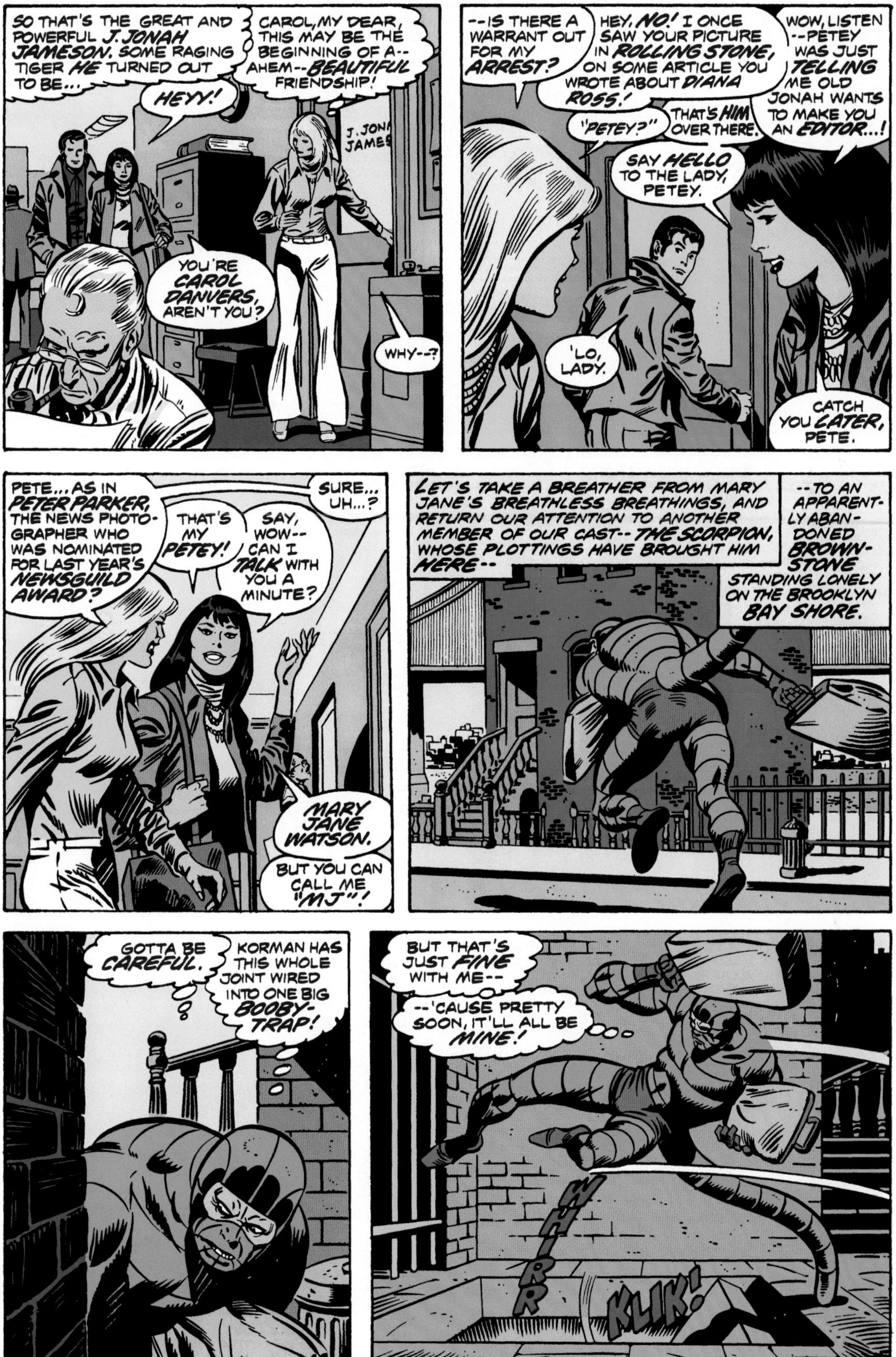

SO THAT'S THE GREAT AND POWERFUL J. JONAH JAMESON. SOME RAGING TIGER HE TURNED OUT TO BE...
CAROL, MY DEAR, THIS MAY BE THE BEGINNING OF A-- AHEM--BEAUTIFUL FRIENDSHIP!
HEYY!
J. JON JAMES
YOU'RE CAROL DANVERS, AREN'T YOU?
WHY--?
--IS THERE A WARRANT OUT FOR MY ARREST?
HEY, NO! I ONCE SAW YOUR PICTURE IN ROLLING STONE, ON SOME ARTICLE YOU WROTE ABOUT DIANA ROSS!
WOW, LISTEN --PETEY WAS JUST TELLING ME OLD JONAH WANTS TO MAKE YOU AN EDITOR...!
"PETEY?"
THAT'S HIM OVER THERE.
SAY HELLO TO THE LADY, PETEY.
'LO, LADY.
CATCH YOU LATER, PETE.
PETE... AS IN PETER PARKER, THE NEWS PHOTOGRAPHER WHO WAS NOMINATED FOR LAST YEAR'S NEWSGUILD AWARD?
SURE... UH...?
THAT'S MY PETEY!
SAY, WOW-- CAN I TALK WITH YOU A MINUTE?
MARY JANE WATSON.
BUT YOU CAN CALL ME "MJ"!
LET'S TAKE A BREATHER FROM MARY JANE'S BREATHLESS BREATHINGS, AND RETURN OUR ATTENTION TO ANOTHER MEMBER OF OUR CAST--THE SCORPION, WHOSE PLOTTINGS HAVE BROUGHT HIM HERE--
--TO AN APPARENTLY ABANDONED BROWNSTONE STANDING LONELY ON THE BROOKLYN BAY SHORE.
GOTTA BE CAREFUL.
KORMAN HAS THIS WHOLE JOINT WIRED INTO ONE BIG BOOBY-TRAP!
BUT THAT'S JUST FINE WITH ME--
--'CAUSE PRETTY SOON, IT'LL ALL BE MINE!
WHHIRR
KLIK!

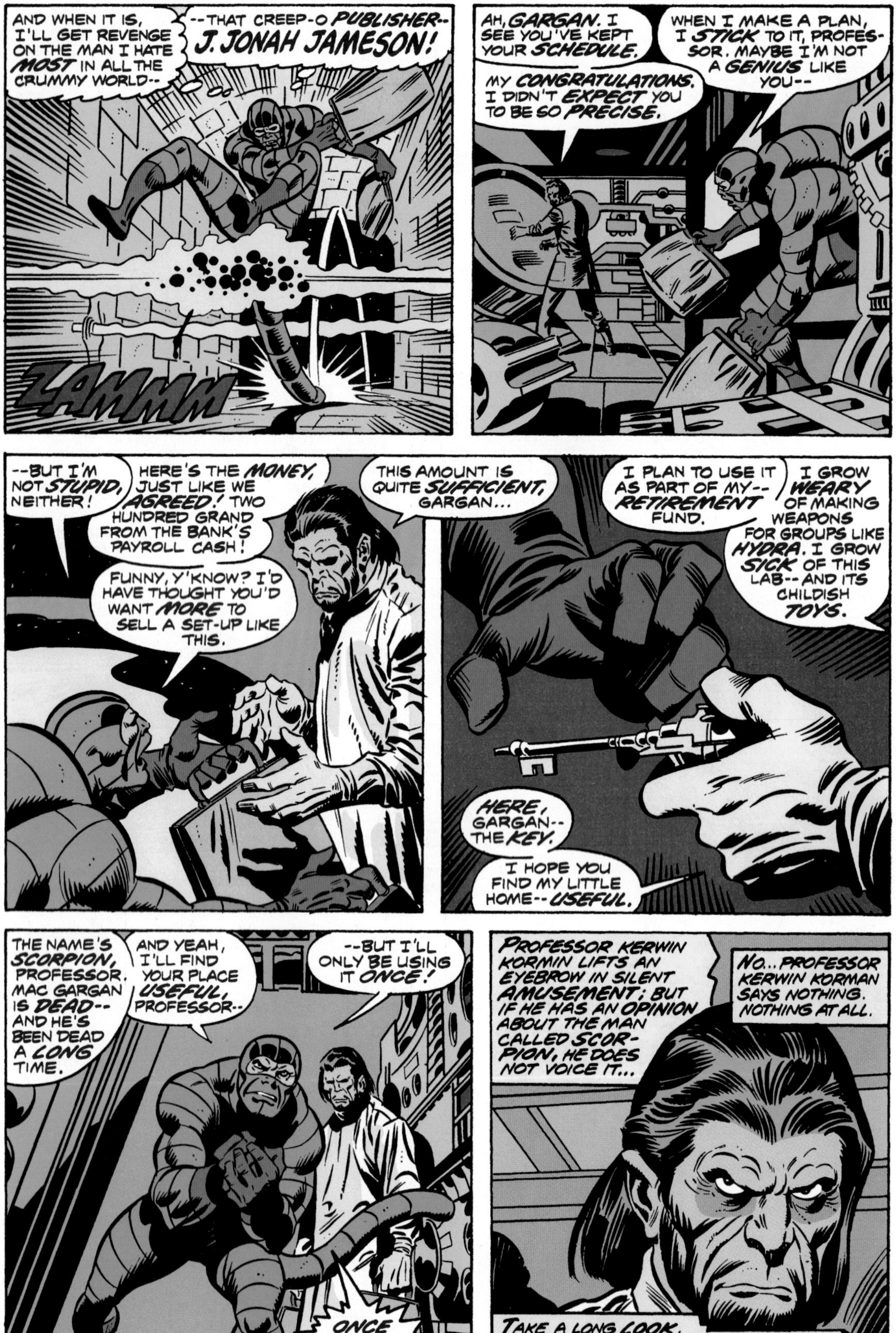
AND WHEN IT IS, I'LL GET REVENGE ON THE MAN I HATE MOST IN ALL THE CRUMMY WORLD--
--THAT CREEP-O PUBLISHER-- J. JONAH JAMESON!
ZAMMM
AH, GARGAN. I SEE YOU'VE KEPT YOUR SCHEDULE.
MY CONGRATULATIONS. I DIDN'T EXPECT YOU TO BE SO PRECISE.
WHEN I MAKE A PLAN, I STICK TO IT, PROFESSOR. MAYBE I'M NOT A GENIUS LIKE YOU--
--BUT I'M NOT STUPID, NEITHER!
HERE'S THE MONEY, JUST LIKE WE AGREED! TWO HUNDRED GRAND FROM THE BANK'S PAYROLL CASH!
FUNNY, Y'KNOW? I'D HAVE THOUGHT YOU'D WANT MORE TO SELL A SET-UP LIKE THIS.
THIS AMOUNT IS QUITE SUFFICIENT, GARGAN...
I PLAN TO USE IT AS PART OF MY-- RETIREMENT FUND.
I GROW WEARY OF MAKING WEAPONS FOR GROUPS LIKE HYDRA. I GROW SICK OF THIS LAB-- AND ITS CHILDISH TOYS.
HERE, GARGAN-- THE KEY.
I HOPE YOU FIND MY LITTLE HOME-- USEFUL.
THE NAME'S SCORPION, PROFESSOR. MAC GARGAN IS DEAD-- AND HE'S BEEN DEAD A LONG TIME.
AND YEAH, I'LL FIND YOUR PLACE USEFUL, PROFESSOR--
--BUT I'LL ONLY BE USING IT ONCE!
ONCE IS ALL I NEED!
PROFESSOR KERWIN KORMIN LIFTS AN EYEBROW IN SILENT AMUSEMENT; BUT IF HE HAS AN OPINION ABOUT THE MAN CALLED SCORPION, HE DOES NOT VOICE IT...
NO... PROFESSOR KERWIN KORMAN SAYS NOTHING. NOTHING AT ALL.
TAKE A LONG LOOK, READER. WE'VE GOT A FEELING WE MAY WELL SEE THIS MAN AGAIN!)

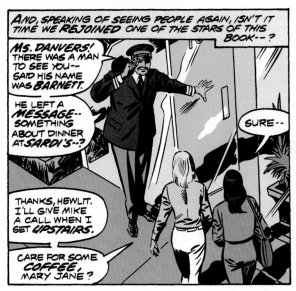

AND, SPEAKING OF SEEING PEOPLE AGAIN, ISN'T IT TIME WE REJOINED ONE OF THE STARS OF THIS BOOK--?

MS. DANVERS! THERE WAS A MAN TO SEE YOU-- SAID HIS NAME WAS BARNETT.

HE LEFT A MESSAGE-- SOMETHING ABOUT DINNER AT SARDI'S--?

SURE--

THANKS, HEWLIT. I'LL GIVE MIKE A CALL WHEN I GET UPSTAIRS.

CARE FOR SOME COFFEE, MARY JANE?

--I'VE NEVER HAD COFFEE IN A CENTRAL PARK PENT-HOUSE BEFORE!

SAY, HOW DO YOU AFFORD A FAN-TASSTIC LAYOUT LIKE THIS? DO EDITORS MAKE THAT MUCH MONEY..?

THEY DON'T, MJ-- BUT SOME LUCKY WRITERS DO.

ROYALTIES FROM MY FIRST BOOK-- ABOUT THE SPACE INDUSTRY.

WOW...

...THAT'S RIGHT. YOU WERE A SECURITY CONSULTANT AT CAPE KENNEDY, WEREN'T YOU?

WHY'D YOU LEAVE ALL THAT, CAROL-- AND HOWCUM YOU BECAME A WRITER?

I REMEMBER READING ABOUT YOU IN THE PAPERS, WHEN THAT WEIRD CAPTAIN MARVEL GUY FIRST SHOWED UP ON EARTH. *

NOT BECAUSE I WANTED TO, MJ--

* AGAIN, CM #1.--GER.

--BUT BECAUSE I HAD TO.

CAPTAIN MARVEL'S APPEARANCE AT THE CAPE--AND MY INABILITY TO CAPTURE HIM-- JUST ABOUT DESTROY-ED MY SECURITY FIELD CAREER.

I KEPT TRYING TO HOLD IT TOGETHER, UNTIL I FINALLY WENT BACK TO MY FIRST LOVE--

WRITING.

TURNS OUT I HAVE MORE TALENT FOR THE PEN THEN THE SWORD--AND I'LL TELL YOU, I'M A LOT HAPPIER THAN--

CAROL!

OHHHH

KRASH

I-I'M ALL RIGHT, MARY JANE. J-JUST A MIGRANE HEAD-ACHE...

I'VE BEEN GETTING A LOT OF THEM... SINCE COMING TO NEW YORK...

YOU WANT ME TO CALL A DOCTOR?

NO!

NO... I'M SORRY ...BUT YOU BETTER JUST GO...

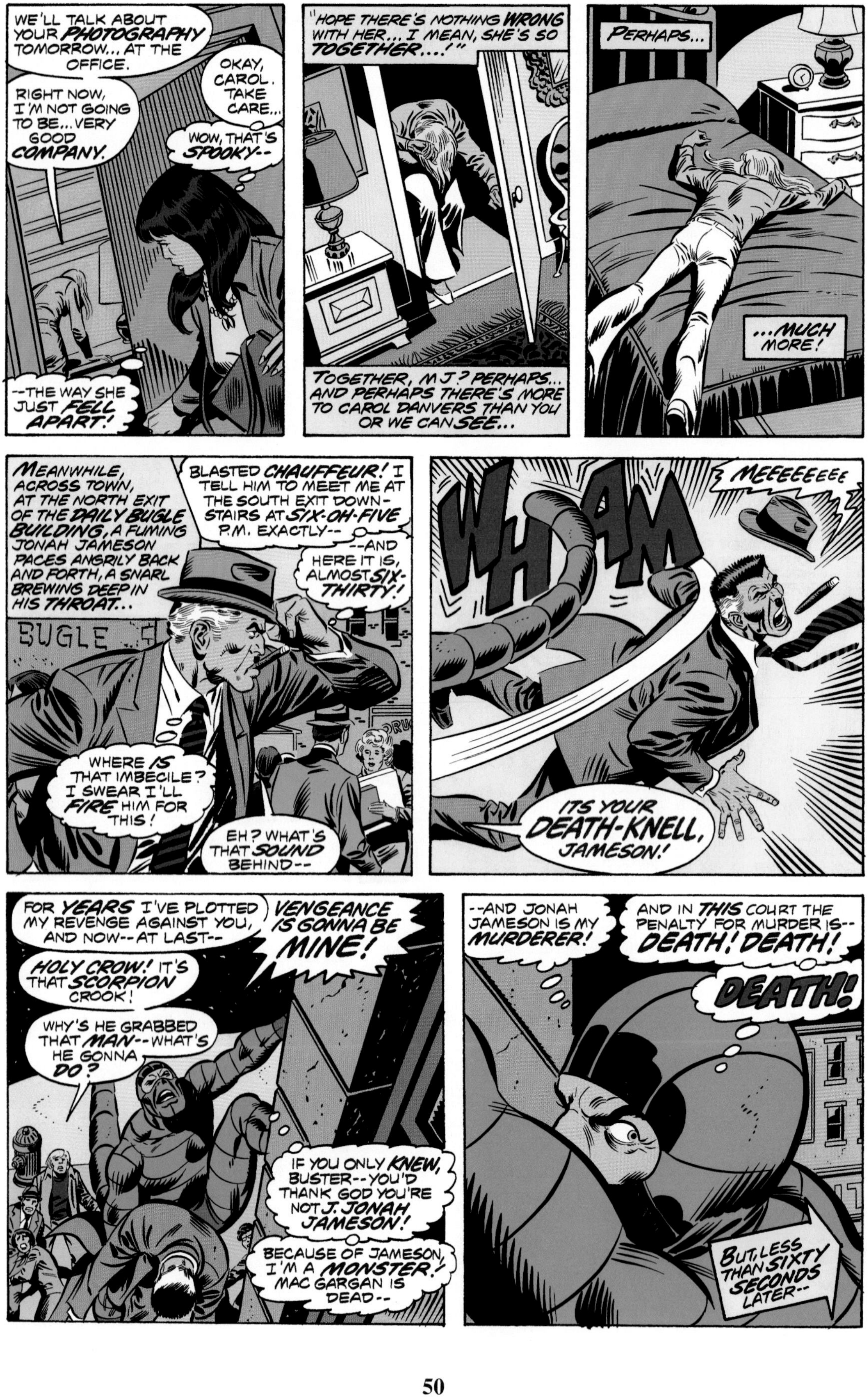
WE'LL TALK ABOUT YOUR PHOTOGRAPHY TOMORROW... AT THE OFFICE.
RIGHT NOW, I'M NOT GOING TO BE... VERY GOOD COMPANY.
OKAY, CAROL. TAKE CARE...
WOW, THAT'S SPOOKY--
--THE WAY SHE JUST FELL APART!
"HOPE THERE'S NOTHING WRONG WITH HER... I MEAN, SHE'S SO TOGETHER....!"
TOGETHER, M J? PERHAPS... AND PERHAPS THERE'S MORE TO CAROL DANVERS THAN YOU OR WE CAN SEE...
PERHAPS...
...MUCH MORE!
MEANWHILE, ACROSS TOWN, AT THE NORTH EXIT OF THE DAILY BUGLE BUILDING, A FUMING JONAH JAMESON PACES ANGRILY BACK AND FORTH, A SNARL BREWING DEEP IN HIS THROAT...
BLASTED CHAUFFEUR! I TELL HIM TO MEET ME AT THE SOUTH EXIT DOWN-STAIRS AT SIX-OH-FIVE P.M. EXACTLY--
--AND HERE IT IS, ALMOST SIX-THIRTY!
BUGLE
WHERE IS THAT IMBECILE? I SWEAR I'LL FIRE HIM FOR THIS!
EH? WHAT'S THAT SOUND BEHIND--
WHAM
MEEEEEEEEE
ITS YOUR DEATH-KNELL, JAMESON!
FOR YEARS I'VE PLOTTED MY REVENGE AGAINST YOU, AND NOW--AT LAST--
VENGEANCE IS GONNA BE MINE!
HOLY CROW! IT'S THAT SCORPION CROOK!
WHY'S HE GRABBED THAT MAN--WHAT'S HE GONNA DO?
IF YOU ONLY KNEW, BUSTER--YOU'D THANK GOD YOU'RE NOT J. JONAH JAMESON!
BECAUSE OF JAMESON, I'M A MONSTER! MAC GARGAN IS DEAD--
--AND JONAH JAMESON IS MY MURDERER!
AND IN THIS COURT THE PENALTY FOR MURDER IS-- DEATH! DEATH!
DEATH!
BUT, LESS THAN SIXTY SECONDS LATER--

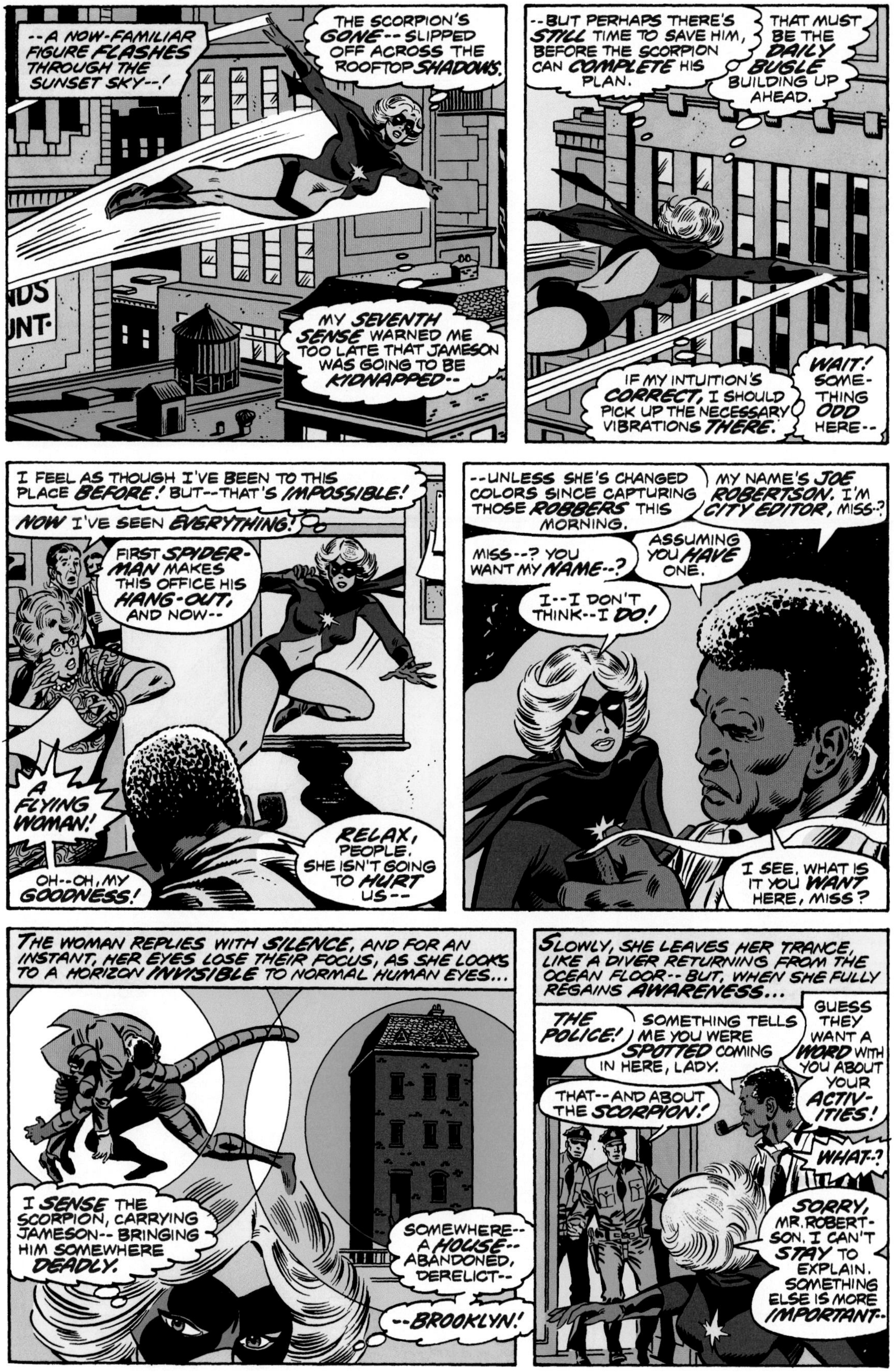
--A NOW-FAMILIAR FIGURE FLASHES THROUGH THE SUNSET SKY--!
THE SCORPION'S GONE--SLIPPED OFF ACROSS THE ROOFTOP SHADOWS.
MY SEVENTH SENSE WARNED ME TOO LATE THAT JAMESON WAS GOING TO BE KIDNAPPED--
--BUT PERHAPS THERE'S STILL TIME TO SAVE HIM, BEFORE THE SCORPION CAN COMPLETE HIS PLAN.
THAT MUST BE THE DAILY BUGLE BUILDING UP AHEAD.
IF MY INTUITION'S CORRECT, I SHOULD PICK UP THE NECESSARY VIBRATIONS THERE.
WAIT! SOMETHING ODD HERE--
I FEEL AS THOUGH I'VE BEEN TO THIS PLACE BEFORE! BUT--THAT'S IMPOSSIBLE!
NOW I'VE SEEN EVERYTHING!
FIRST SPIDER-MAN MAKES THIS OFFICE HIS HANG-OUT, AND NOW--
A FLYING WOMAN!
OH--OH, MY GOODNESS!
RELAX, PEOPLE. SHE ISN'T GOING TO HURT US--
--UNLESS SHE'S CHANGED COLORS SINCE CAPTURING THOSE ROBBERS THIS MORNING.
MY NAME'S JOE ROBERTSON. I'M CITY EDITOR, MISS-?
MISS--? YOU WANT MY NAME--?
ASSUMING YOU HAVE ONE.
I--I DON'T THINK--I DO!
I SEE. WHAT IS IT YOU WANT HERE, MISS?
THE WOMAN REPLIES WITH SILENCE, AND FOR AN INSTANT, HER EYES LOSE THEIR FOCUS, AS SHE LOOKS TO A HORIZON INVISIBLE TO NORMAL HUMAN EYES...
I SENSE THE SCORPION, CARRYING JAMESON-- BRINGING HIM SOMEWHERE DEADLY.
SOMEWHERE-- A HOUSE-- ABANDONED, DERELICT--
--BROOKLYN!
SLOWLY, SHE LEAVES HER TRANCE, LIKE A DIVER RETURNING FROM THE OCEAN FLOOR-- BUT, WHEN SHE FULLY REGAINS AWARENESS...
THE POLICE!
SOMETHING TELLS ME YOU WERE SPOTTED COMING IN HERE, LADY.
GUESS THEY WANT A WORD WITH YOU ABOUT YOUR ACTIVITIES!
THAT--AND ABOUT THE SCORPION!
WHAT-?
SORRY, MR. ROBERTSON. I CAN'T STAY TO EXPLAIN. SOMETHING ELSE IS MORE IMPORTANT--

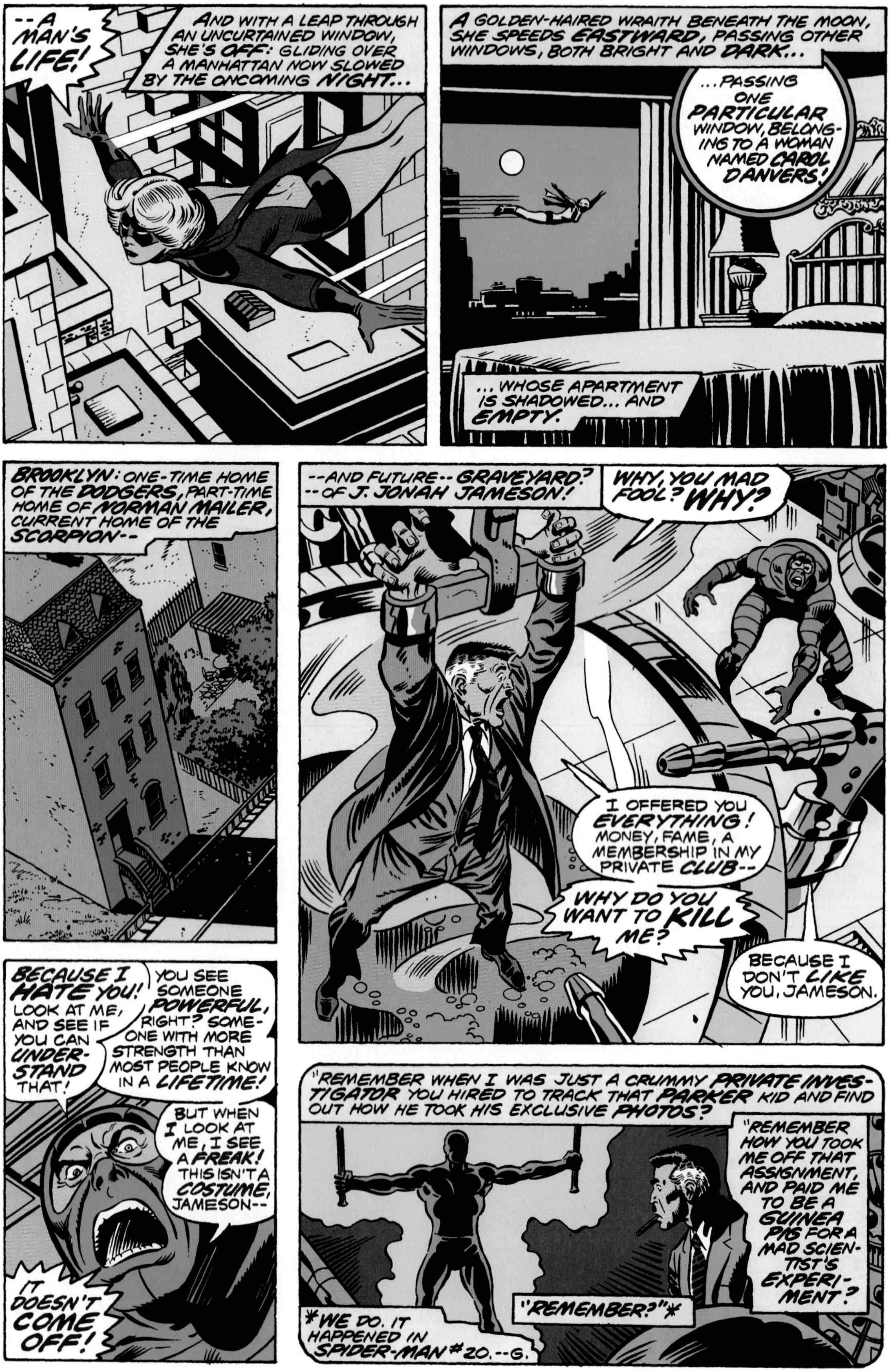
--A MAN'S LIFE!
AND WITH A LEAP THROUGH AN UNCURTAINED WINDOW, SHE'S OFF: GLIDING OVER A MANHATTAN NOW SLOWED BY THE ONCOMING NIGHT...
A GOLDEN-HAIRED WRAITH BENEATH THE MOON, SHE SPEEDS EASTWARD, PASSING OTHER WINDOWS, BOTH BRIGHT AND DARK...
...PASSING ONE PARTICULAR WINDOW, BELONGING TO A WOMAN NAMED CAROL DANVERS!
...WHOSE APARTMENT IS SHADOWED... AND EMPTY.
BROOKLYN: ONE-TIME HOME OF THE DODGERS, PART-TIME HOME OF NORMAN MAILER, CURRENT HOME OF THE SCORPION--
--AND FUTURE--GRAVEYARD?--OF J. JONAH JAMESON!
WHY, YOU MAD FOOL? WHY?
I OFFERED YOU EVERYTHING! MONEY, FAME, A MEMBERSHIP IN MY PRIVATE CLUB--
WHY DO YOU WANT TO KILL ME?
BECAUSE I DON'T LIKE YOU, JAMESON.
BECAUSE I HATE YOU! LOOK AT ME, AND SEE IF YOU CAN UNDERSTAND THAT!
YOU SEE SOMEONE POWERFUL, RIGHT? SOMEONE WITH MORE STRENGTH THAN MOST PEOPLE KNOW IN A LIFETIME!
BUT WHEN I LOOK AT ME, I SEE A FREAK! THIS ISN'T A COSTUME, JAMESON--
IT DOESN'T COME OFF!
"REMEMBER WHEN I WAS JUST A CRUMMY PRIVATE INVESTIGATOR YOU HIRED TO TRACK THAT PARKER KID AND FIND OUT HOW HE TOOK HIS EXCLUSIVE PHOTOS?
"REMEMBER HOW YOU TOOK ME OFF THAT ASSIGNMENT, AND PAID ME TO BE A GUINEA PIG FOR A MAD SCIENTIST'S EXPERIMENT?
"REMEMBER?"*
*WE DO. IT HAPPENED IN SPIDER-MAN #20.--G.

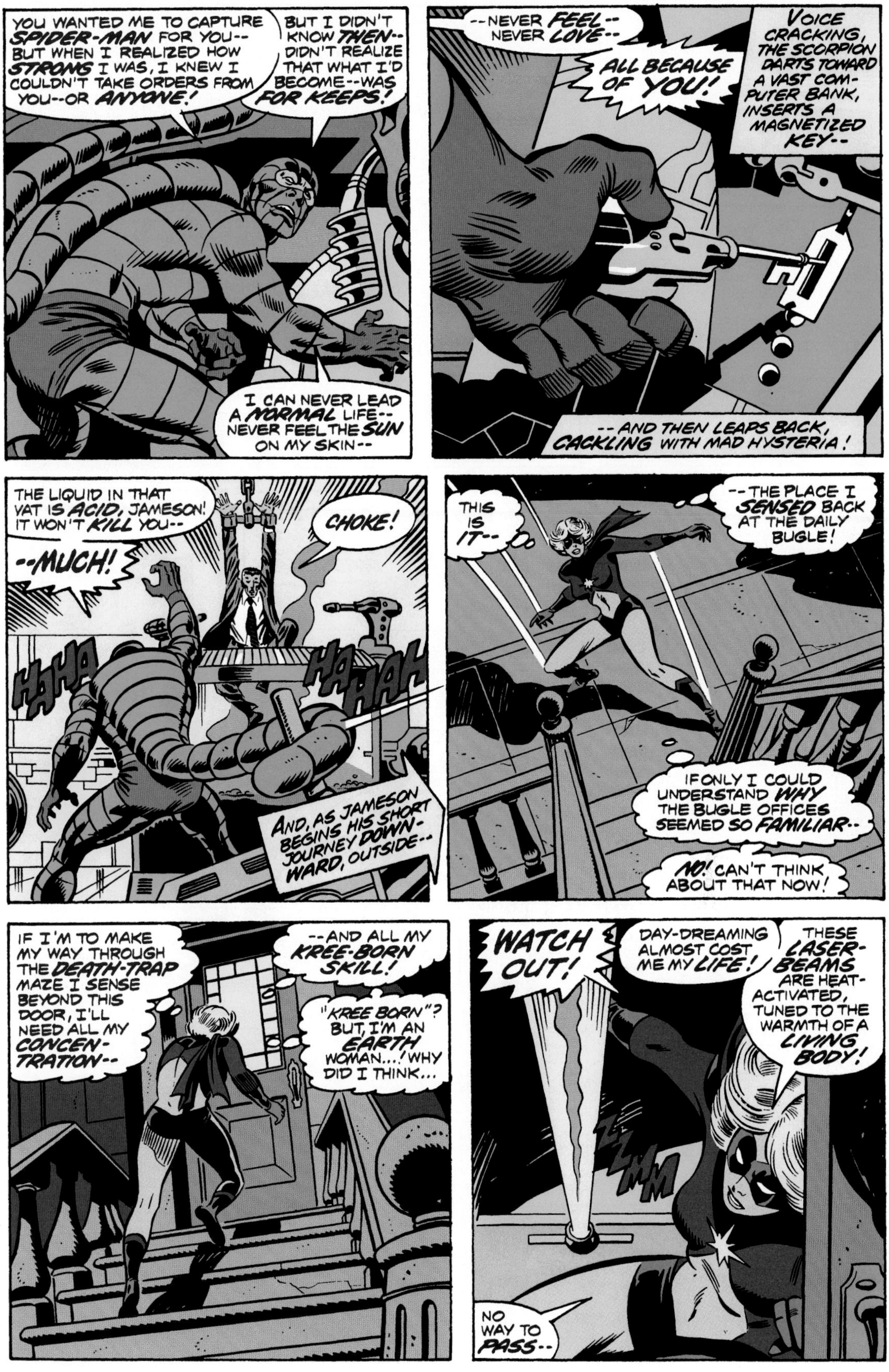
YOU WANTED ME TO CAPTURE SPIDER-MAN FOR YOU-- BUT WHEN I REALIZED HOW STRONG I WAS, I KNEW I COULDN'T TAKE ORDERS FROM YOU--OR ANYONE!
BUT I DIDN'T KNOW THEN-- DIDN'T REALIZE THAT WHAT I'D BECOME--WAS FOR KEEPS!
I CAN NEVER LEAD A NORMAL LIFE-- NEVER FEEL THE SUN ON MY SKIN--
--NEVER FEEL-- NEVER LOVE--
ALL BECAUSE OF YOU!
VOICE CRACKING, THE SCORPION DARTS TOWARD A VAST COMPUTER BANK, INSERTS A MAGNETIZED KEY--
--AND THEN LEAPS BACK, CACKLING WITH MAD HYSTERIA!
THE LIQUID IN THAT VAT IS ACID, JAMESON! IT WON'T KILL YOU--
--MUCH!
CHOKE!
HAHA
HAHAHAH
AND, AS JAMESON BEGINS HIS SHORT JOURNEY DOWNWARD, OUTSIDE--
THIS IS IT--
--THE PLACE I SENSED BACK AT THE DAILY BUGLE!
IF ONLY I COULD UNDERSTAND WHY THE BUGLE OFFICES SEEMED SO FAMILIAR--
NO! CAN'T THINK ABOUT THAT NOW!
IF I'M TO MAKE MY WAY THROUGH THE DEATH-TRAP MAZE I SENSE BEYOND THIS DOOR, I'LL NEED ALL MY CONCENTRATION--
--AND ALL MY KREE-BORN SKILL!
"KREE BORN"? BUT, I'M AN EARTH WOMAN...! WHY DID I THINK...
WATCH OUT!
DAY-DREAMING ALMOST COST ME MY LIFE!
THESE LASER-BEAMS ARE HEAT-ACTIVATED, TUNED TO THE WARMTH OF A LIVING BODY!
ZZMM
NO WAY TO PASS--

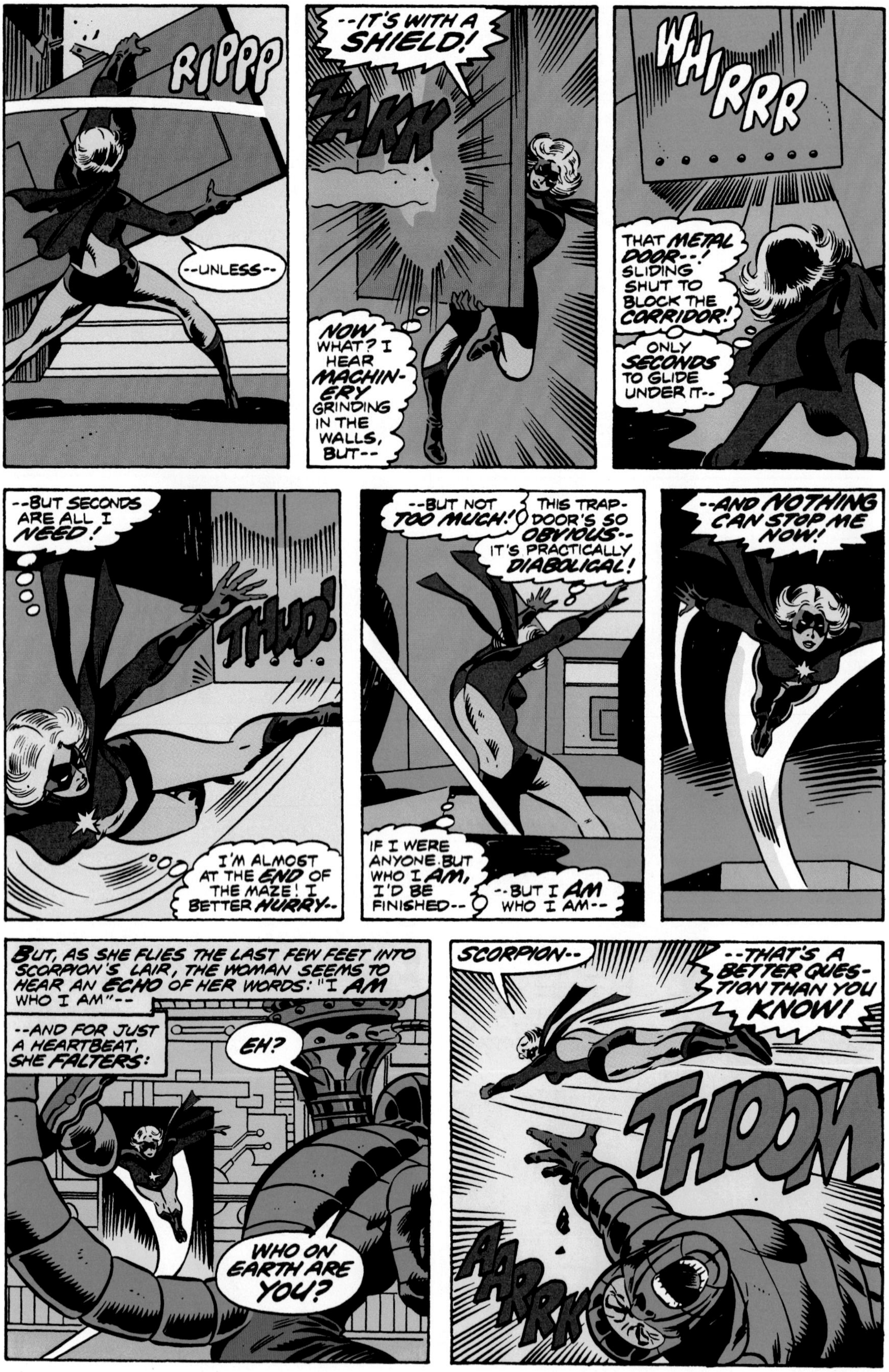
RIPPP
--UNLESS--
--IT'S WITH A SHIELD!
ZAKK
NOW WHAT? I HEAR MACHINERY GRINDING IN THE WALLS, BUT--
WHIRRRR
THAT METAL DOOR--! SLIDING SHUT TO BLOCK THE CORRIDOR!
ONLY SECONDS TO GLIDE UNDER IT--
--BUT SECONDS ARE ALL I NEED!
THUD!
I'M ALMOST AT THE END OF THE MAZE! I BETTER HURRY--
--BUT NOT TOO MUCH!
THIS TRAP-DOOR'S SO OBVIOUS--IT'S PRACTICALLY DIABOLICAL!
IF I WERE ANYONE BUT WHO I AM, I'D BE FINISHED--
--BUT I AM WHO I AM--
--AND NOTHING CAN STOP ME NOW!
BUT, AS SHE FLIES THE LAST FEW FEET INTO SCORPION'S LAIR, THE WOMAN SEEMS TO HEAR AN ECHO OF HER WORDS: "I AM WHO I AM"--
--AND FOR JUST A HEARTBEAT, SHE FALTERS:
EH?
WHO ON EARTH ARE YOU?
SCORPION--
--THAT'S A BETTER QUESTION THAN YOU KNOW!
THOOM
AARRRK

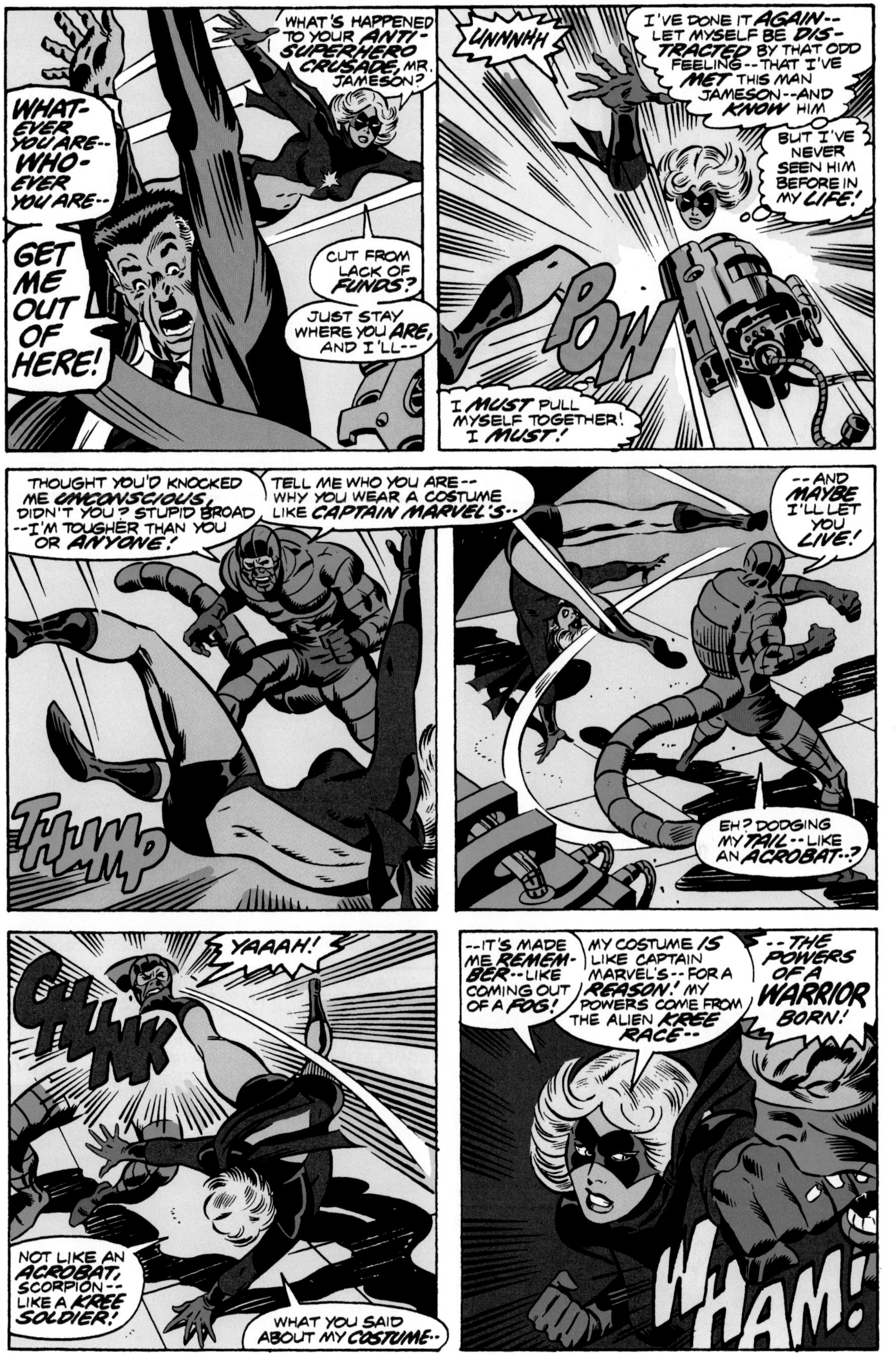
WHAT'S HAPPENED TO YOUR ANTI-SUPERHERO CRUSADE, MR. JAMESON?
WHATEVER YOU ARE-- WHOEVER YOU ARE--
GET ME OUT OF HERE!
CUT FROM LACK OF FUNDS?
JUST STAY WHERE YOU ARE, AND I'LL--
UNNNHH
I'VE DONE IT AGAIN-- LET MYSELF BE DISTRACTED BY THAT ODD FEELING--THAT I'VE MET THIS MAN JAMESON--AND KNOW HIM
BUT I'VE NEVER SEEN HIM BEFORE IN MY LIFE!
POW
I MUST PULL MYSELF TOGETHER! I MUST!
THOUGHT YOU'D KNOCKED ME UNCONSCIOUS, DIDN'T YOU? STUPID BROAD --I'M TOUGHER THAN YOU OR ANYONE!
TELL ME WHO YOU ARE-- WHY YOU WEAR A COSTUME LIKE CAPTAIN MARVEL'S--
THUMP
--AND MAYBE I'LL LET YOU LIVE!
EH? DODGING MY TAIL--LIKE AN ACROBAT--?
YAAAH!
CHUNK
NOT LIKE AN ACROBAT, SCORPION-- LIKE A KREE SOLDIER!
WHAT YOU SAID ABOUT MY COSTUME--
--IT'S MADE ME REMEMBER--LIKE COMING OUT OF A FOG!
MY COSTUME IS LIKE CAPTAIN MARVEL'S--FOR A REASON! MY POWERS COME FROM THE ALIEN KREE RACE--
--THE POWERS OF A WARRIOR BORN!
WHAM!

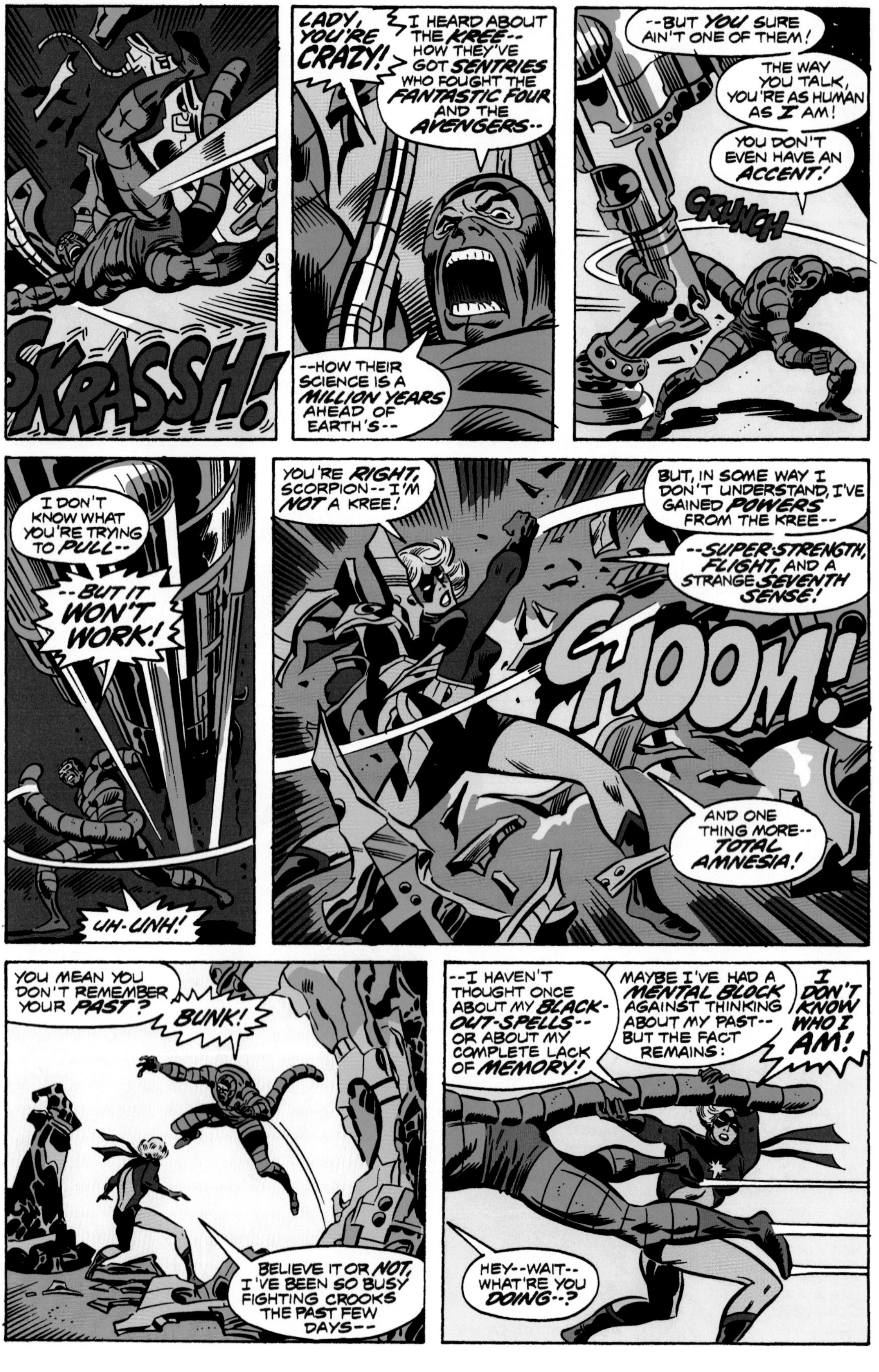
SKRASSH!
LADY, YOU'RE CRAZY!
I HEARD ABOUT THE KREE-- HOW THEY'VE GOT SENTRIES WHO FOUGHT THE FANTASTIC FOUR AND THE AVENGERS--
--HOW THEIR SCIENCE IS A MILLION YEARS AHEAD OF EARTH'S--
--BUT YOU SURE AIN'T ONE OF THEM!
THE WAY YOU TALK, YOU'RE AS HUMAN AS I AM!
YOU DON'T EVEN HAVE AN ACCENT!
CRUNCH
I DON'T KNOW WHAT YOU'RE TRYING TO PULL--
--BUT IT WON'T WORK!
UH-UNH!
YOU'RE RIGHT, SCORPION--I'M NOT A KREE!
BUT, IN SOME WAY I DON'T UNDERSTAND, I'VE GAINED POWERS FROM THE KREE--
--SUPER-STRENGTH, FLIGHT, AND A STRANGE SEVENTH SENSE!
CHOOM!
AND ONE THING MORE-- TOTAL AMNESIA!
YOU MEAN YOU DON'T REMEMBER YOUR PAST?
BUNK!
BELIEVE IT OR NOT, I'VE BEEN SO BUSY FIGHTING CROOKS THE PAST FEW DAYS--
--I HAVEN'T THOUGHT ONCE ABOUT MY BLACK-OUT-SPELLS-- OR ABOUT MY COMPLETE LACK OF MEMORY!
MAYBE I'VE HAD A MENTAL BLOCK AGAINST THINKING ABOUT MY PAST-- BUT THE FACT REMAINS:
I DON'T KNOW WHO I AM!
HEY--WAIT-- WHAT'RE YOU DOING--?

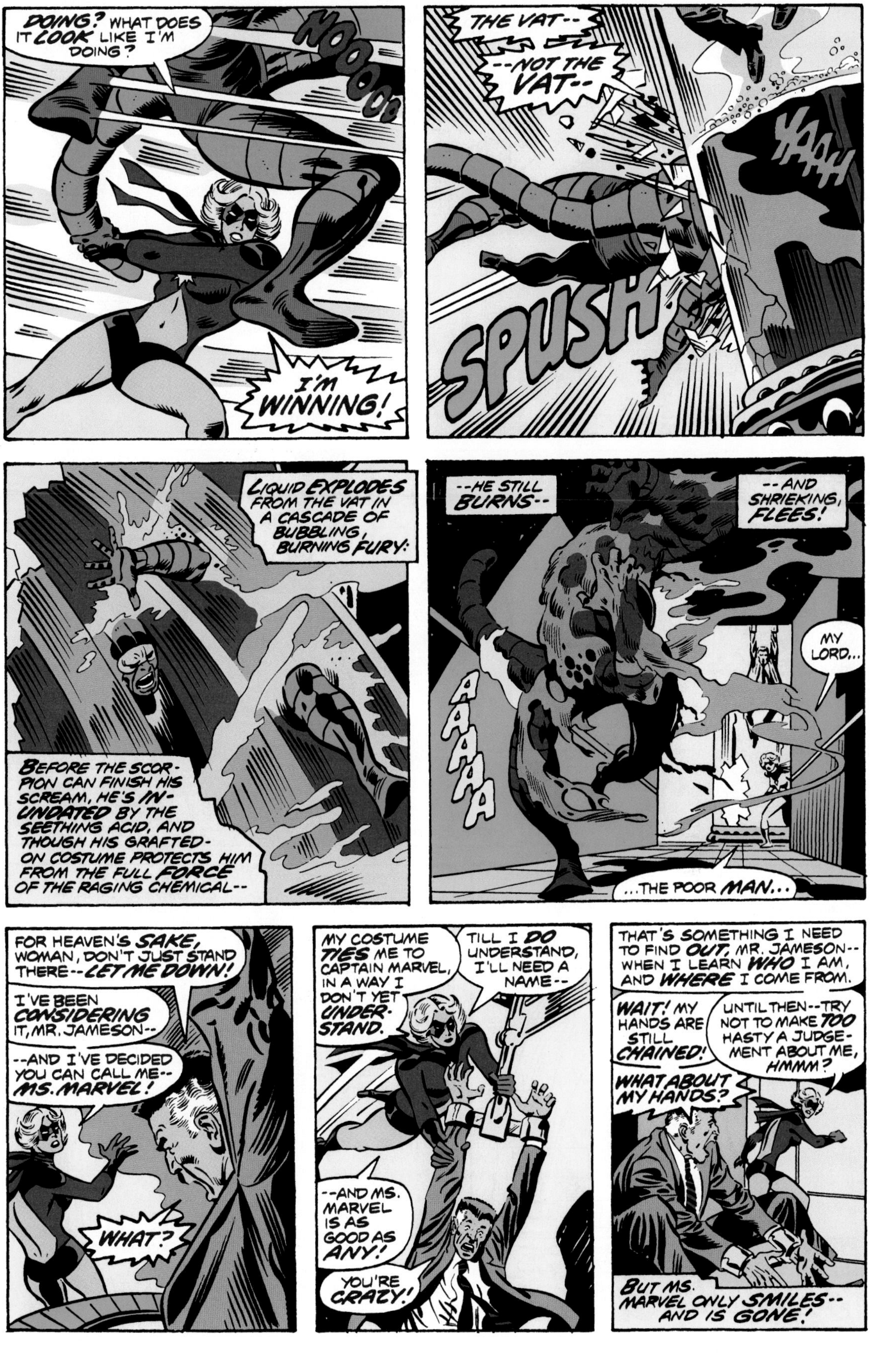
DOING? WHAT DOES IT LOOK LIKE I'M DOING?
NOOOOO
I'M WINNING!
THE VAT--
--NOT THE VAT--
YAAAH
SPUSH
LIQUID EXPLODES FROM THE VAT IN A CASCADE OF BUBBLING, BURNING FURY:
BEFORE THE SCORPION CAN FINISH HIS SCREAM, HE'S INUNDATED BY THE SEETHING ACID, AND THOUGH HIS GRAFTED-ON COSTUME PROTECTS HIM FROM THE FULL FORCE OF THE RAGING CHEMICAL--
--HE STILL BURNS--
--AND SHRIEKING, FLEES!
AAAAA
MY LORD...
...THE POOR MAN...
FOR HEAVEN'S SAKE, WOMAN, DON'T JUST STAND THERE--LET ME DOWN!
I'VE BEEN CONSIDERING IT, MR. JAMESON--
--AND I'VE DECIDED YOU CAN CALL ME--MS. MARVEL!
WHAT?
MY COSTUME TIES ME TO CAPTAIN MARVEL, IN A WAY I DON'T YET UNDERSTAND.
TILL I DO UNDERSTAND, I'LL NEED A NAME--
--AND MS. MARVEL IS AS GOOD AS ANY!
YOU'RE CRAZY!
THAT'S SOMETHING I NEED TO FIND OUT, MR. JAMESON--WHEN I LEARN WHO I AM, AND WHERE I COME FROM.
WAIT! MY HANDS ARE STILL CHAINED!
UNTIL THEN--TRY NOT TO MAKE TOO HASTY A JUDGEMENT ABOUT ME, HMMM?
WHAT ABOUT MY HANDS?
BUT MS. MARVEL ONLY SMILES--AND IS GONE!

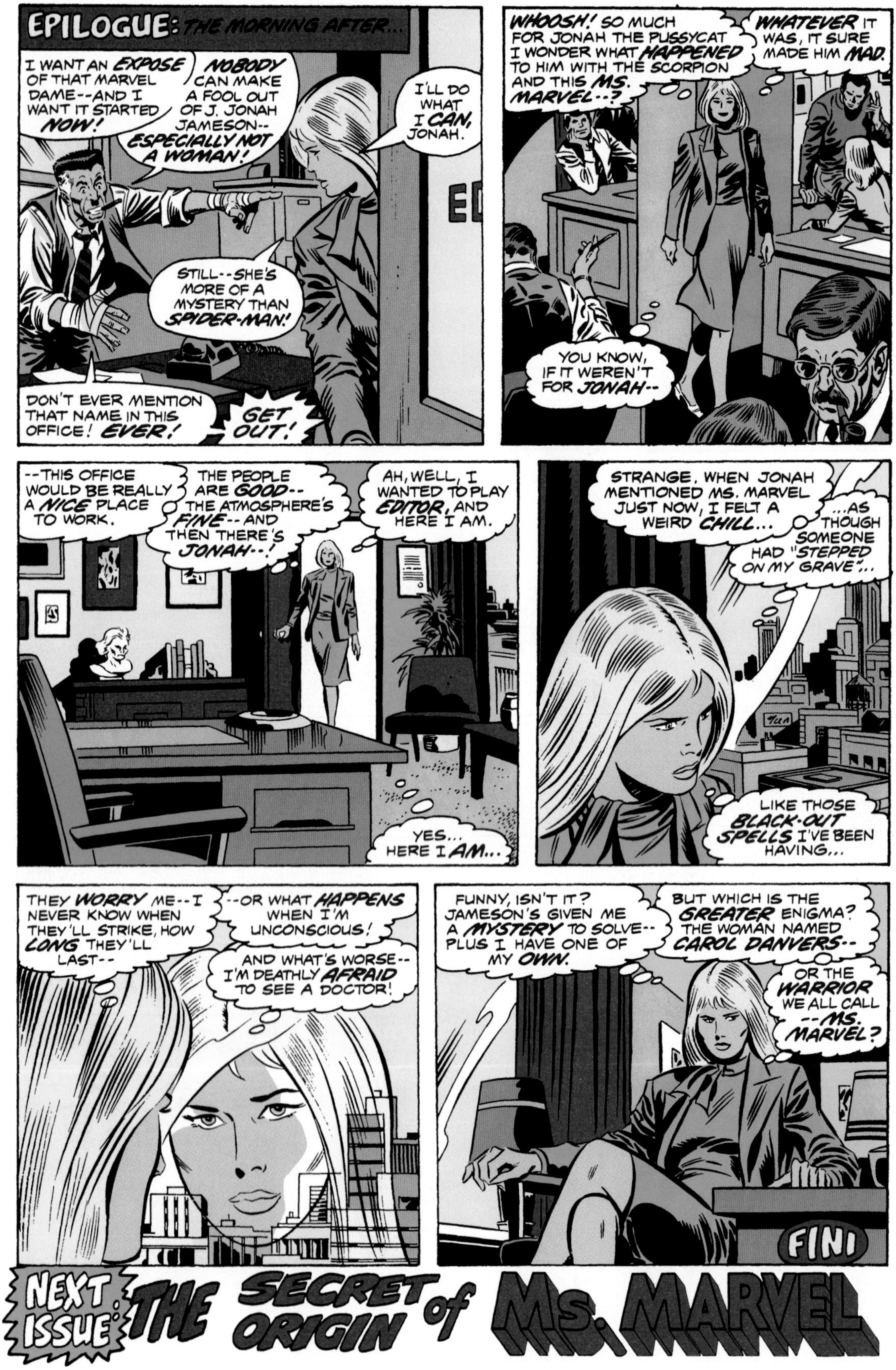
EPILOGUE: THE MORNING AFTER...
I WANT AN EXPOSE OF THAT MARVEL DAME--AND I WANT IT STARTED NOW!
NOBODY CAN MAKE A FOOL OUT OF J. JONAH JAMESON-- ESPECIALLY NOT A WOMAN!
I'LL DO WHAT I CAN, JONAH.
STILL--SHE'S MORE OF A MYSTERY THAN SPIDER-MAN!
DON'T EVER MENTION THAT NAME IN THIS OFFICE! EVER!
GET OUT!
WHOOSH! SO MUCH FOR JONAH THE PUSSYCAT. I WONDER WHAT HAPPENED TO HIM WITH THE SCORPION AND THIS MS. MARVEL--?
WHATEVER IT WAS, IT SURE MADE HIM MAD.
YOU KNOW, IF IT WEREN'T FOR JONAH--
--THIS OFFICE WOULD BE REALLY A NICE PLACE TO WORK.
THE PEOPLE ARE GOOD-- THE ATMOSPHERE'S FINE--AND THEN THERE'S JONAH--!
AH, WELL, I WANTED TO PLAY EDITOR, AND HERE I AM.
YES... HERE I AM...
STRANGE. WHEN JONAH MENTIONED MS. MARVEL JUST NOW, I FELT A WEIRD CHILL...
...AS THOUGH SOMEONE HAD "STEPPED ON MY GRAVE"...
LIKE THOSE BLACK-OUT SPELLS I'VE BEEN HAVING...
THEY WORRY ME--I NEVER KNOW WHEN THEY'LL STRIKE, HOW LONG THEY'LL LAST--
--OR WHAT HAPPENS WHEN I'M UNCONSCIOUS!
AND WHAT'S WORSE-- I'M DEATHLY AFRAID TO SEE A DOCTOR!
FUNNY, ISN'T IT? JAMESON'S GIVEN ME A MYSTERY TO SOLVE-- PLUS I HAVE ONE OF MY OWN.
BUT WHICH IS THE GREATER ENIGMA? THE WOMAN NAMED CAROL DANVERS--
OR THE WARRIOR WE ALL CALL --MS. MARVEL?
FINI
NEXT ISSUE: THE SECRET ORIGIN of MS. MARVEL

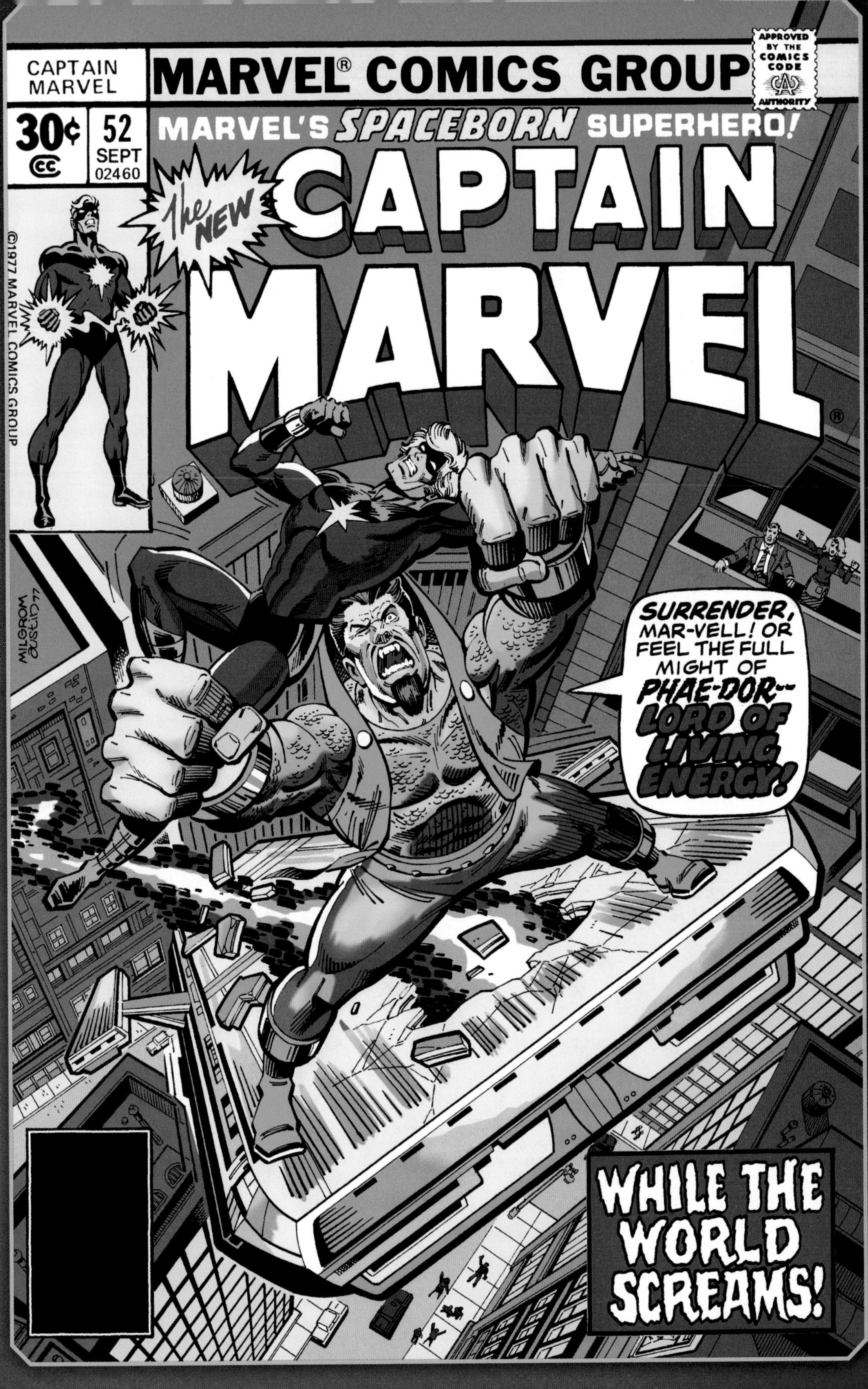
CAPTAIN MARVEL
MARVEL® COMICS GROUP
APPROVED BY THE COMICS CODE AUTHORITY
30¢
52
SEPT
02460
MARVEL'S SPACEBORN SUPERHERO!
The NEW
CAPTAIN MARVEL®
©1977 MARVEL COMICS GROUP
MILGROM
SURRENDER, MAR-VELL! OR FEEL THE FULL MIGHT OF PHAE-DOR-- LORD OF LIVING ENERGY!
WHILE THE WORLD SCREAMS!

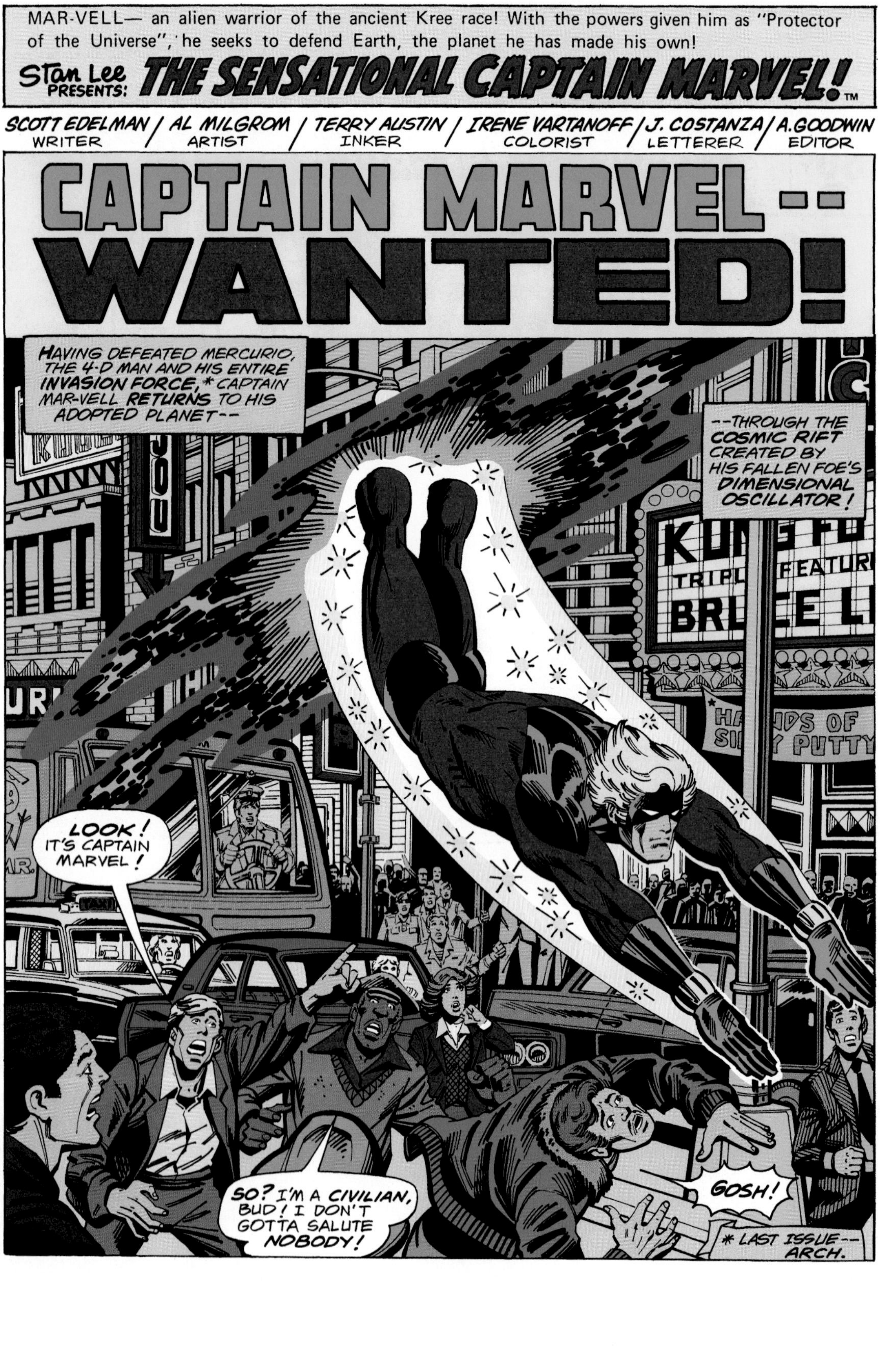

MAR-VELL— an alien warrior of the ancient Kree race! With the powers given him as "Protector of the Universe", he seeks to defend Earth, the planet he has made his own!
Stan Lee PRESENTS: THE SENSATIONAL CAPTAIN MARVEL! TM
SCOTT EDELMAN WRITER / AL MILGROM ARTIST / TERRY AUSTIN INKER / IRENE VARTANOFF COLORIST / J. COSTANZA LETTERER / A. GOODWIN EDITOR
CAPTAIN MARVEL -- WANTED!
HAVING DEFEATED MERCURIO, THE 4-D MAN AND HIS ENTIRE INVASION FORCE,* CAPTAIN MAR-VELL RETURNS TO HIS ADOPTED PLANET--
--THROUGH THE COSMIC RIFT CREATED BY HIS FALLEN FOE'S DIMENSIONAL OSCILLATOR!
LOOK! IT'S CAPTAIN MARVEL!
SO? I'M A CIVILIAN, BUD! I DON'T GOTTA SALUTE NOBODY!
GOSH!
*LAST ISSUE-- ARCH.

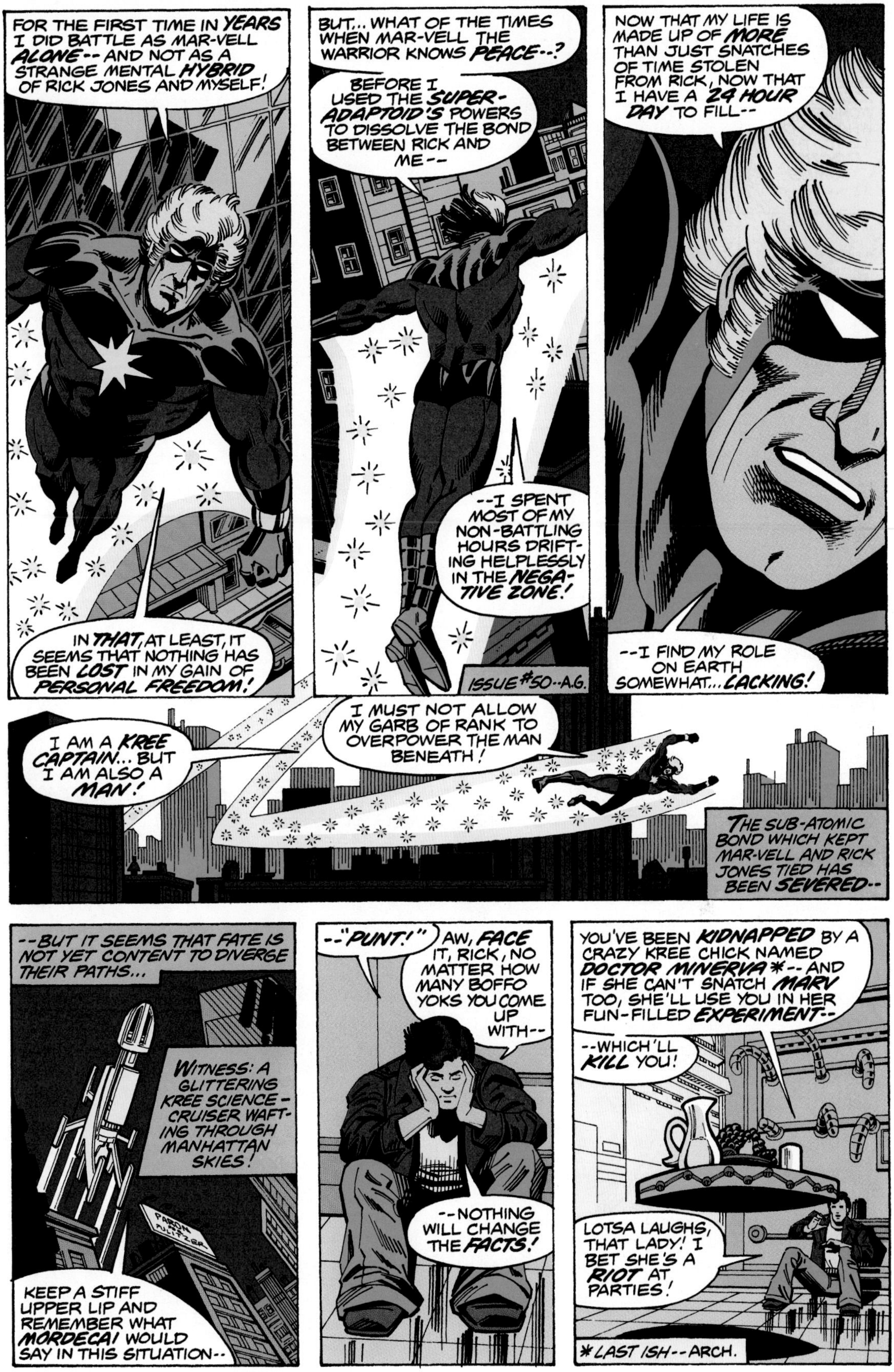
FOR THE FIRST TIME IN YEARS I DID BATTLE AS MAR-VELL ALONE-- AND NOT AS A STRANGE MENTAL HYBRID OF RICK JONES AND MYSELF!
IN THAT, AT LEAST, IT SEEMS THAT NOTHING HAS BEEN LOST IN MY GAIN OF PERSONAL FREEDOM!
BUT... WHAT OF THE TIMES WHEN MAR-VELL THE WARRIOR KNOWS PEACE--?
BEFORE I USED THE SUPER-ADAPTOID'S POWERS TO DISSOLVE THE BOND BETWEEN RICK AND ME--
--I SPENT MOST OF MY NON-BATTLING HOURS DRIFTING HELPLESSLY IN THE NEGATIVE ZONE!
ISSUE #50--A.G.
NOW THAT MY LIFE IS MADE UP OF MORE THAN JUST SNATCHES OF TIME STOLEN FROM RICK, NOW THAT I HAVE A 24 HOUR DAY TO FILL--
--I FIND MY ROLE ON EARTH SOMEWHAT... LACKING!
I AM A KREE CAPTAIN... BUT I AM ALSO A MAN!
I MUST NOT ALLOW MY GARB OF RANK TO OVERPOWER THE MAN BENEATH!
THE SUB-ATOMIC BOND WHICH KEPT MAR-VELL AND RICK JONES TIED HAS BEEN SEVERED--
--BUT IT SEEMS THAT FATE IS NOT YET CONTENT TO DIVERGE THEIR PATHS...
WITNESS: A GLITTERING KREE SCIENCE-CRUISER WAFTING THROUGH MANHATTAN SKIES!
KEEP A STIFF UPPER LIP AND REMEMBER WHAT MORDECAI WOULD SAY IN THIS SITUATION--
--"PUNT!"
AW, FACE IT, RICK, NO MATTER HOW MANY BOFFO YOKS YOU COME UP WITH--
--NOTHING WILL CHANGE THE FACTS!
YOU'VE BEEN KIDNAPPED BY A CRAZY KREE CHICK NAMED DOCTOR MINERVA*-- AND IF SHE CAN'T SNATCH MARV TOO, SHE'LL USE YOU IN HER FUN-FILLED EXPERIMENT--
--WHICH'LL KILL YOU!
LOTSA LAUGHS, THAT LADY! I BET SHE'S A RIOT AT PARTIES!
*LAST ISH--ARCH.

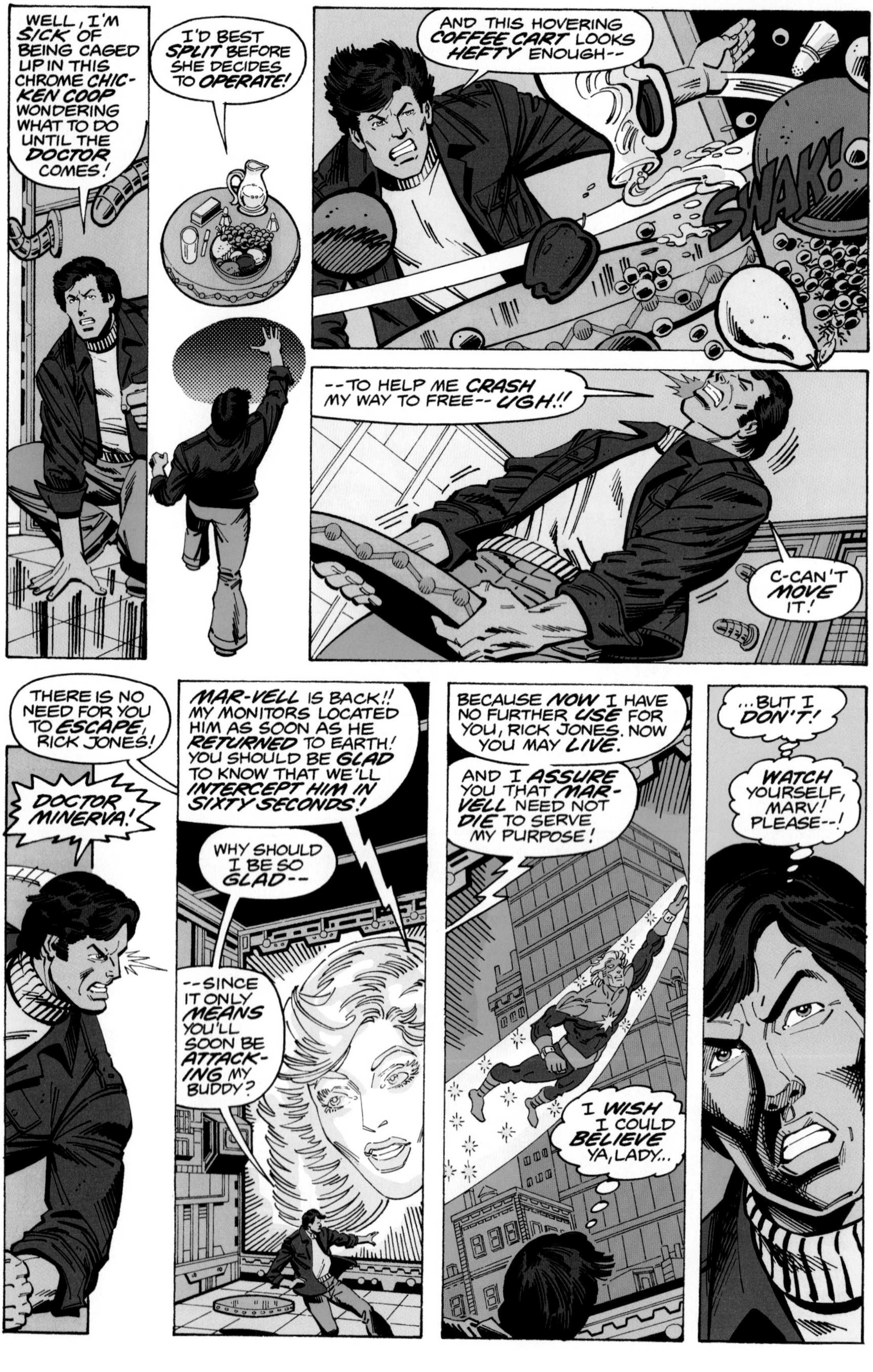
WELL, I'M SICK OF BEING CAGED UP IN THIS CHROME CHIC-KEN COOP WONDERING WHAT TO DO UNTIL THE DOCTOR COMES!
I'D BEST SPLIT BEFORE SHE DECIDES TO OPERATE!
AND THIS HOVERING COFFEE CART LOOKS HEFTY ENOUGH--
SWAK!
--TO HELP ME CRASH MY WAY TO FREE-- UGH!!
C-CAN'T MOVE IT!
THERE IS NO NEED FOR YOU TO ESCAPE, RICK JONES!
DOCTOR MINERVA!
MAR-VELL IS BACK!! MY MONITORS LOCATED HIM AS SOON AS HE RETURNED TO EARTH! YOU SHOULD BE GLAD TO KNOW THAT WE'LL INTERCEPT HIM IN SIXTY SECONDS!
WHY SHOULD I BE SO GLAD--
--SINCE IT ONLY MEANS YOU'LL SOON BE ATTACK-ING MY BUDDY?
BECAUSE NOW I HAVE NO FURTHER USE FOR YOU, RICK JONES. NOW YOU MAY LIVE.
AND I ASSURE YOU THAT MAR-VELL NEED NOT DIE TO SERVE MY PURPOSE!
I WISH I COULD BELIEVE YA, LADY...
...BUT I DON'T!
WATCH YOURSELF, MARV! PLEASE--!

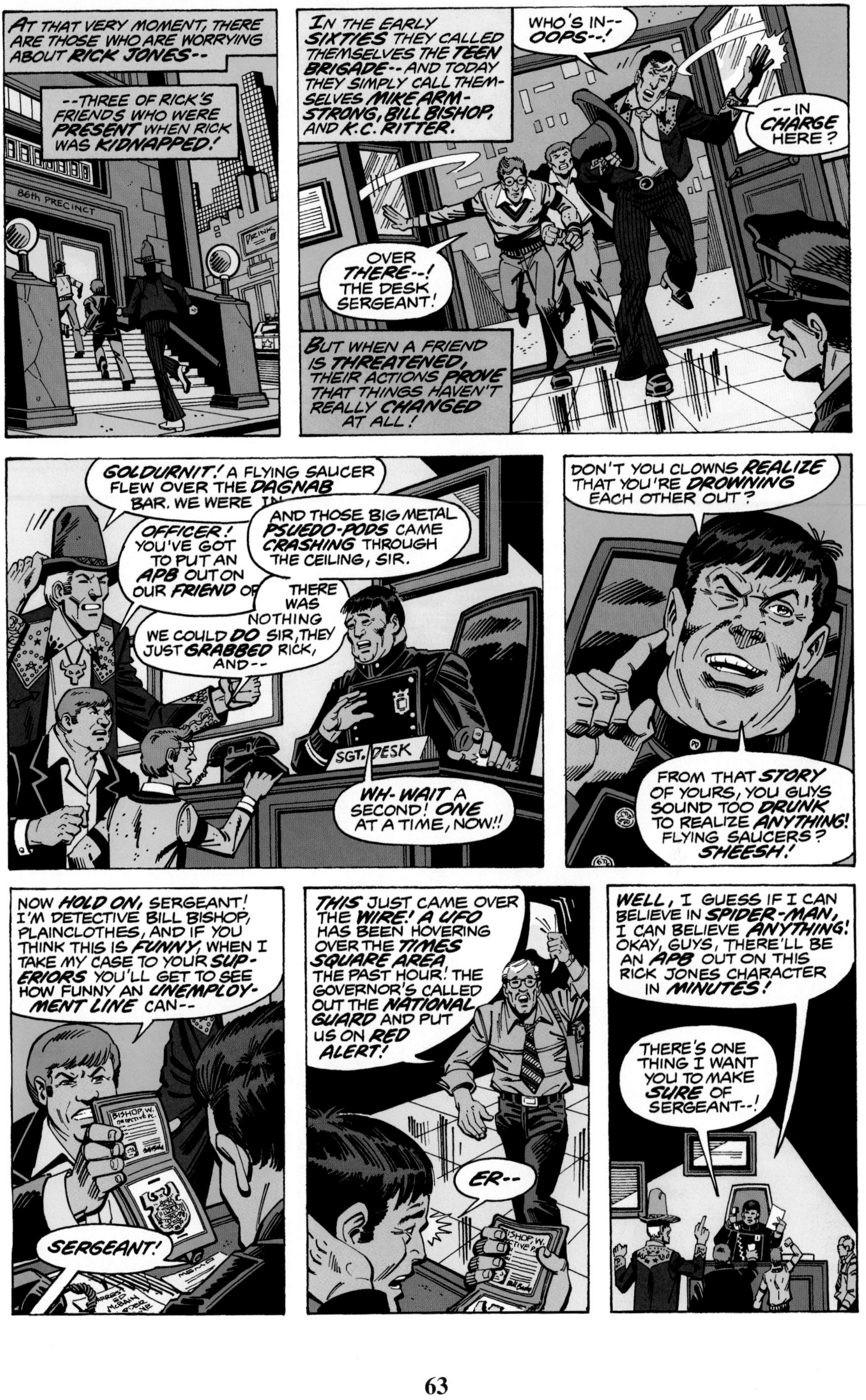

AT THAT VERY MOMENT, THERE ARE THOSE WHO ARE WORRYING ABOUT RICK JONES--
--THREE OF RICK'S FRIENDS WHO WERE PRESENT WHEN RICK WAS KIDNAPPED!
86th PRECINCT
IN THE EARLY SIXTIES THEY CALLED THEMSELVES THE TEEN BRIGADE--AND TODAY THEY SIMPLY CALL THEMSELVES MIKE ARMSTRONG, BILL BISHOP, AND K.C. RITTER.
WHO'S IN-- OOPS--!
--IN CHARGE HERE?
OVER THERE--! THE DESK SERGEANT!
BUT WHEN A FRIEND IS THREATENED, THEIR ACTIONS PROVE THAT THINGS HAVEN'T REALLY CHANGED AT ALL!
GOLDURNIT! A FLYING SAUCER FLEW OVER THE DAGNAB BAR. WE WERE IN
OFFICER! YOU'VE GOT TO PUT AN APB OUT ON OUR FRIEND OF
AND THOSE BIG METAL PSUEDO-PODS CAME CRASHING THROUGH THE CEILING, SIR.
THERE WAS NOTHING WE COULD DO SIR, THEY JUST GRABBED RICK, AND--
SGT. DESK
WH-WAIT A SECOND! ONE AT A TIME, NOW!!
DON'T YOU CLOWNS REALIZE THAT YOU'RE DROWNING EACH OTHER OUT?
FROM THAT STORY OF YOURS, YOU GUYS SOUND TOO DRUNK TO REALIZE ANYTHING! FLYING SAUCERS? SHEESH!
NOW HOLD ON, SERGEANT! I'M DETECTIVE BILL BISHOP, PLAINCLOTHES, AND IF YOU THINK THIS IS FUNNY, WHEN I TAKE MY CASE TO YOUR SUPERIORS YOU'LL GET TO SEE HOW FUNNY AN UNEMPLOYMENT LINE CAN--
SERGEANT!
THIS JUST CAME OVER THE WIRE! A UFO HAS BEEN HOVERING OVER THE TIMES SQUARE AREA THE PAST HOUR! THE GOVERNOR'S CALLED OUT THE NATIONAL GUARD AND PUT US ON RED ALERT!
ER--
WELL, I GUESS IF I CAN BELIEVE IN SPIDER-MAN, I CAN BELIEVE ANYTHING! OKAY, GUYS, THERE'LL BE AN APB OUT ON THIS RICK JONES CHARACTER IN MINUTES!
THERE'S ONE THING I WANT YOU TO MAKE SURE OF SERGEANT--!

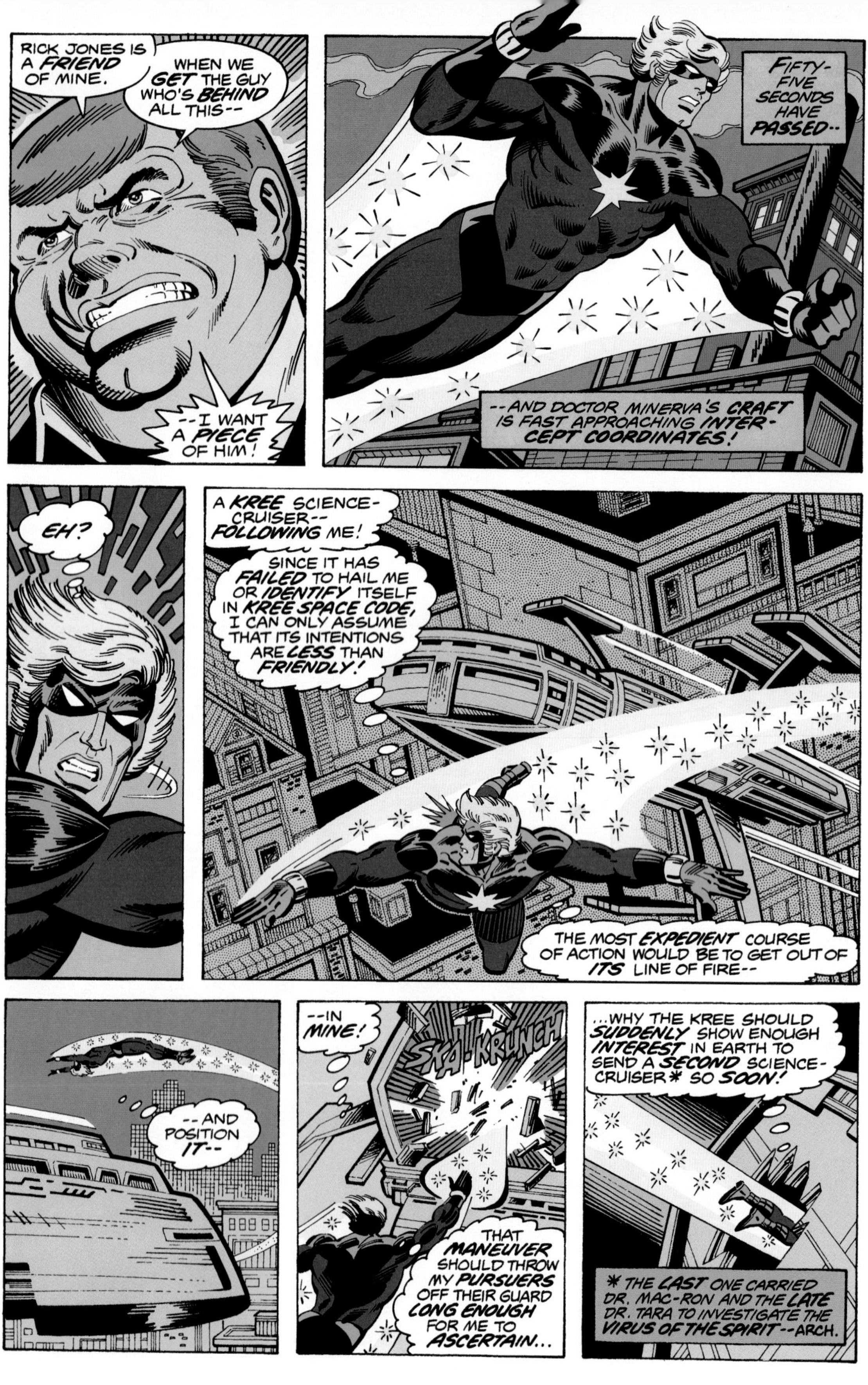
RICK JONES IS A FRIEND OF MINE.
WHEN WE GET THE GUY WHO'S BEHIND ALL THIS--
--I WANT A PIECE OF HIM!
FIFTY-FIVE SECONDS HAVE PASSED--
--AND DOCTOR MINERVA'S CRAFT IS FAST APPROACHING INTER-CEPT COORDINATES!
EH?
A KREE SCIENCE-CRUISER--FOLLOWING ME!
SINCE IT HAS FAILED TO HAIL ME OR IDENTIFY ITSELF IN KREE SPACE CODE, I CAN ONLY ASSUME THAT ITS INTENTIONS ARE LESS THAN FRIENDLY!
THE MOST EXPEDIENT COURSE OF ACTION WOULD BE TO GET OUT OF ITS LINE OF FIRE--
--AND POSITION IT--
--IN MINE!
SKA-KRUNCH
THAT MANEUVER SHOULD THROW MY PURSUERS OFF THEIR GUARD LONG ENOUGH FOR ME TO ASCERTAIN...
...WHY THE KREE SHOULD SUDDENLY SHOW ENOUGH INTEREST IN EARTH TO SEND A SECOND SCIENCE-CRUISER* SO SOON!
* THE LAST ONE CARRIED DR. MAC-RON AND THE LATE DR. TARA TO INVESTIGATE THE VIRUS OF THE SPIRIT--ARCH.

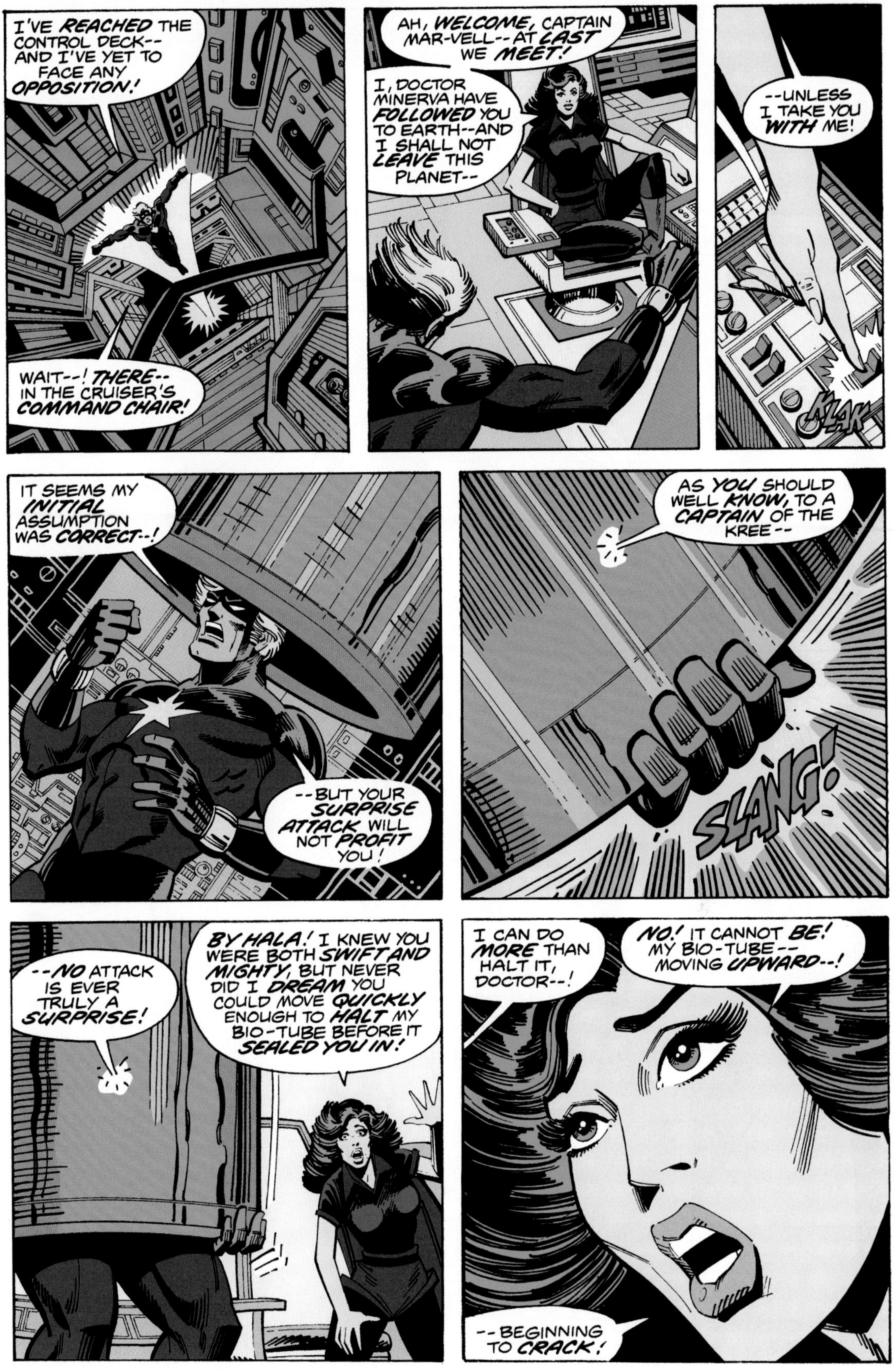
I'VE REACHED THE CONTROL DECK-- AND I'VE YET TO FACE ANY OPPOSITION!
WAIT--! THERE-- IN THE CRUISER'S COMMAND CHAIR!
AH, WELCOME, CAPTAIN MAR-VELL--AT LAST WE MEET!
I, DOCTOR MINERVA HAVE FOLLOWED YOU TO EARTH--AND I SHALL NOT LEAVE THIS PLANET--
--UNLESS I TAKE YOU WITH ME!
KLAK
IT SEEMS MY INITIAL ASSUMPTION WAS CORRECT--!
--BUT YOUR SURPRISE ATTACK WILL NOT PROFIT YOU!
AS YOU SHOULD WELL KNOW, TO A CAPTAIN OF THE KREE--
SLANG!
--NO ATTACK IS EVER TRULY A SURPRISE!
BY HALA! I KNEW YOU WERE BOTH SWIFT AND MIGHTY, BUT NEVER DID I DREAM YOU COULD MOVE QUICKLY ENOUGH TO HALT MY BIO-TUBE BEFORE IT SEALED YOU IN!
I CAN DO MORE THAN HALT IT, DOCTOR--!
NO! IT CANNOT BE! MY BIO-TUBE-- MOVING UPWARD--!
--BEGINNING TO CRACK!

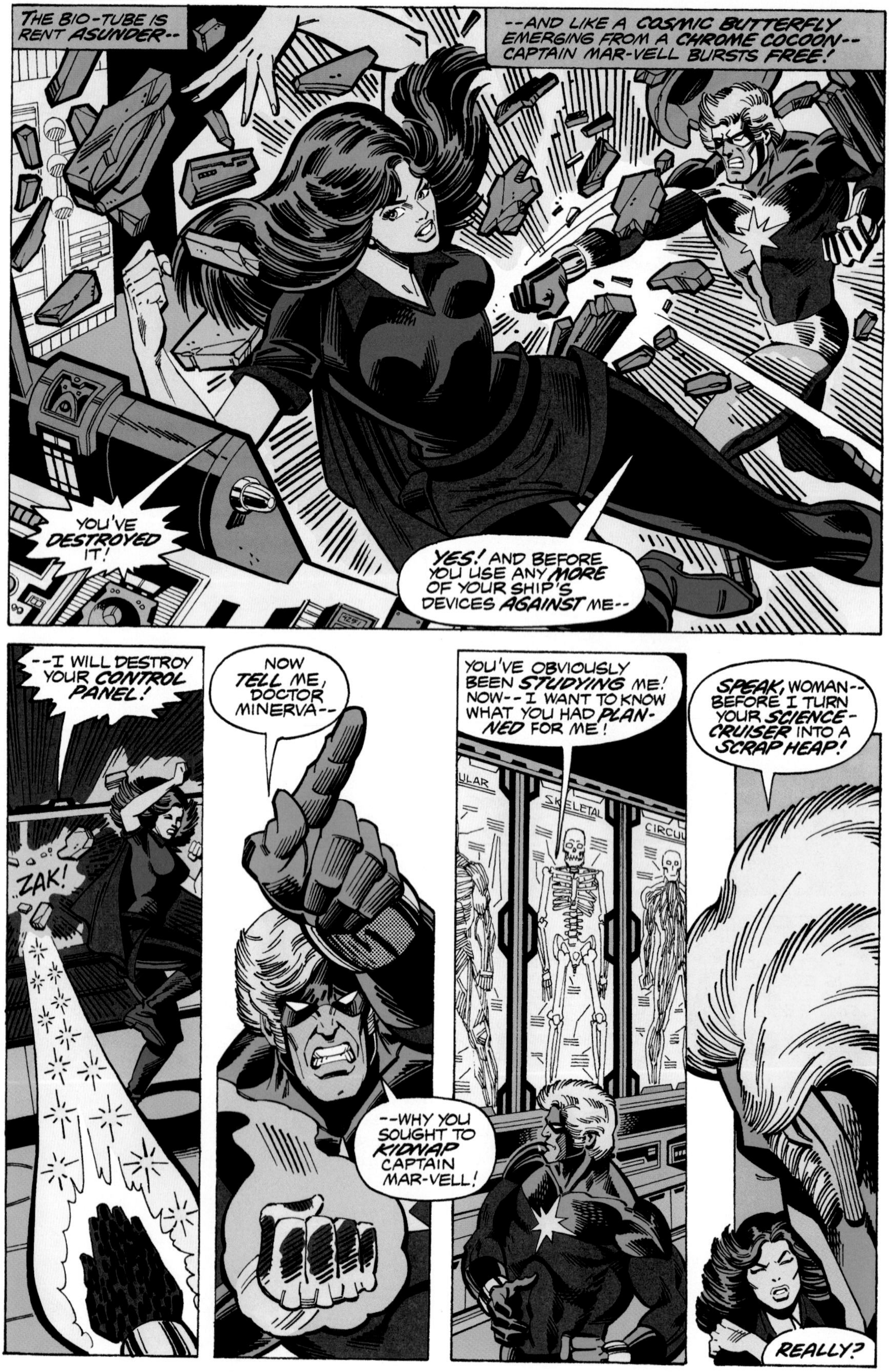

THE BIO-TUBE IS RENT ASUNDER--
--AND LIKE A COSMIC BUTTERFLY EMERGING FROM A CHROME COCOON-- CAPTAIN MAR-VELL BURSTS FREE!
YOU'VE DESTROYED IT!
YES! AND BEFORE YOU USE ANY MORE OF YOUR SHIP'S DEVICES AGAINST ME--
--I WILL DESTROY YOUR CONTROL PANEL!
ZAK!
NOW TELL ME, DOCTOR MINERVA--
--WHY YOU SOUGHT TO KIDNAP CAPTAIN MAR-VELL!
YOU'VE OBVIOUSLY BEEN STUDYING ME! NOW-- I WANT TO KNOW WHAT YOU HAD PLANNED FOR ME!
ULAR
SKELETAL
CIRCUL
SPEAK, WOMAN-- BEFORE I TURN YOUR SCIENCE-CRUISER INTO A SCRAP HEAP!
REALLY?

I THINK *NOT!* DID YOU TRULY *BELIEVE* I WOULD ALLOW DAMAGE TO THE *CONTROLS* TO *ROB* ME OF *COMMAND* OF MY SHIP?

A *MINIATURIZED* SET GRANTING ME *MENTAL* CONTROL HAS BEEN IMPLANTED *HERE--*

--AND IT WILL ENABLE ME TO *SHOW* YOU WHY YOU *DARE* NOT DEFY ME!

RICK!!

ER--HI, MARV!

REFUSE TO *OBEY* ME, AND THE LAD SHALL BE RIPPED TO *SHREDS.* DO NOT *DOUBT* MY WORD, MAR-VELL--I WOULD RISK *ALL* TO PROVE MY *THEORIES!*

I AM A BIO-GENETICIST! THE SUPREME INTELLIGENCE HAS CLAIMED THAT WE KREE ARE TRAPPED ON A LOW RUNG OF THE EVOLUTIONARY LADDER, AND THAT THE EARTHLINGS WILL SOON SURPASS US! I SWORE TO PROVE HIM *WRONG*--AND I BELIEVE THAT I HAVE!

I HAVE DISCOVERED THAT AMONG ALL THE KREE, THERE ARE TWO WITH GENE PATTERNS WHOSE UNION WOULD PRODUCE *SUPERIOR OFFSPRING!* THESE CHILDREN WOULD BE THE FOUNDATION FROM WHICH THE KREE WOULD RENEW ITS EVOLUTIONARY ASCENT!

I FIND YOU *DESPICABLE,* MAR-VELL! I CONSIDER YOU A *TRAITOR* TO THE KREE... AND I EXPECT YOU TO RESIST MY PLAN TO ADVANCE OUR SPECIES--BUT THE ONLY *HOPE* FOR THE KREE RACE--

--IS YOU AND I!

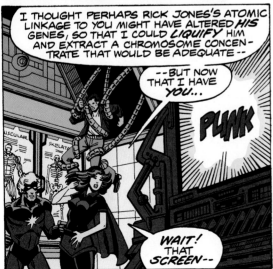

I THOUGHT PERHAPS RICK JONES'S ATOMIC LINKAGE TO YOU MIGHT HAVE ALTERED *HIS* GENES, SO THAT I COULD *LIQUIFY* HIM AND EXTRACT A CHROMOSOME CONCENTRATE THAT WOULD BE ADEQUATE--

--BUT NOW THAT I HAVE *YOU...*

PLINK

WAIT! THAT *SCREEN--*

A *COMMUNIQUÉ* FROM PHAE-DOR, HEAD OF THE *SUPREME SCIENCE COUNCIL**!

ABANDON MY--? *NEVER!*

YES, DR. MINERVA-- IT IS *I!* I HAVE AN URGENT COMMAND FROM THE COUNCIL! *ABANDON* YOUR PROJECT! RETURN IMMEDIATELY TO THE HOMEWORLD WITH MAR-VELL AS YOUR *CAPTIVE!*

*REMEMBER HIM FROM *INHUMANS* #3 ON?--ARCH.

67

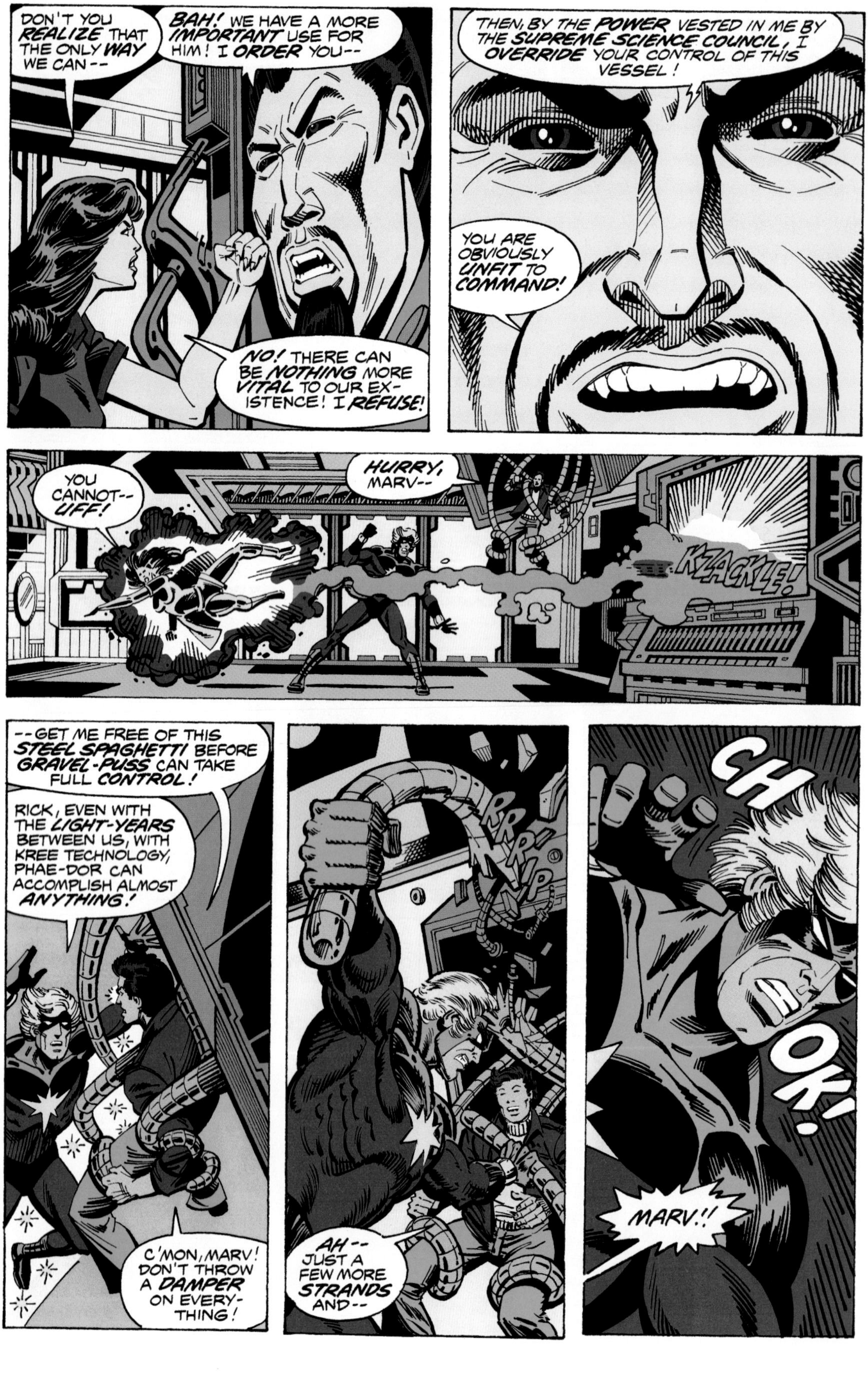
DON'T YOU REALIZE THAT THE ONLY WAY WE CAN--
BAH! WE HAVE A MORE IMPORTANT USE FOR HIM! I ORDER YOU--
NO! THERE CAN BE NOTHING MORE VITAL TO OUR EXISTENCE! I REFUSE!
THEN, BY THE POWER VESTED IN ME BY THE SUPREME SCIENCE COUNCIL, I OVERRIDE YOUR CONTROL OF THIS VESSEL!
YOU ARE OBVIOUSLY UNFIT TO COMMAND!
YOU CANNOT-- UFF!
HURRY, MARV--
KZACKLE!
--GET ME FREE OF THIS STEEL SPAGHETTI BEFORE GRAVEL-PUSS CAN TAKE FULL CONTROL!
RICK, EVEN WITH THE LIGHT-YEARS BETWEEN US, WITH KREE TECHNOLOGY, PHAE-DOR CAN ACCOMPLISH ALMOST ANYTHING!
C'MON, MARV! DON'T THROW A DAMPER ON EVERYTHING!
RRRIP
AH-- JUST A FEW MORE STRANDS AND--
CHOK!
MARV!!

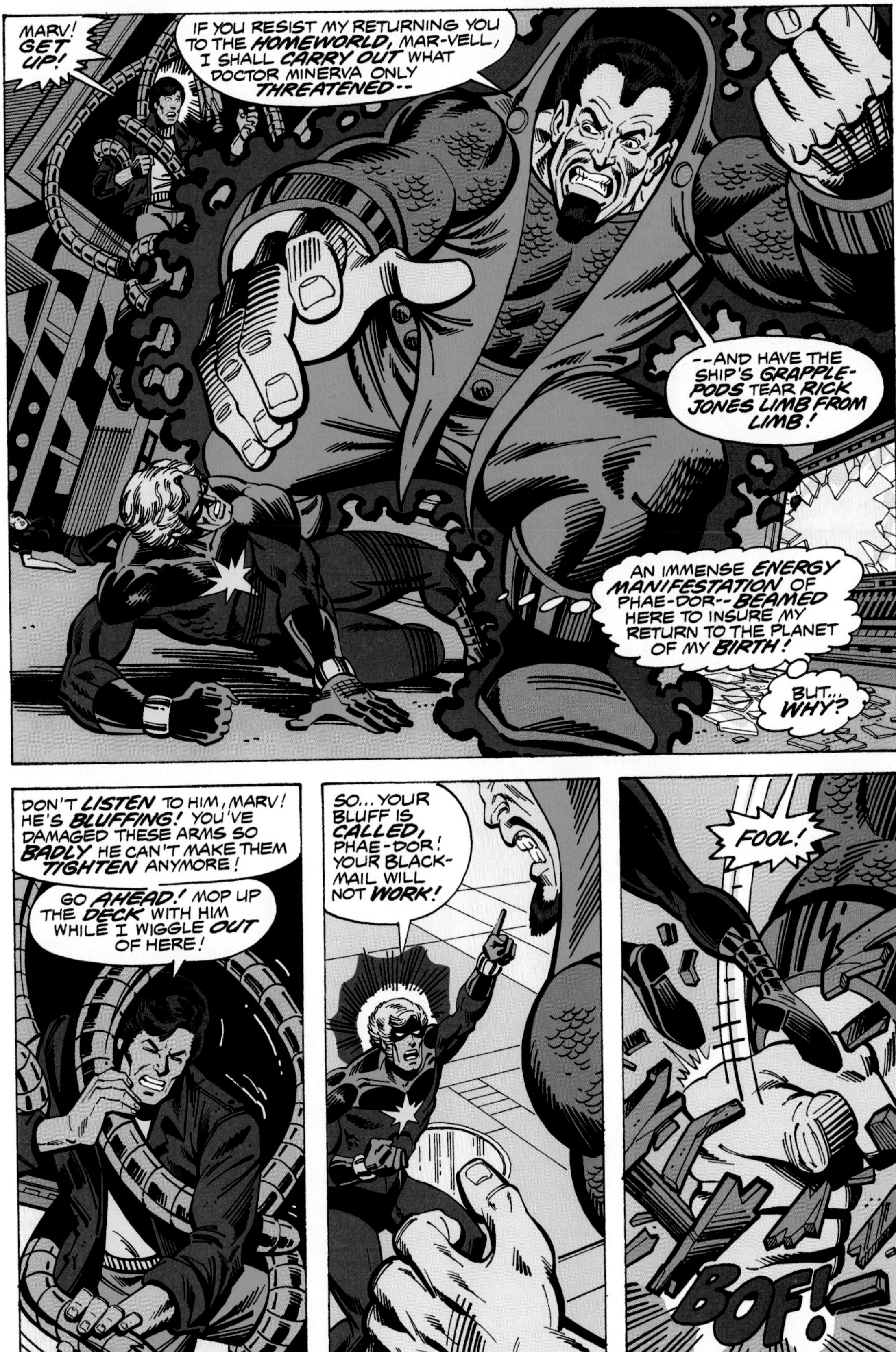
MARV! GET UP!
IF YOU RESIST MY RETURNING YOU TO THE HOMEWORLD, MAR-VELL, I SHALL CARRY OUT WHAT DOCTOR MINERVA ONLY THREATENED--
--AND HAVE THE SHIP'S GRAPPLE-PODS TEAR RICK JONES LIMB FROM LIMB!
AN IMMENSE ENERGY MANIFESTATION OF PHAE-DOR--BEAMED HERE TO INSURE MY RETURN TO THE PLANET OF MY BIRTH!
BUT... WHY?
DON'T LISTEN TO HIM, MARV! HE'S BLUFFING! YOU'VE DAMAGED THESE ARMS SO BADLY HE CAN'T MAKE THEM TIGHTEN ANYMORE!
GO AHEAD! MOP UP THE DECK WITH HIM WHILE I WIGGLE OUT OF HERE!
SO... YOUR BLUFF IS CALLED, PHAE-DOR! YOUR BLACK-MAIL WILL NOT WORK!
FOOL!
BOF!

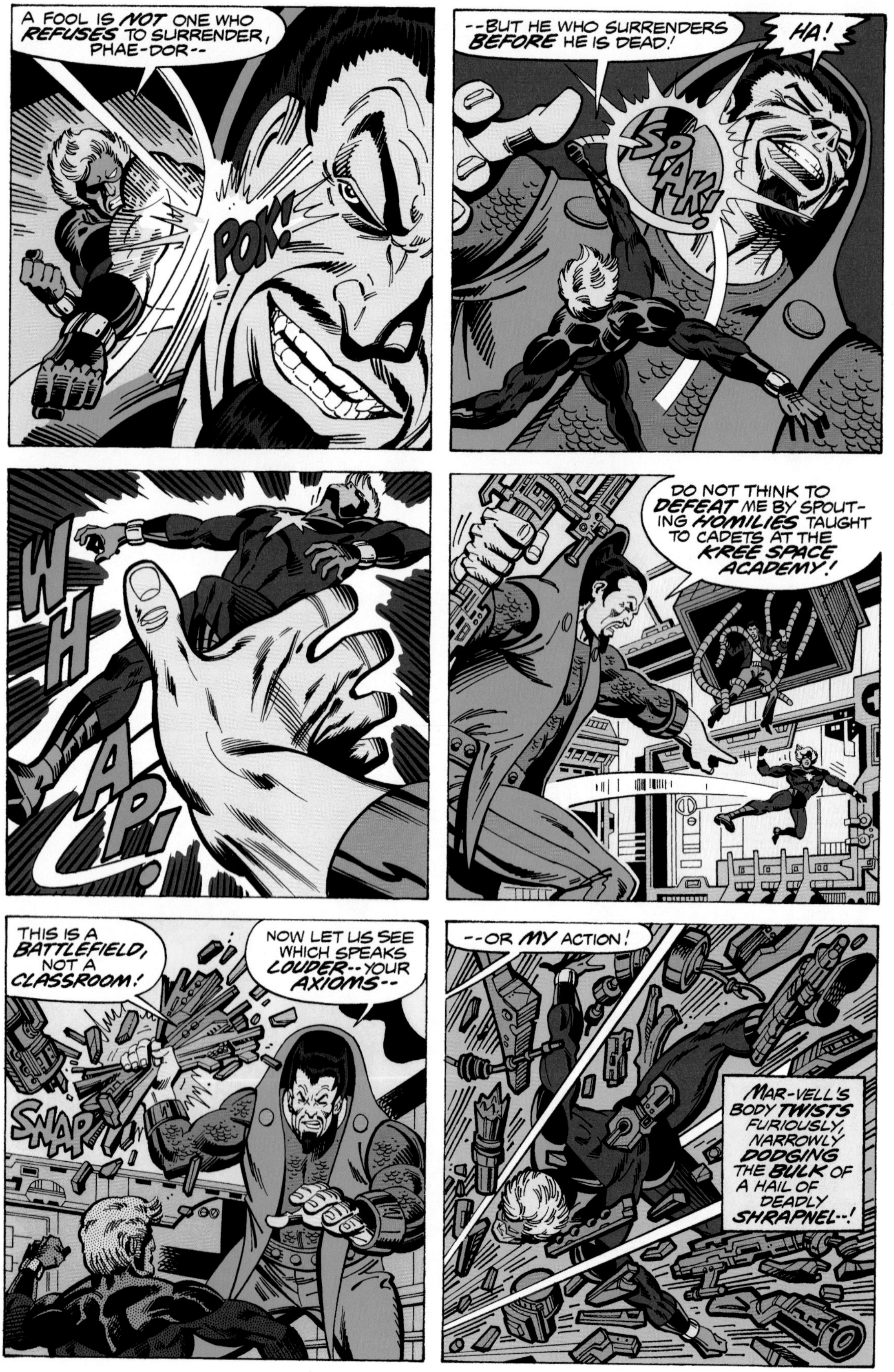
A FOOL IS NOT ONE WHO REFUSES TO SURRENDER, PHAE-DOR--
POK!
--BUT HE WHO SURRENDERS BEFORE HE IS DEAD!
HA!
SPAK!
WHAP!
DO NOT THINK TO DEFEAT ME BY SPOUTING HOMILIES TAUGHT TO CADETS AT THE KREE SPACE ACADEMY!
THIS IS A BATTLEFIELD, NOT A CLASSROOM!
NOW LET US SEE WHICH SPEAKS LOUDER--YOUR AXIOMS--
SNAP!
--OR MY ACTION!
MAR-VELL'S BODY TWISTS FURIOUSLY, NARROWLY DODGING THE BULK OF A HAIL OF DEADLY SHRAPNEL--!

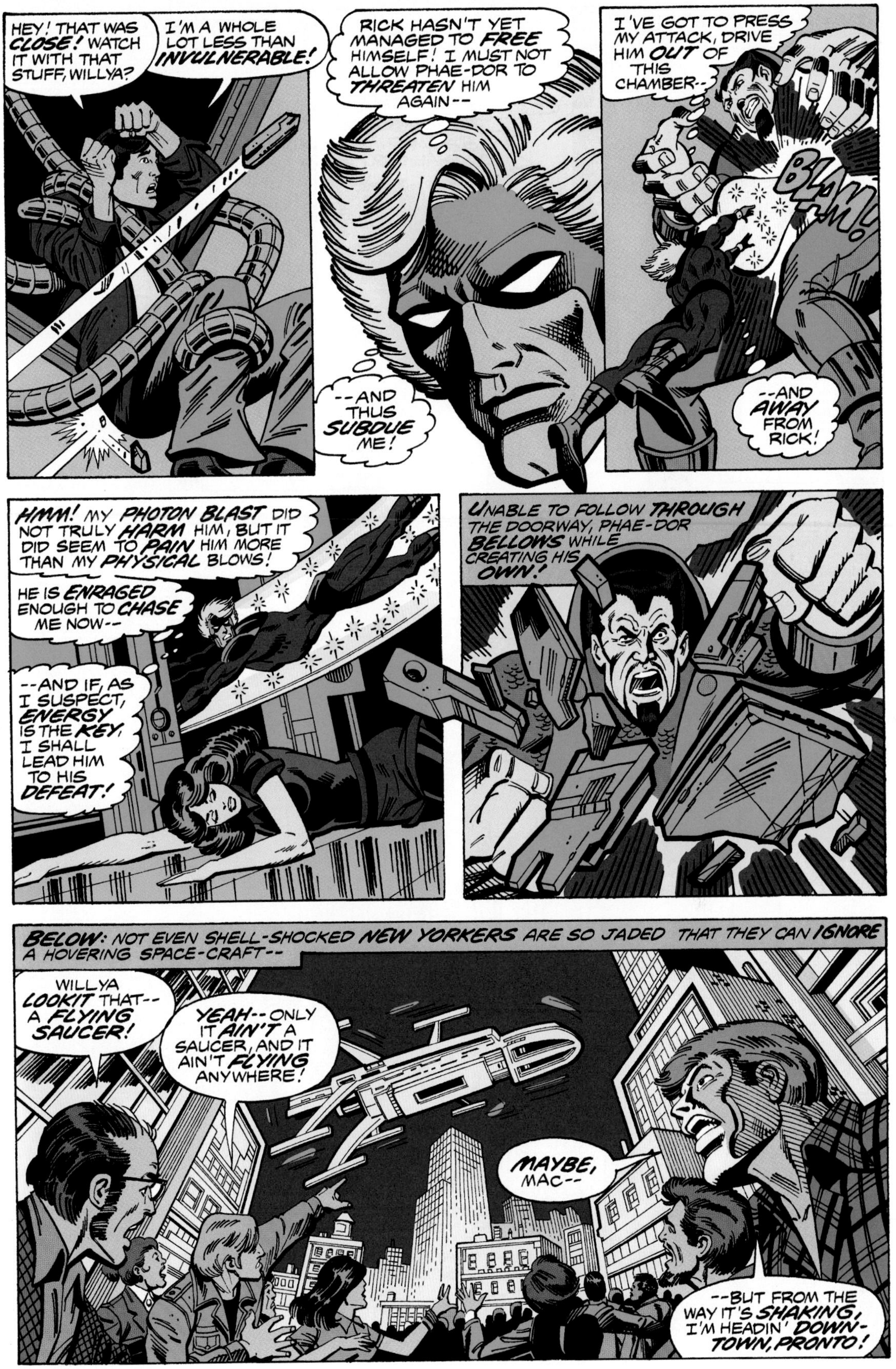
HEY! THAT WAS CLOSE! WATCH IT WITH THAT STUFF, WILLYA?
I'M A WHOLE LOT LESS THAN INVULNERABLE!
RICK HASN'T YET MANAGED TO FREE HIMSELF! I MUST NOT ALLOW PHAE-DOR TO THREATEN HIM AGAIN--
--AND THUS SUBDUE ME!
I'VE GOT TO PRESS MY ATTACK, DRIVE HIM OUT OF THIS CHAMBER--
BLAMM!
--AND AWAY FROM RICK!
HMM! MY PHOTON BLAST DID NOT TRULY HARM HIM, BUT IT DID SEEM TO PAIN HIM MORE THAN MY PHYSICAL BLOWS!
HE IS ENRAGED ENOUGH TO CHASE ME NOW--
--AND IF, AS I SUSPECT, ENERGY IS THE KEY, I SHALL LEAD HIM TO HIS DEFEAT!
UNABLE TO FOLLOW THROUGH THE DOORWAY, PHAE-DOR BELLOWS WHILE CREATING HIS OWN!
BELOW: NOT EVEN SHELL-SHOCKED NEW YORKERS ARE SO JADED THAT THEY CAN IGNORE A HOVERING SPACE-CRAFT--
WILLYA LOOKIT THAT-- A FLYING SAUCER!
YEAH-- ONLY IT AIN'T A SAUCER, AND IT AIN'T FLYING ANYWHERE!
MAYBE, MAC--
--BUT FROM THE WAY IT'S SHAKING, I'M HEADIN' DOWN-TOWN, PRONTO!

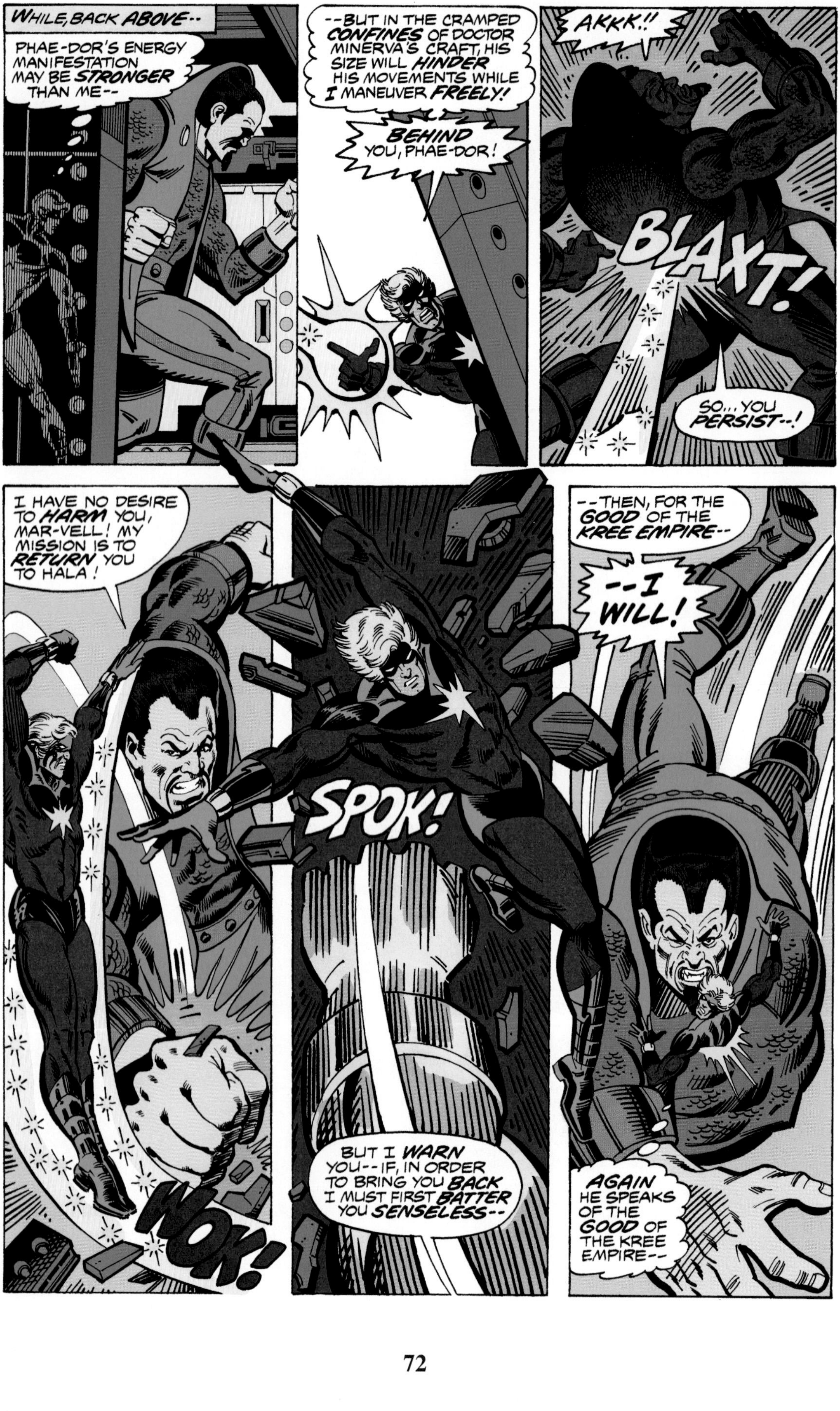
WHILE, BACK ABOVE--
PHAE-DOR'S ENERGY MANIFESTATION MAY BE STRONGER THAN ME--
--BUT IN THE CRAMPED CONFINES OF DOCTOR MINERVA'S CRAFT, HIS SIZE WILL HINDER HIS MOVEMENTS WHILE I MANEUVER FREELY!
BEHIND YOU, PHAE-DOR!
AKKK!!
BLAXT!
SO... YOU PERSIST--!
I HAVE NO DESIRE TO HARM YOU, MAR-VELL! MY MISSION IS TO RETURN YOU TO HALA!
WOK!
SPOK!
BUT I WARN YOU--IF, IN ORDER TO BRING YOU BACK I MUST FIRST BATTER YOU SENSELESS--
--THEN, FOR THE GOOD OF THE KREE EMPIRE--
--I WILL!
AGAIN HE SPEAKS OF THE GOOD OF THE KREE EMPIRE--

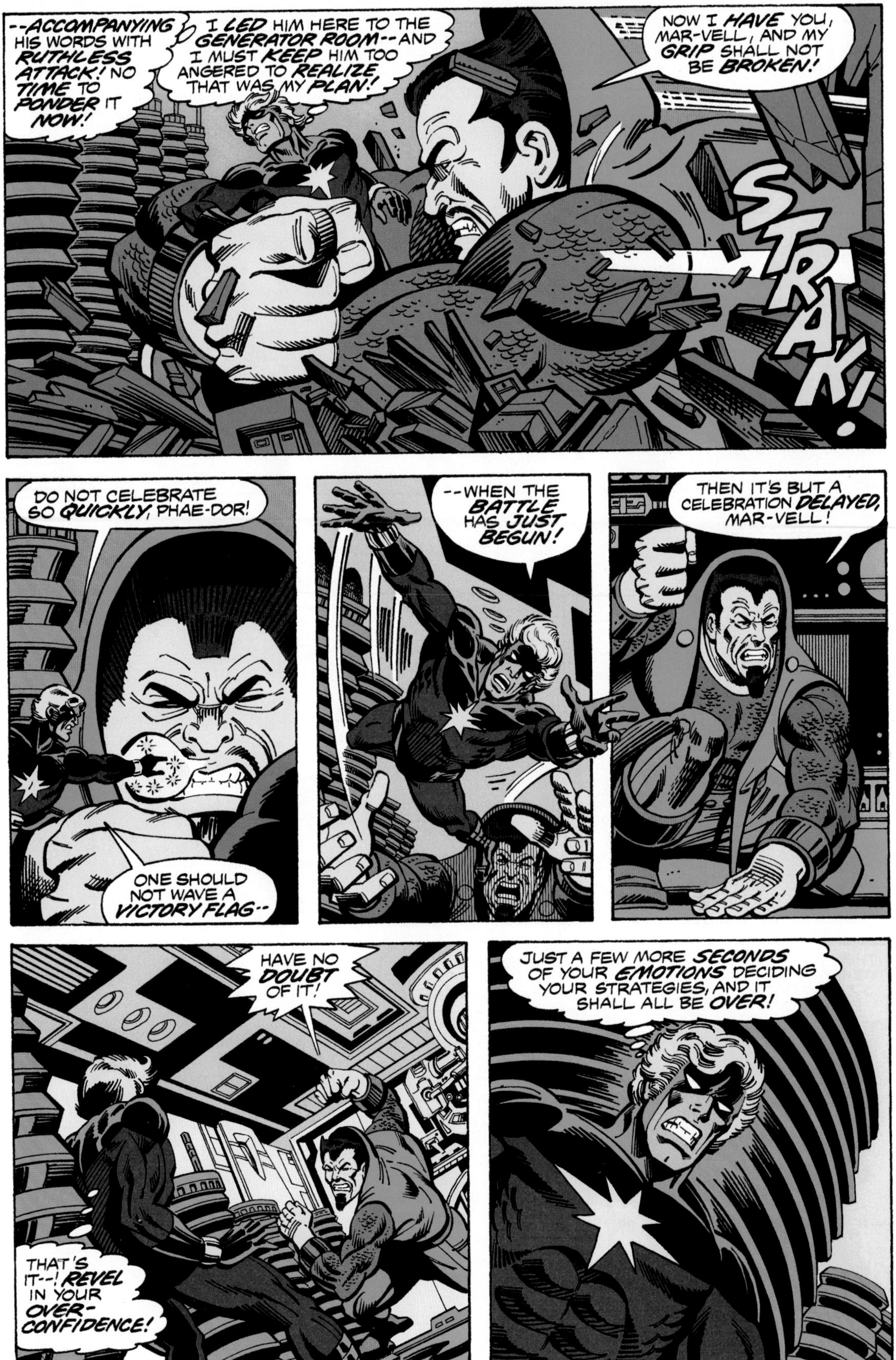
--ACCOMPANYING HIS WORDS WITH RUTHLESS ATTACK! NO TIME TO PONDER IT NOW!
I LED HIM HERE TO THE GENERATOR ROOM--AND I MUST KEEP HIM TOO ANGERED TO REALIZE THAT WAS MY PLAN!
NOW I HAVE YOU, MAR-VELL, AND MY GRIP SHALL NOT BE BROKEN!
STRAK!
DO NOT CELEBRATE SO QUICKLY, PHAE-DOR!
ONE SHOULD NOT WAVE A VICTORY FLAG--
--WHEN THE BATTLE HAS JUST BEGUN!
THEN IT'S BUT A CELEBRATION DELAYED, MAR-VELL!
HAVE NO DOUBT OF IT!
THAT'S IT--! REVEL IN YOUR OVER-CONFIDENCE!
JUST A FEW MORE SECONDS OF YOUR EMOTIONS DECIDING YOUR STRATEGIES, AND IT SHALL ALL BE OVER!

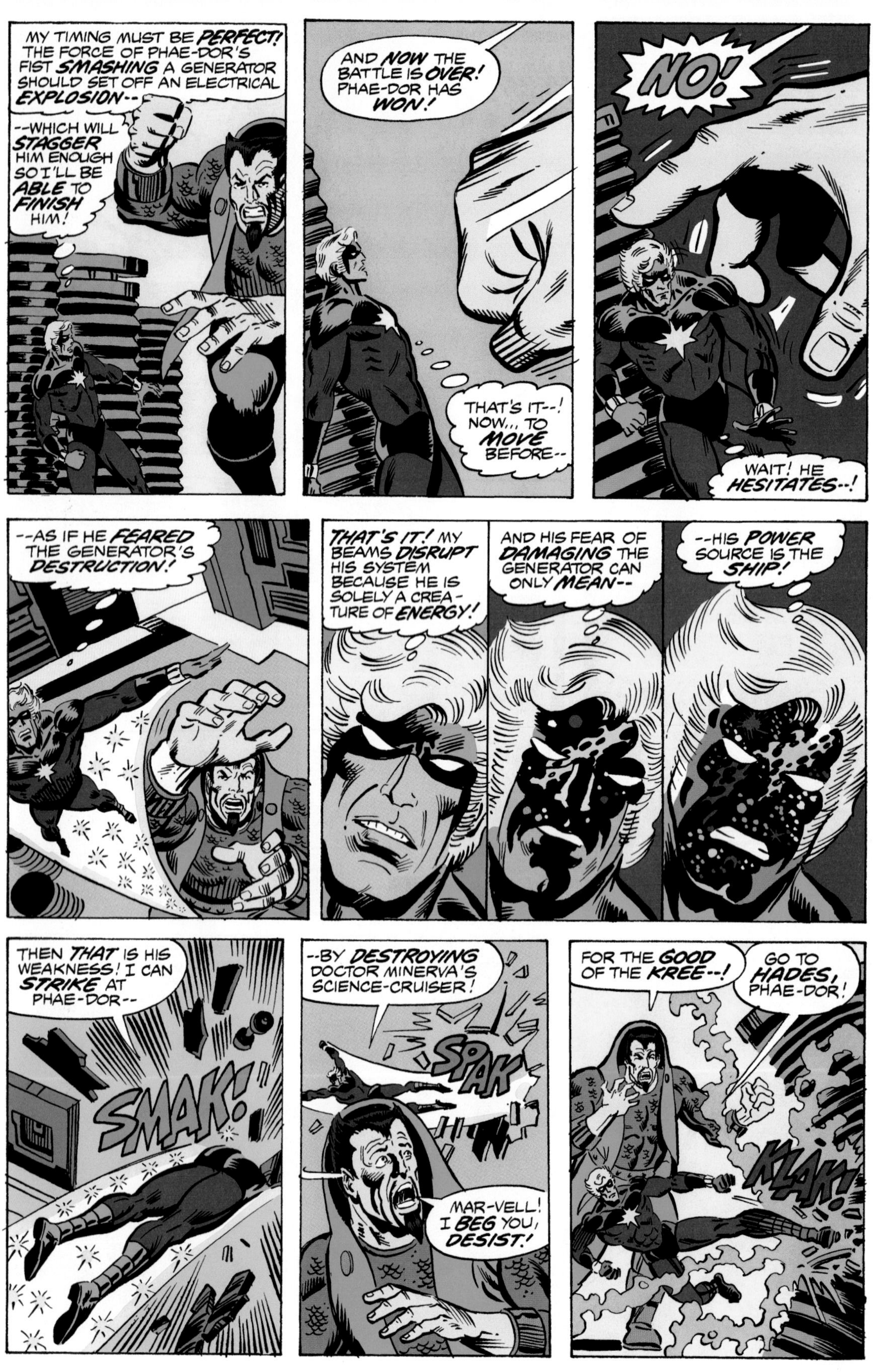
MY TIMING MUST BE PERFECT! THE FORCE OF PHAE-DOR'S FIST SMASHING A GENERATOR SHOULD SET OFF AN ELECTRICAL EXPLOSION--
--WHICH WILL STAGGER HIM ENOUGH SO I'LL BE ABLE TO FINISH HIM!
AND NOW THE BATTLE IS OVER! PHAE-DOR HAS WON!
THAT'S IT--! NOW... TO MOVE BEFORE--
NO!
WAIT! HE HESITATES--!
--AS IF HE FEARED THE GENERATOR'S DESTRUCTION!
THAT'S IT! MY BEAMS DISRUPT HIS SYSTEM BECAUSE HE IS SOLELY A CREA-TURE OF ENERGY!
AND HIS FEAR OF DAMAGING THE GENERATOR CAN ONLY MEAN--
--HIS POWER SOURCE IS THE SHIP!
THEN THAT IS HIS WEAKNESS! I CAN STRIKE AT PHAE-DOR--
SMAK!
--BY DESTROYING DOCTOR MINERVA'S SCIENCE-CRUISER!
SPAK
MAR-VELL! I BEG YOU, DESIST!
FOR THE GOOD OF THE KREE--!
GO TO HADES, PHAE-DOR!
KLAK!

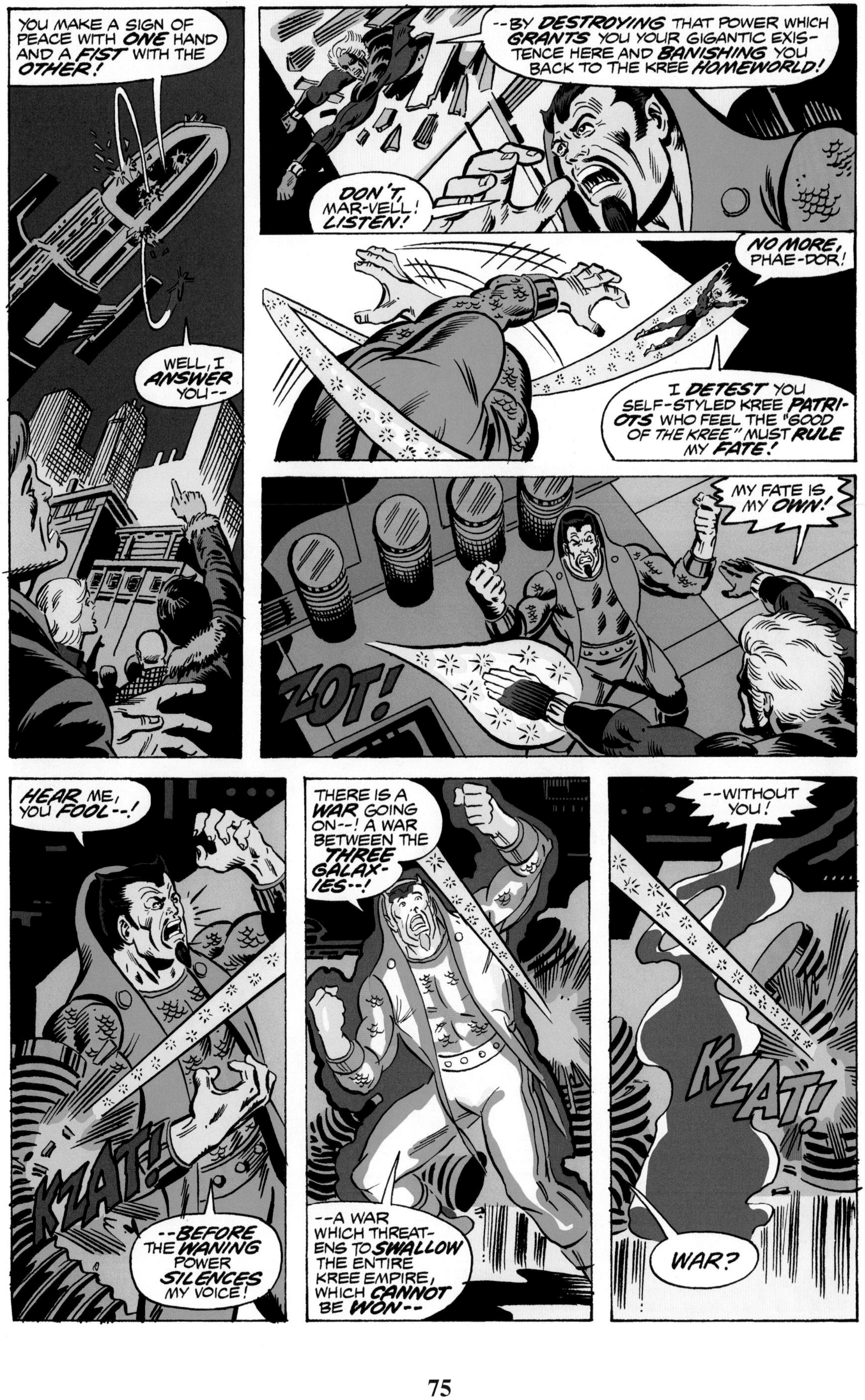
YOU MAKE A SIGN OF PEACE WITH ONE HAND AND A FIST WITH THE OTHER!
WELL, I ANSWER YOU--
--BY DESTROYING THAT POWER WHICH GRANTS YOU YOUR GIGANTIC EXISTENCE HERE AND BANISHING YOU BACK TO THE KREE HOMEWORLD!
DON'T, MAR-VELL! LISTEN!
NO MORE, PHAE-DOR!
I DETEST YOU SELF-STYLED KREE PATRIOTS WHO FEEL THE "GOOD OF THE KREE" MUST RULE MY FATE!
MY FATE IS MY OWN!
ZOT!
HEAR ME, YOU FOOL--!
KZAT!
--BEFORE THE WANING POWER SILENCES MY VOICE!
THERE IS A WAR GOING ON--! A WAR BETWEEN THE THREE GALAXIES--!
--A WAR WHICH THREATENS TO SWALLOW THE ENTIRE KREE EMPIRE, WHICH CANNOT BE WON--
--WITHOUT YOU!
KZAT!
WAR?

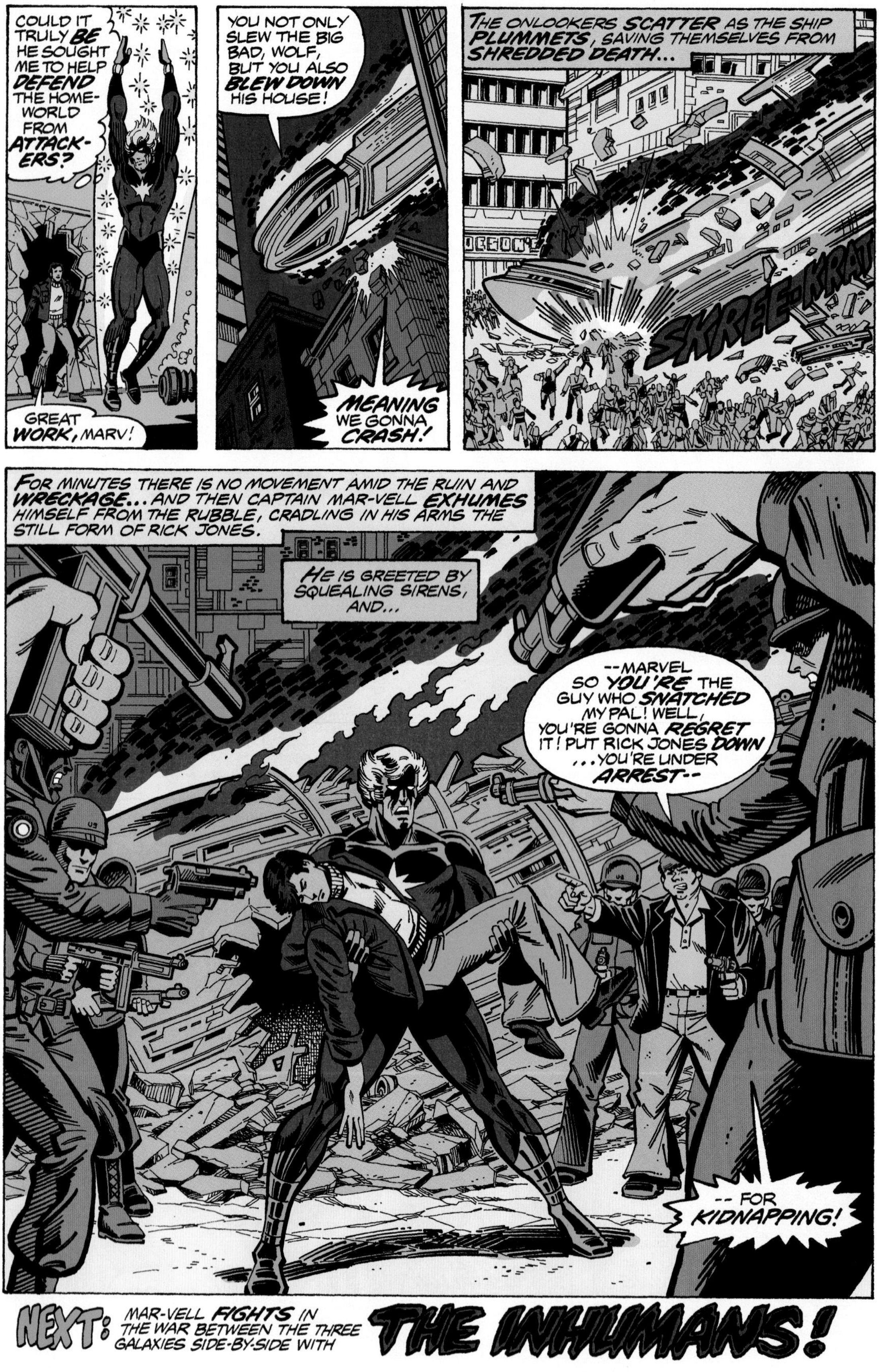
COULD IT TRULY BE HE SOUGHT ME TO HELP DEFEND THE HOME-WORLD FROM ATTACK-ERS?
GREAT WORK, MARV!
YOU NOT ONLY SLEW THE BIG BAD, WOLF, BUT YOU ALSO BLEW DOWN HIS HOUSE!
MEANING WE GONNA CRASH!
THE ONLOOKERS SCATTER AS THE SHIP PLUMMETS, SAVING THEMSELVES FROM SHREDDED DEATH...
SKREEE-KRAT
FOR MINUTES THERE IS NO MOVEMENT AMID THE RUIN AND WRECKAGE... AND THEN CAPTAIN MAR-VELL EXHUMES HIMSELF FROM THE RUBBLE, CRADLING IN HIS ARMS THE STILL FORM OF RICK JONES.
HE IS GREETED BY SQUEALING SIRENS, AND...
--MARVEL SO YOU'RE THE GUY WHO SNATCHED MY PAL! WELL, YOU'RE GONNA REGRET IT! PUT RICK JONES DOWN ...YOU'RE UNDER ARREST--
-- FOR KIDNAPPING!
NEXT: MAR-VELL FIGHTS IN THE WAR BETWEEN THE THREE GALAXIES SIDE-BY-SIDE WITH THE INHUMANS!

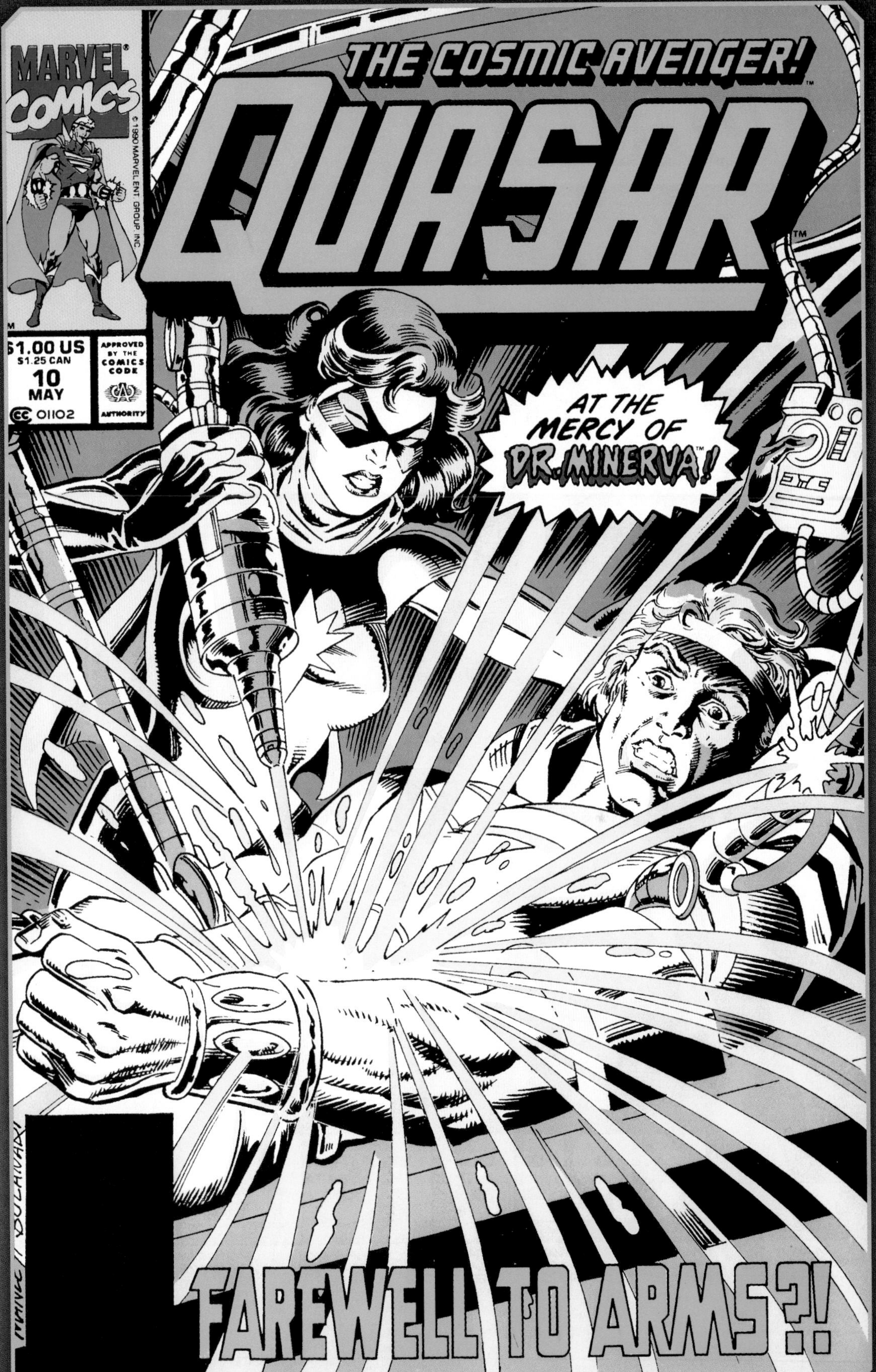
MARVEL COMICS
THE COSMIC AVENGER!
QUASAR
© 1990 MARVELENT GROUP, INC
$1.00 US
$1.25 CAN
10
MAY
01102
APPROVED BY THE COMICS CODE AUTHORITY
AT THE MERCY OF DR. MINERVA!
FAREWELL TO ARMS?!

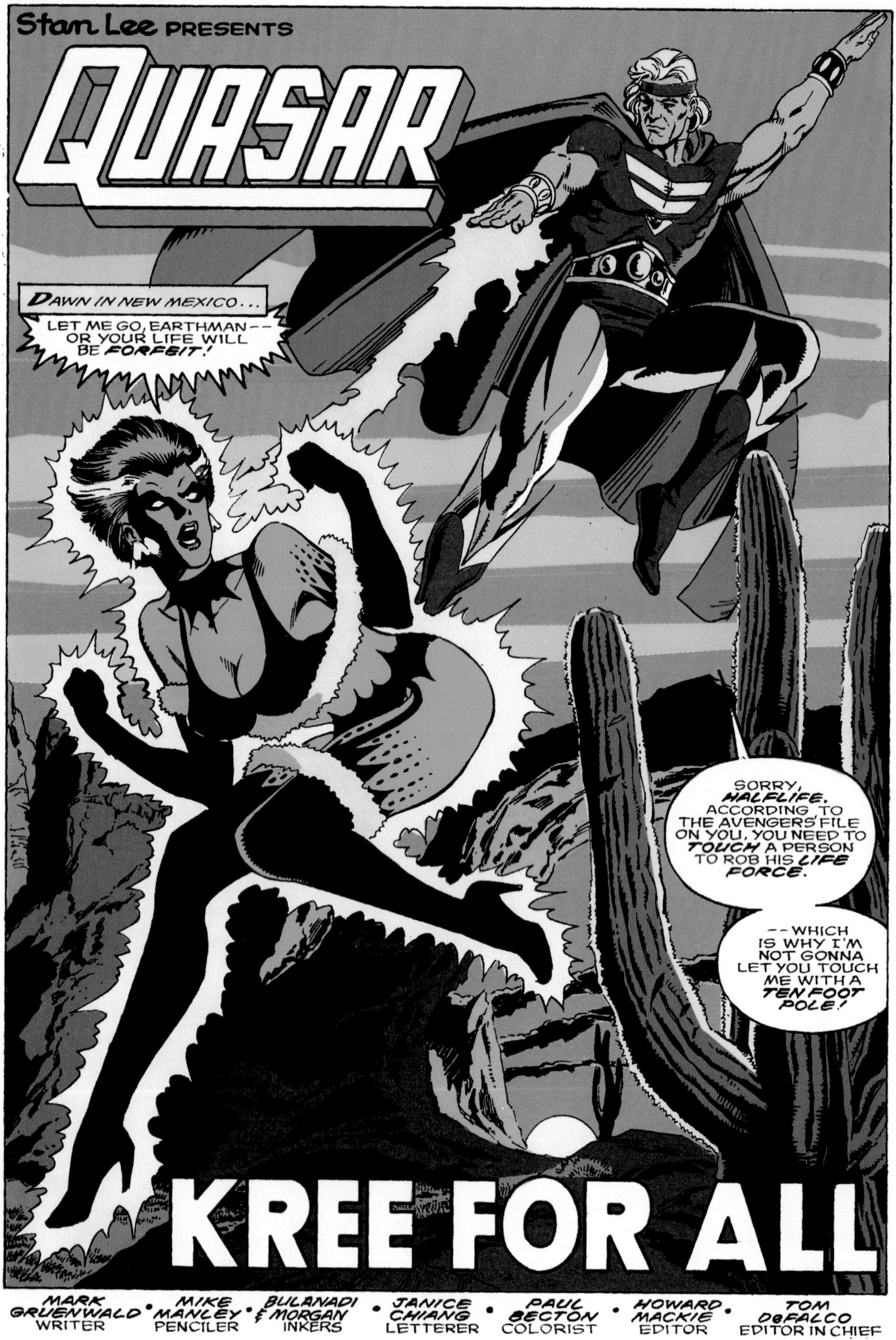
Stan Lee PRESENTS
QUASAR
DAWN IN NEW MEXICO...
LET ME GO, EARTHMAN-- OR YOUR LIFE WILL BE FORFEIT!
SORRY, HALFLIFE. ACCORDING TO THE AVENGERS' FILE ON YOU, YOU NEED TO TOUCH A PERSON TO ROB HIS LIFE FORCE.
--WHICH IS WHY I'M NOT GONNA LET YOU TOUCH ME WITH A TEN FOOT POLE!
KREE FOR ALL

MARK GRUENWALD WRITER • MIKE MANLEY PENCILER • BULANADI & MORGAN INKERS • JANICE CHIANG LETTERER • PAUL BECTON COLORIST • HOWARD MACKIE EDITOR • TOM DeFALCO EDITOR IN CHIEF

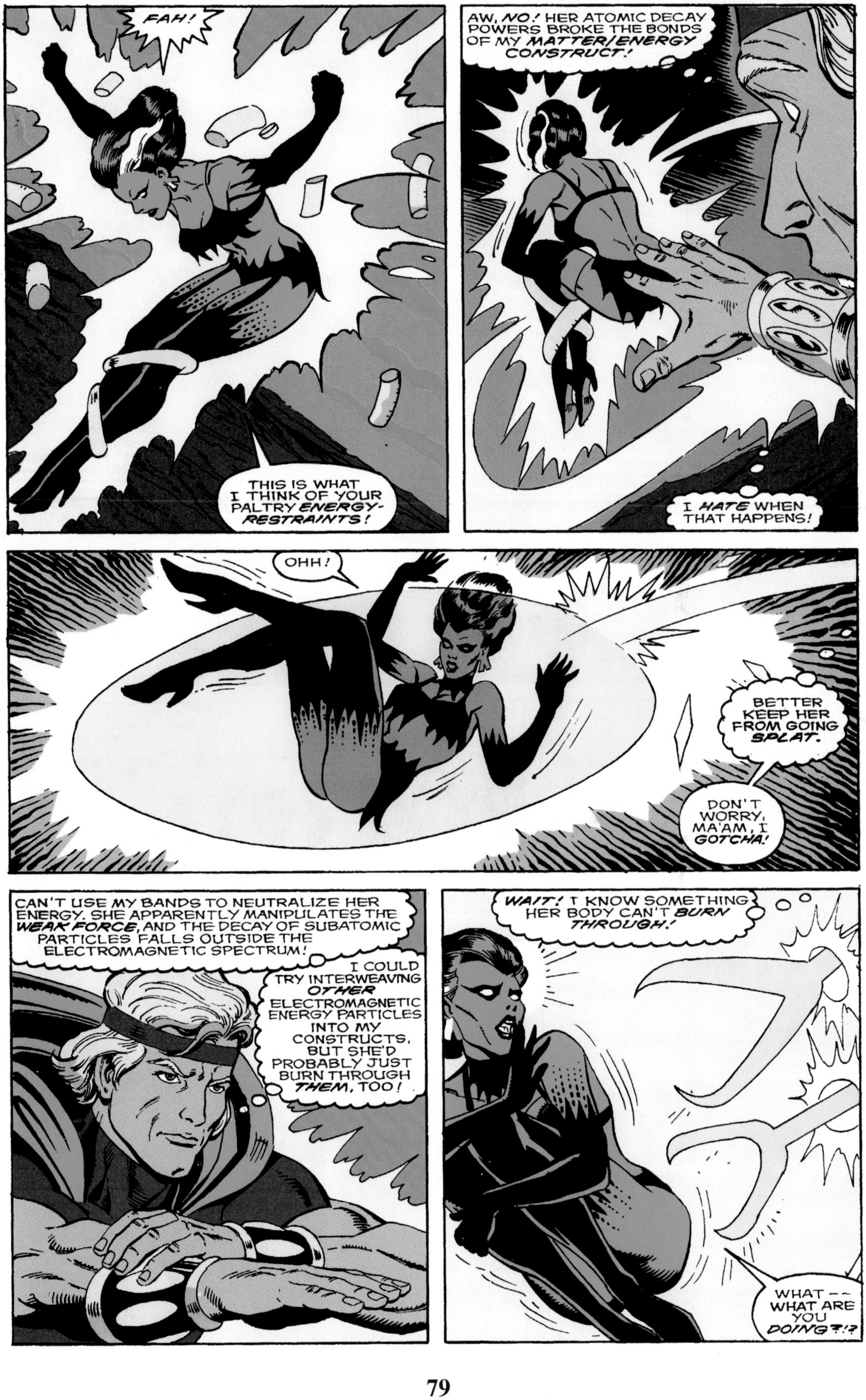
FAH!
THIS IS WHAT I THINK OF YOUR PALTRY ENERGY-RESTRAINTS!
AW, NO! HER ATOMIC DECAY POWERS BROKE THE BONDS OF MY MATTER/ENERGY CONSTRUCT!
I HATE WHEN THAT HAPPENS!
OHH!
BETTER KEEP HER FROM GOING SPLAT.
DON'T WORRY, MA'AM, I GOTCHA!
CAN'T USE MY BANDS TO NEUTRALIZE HER ENERGY. SHE APPARENTLY MANIPULATES THE WEAK FORCE, AND THE DECAY OF SUBATOMIC PARTICLES FALLS OUTSIDE THE ELECTROMAGNETIC SPECTRUM!
I COULD TRY INTERWEAVING OTHER ELECTROMAGNETIC ENERGY PARTICLES INTO MY CONSTRUCTS, BUT SHE'D PROBABLY JUST BURN THROUGH THEM, TOO!
WAIT! I KNOW SOMETHING HER BODY CAN'T BURN THROUGH!
WHAT -- WHAT ARE YOU DOING?!?

SORRY TO GET SO *PERSONAL*, MA'AM...

...BUT I HAVE TO BORROW THOSE ULTRAFASHIONABLE DESIGNER *HIP-BOOTS* OF YOURS A MOMENT.

THERE. UNLESS THE OUTFIT OF YOURS WAS ONCE CONSIDERABLY MORE SUBSTANTIAL, I FIGURE YOUR ALIEN GARMENTS ARE *PROOF* AGAINST YOUR DISINTEGRATIONAL ABILITIES. AM I *CORRECT*?

YOU SHALL *PAY* FOR THIS INDIGNITY.

DO YOU TAKE *CREDIT CARDS*?

AIIEH! WHERE ARE YOU TAKING ME?

A NICE COZY PLACE I KNOW DESIGNED TO HOLD *SUPERHUMAN SUSPECTS* LIKE YOURSELF--

--THE VAULT.

DON'T WORRY, MISS. YOU'LL ONLY BE HELD HERE UNTIL YOU CAN STAND *TRIAL* FOR THE *MURDERS* YOU'RE SUSPECTED OF.

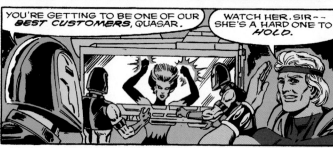

YOU'RE GETTING TO BE ONE OF OUR *BEST CUSTOMERS*, QUASAR.

WATCH HER, SIR-- SHE'S A HARD ONE TO *HOLD*.

I'LL *FAX* YOU A STATEMENT LATER TODAY...

...GOTTA BE *OFF*!

THERE HE GOES, *OBLIVIOUS* TO US.

APPARENTLY HALFLIFE NEVER REVEALED TO HIM WHAT SHE WAS OUT IN THE DESERT *LOOKING FOR*!

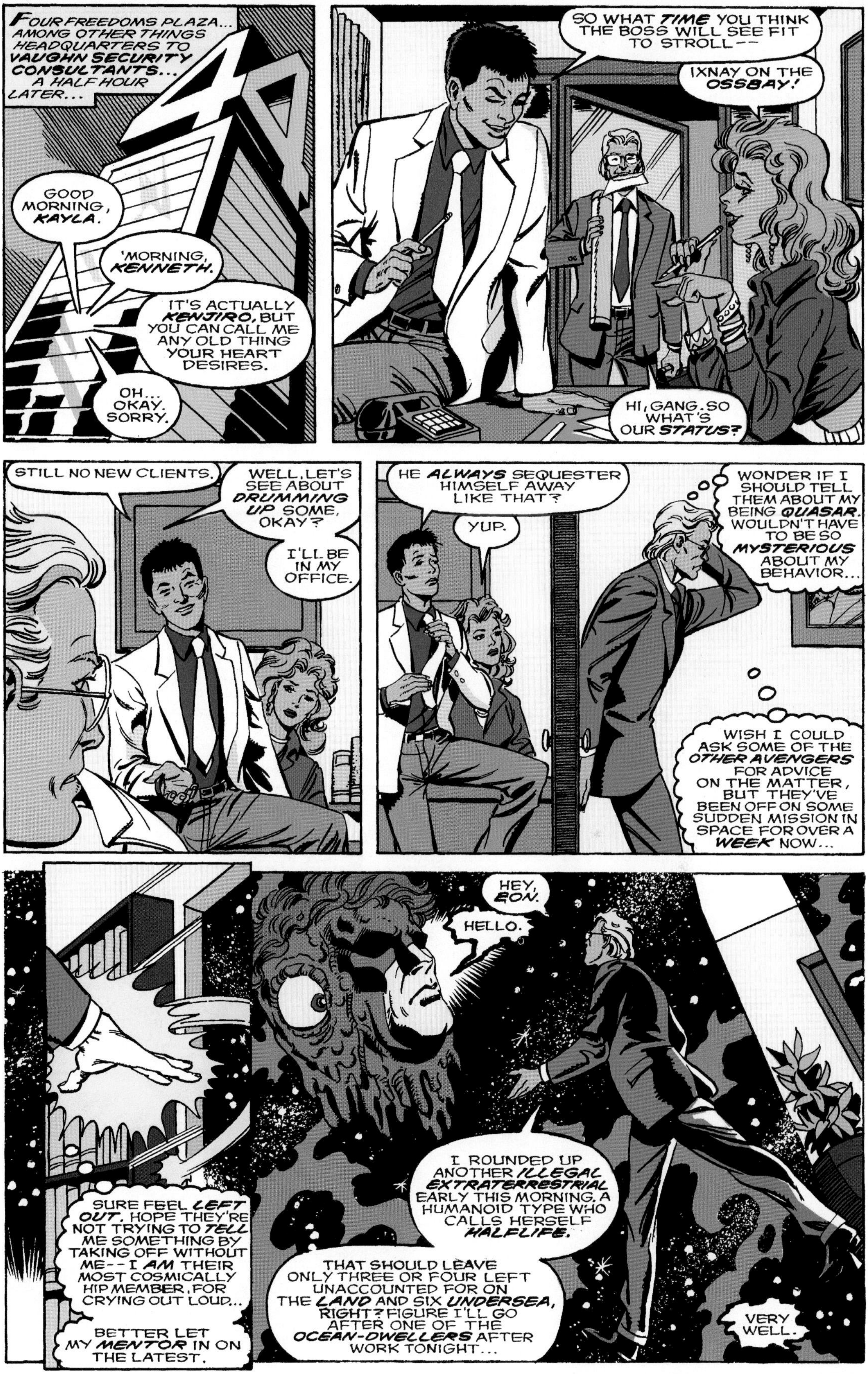
FOUR FREEDOMS PLAZA... AMONG OTHER THINGS HEADQUARTERS TO VAUGHN SECURITY CONSULTANTS... A HALF HOUR LATER...
GOOD MORNING, KAYLA.
'MORNING, KENNETH.
IT'S ACTUALLY KENJIRO, BUT YOU CAN CALL ME ANY OLD THING YOUR HEART DESIRES.
OH... OKAY. SORRY.
SO WHAT TIME YOU THINK THE BOSS WILL SEE FIT TO STROLL--
IXNAY ON THE OSSBAY!
HI, GANG. SO WHAT'S OUR STATUS?
STILL NO NEW CLIENTS.
WELL, LET'S SEE ABOUT DRUMMING UP SOME, OKAY?
I'LL BE IN MY OFFICE.
HE ALWAYS SEQUESTER HIMSELF AWAY LIKE THAT?
YUP.
WONDER IF I SHOULD TELL THEM ABOUT MY BEING QUASAR. WOULDN'T HAVE TO BE SO MYSTERIOUS ABOUT MY BEHAVIOR...
WISH I COULD ASK SOME OF THE OTHER AVENGERS FOR ADVICE ON THE MATTER, BUT THEY'VE BEEN OFF ON SOME SUDDEN MISSION IN SPACE FOR OVER A WEEK NOW...
SURE FEEL LEFT OUT. HOPE THEY'RE NOT TRYING TO TELL ME SOMETHING BY TAKING OFF WITHOUT ME-- I AM THEIR MOST COSMICALLY HIP MEMBER, FOR CRYING OUT LOUD...
BETTER LET MY MENTOR IN ON THE LATEST.
HEY, EON.
HELLO.
I ROUNDED UP ANOTHER ILLEGAL EXTRATERRESTRIAL EARLY THIS MORNING. A HUMANOID TYPE WHO CALLS HERSELF HALFLIFE.
THAT SHOULD LEAVE ONLY THREE OR FOUR LEFT UNACCOUNTED FOR ON THE LAND AND SIX UNDERSEA, RIGHT? FIGURE I'LL GO AFTER ONE OF THE OCEAN-DWELLERS AFTER WORK TONIGHT...
VERY WELL.

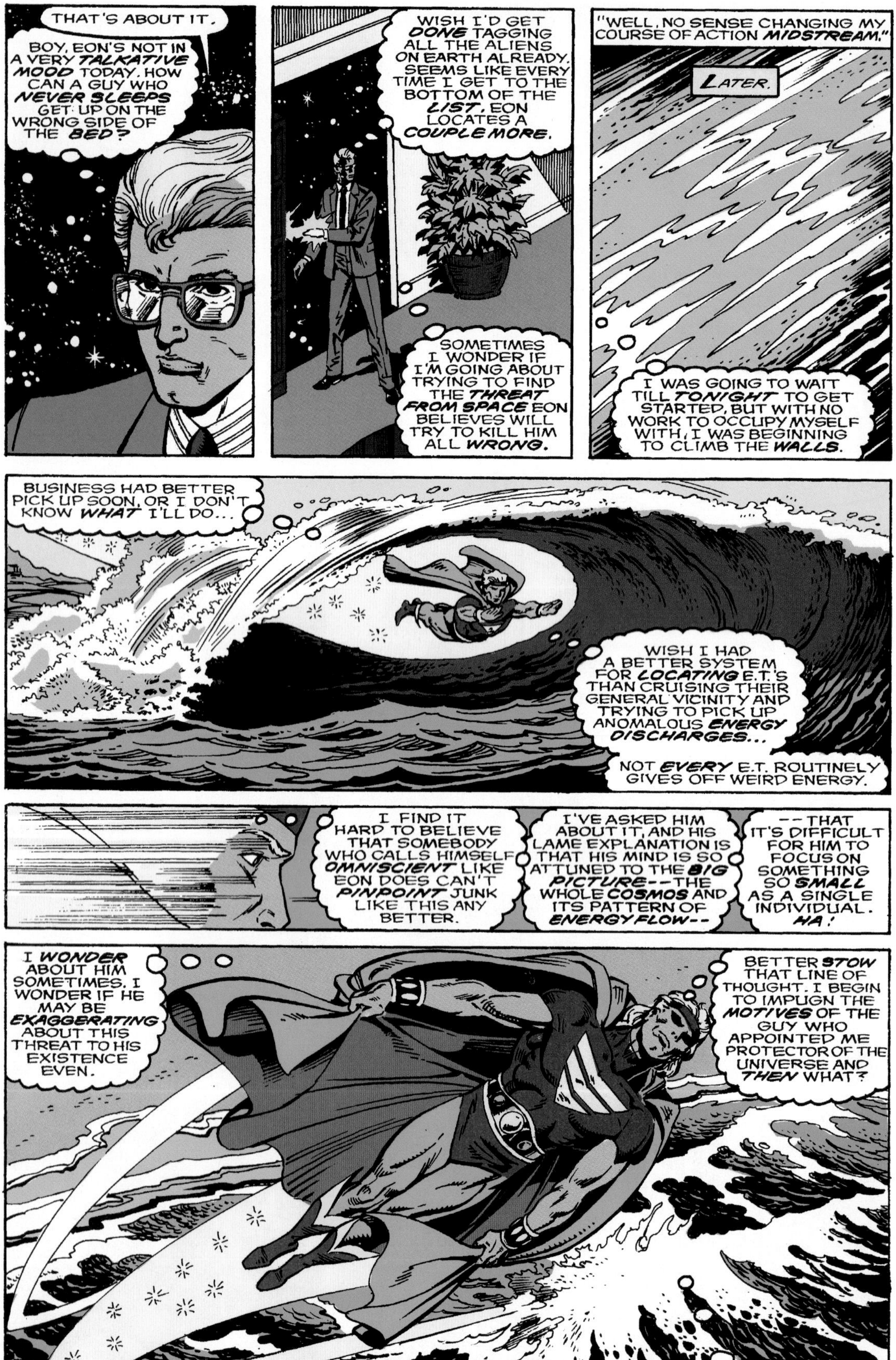
THAT'S ABOUT IT.
BOY, EON'S NOT IN A VERY TALKATIVE MOOD TODAY. HOW CAN A GUY WHO NEVER SLEEPS GET UP ON THE WRONG SIDE OF THE BED?
WISH I'D GET DONE TAGGING ALL THE ALIENS ON EARTH ALREADY. SEEMS LIKE EVERY TIME I GET TO THE BOTTOM OF THE LIST, EON LOCATES A COUPLE MORE.
SOMETIMES I WONDER IF I'M GOING ABOUT TRYING TO FIND THE THREAT FROM SPACE EON BELIEVES WILL TRY TO KILL HIM ALL WRONG.
"WELL, NO SENSE CHANGING MY COURSE OF ACTION MIDSTREAM."
LATER.
I WAS GOING TO WAIT TILL TONIGHT TO GET STARTED, BUT WITH NO WORK TO OCCUPY MYSELF WITH, I WAS BEGINNING TO CLIMB THE WALLS.
BUSINESS HAD BETTER PICK UP SOON, OR I DON'T KNOW WHAT I'LL DO...
WISH I HAD A BETTER SYSTEM FOR LOCATING E.T.'S THAN CRUISING THEIR GENERAL VICINITY AND TRYING TO PICK UP ANOMALOUS ENERGY DISCHARGES...
NOT EVERY E.T. ROUTINELY GIVES OFF WEIRD ENERGY.
I FIND IT HARD TO BELIEVE THAT SOMEBODY WHO CALLS HIMSELF OMNISCIENT LIKE EON DOES CAN'T PINPOINT JUNK LIKE THIS ANY BETTER.
I'VE ASKED HIM ABOUT IT, AND HIS LAME EXPLANATION IS THAT HIS MIND IS SO ATTUNED TO THE BIG PICTURE--THE WHOLE COSMOS AND ITS PATTERN OF ENERGY FLOW--
--THAT IT'S DIFFICULT FOR HIM TO FOCUS ON SOMETHING SO SMALL AS A SINGLE INDIVIDUAL. HA!
I WONDER ABOUT HIM SOMETIMES. I WONDER IF HE MAY BE EXAGGERATING ABOUT THIS THREAT TO HIS EXISTENCE EVEN.
BETTER STOW THAT LINE OF THOUGHT. I BEGIN TO IMPUGN THE MOTIVES OF THE GUY WHO APPOINTED ME PROTECTOR OF THE UNIVERSE AND THEN WHAT?
THEN NOTHING MAKES SENSE.

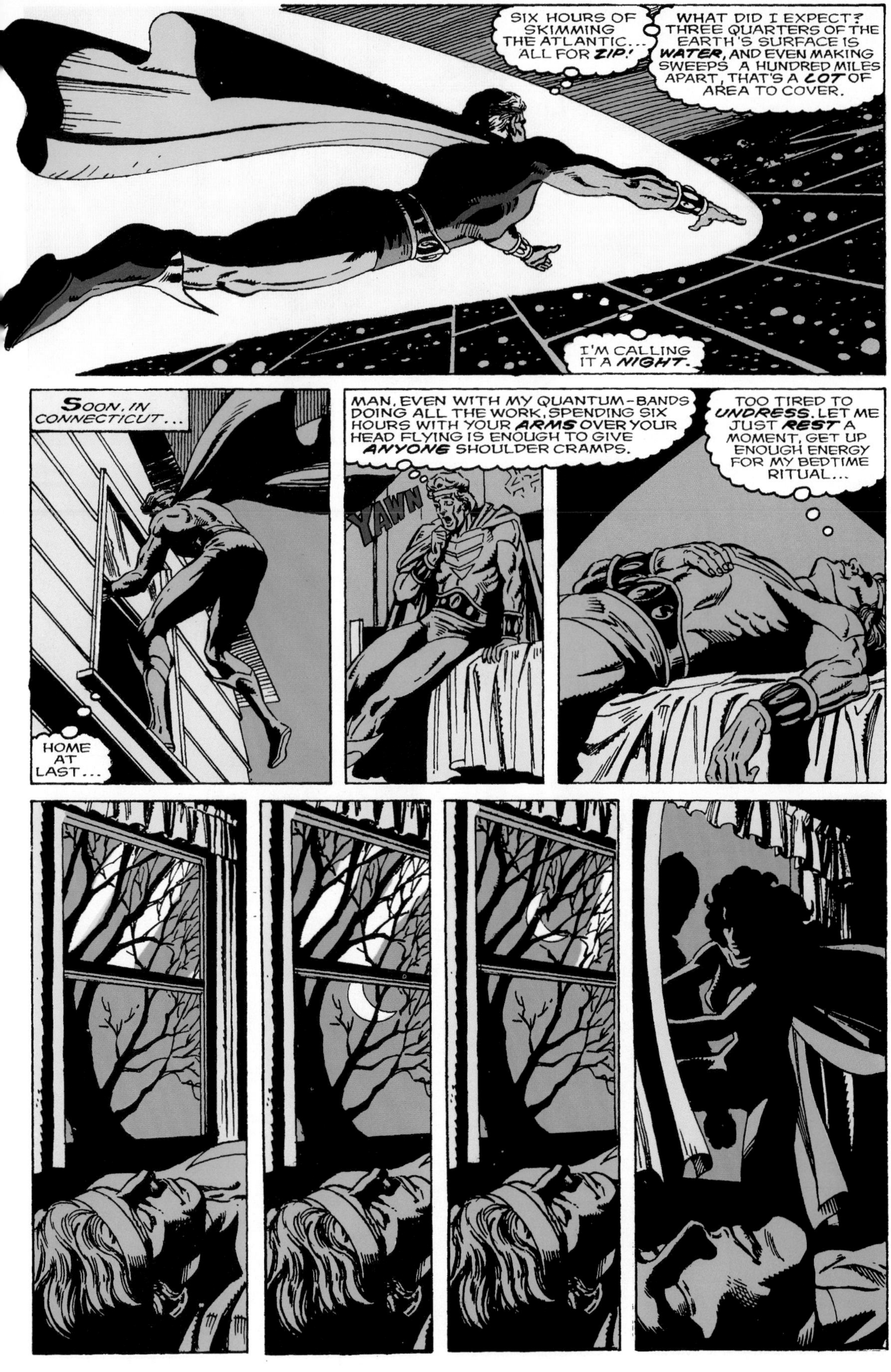
SIX HOURS OF SKIMMING THE ATLANTIC... ALL FOR ZIP!
WHAT DID I EXPECT? THREE QUARTERS OF THE EARTH'S SURFACE IS WATER, AND EVEN MAKING SWEEPS A HUNDRED MILES APART, THAT'S A LOT OF AREA TO COVER.
I'M CALLING IT A NIGHT.
SOON, IN CONNECTICUT...
HOME AT LAST...
MAN, EVEN WITH MY QUANTUM-BANDS DOING ALL THE WORK, SPENDING SIX HOURS WITH YOUR ARMS OVER YOUR HEAD FLYING IS ENOUGH TO GIVE ANYONE SHOULDER CRAMPS.
YAWN
TOO TIRED TO UNDRESS. LET ME JUST REST A MOMENT, GET UP ENOUGH ENERGY FOR MY BEDTIME RITUAL...

SHOOSH

PATHETICALLY SIMPLE.

⟨HE'S OURS, CAPTAIN.⟩*

*TRANSLATED FROM THE KREE LANGUAGE.

⟨I HAVE HIM.⟩

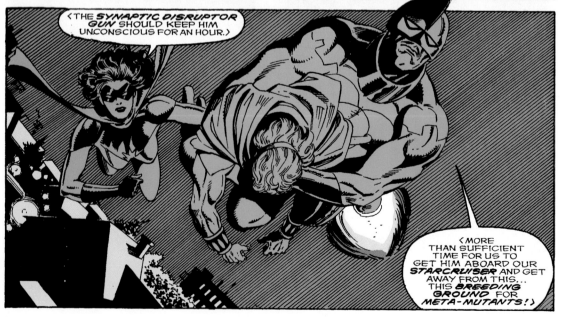

⟨THE SYNAPTIC DISRUPTOR GUN SHOULD KEEP HIM UNCONSCIOUS FOR AN HOUR.⟩

⟨MORE THAN SUFFICIENT TIME FOR US TO GET HIM ABOARD OUR STARCRUISER AND GET AWAY FROM THIS... THIS BREEDING GROUND FOR META-MUTANTS!⟩

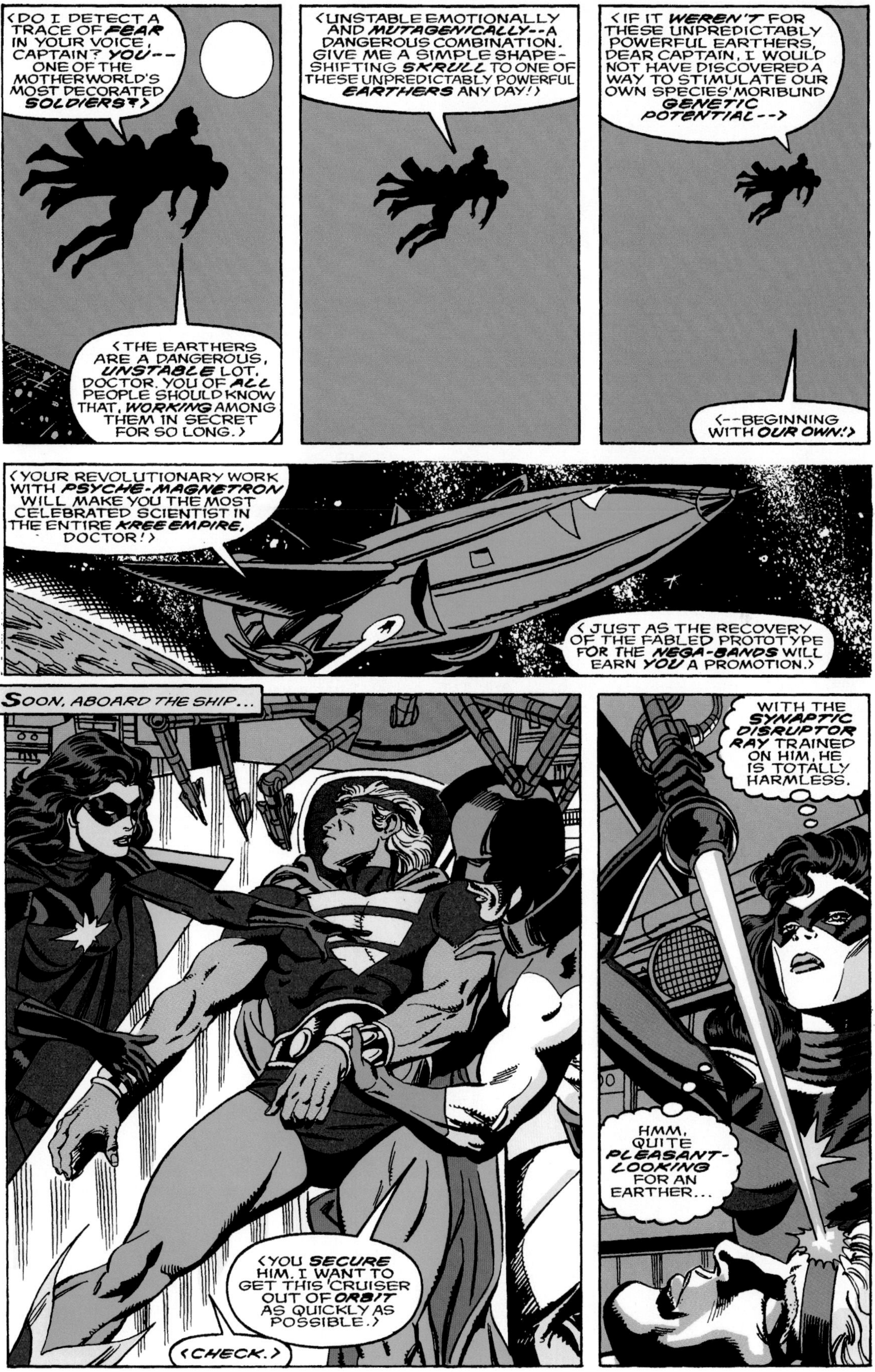

‹DO I DETECT A TRACE OF FEAR IN YOUR VOICE, CAPTAIN? YOU-- ONE OF THE MOTHERWORLD'S MOST DECORATED SOLDIERS?›
‹THE EARTHERS ARE A DANGEROUS, UNSTABLE LOT, DOCTOR. YOU OF ALL PEOPLE SHOULD KNOW THAT, WORKING AMONG THEM IN SECRET FOR SO LONG.›
‹UNSTABLE EMOTIONALLY AND MUTAGENICALLY--A DANGEROUS COMBINATION. GIVE ME A SIMPLE SHAPE-SHIFTING SKRULL TO ONE OF THESE UNPREDICTABLY POWERFUL EARTHERS ANY DAY!›
‹IF IT WEREN'T FOR THESE UNPREDICTABLY POWERFUL EARTHERS, DEAR CAPTAIN, I WOULD NOT HAVE DISCOVERED A WAY TO STIMULATE OUR OWN SPECIES' MORIBUND GENETIC POTENTIAL-->
‹--BEGINNING WITH OUR OWN!›
‹YOUR REVOLUTIONARY WORK WITH PSYCHE-MAGNETRON WILL MAKE YOU THE MOST CELEBRATED SCIENTIST IN THE ENTIRE KREE EMPIRE, DOCTOR!›
‹JUST AS THE RECOVERY OF THE FABLED PROTOTYPE FOR THE NEGA-BANDS WILL EARN YOU A PROMOTION.›
SOON, ABOARD THE SHIP...
‹YOU SECURE HIM. I WANT TO GET THIS CRUISER OUT OF ORBIT AS QUICKLY AS POSSIBLE.›
‹CHECK.›
WITH THE SYNAPTIC DISRUPTOR RAY TRAINED ON HIM, HE IS TOTALLY HARMLESS.
HMM, QUITE PLEASANT-LOOKING FOR AN EARTHER...

<--HYPERDRIVE ACCELERATION.>

<DOCTOR MINERVA, WE'RE LEAVING EARTH ORBIT. STRAP YOURSELF DOWN IN PREPARATION FOR--->

AND SOON...

<DO YOU REALLY THINK THOSE WRIST-BANDS HE WEARS ARE THE LEGENDARY POWER-BANDS OF RINN?>

<I WAS NOT AWARE OF YOUR INTEREST IN CRYPTO-HISTORY, CAPTAIN ATLAS.>

<ACCORDING TO LORE, THEY WERE LAST SEEN IN THIS VICINITY SEVERAL MILLENNIA AGO. SENTRY 213, I BELIEVE IT WAS, RECOVERED IT AND PUT IN A WEAPONS DEPOT SOMEWHERE IN THIS SYSTEM.>

<YES. I STUDIED GALACTIC WEAPONRY AT THE ACADEMY. AS I RECALL, MY PROFESSOR RANKED THE POWER-BANDS RIGHT UP THERE WITH THE SOUL-GEMS, THE SKRULLIAN CUBE, AND THE ULTIMATE NULLIFIER.>

<WELL, IF THIS LUBRICANT DOES WHAT IT'S SUPPOSED TO DO-->

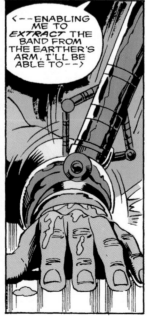

<--ENABLING ME TO EXTRACT THE BAND FROM THE EARTHER'S ARM, I'LL BE ABLE TO-->

<HMM! IT'S NOT MOVING. LET ME-- PAMA, I CANNOT EVEN GET THIS DEPRESSOR UNDER IT!>

<IT'S AS IF THE METAL WERE BONDED TO HIS ARM!>

86

‹IT WOULD SEEM MY ONLY RECOURSE IS TO **SEVER** THE FOREARM ABOVE AND BELOW THE POWER-BAND, THEN SCOOP OUT THE **ORGANIC MATERIAL** BETWEEN...›

‹**PITY.**›

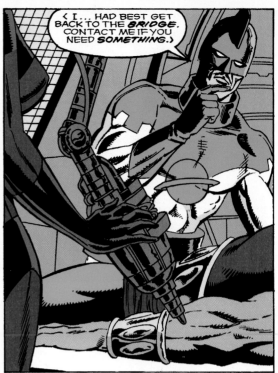

‹ I... HAD BEST GET BACK TO THE **BRIDGE.** CONTACT ME IF YOU NEED **SOMETHING.**›

HMMMPH! MY COLLEAGUE, THE PROFESSIONAL **SOLDIER,** WOULD APPEAR TO BE SOMEWHAT **SQUEAMISH** ABOUT BLOODSHED. GO FIGURE.

‹ WELL, EARTHER, I HATE TO HAVE TO **DO** THIS, BUT YOU LEAVE ME **NO CHOICE.**›

‹DON'T WORRY. EVEN THOUGH I HAVEN'T PERFORMED A PROCEEDURE LIKE THIS SINCE **MIDDLE SCHOOL,** I GUARANTEE YOU WON'T **FEEL** A THING...›

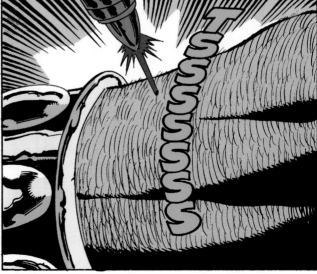

TSSSSSS

87

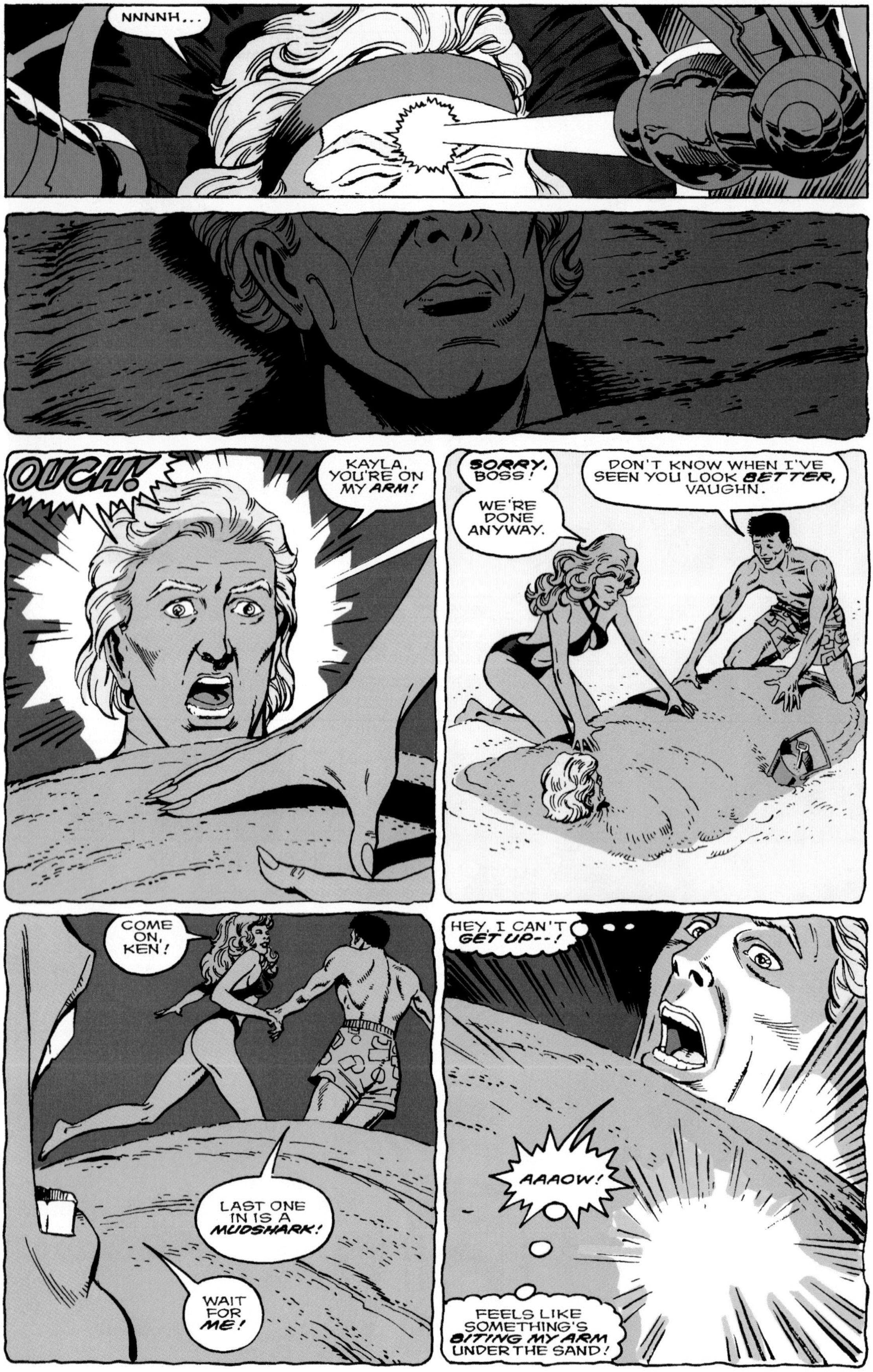
NNNNH...
OUCH!
KAYLA, YOU'RE ON MY ARM!
SORRY, BOSS!
WE'RE DONE ANYWAY.
DON'T KNOW WHEN I'VE SEEN YOU LOOK BETTER, VAUGHN.
COME ON, KEN!
LAST ONE IN IS A MUDSHARK!
WAIT FOR ME!
HEY, I CAN'T GET UP--!
AAAOW!
FEELS LIKE SOMETHING'S BITING MY ARM UNDER THE SAND!

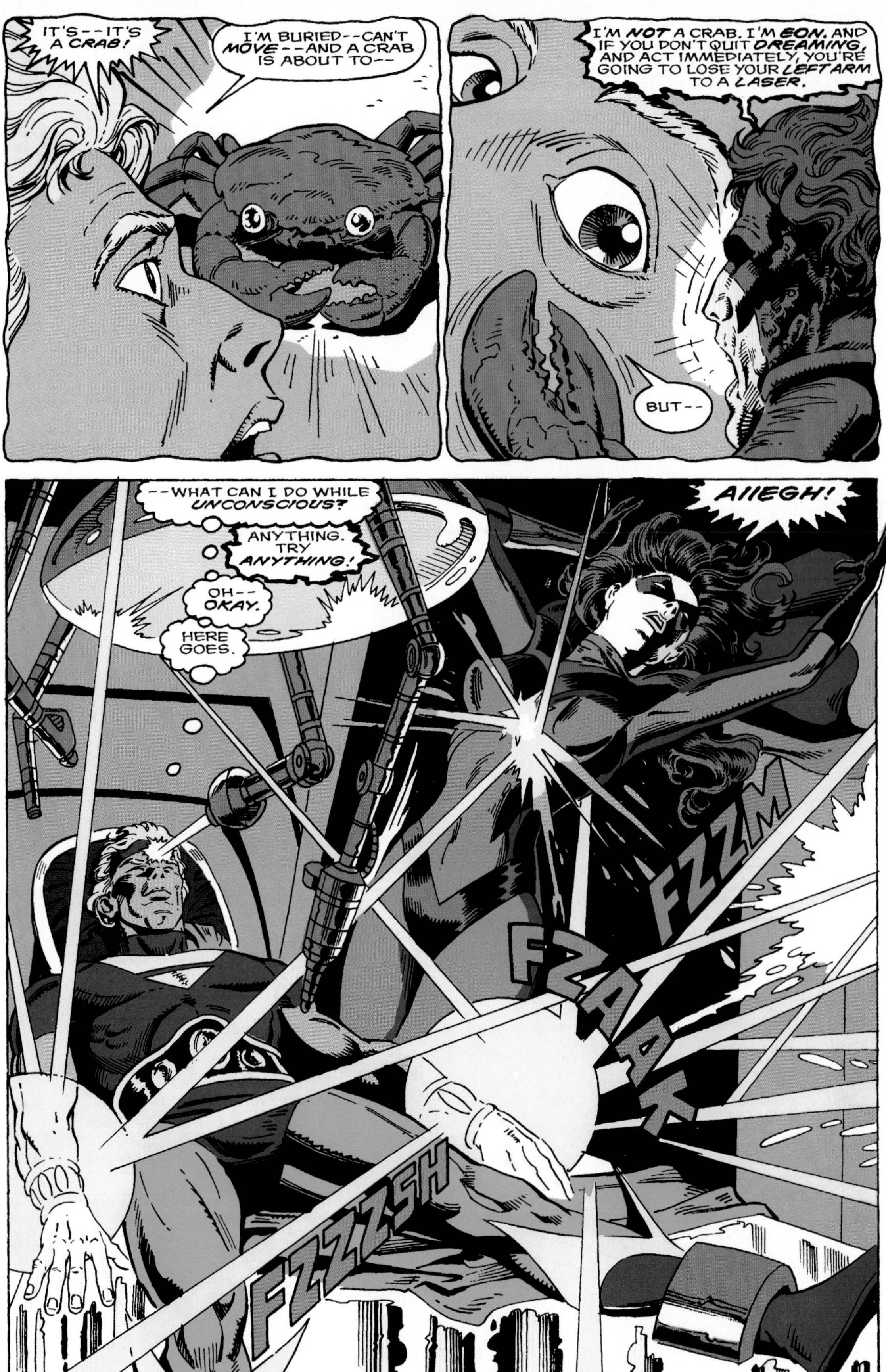
IT'S--IT'S A CRAB!
I'M BURIED--CAN'T MOVE--AND A CRAB IS ABOUT TO--
I'M NOT A CRAB. I'M EON. AND IF YOU DON'T QUIT DREAMING, AND ACT IMMEDIATELY, YOU'RE GOING TO LOSE YOUR LEFT ARM TO A LASER.
BUT--
--WHAT CAN I DO WHILE UNCONSCIOUS?
ANYTHING. TRY ANYTHING!
OH--OKAY.
HERE GOES.
AIIEGH!
FZZM
FZAAAK
FZZZSH

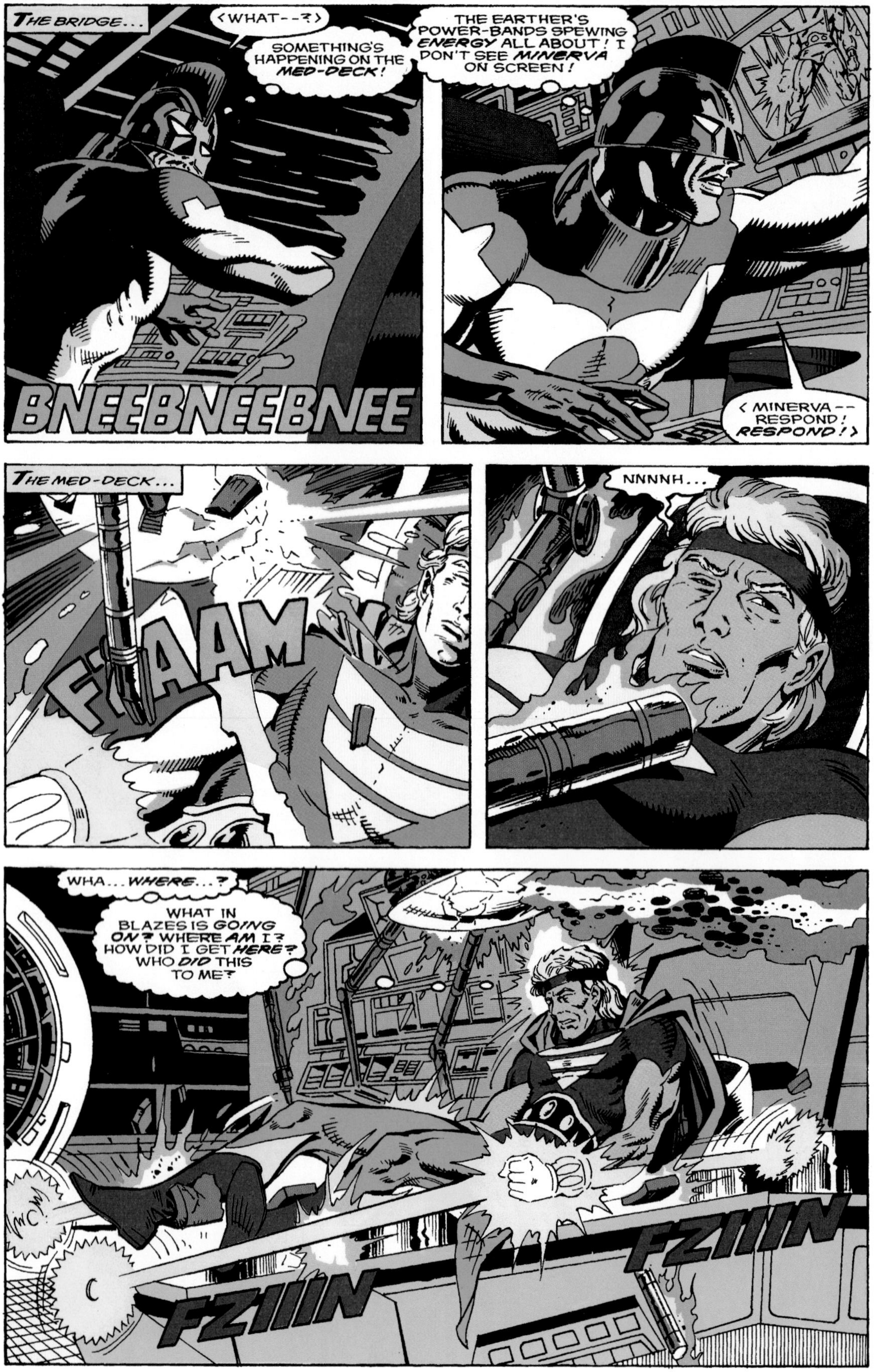
THE BRIDGE...
<WHAT--?>
SOMETHING'S HAPPENING ON THE MED-DECK!
THE EARTHER'S POWER-BANDS SPEWING ENERGY ALL ABOUT! I DON'T SEE MINERVA ON SCREEN!
BNEEBNEEBNEE
<MINERVA-- RESPOND! RESPOND!>
THE MED-DECK...
FTAAM
NNNNH...
WHA...WHERE...?
WHAT IN BLAZES IS GOING ON? WHERE AM I? HOW DID I GET HERE? WHO DID THIS TO ME?
FZIIIN
FZIIIN

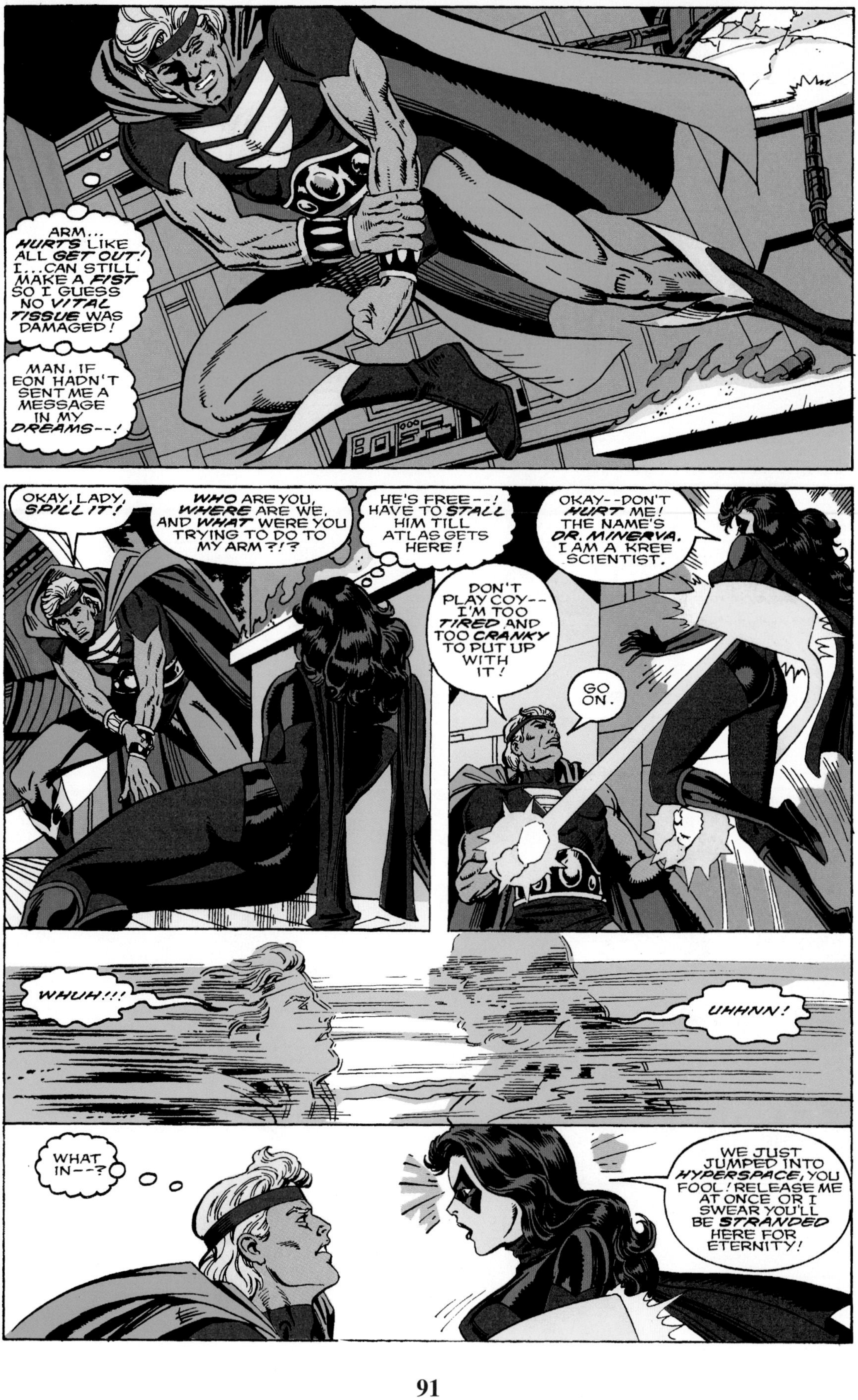
ARM... HURTS LIKE ALL GET OUT! I...CAN STILL MAKE A FIST SO I GUESS NO VITAL TISSUE WAS DAMAGED!
MAN, IF EON HADN'T SENT ME A MESSAGE IN MY DREAMS--!
OKAY, LADY, SPILL IT!
WHO ARE YOU, WHERE ARE WE, AND WHAT WERE YOU TRYING TO DO TO MY ARM?!?
HE'S FREE--! HAVE TO STALL HIM TILL ATLAS GETS HERE!
OKAY--DON'T HURT ME! THE NAME'S DR. MINERVA. I AM A KREE SCIENTIST.
DON'T PLAY COY-- I'M TOO TIRED AND TOO CRANKY TO PUT UP WITH IT!
GO ON.
WHUH!!!
UHHNN!
WHAT IN--?
WE JUST JUMPED INTO HYPERSPACE, YOU FOOL! RELEASE ME AT ONCE OR I SWEAR YOU'LL BE STRANDED HERE FOR ETERNITY!

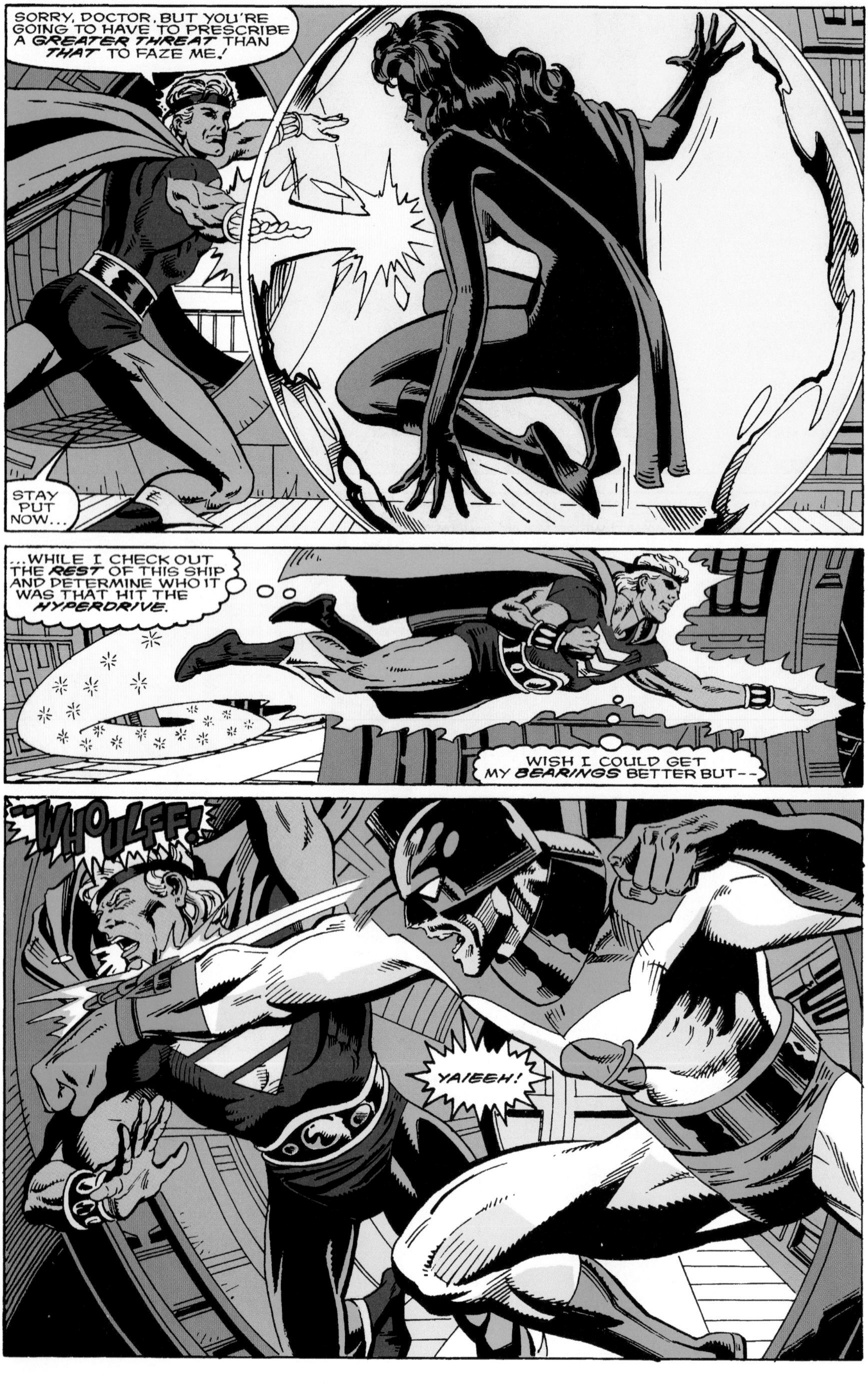
SORRY, DOCTOR, BUT YOU'RE GOING TO HAVE TO PRESCRIBE A GREATER THREAT THAN THAT TO FAZE ME!
STAY PUT NOW...
...WHILE I CHECK OUT THE REST OF THIS SHIP AND DETERMINE WHO IT WAS THAT HIT THE HYPERDRIVE.
WISH I COULD GET MY BEARINGS BETTER BUT--
WHOULFF!
YAIEEH!

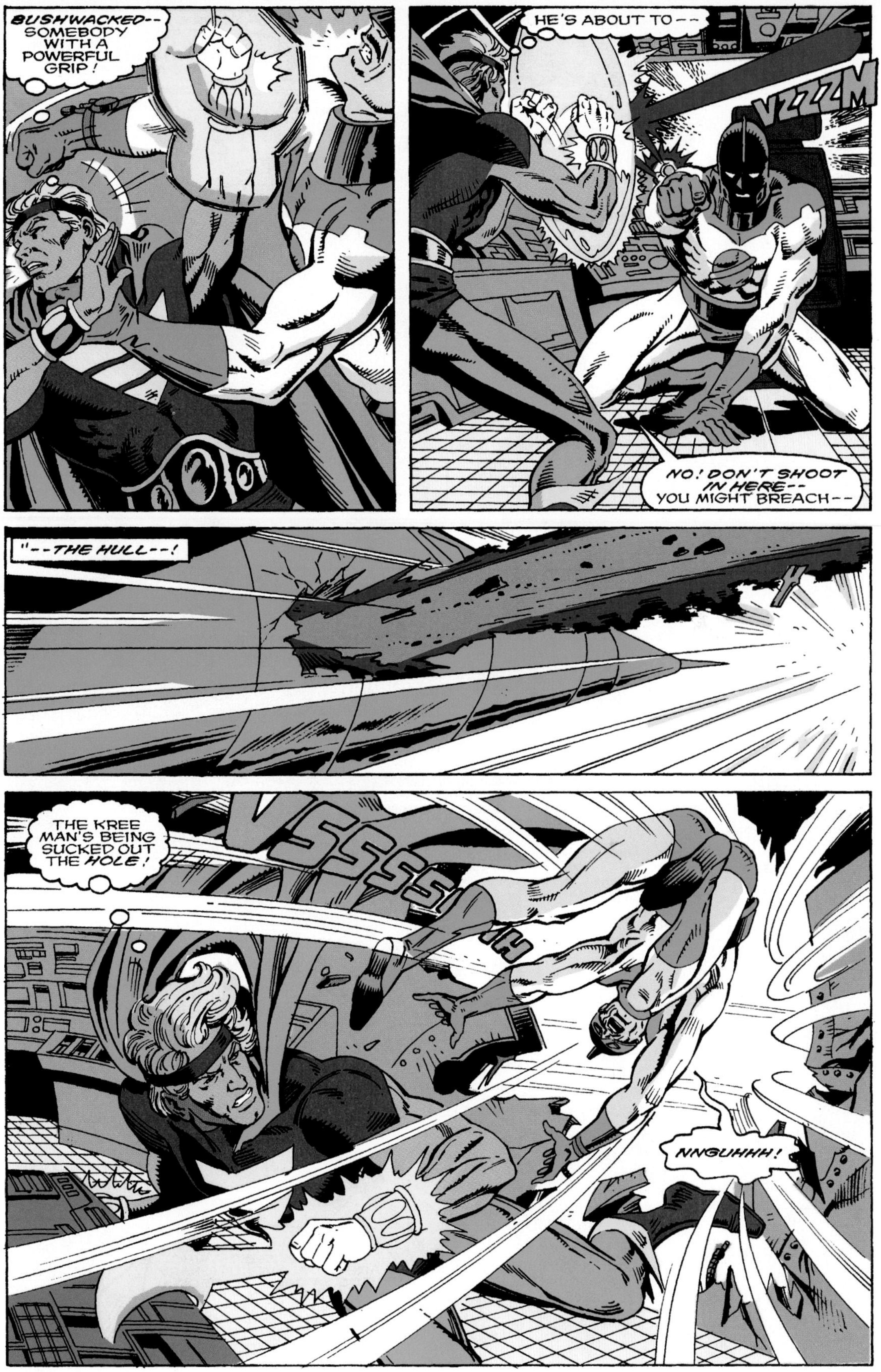
BUSHWACKED-- SOMEBODY WITH A POWERFUL GRIP!
HE'S ABOUT TO--
VZZZM
NO! DON'T SHOOT IN HERE-- YOU MIGHT BREACH--
"--THE HULL--!
THE KREE MAN'S BEING SUCKED OUT THE HOLE!
VSSSSHH
NNGUHHH!

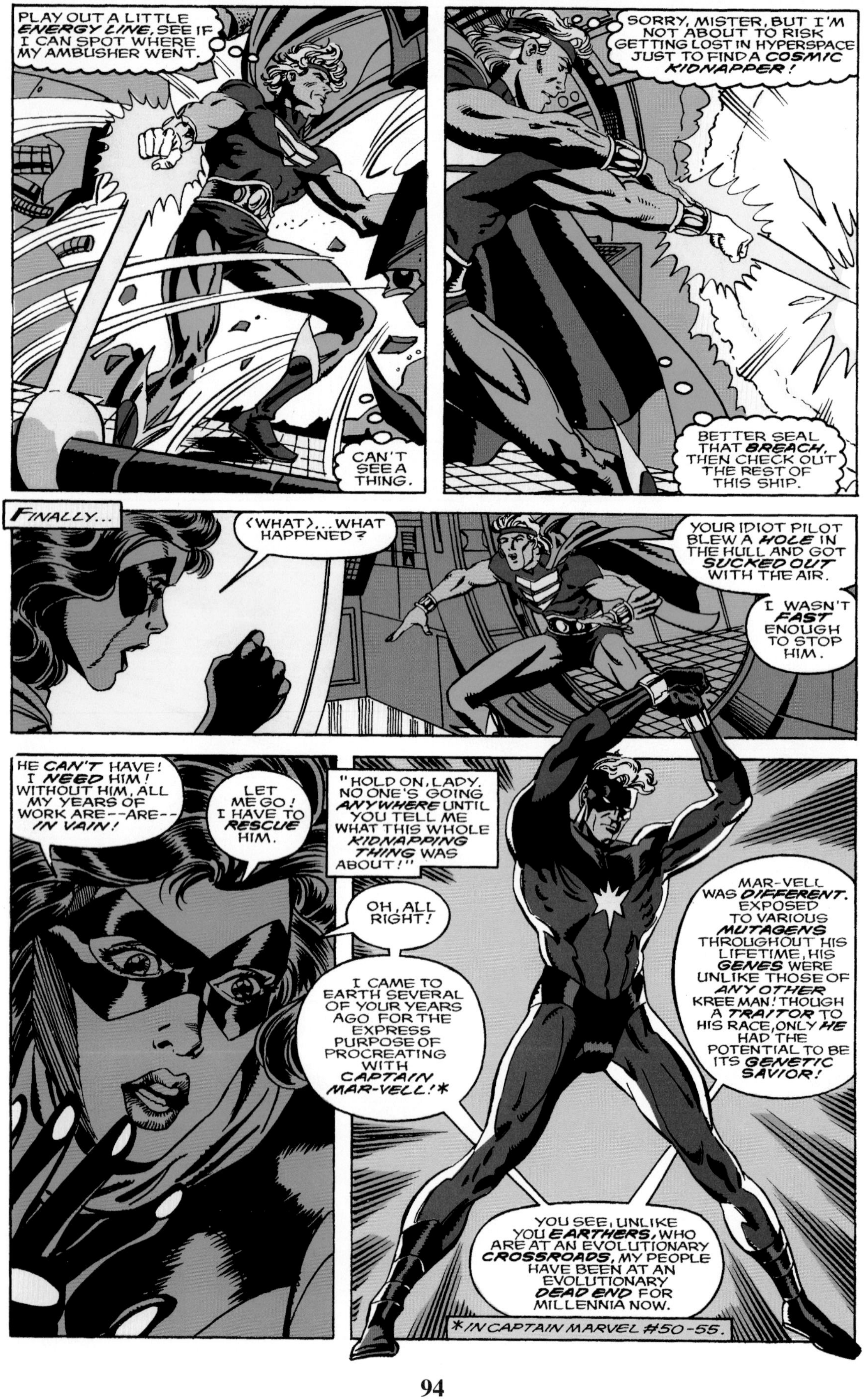
PLAY OUT A LITTLE ENERGY LINE, SEE IF I CAN SPOT WHERE MY AMBUSHER WENT.
CAN'T SEE A THING.
SORRY, MISTER, BUT I'M NOT ABOUT TO RISK GETTING LOST IN HYPERSPACE JUST TO FIND A COSMIC KIDNAPPER!
BETTER SEAL THAT BREACH, THEN CHECK OUT THE REST OF THIS SHIP.
FINALLY...
⟨WHAT⟩...WHAT HAPPENED?
YOUR IDIOT PILOT BLEW A HOLE IN THE HULL AND GOT SUCKED OUT WITH THE AIR.
I WASN'T FAST ENOUGH TO STOP HIM.
HE CAN'T HAVE! I NEED HIM! WITHOUT HIM, ALL MY YEARS OF WORK ARE--ARE--IN VAIN!
LET ME GO! I HAVE TO RESCUE HIM.
"HOLD ON, LADY. NO ONE'S GOING ANYWHERE UNTIL YOU TELL ME WHAT THIS WHOLE KIDNAPPING THING WAS ABOUT!"
OH, ALL RIGHT!
I CAME TO EARTH SEVERAL OF YOUR YEARS AGO FOR THE EXPRESS PURPOSE OF PROCREATING WITH CAPTAIN MAR-VELL!*
MAR-VELL WAS DIFFERENT. EXPOSED TO VARIOUS MUTAGENS THROUGHOUT HIS LIFETIME, HIS GENES WERE UNLIKE THOSE OF ANY OTHER KREE MAN! THOUGH A TRAITOR TO HIS RACE, ONLY HE HAD THE POTENTIAL TO BE ITS GENETIC SAVIOR!
YOU SEE, UNLIKE YOU EARTHERS, WHO ARE AT AN EVOLUTIONARY CROSSROADS, MY PEOPLE HAVE BEEN AT AN EVOLUTIONARY DEAD END FOR MILLENNIA NOW.
*IN CAPTAIN MARVEL #50-55.

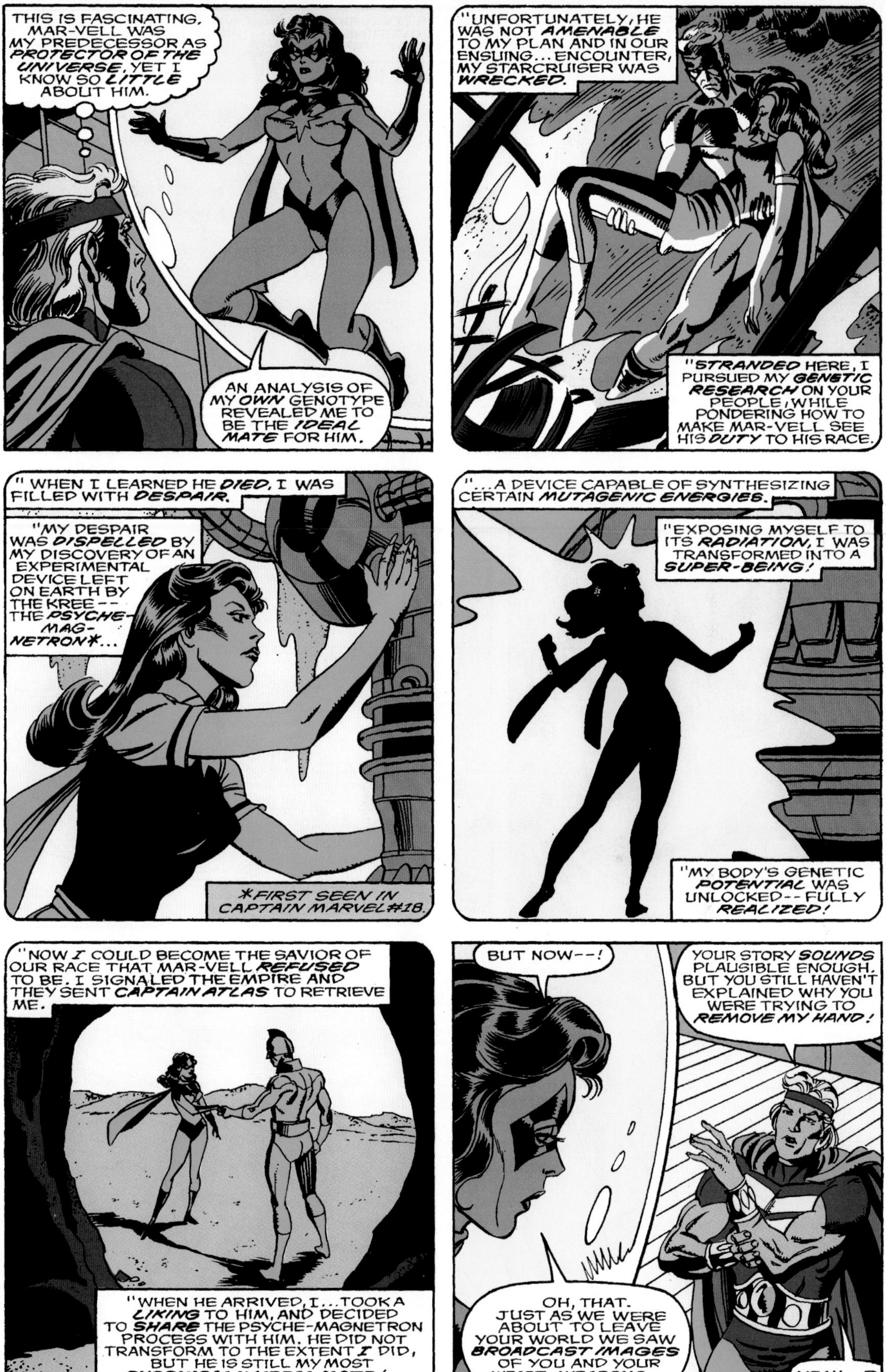

THIS IS FASCINATING. MAR-VELL WAS MY PREDECESSOR AS PROTECTOR OF THE UNIVERSE, YET I KNOW SO LITTLE ABOUT HIM.
AN ANALYSIS OF MY OWN GENOTYPE REVEALED ME TO BE THE IDEAL MATE FOR HIM.
"UNFORTUNATELY, HE WAS NOT AMENABLE TO MY PLAN AND IN OUR ENSUING... ENCOUNTER, MY STARCRUISER WAS WRECKED.
"STRANDED HERE, I PURSUED MY GENETIC RESEARCH ON YOUR PEOPLE, WHILE PONDERING HOW TO MAKE MAR-VELL SEE HIS DUTY TO HIS RACE.
" WHEN I LEARNED HE DIED, I WAS FILLED WITH DESPAIR.
"MY DESPAIR WAS DISPELLED BY MY DISCOVERY OF AN EXPERIMENTAL DEVICE LEFT ON EARTH BY THE KREE -- THE PSYCHE-MAGNETRON*...
*FIRST SEEN IN CAPTAIN MARVEL #18.
"...A DEVICE CAPABLE OF SYNTHESIZING CERTAIN MUTAGENIC ENERGIES.
"EXPOSING MYSELF TO ITS RADIATION, I WAS TRANSFORMED INTO A SUPER-BEING!
"MY BODY'S GENETIC POTENTIAL WAS UNLOCKED-- FULLY REALIZED!
"NOW I COULD BECOME THE SAVIOR OF OUR RACE THAT MAR-VELL REFUSED TO BE. I SIGNALED THE EMPIRE AND THEY SENT CAPTAIN ATLAS TO RETRIEVE ME.
"WHEN HE ARRIVED, I... TOOK A LIKING TO HIM, AND DECIDED TO SHARE THE PSYCHE-MAGNETRON PROCESS WITH HIM. HE DID NOT TRANSFORM TO THE EXTENT I DID, BUT HE IS STILL MY MOST EUGENICALLY IDEAL MATE!
BUT NOW--!
YOUR STORY SOUNDS PLAUSIBLE ENOUGH. BUT YOU STILL HAVEN'T EXPLAINED WHY YOU WERE TRYING TO REMOVE MY HAND!
OH, THAT. JUST AS WE WERE ABOUT TO LEAVE YOUR WORLD WE SAW BROADCAST IMAGES OF YOU AND YOUR WRIST-WEAPONS...
YEAH...?

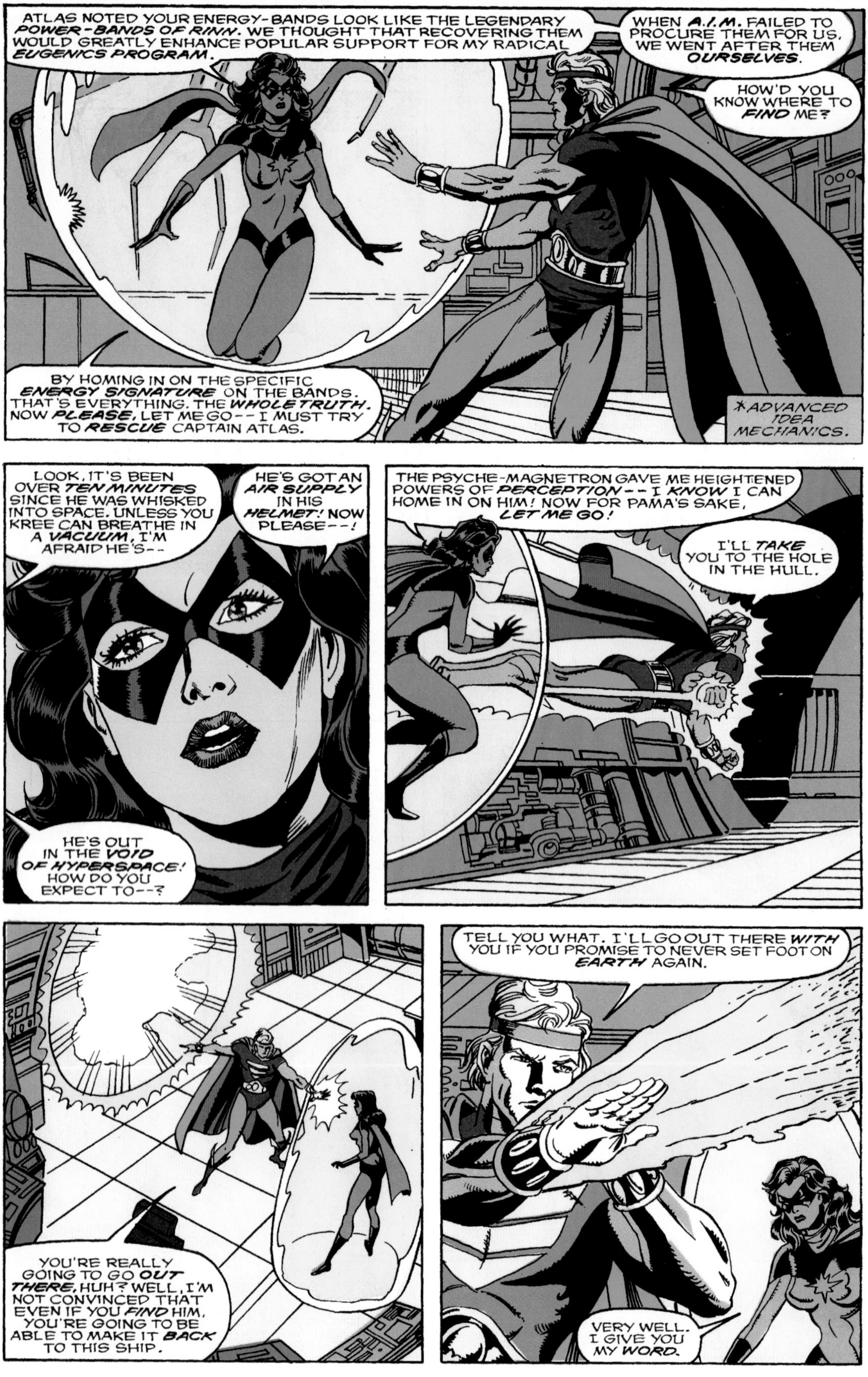
ATLAS NOTED YOUR ENERGY-BANDS LOOK LIKE THE LEGENDARY POWER-BANDS OF RINN. WE THOUGHT THAT RECOVERING THEM WOULD GREATLY ENHANCE POPULAR SUPPORT FOR MY RADICAL EUGENICS PROGRAM.
WHEN A.I.M. FAILED TO PROCURE THEM FOR US, WE WENT AFTER THEM OURSELVES.
HOW'D YOU KNOW WHERE TO FIND ME?
BY HOMING IN ON THE SPECIFIC ENERGY SIGNATURE ON THE BANDS. THAT'S EVERYTHING. THE WHOLE TRUTH. NOW PLEASE, LET ME GO-- I MUST TRY TO RESCUE CAPTAIN ATLAS.
*ADVANCED IDEA MECHANICS.
LOOK, IT'S BEEN OVER TEN MINUTES SINCE HE WAS WHISKED INTO SPACE. UNLESS YOU KREE CAN BREATHE IN A VACUUM, I'M AFRAID HE'S--
HE'S GOT AN AIR SUPPLY IN HIS HELMET! NOW PLEASE--!
HE'S OUT IN THE VOID OF HYPERSPACE! HOW DO YOU EXPECT TO--?
THE PSYCHE-MAGNETRON GAVE ME HEIGHTENED POWERS OF PERCEPTION-- I KNOW I CAN HOME IN ON HIM! NOW FOR PAMA'S SAKE, LET ME GO!
I'LL TAKE YOU TO THE HOLE IN THE HULL.
YOU'RE REALLY GOING TO GO OUT THERE, HUH? WELL, I'M NOT CONVINCED THAT EVEN IF YOU FIND HIM, YOU'RE GOING TO BE ABLE TO MAKE IT BACK TO THIS SHIP.
TELL YOU WHAT. I'LL GO OUT THERE WITH YOU IF YOU PROMISE TO NEVER SET FOOT ON EARTH AGAIN.
VERY WELL. I GIVE YOU MY WORD.

MOMENTS LATER...

AM I *NUTS* FOR DOING THIS, HELPING OUT TWO MEMBERS OF AN *ALIEN RACE* KNOWN TO BE *HOSTILE* TOWARD EARTH, WHO PERSONALLY JUST TRIED TO *DO ME IN...*?

I'M REASONABLY CERTAIN I DON'T NEED *THEM* TO GET OUT OF HYPERSPACE...AND NO MATTER *WHERE* I POPPED OUT, I'M SURE *EON* COULD DIRECT ME BACK *HOME.*

MAYBE I JUST DON'T WANT TO LEAVE HER FRIEND TO *DIE* KNOWING I MIGHT HAVE DONE SOMETHING TO *SAVE* HIM.

OR MAYBE I'M DOING IT BECAUSE I THINK IT'S WHAT *CAPTAIN MAR-VELL* WOULD HAVE DONE.

DON'T KNOW IF *MINERVA* WILL REALLY BE ABLE TO *FIND* HIM IN THIS INCOMPREHENSIBLE VOID...

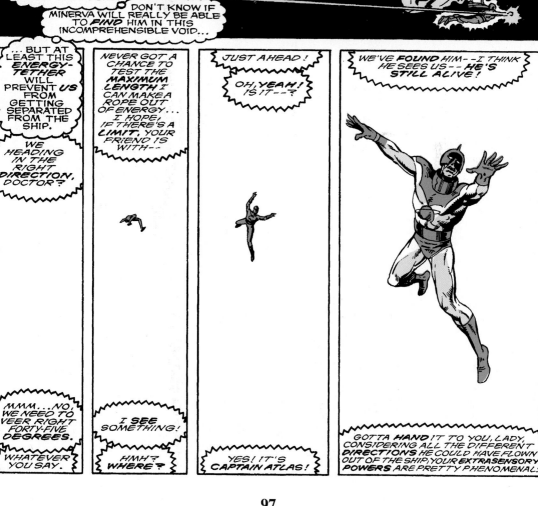

...BUT AT LEAST THIS *ENERGY-TETHER* WILL PREVENT *US* FROM GETTING SEPARATED FROM THE SHIP.

WE HEADING IN THE RIGHT *DIRECTION,* DOCTOR?

MMM...NO, WE NEED TO VEER RIGHT FORTY-FIVE *DEGREES.*

WHATEVER YOU SAY.

NEVER GOT A CHANCE TO TEST THE *MAXIMUM LENGTH* I CAN MAKE A ROPE OUT OF ENERGY... I HOPE, IF THERE'S A *LIMIT,* YOUR FRIEND IS WITH--

I SEE *SOMETHING!*

HMH? *WHERE?*

JUST AHEAD!

OH, YEAH! IS IT--?

YES! IT'S *CAPTAIN ATLAS!*

WE'VE *FOUND* HIM--I THINK HE SEES US--*HE'S STILL ALIVE!*

GOTTA *HAND* IT TO YOU, LADY, CONSIDERING ALL THE DIFFERENT *DIRECTIONS* HE COULD HAVE FLOWN OUT OF THE SHIP, YOUR *EXTRASENSORY POWERS* ARE PRETTY PHENOMENAL!

EASY NOW, SIR--THE GUY WHOSE *JAW* YOU TRIED TO *DISLOCATE* WILL HAVE YOU BACK IN YOUR COZY LITTLE *SPACECRAFT*--

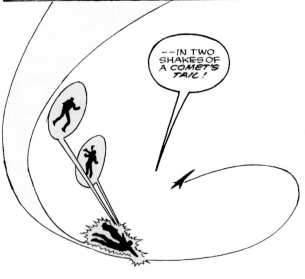

--IN TWO SHAKES OF A *COMET'S TAIL!*

AND...

⟨CAPTAIN, ARE YOU--⟩

⟨I AM FINE.⟩

HERE'S THE *SCOOP*, YOU TWO. THESE TWO QUANTUM-BANDS GIVE ME MORE *POWER* THAN YOU KNOW WHAT TO DO WITH. YOU DON'T WANT TO GET ME ANY *ANGRIER* THAN YOU ALREADY HAVE.

GO BACK TO YOUR EMPIRE, *MATE*, SET UP A *NURSERY*--I DON'T CARE. BUT JUST DON'T LET ME *CATCH* YOU IN THE VICINITY OF EARTH-- *EVER AGAIN*--

--OR YOU'RE GOING TO WISH I'D DITCHED YOU BOTH IN *HYPERSPACE*. AM I MAKING MYSELF *UNDERSTOOD?*

YES.

"OKAY THEN. GET OUT OF *HYPERDRIVE* AND LET ME OFF."

98

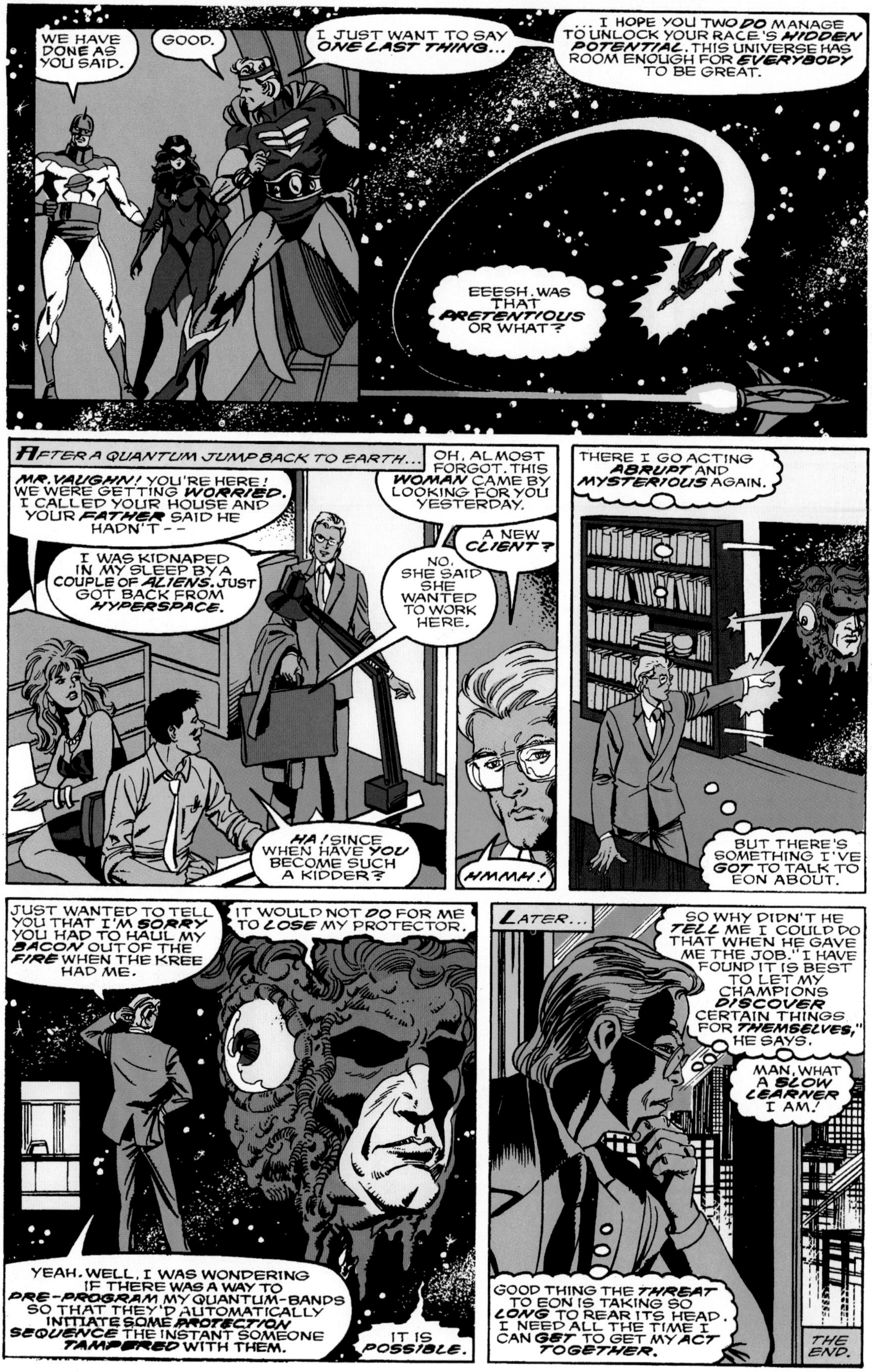
WE HAVE DONE AS YOU SAID.
GOOD.
I JUST WANT TO SAY ONE LAST THING...
... I HOPE YOU TWO DO MANAGE TO UNLOCK YOUR RACE'S HIDDEN POTENTIAL. THIS UNIVERSE HAS ROOM ENOUGH FOR EVERYBODY TO BE GREAT.
EEESH. WAS THAT PRETENTIOUS OR WHAT?
AFTER A QUANTUM JUMP BACK TO EARTH...
MR. VAUGHN! YOU'RE HERE! WE WERE GETTING WORRIED. I CALLED YOUR HOUSE AND YOUR FATHER SAID HE HADN'T - -
I WAS KIDNAPED IN MY SLEEP BY A COUPLE OF ALIENS. JUST GOT BACK FROM HYPERSPACE.
HA! SINCE WHEN HAVE YOU BECOME SUCH A KIDDER?
OH, ALMOST FORGOT. THIS WOMAN CAME BY LOOKING FOR YOU YESTERDAY.
A NEW CLIENT?
NO. SHE SAID SHE WANTED TO WORK HERE.
HMMM!
THERE I GO ACTING ABRUPT AND MYSTERIOUS AGAIN.
BUT THERE'S SOMETHING I'VE GOT TO TALK TO EON ABOUT.
JUST WANTED TO TELL YOU THAT I'M SORRY YOU HAD TO HAUL MY BACON OUT OF THE FIRE WHEN THE KREE HAD ME.
IT WOULD NOT DO FOR ME TO LOSE MY PROTECTOR.
YEAH. WELL, I WAS WONDERING IF THERE WAS A WAY TO PRE-PROGRAM MY QUANTUM-BANDS SO THAT THEY'D AUTOMATICALLY INITIATE SOME PROTECTION SEQUENCE THE INSTANT SOMEONE TAMPERED WITH THEM.
IT IS POSSIBLE.
LATER...
SO WHY DIDN'T HE TELL ME I COULD DO THAT WHEN HE GAVE ME THE JOB. "I HAVE FOUND IT IS BEST TO LET MY CHAMPIONS DISCOVER CERTAIN THINGS FOR THEMSELVES," HE SAYS.
MAN, WHAT A SLOW LEARNER I AM!
GOOD THING THE THREAT TO EON IS TAKING SO LONG TO REAR ITS HEAD. I NEED ALL THE TIME I CAN GET TO GET MY ACT TOGETHER.
THE END.

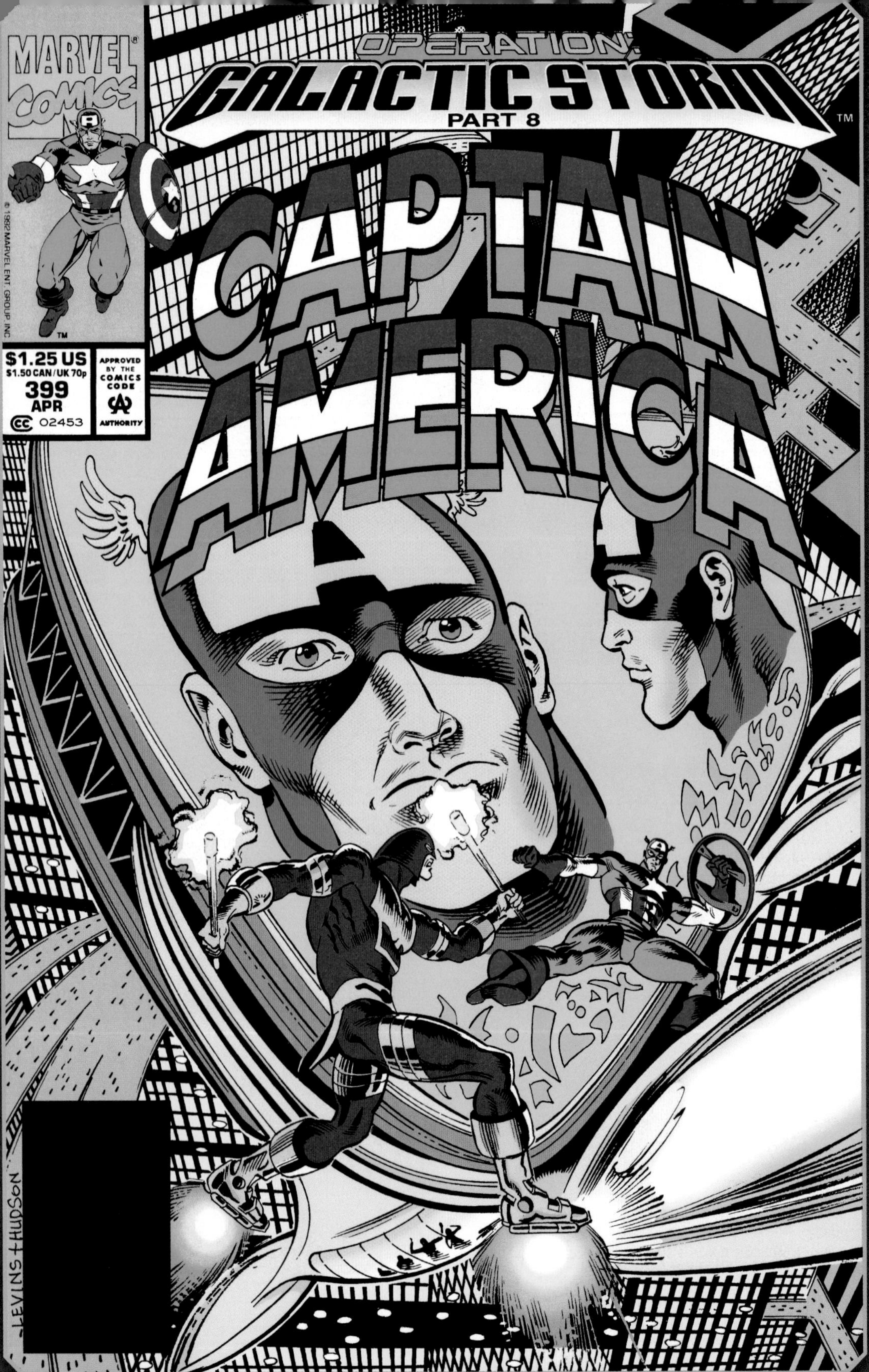
MARVEL COMICS
OPERATION: GALACTIC STORM
PART 8
TM
CAPTAIN AMERICA
$1.25 US
$1.50 CAN/UK 70p
399
APR
02453
APPROVED BY THE COMICS CODE AUTHORITY
© 1992 MARVEL ENT. GROUP INC.
LEVINS+HUDSON

TWO GALACTIC EMPIRES — THE MILITARISTIC KREE AND THE MATRIARCHAL SHI'AR — ARE AT WAR, A WAR THAT THREATENS ALL LIFE ON EARTH. THE MIGHTY AVENGERS HAVE SPLIT INTO TWO ENVOYS TO NEGOTIATE WITH THE HEADS OF EACH EMPIRE. IN THE GROUP SENT TO THE KREE EMPIRE — IRON MAN, SERSI, HERCULES, THE BLACK KNIGHT, CRYSTAL, GOLIATH, AND. . .CAPTAIN AMERICA!

Stan Lee PRESENTS:

OPERATION: GALACTIC STORM PART 8

CAPTAIN AMERICA

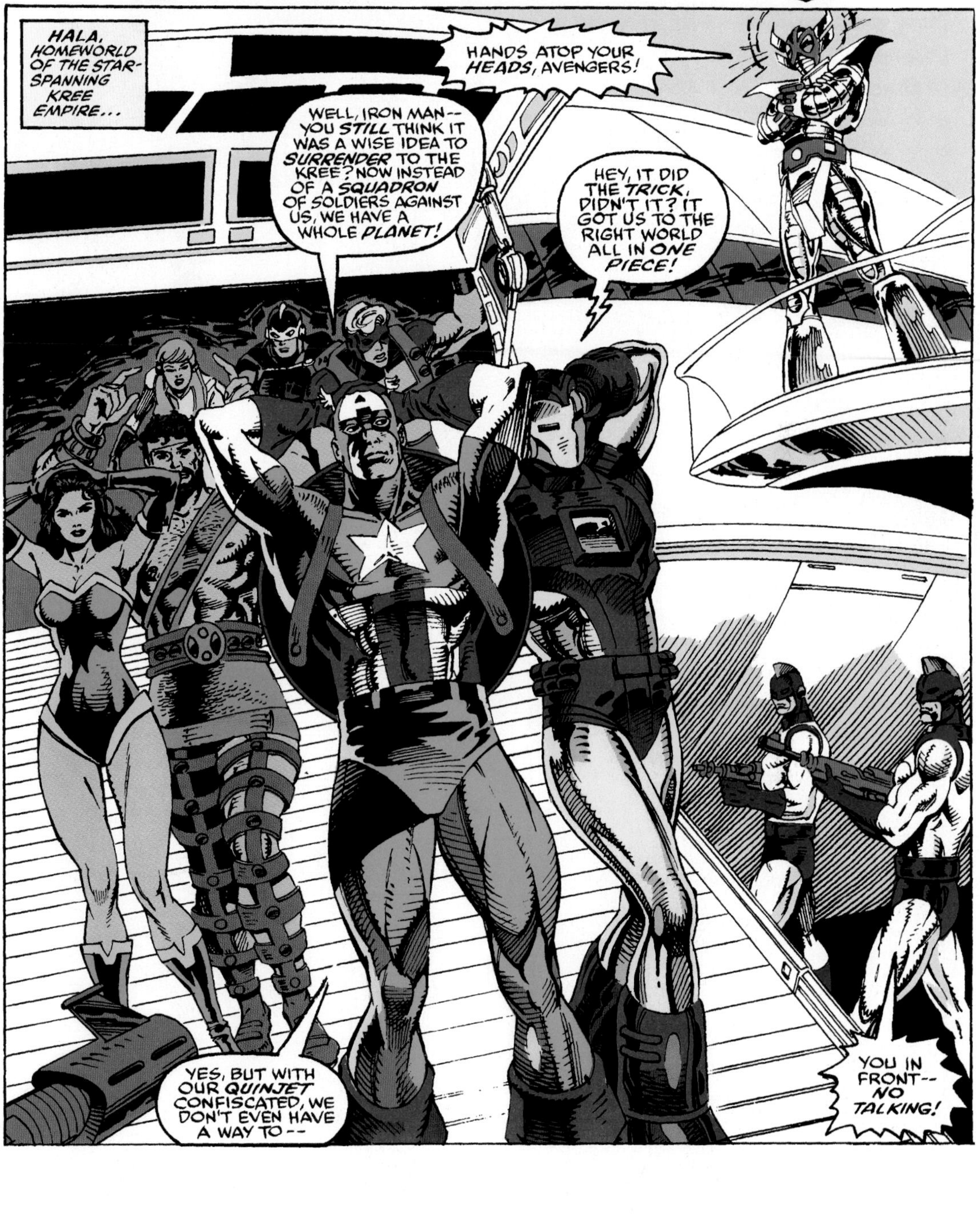

HALA, HOMEWORLD OF THE STAR-SPANNING KREE EMPIRE...
HANDS ATOP YOUR HEADS, AVENGERS!
WELL, IRON MAN-- YOU STILL THINK IT WAS A WISE IDEA TO SURRENDER TO THE KREE? NOW INSTEAD OF A SQUADRON OF SOLDIERS AGAINST US, WE HAVE A WHOLE PLANET!
HEY, IT DID THE TRICK, DIDN'T IT? IT GOT US TO THE RIGHT WORLD ALL IN ONE PIECE!
YES, BUT WITH OUR QUINJET CONFISCATED, WE DON'T EVEN HAVE A WAY TO --
YOU IN FRONT-- NO TALKING!

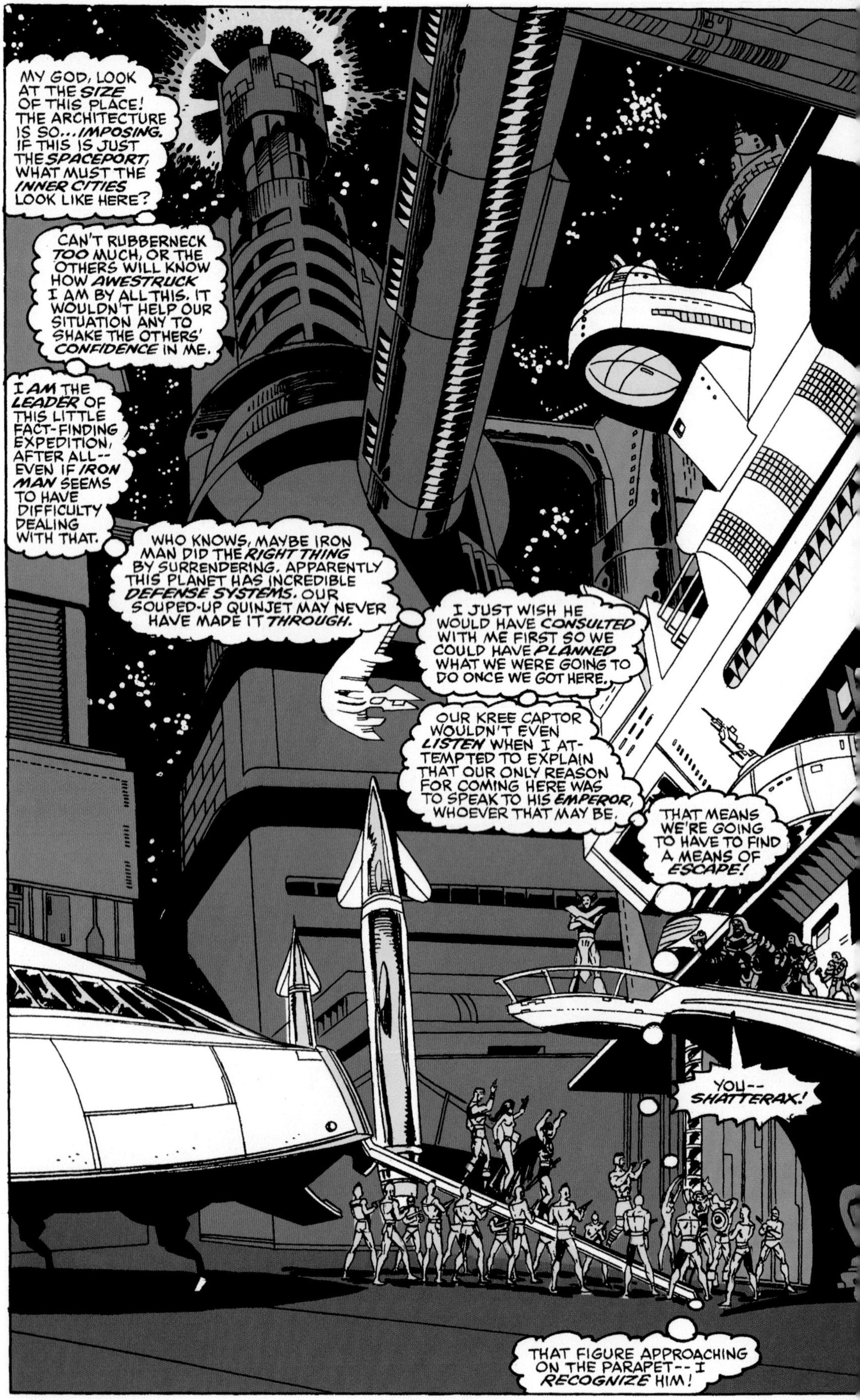
MY GOD, LOOK AT THE SIZE OF THIS PLACE! THE ARCHITECTURE IS SO... IMPOSING. IF THIS IS JUST THE SPACEPORT, WHAT MUST THE INNER CITIES LOOK LIKE HERE?
CAN'T RUBBERNECK TOO MUCH, OR THE OTHERS WILL KNOW HOW AWESTRUCK I AM BY ALL THIS. IT WOULDN'T HELP OUR SITUATION ANY TO SHAKE THE OTHERS' CONFIDENCE IN ME.
I AM THE LEADER OF THIS LITTLE FACT-FINDING EXPEDITION, AFTER ALL-- EVEN IF IRON MAN SEEMS TO HAVE DIFFICULTY DEALING WITH THAT.
WHO KNOWS, MAYBE IRON MAN DID THE RIGHT THING BY SURRENDERING. APPARENTLY THIS PLANET HAS INCREDIBLE DEFENSE SYSTEMS. OUR SOUPED-UP QUINJET MAY NEVER HAVE MADE IT THROUGH.
I JUST WISH HE WOULD HAVE CONSULTED WITH ME FIRST SO WE COULD HAVE PLANNED WHAT WE WERE GOING TO DO ONCE WE GOT HERE.
OUR KREE CAPTOR WOULDN'T EVEN LISTEN WHEN I AT-TEMPTED TO EXPLAIN THAT OUR ONLY REASON FOR COMING HERE WAS TO SPEAK TO HIS EMPEROR, WHOEVER THAT MAY BE.
THAT MEANS WE'RE GOING TO HAVE TO FIND A MEANS OF ESCAPE!
YOU-- SHATTERAX!
THAT FIGURE APPROACHING ON THE PARAPET-- I RECOGNIZE HIM!

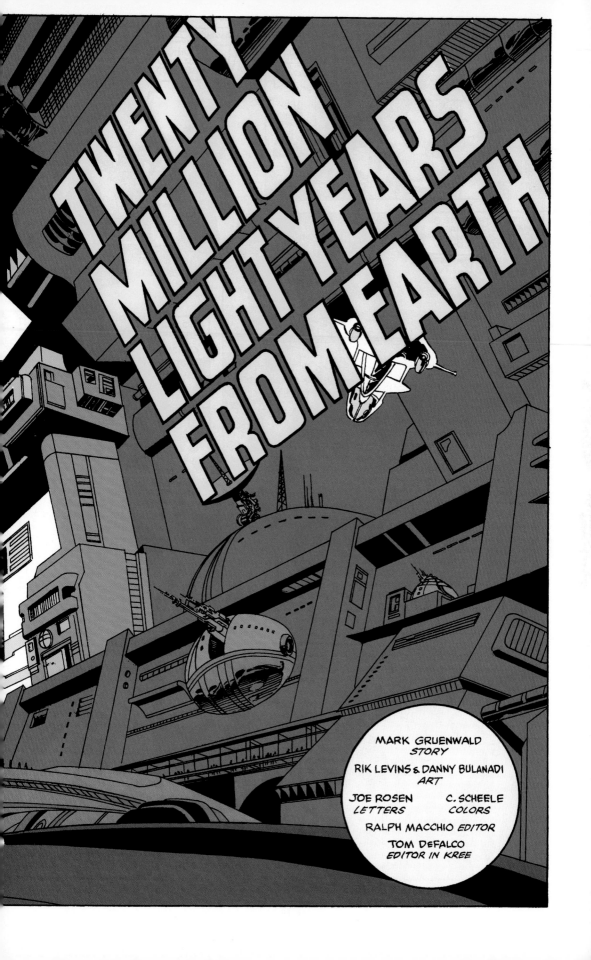

TWENTY MILLION LIGHT YEARS FROM EARTH

MARK GRUENWALD
STORY

RIK LEVINS & DANNY BULANADI
ART

JOE ROSEN   C. SCHEELE
LETTERS   COLORS

RALPH MACCHIO EDITOR

TOM DEFALCO
EDITOR IN KREE

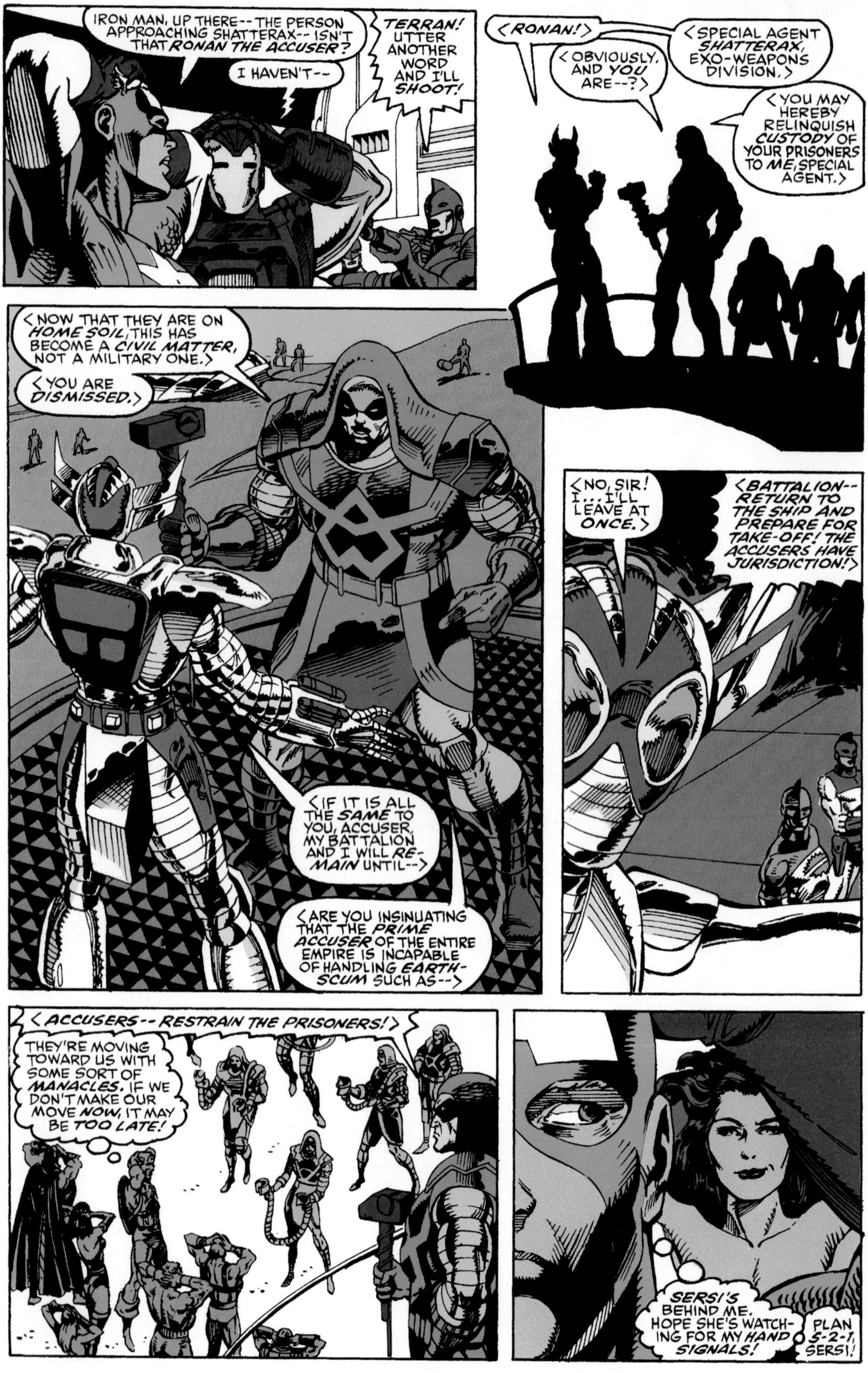
IRON MAN, UP THERE-- THE PERSON APPROACHING SHATTERAX-- ISN'T THAT RONAN THE ACCUSER?
I HAVEN'T--
TERRAN! UTTER ANOTHER WORD AND I'LL SHOOT!
<RONAN!>
<SPECIAL AGENT SHATTERAX, EXO-WEAPONS DIVISION.>
<OBVIOUSLY. AND YOU ARE--?>
<YOU MAY HEREBY RELINQUISH CUSTODY OF YOUR PRISONERS TO ME, SPECIAL AGENT.>
<NOW THAT THEY ARE ON HOME SOIL, THIS HAS BECOME A CIVIL MATTER, NOT A MILITARY ONE.>
<YOU ARE DISMISSED.>
<IF IT IS ALL THE SAME TO YOU, ACCUSER, MY BATTALION AND I WILL RE-MAIN UNTIL-->
<ARE YOU INSINUATING THAT THE PRIME ACCUSER OF THE ENTIRE EMPIRE IS INCAPABLE OF HANDLING EARTH-SCUM SUCH AS-->
<NO, SIR! I... I'LL LEAVE AT ONCE.>
<BATTALION-- RETURN TO THE SHIP AND PREPARE FOR TAKE-OFF! THE ACCUSERS HAVE JURISDICTION!>
<ACCUSERS-- RESTRAIN THE PRISONERS!>
THEY'RE MOVING TOWARD US WITH SOME SORT OF MANACLES. IF WE DON'T MAKE OUR MOVE NOW, IT MAY BE TOO LATE!
SERSI'S BEHIND ME. HOPE SHE'S WATCHING FOR MY HAND SIGNALS!
PLAN S-2-7, SERSI!

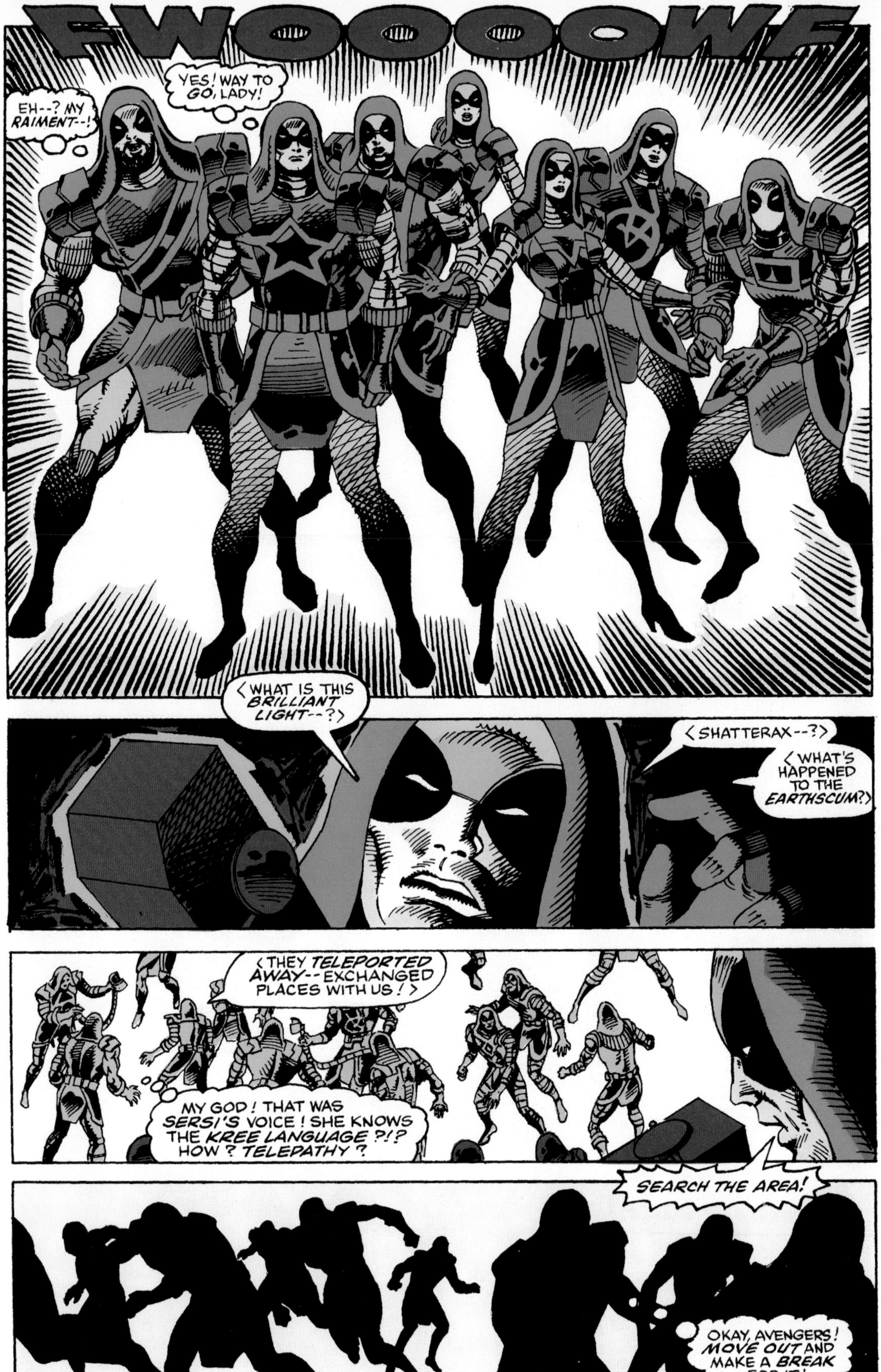
FWOOOOWF
EH--? MY RAIMENT--!
YES! WAY TO GO, LADY!
⟨WHAT IS THIS BRILLIANT LIGHT--?⟩
⟨SHATTERAX--?⟩
⟨WHAT'S HAPPENED TO THE EARTHSCUM?⟩
⟨THEY TELEPORTED AWAY--EXCHANGED PLACES WITH US!⟩
MY GOD! THAT WAS SERSI'S VOICE! SHE KNOWS THE KREE LANGUAGE ?!? HOW? TELEPATHY?
SEARCH THE AREA!
OKAY, AVENGERS! MOVE OUT AND MAKE A BREAK FOR IT!

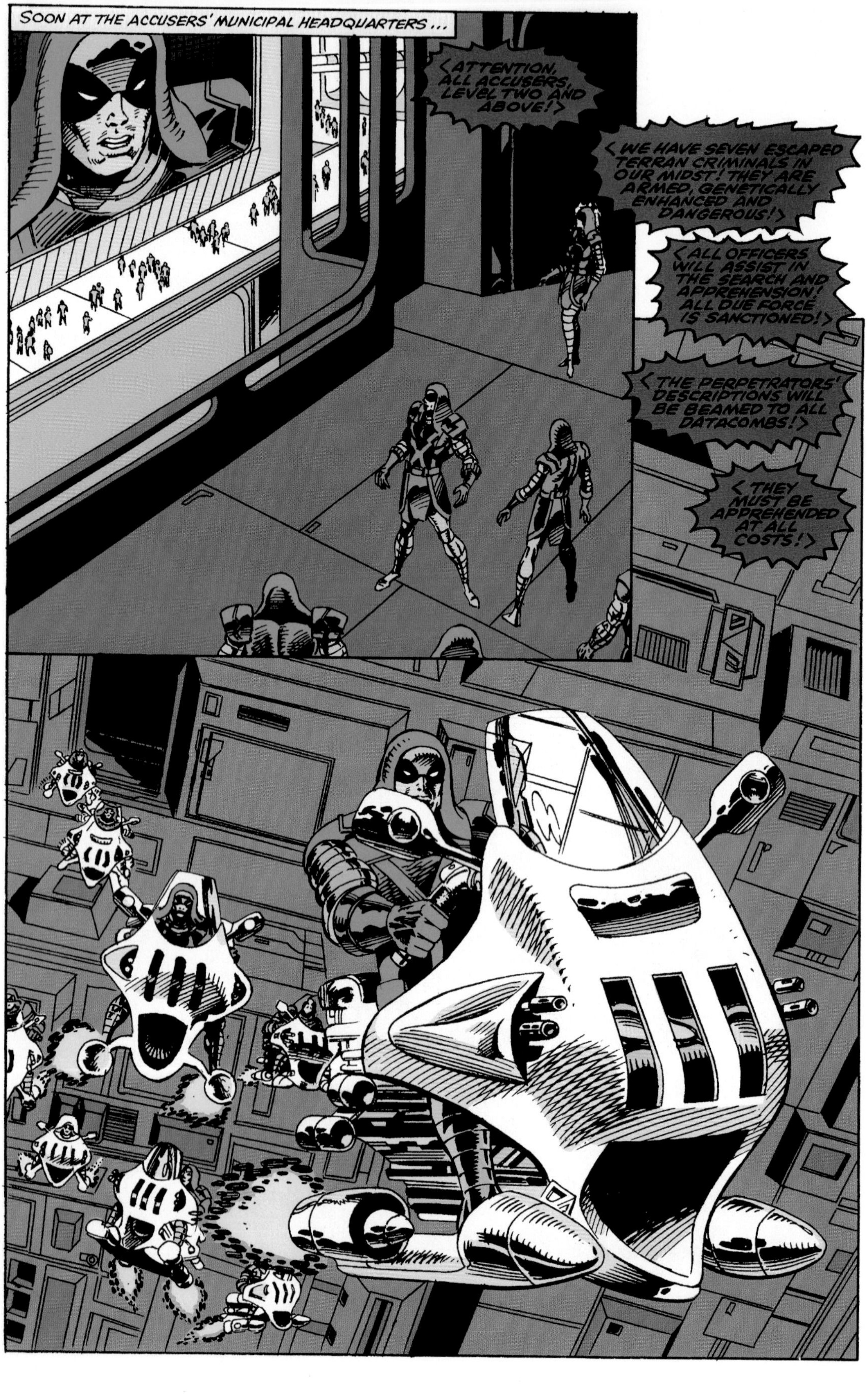
SOON AT THE ACCUSERS' MUNICIPAL HEADQUARTERS...
<ATTENTION, ALL ACCUSERS, LEVEL TWO AND ABOVE!>
<WE HAVE SEVEN ESCAPED TERRAN CRIMINALS IN OUR MIDST! THEY ARE ARMED, GENETICALLY ENHANCED AND DANGEROUS!>
<ALL OFFICERS WILL ASSIST IN THE SEARCH AND APPREHENSION! ALL DUE FORCE IS SANCTIONED!>
<THE PERPETRATORS' DESCRIPTIONS WILL BE BEAMED TO ALL DATACOMBS!>
<THEY MUST BE APPREHENDED AT ALL COSTS!>

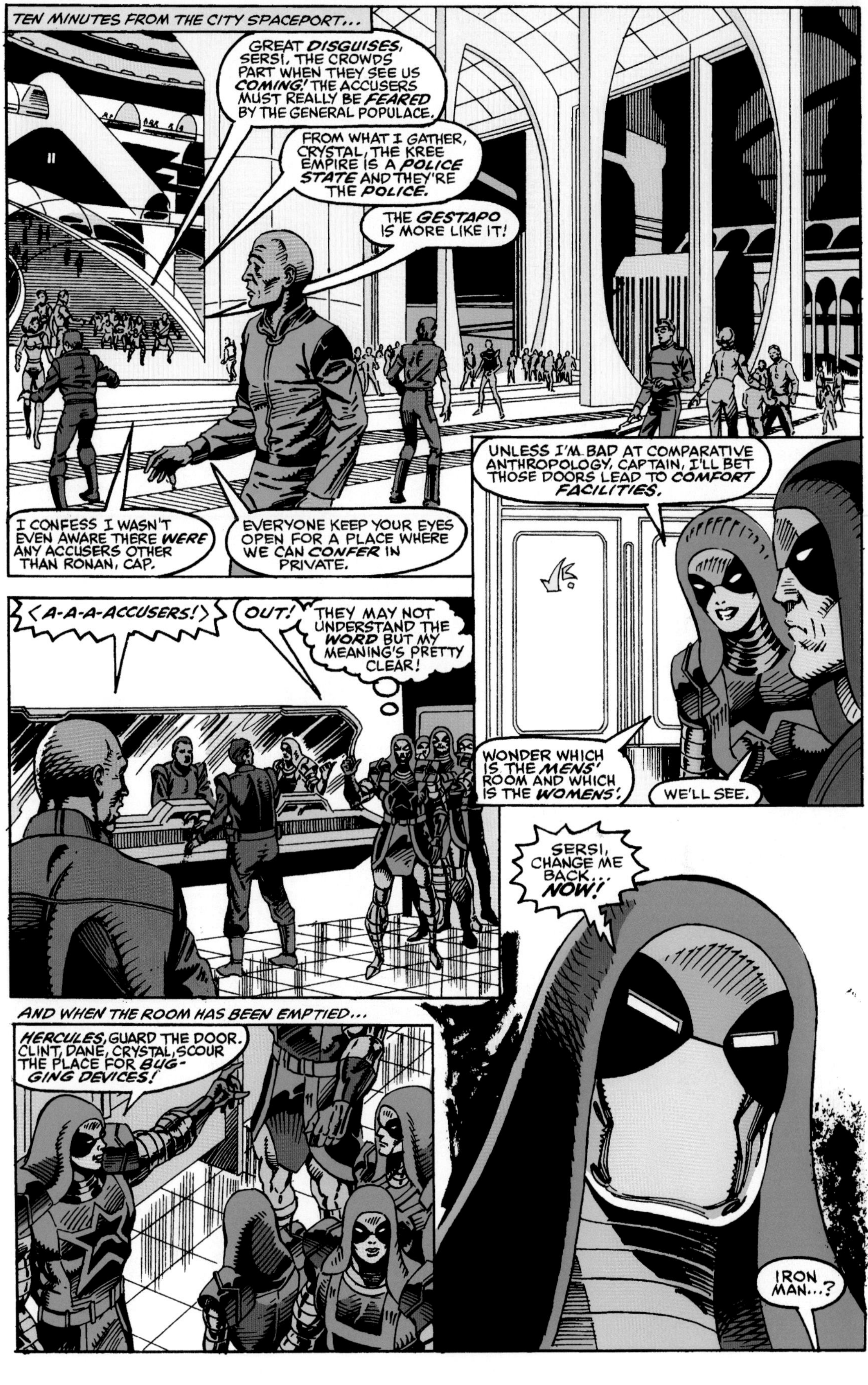
TEN MINUTES FROM THE CITY SPACEPORT...
GREAT DISGUISES, SERSI. THE CROWDS PART WHEN THEY SEE US COMING! THE ACCUSERS MUST REALLY BE FEARED BY THE GENERAL POPULACE.
FROM WHAT I GATHER, CRYSTAL, THE KREE EMPIRE IS A POLICE STATE AND THEY'RE THE POLICE.
THE GESTAPO IS MORE LIKE IT!
I CONFESS I WASN'T EVEN AWARE THERE WERE ANY ACCUSERS OTHER THAN RONAN, CAP.
EVERYONE KEEP YOUR EYES OPEN FOR A PLACE WHERE WE CAN CONFER IN PRIVATE.
UNLESS I'M BAD AT COMPARATIVE ANTHROPOLOGY, CAPTAIN, I'LL BET THOSE DOORS LEAD TO COMFORT FACILITIES.
WONDER WHICH IS THE MENS' ROOM AND WHICH IS THE WOMENS'.
WE'LL SEE.
<A-A-A-ACCUSERS!>
OUT!
THEY MAY NOT UNDERSTAND THE WORD BUT MY MEANING'S PRETTY CLEAR!
AND WHEN THE ROOM HAS BEEN EMPTIED...
HERCULES, GUARD THE DOOR. CLINT, DANE, CRYSTAL, SCOUR THE PLACE FOR BUG-GING DEVICES!
SERSI, CHANGE ME BACK... NOW!
IRON MAN...?

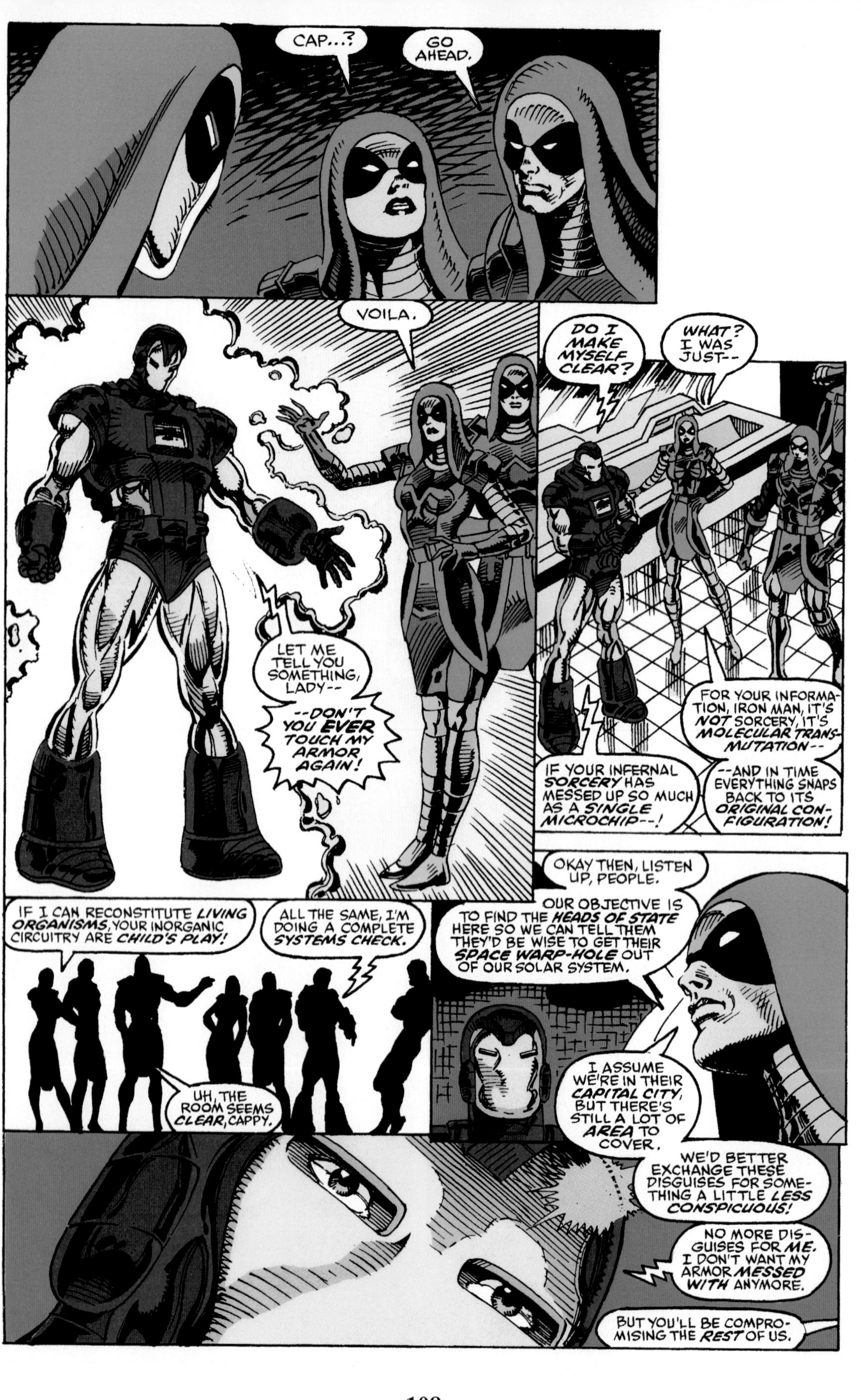
CAP...?
GO AHEAD.
VOILA.
LET ME TELL YOU SOMETHING, LADY--
--DON'T YOU EVER TOUCH MY ARMOR AGAIN!
DO I MAKE MYSELF CLEAR?
WHAT? I WAS JUST--
IF YOUR INFERNAL SORCERY HAS MESSED UP SO MUCH AS A SINGLE MICROCHIP--!
FOR YOUR INFORMATION, IRON MAN, IT'S NOT SORCERY, IT'S MOLECULAR TRANSMUTATION--
--AND IN TIME EVERYTHING SNAPS BACK TO ITS ORIGINAL CONFIGURATION!
IF I CAN RECONSTITUTE LIVING ORGANISMS, YOUR INORGANIC CIRCUITRY ARE CHILD'S PLAY!
ALL THE SAME, I'M DOING A COMPLETE SYSTEMS CHECK.
UH, THE ROOM SEEMS CLEAR, CAPPY.
OKAY THEN, LISTEN UP, PEOPLE.
OUR OBJECTIVE IS TO FIND THE HEADS OF STATE HERE SO WE CAN TELL THEM THEY'D BE WISE TO GET THEIR SPACE WARP-HOLE OUT OF OUR SOLAR SYSTEM.
I ASSUME WE'RE IN THEIR CAPITAL CITY, BUT THERE'S STILL A LOT OF AREA TO COVER.
WE'D BETTER EXCHANGE THESE DISGUISES FOR SOMETHING A LITTLE LESS CONSPICUOUS!
NO MORE DISGUISES FOR ME. I DON'T WANT MY ARMOR MESSED WITH ANYMORE.
BUT YOU'LL BE COMPROMISING THE REST OF US.

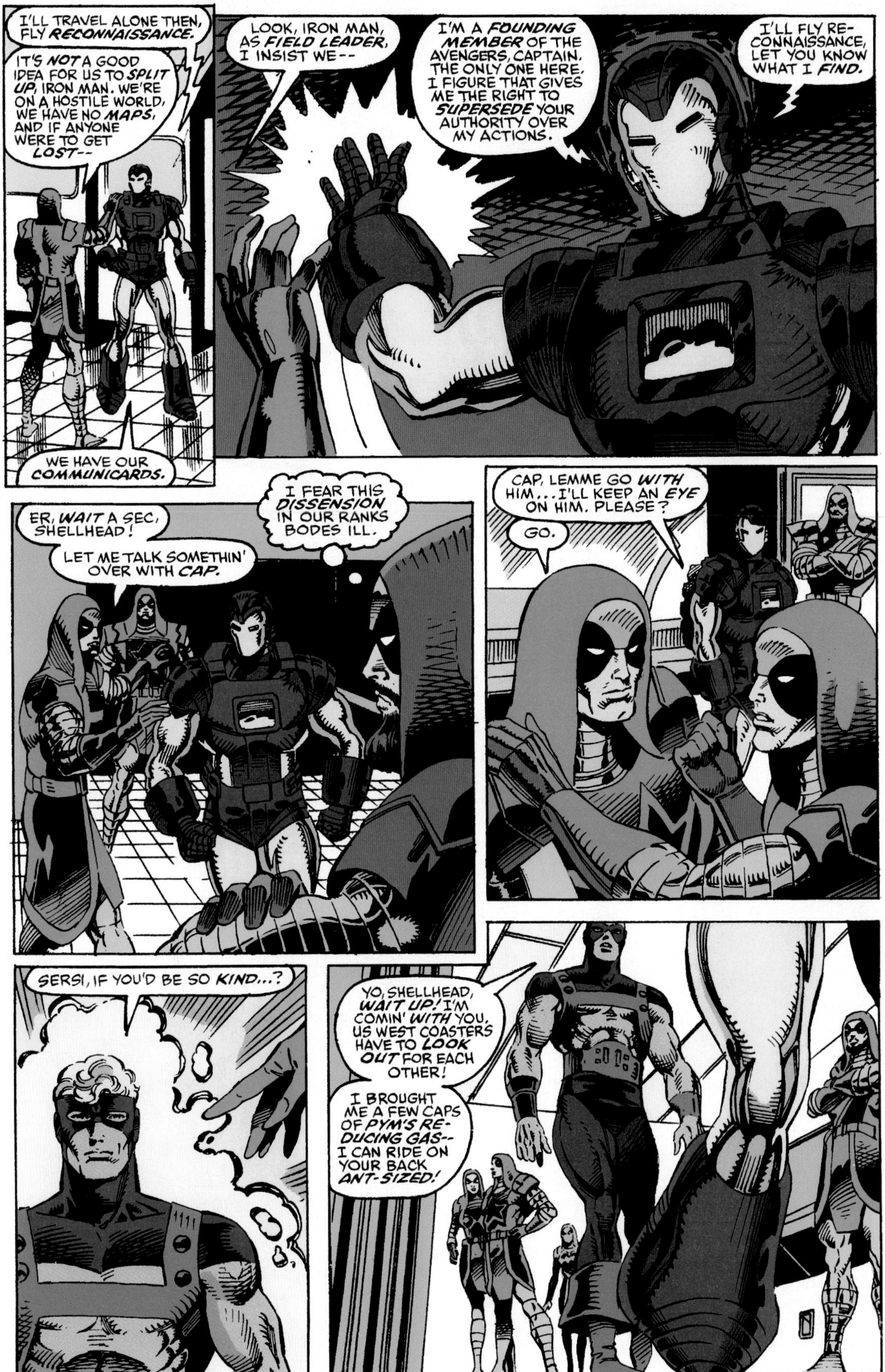

I'LL TRAVEL ALONE THEN, FLY RECONNAISSANCE.
IT'S NOT A GOOD IDEA FOR US TO SPLIT UP, IRON MAN. WE'RE ON A HOSTILE WORLD, WE HAVE NO MAPS, AND IF ANYONE WERE TO GET LOST--
WE HAVE OUR COMMUNICARDS.
LOOK, IRON MAN, AS FIELD LEADER, I INSIST WE--
I'M A FOUNDING MEMBER OF THE AVENGERS, CAPTAIN. THE ONLY ONE HERE. I FIGURE THAT GIVES ME THE RIGHT TO SUPERSEDE YOUR AUTHORITY OVER MY ACTIONS.
I'LL FLY RE-CONNAISSANCE, LET YOU KNOW WHAT I FIND.
ER, WAIT A SEC, SHELLHEAD!
LET ME TALK SOMETHIN' OVER WITH CAP.
I FEAR THIS DISSENSION IN OUR RANKS BODES ILL.
CAP, LEMME GO WITH HIM... I'LL KEEP AN EYE ON HIM. PLEASE?
GO.
SERSI, IF YOU'D BE SO KIND...?
YO, SHELLHEAD, WAIT UP! I'M COMIN' WITH YOU. US WEST COASTERS HAVE TO LOOK OUT FOR EACH OTHER!
I BROUGHT ME A FEW CAPS OF PYM'S RE-DUCING GAS-- I CAN RIDE ON YOUR BACK ANT-SIZED!

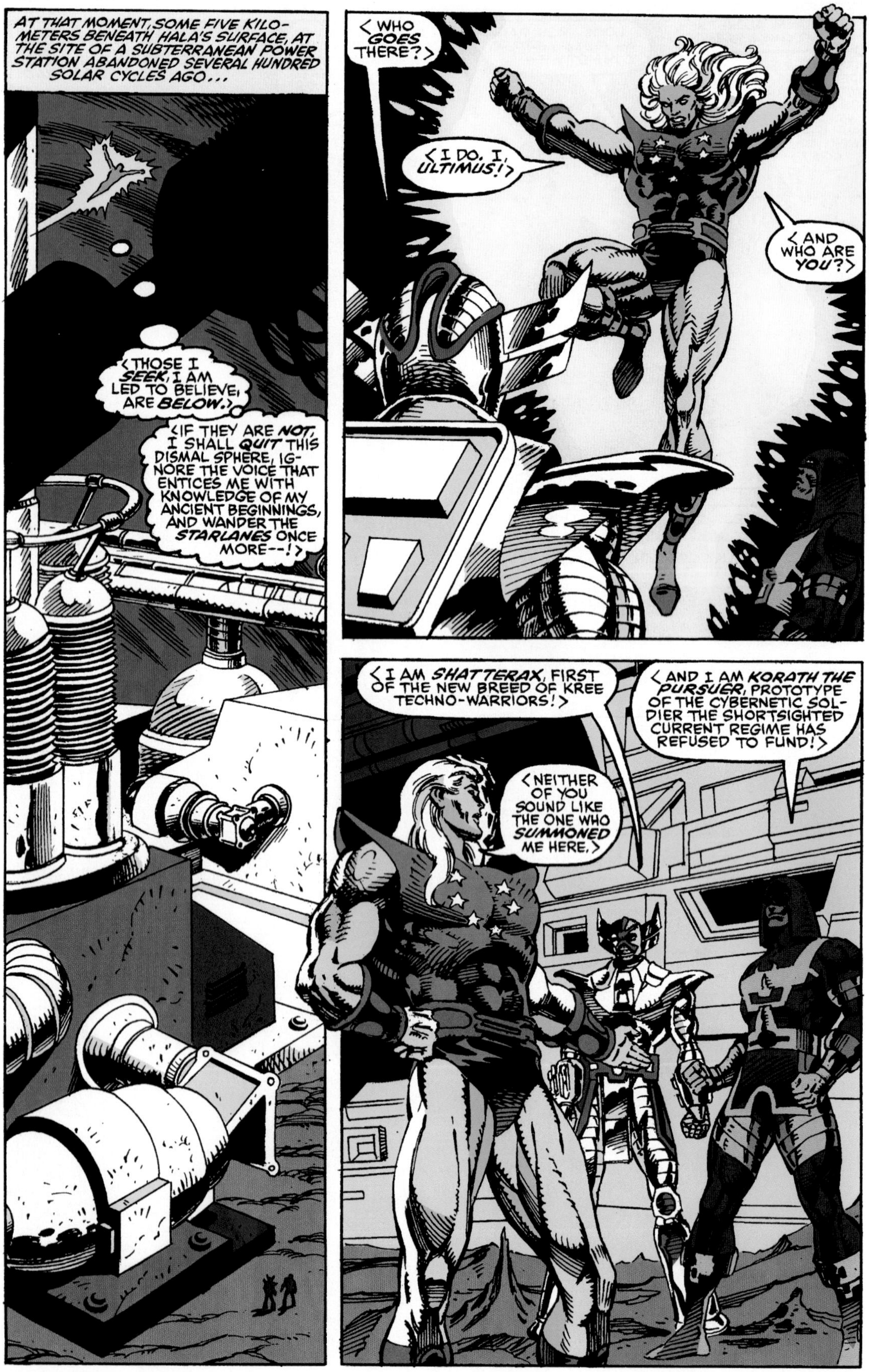
AT THAT MOMENT, SOME FIVE KILOMETERS BENEATH HALA'S SURFACE, AT THE SITE OF A SUBTERRANEAN POWER STATION ABANDONED SEVERAL HUNDRED SOLAR CYCLES AGO...
<THOSE I SEEK, I AM LED TO BELIEVE, ARE BELOW.>
<IF THEY ARE NOT, I SHALL QUIT THIS DISMAL SPHERE, IGNORE THE VOICE THAT ENTICES ME WITH KNOWLEDGE OF MY ANCIENT BEGINNINGS, AND WANDER THE STARLANES ONCE MORE--!>
<WHO GOES THERE?>
<I DO. I, ULTIMUS!>
<AND WHO ARE YOU?>
<I AM SHATTERAX, FIRST OF THE NEW BREED OF KREE TECHNO-WARRIORS!>
<AND I AM KORATH THE PURSUER, PROTOTYPE OF THE CYBERNETIC SOLDIER THE SHORTSIGHTED CURRENT REGIME HAS REFUSED TO FUND!>
<NEITHER OF YOU SOUND LIKE THE ONE WHO SUMMONED ME HERE.>

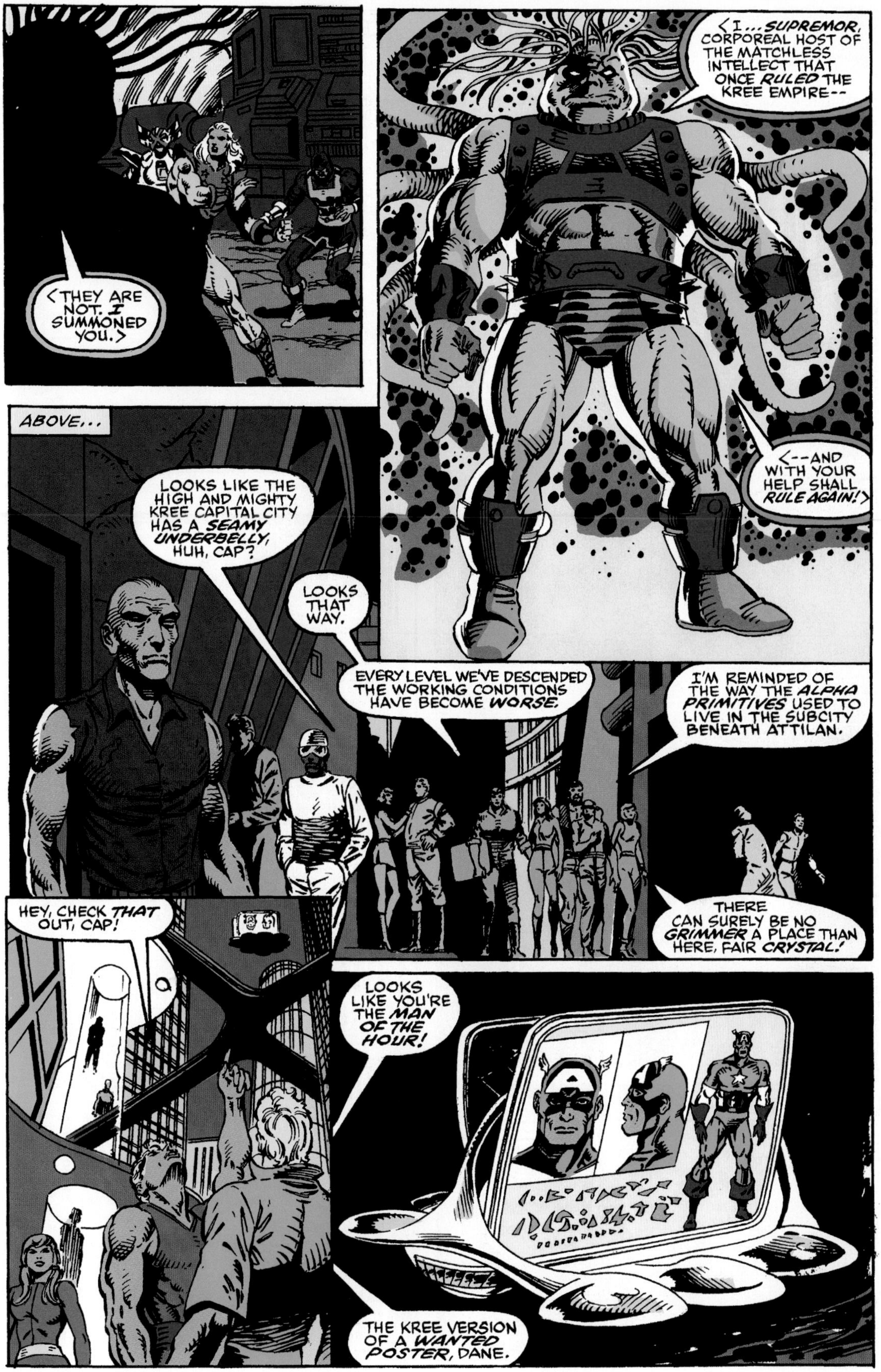

<THEY ARE NOT. I SUMMONED YOU.>
<I... SUPREMOR, CORPOREAL HOST OF THE MATCHLESS INTELLECT THAT ONCE RULED THE KREE EMPIRE--
<--AND WITH YOUR HELP SHALL RULE AGAIN!>
ABOVE...
LOOKS LIKE THE HIGH AND MIGHTY KREE CAPITAL CITY HAS A SEAMY UNDERBELLY, HUH, CAP?
LOOKS THAT WAY.
EVERY LEVEL WE'VE DESCENDED THE WORKING CONDITIONS HAVE BECOME WORSE.
I'M REMINDED OF THE WAY THE ALPHA PRIMITIVES USED TO LIVE IN THE SUBCITY BENEATH ATTILAN.
THERE CAN SURELY BE NO GRIMMER A PLACE THAN HERE, FAIR CRYSTAL!
HEY, CHECK THAT OUT, CAP!
LOOKS LIKE YOU'RE THE MAN OF THE HOUR!
THE KREE VERSION OF A WANTED POSTER, DANE.

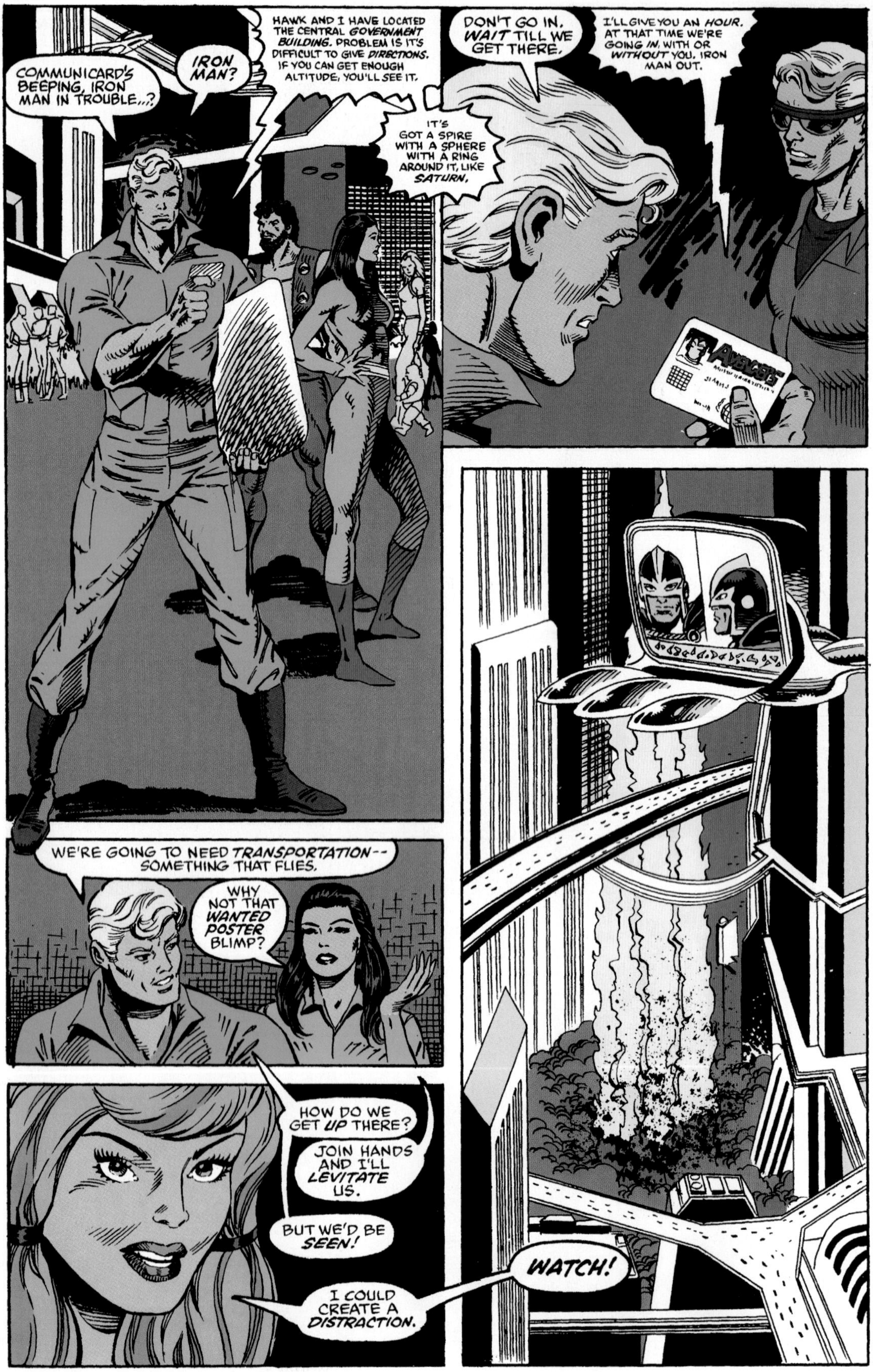
COMMUNICARD'S BEEPING, IRON MAN IN TROUBLE...?
IRON MAN?
HAWK AND I HAVE LOCATED THE CENTRAL GOVERNMENT BUILDING. PROBLEM IS IT'S DIFFICULT TO GIVE DIRECTIONS. IF YOU CAN GET ENOUGH ALTITUDE, YOU'LL SEE IT.
IT'S GOT A SPIRE WITH A SPHERE WITH A RING AROUND IT, LIKE SATURN.
DON'T GO IN. WAIT TILL WE GET THERE.
I'LL GIVE YOU AN HOUR. AT THAT TIME WE'RE GOING IN, WITH OR WITHOUT YOU. IRON MAN OUT.
WE'RE GOING TO NEED TRANSPORTATION-- SOMETHING THAT FLIES.
WHY NOT THAT WANTED POSTER BLIMP?
HOW DO WE GET UP THERE?
JOIN HANDS AND I'LL LEVITATE US.
BUT WE'D BE SEEN!
I COULD CREATE A DISTRACTION.
WATCH!

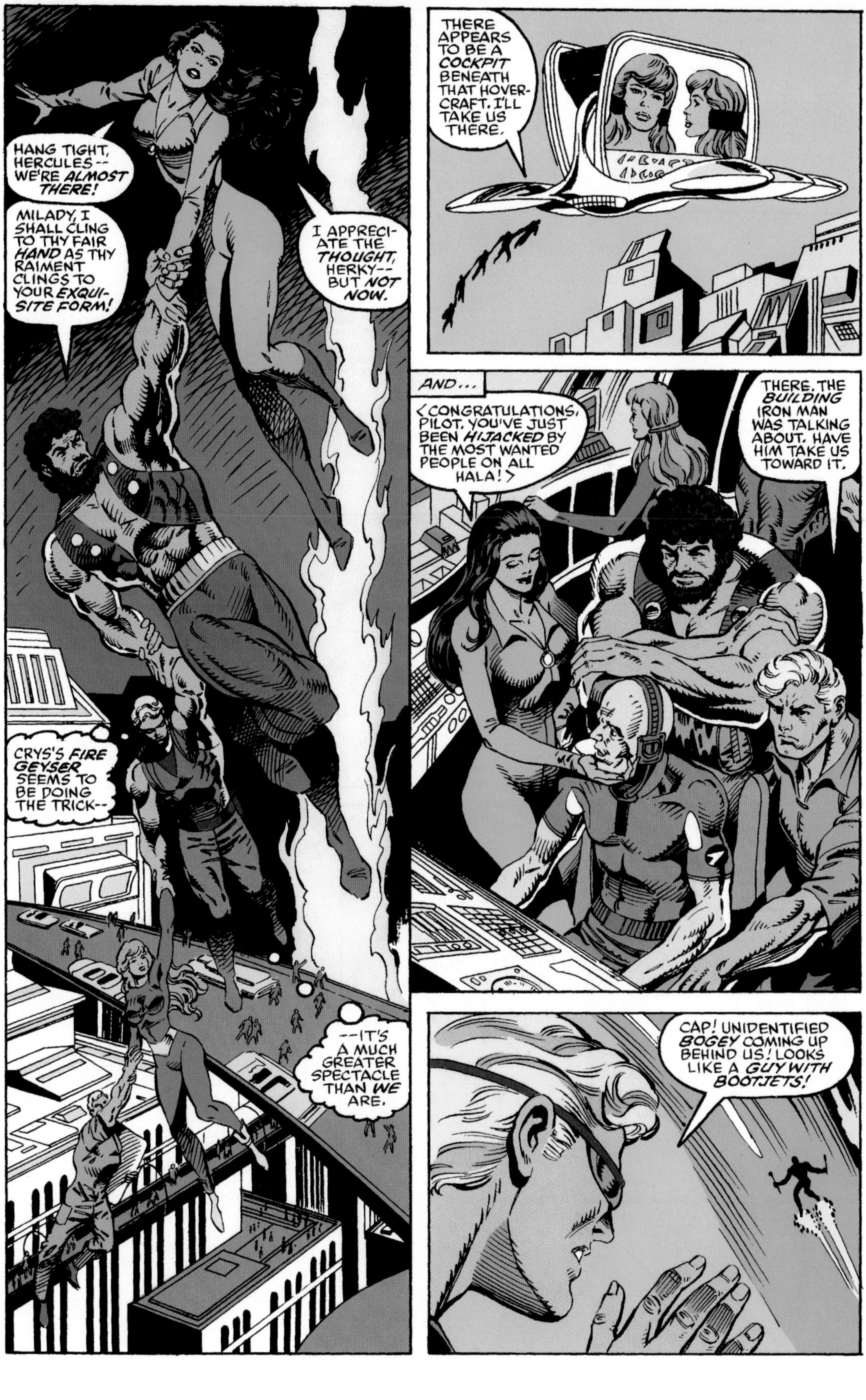
HANG TIGHT, HERCULES-- WE'RE ALMOST THERE!
MILADY, I SHALL CLING TO THY FAIR HAND AS THY RAIMENT CLINGS TO YOUR EXQUISITE FORM!
I APPRECIATE THE THOUGHT, HERKY-- BUT NOT NOW.
CRYS'S FIRE GEYSER SEEMS TO BE DOING THE TRICK--
--IT'S A MUCH GREATER SPECTACLE THAN WE ARE.
THERE APPEARS TO BE A COCKPIT BENEATH THAT HOVER-CRAFT. I'LL TAKE US THERE.
AND...
<CONGRATULATIONS, PILOT. YOU'VE JUST BEEN HIJACKED BY THE MOST WANTED PEOPLE ON ALL HALA!>
THERE. THE BUILDING IRON MAN WAS TALKING ABOUT. HAVE HIM TAKE US TOWARD IT.
CAP! UNIDENTIFIED BOGEY COMING UP BEHIND US! LOOKS LIKE A GUY WITH BOOTJETS!

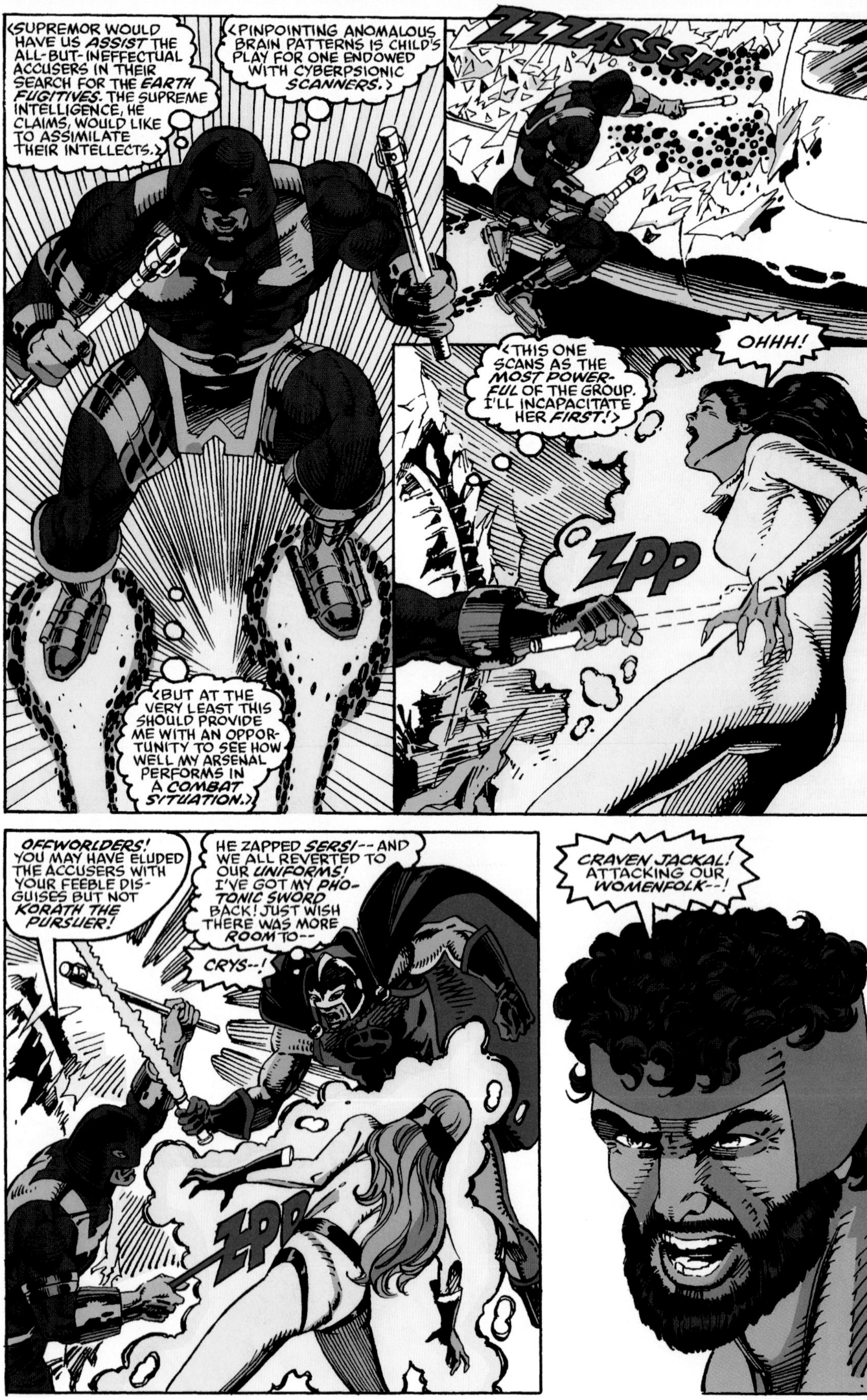
ZZZASSSH
<SUPREMOR WOULD HAVE US ASSIST THE ALL-BUT-INEFFECTUAL ACCUSERS IN THEIR SEARCH FOR THE EARTH FUGITIVES. THE SUPREME INTELLIGENCE, HE CLAIMS, WOULD LIKE TO ASSIMILATE THEIR INTELLECTS.>
<PINPOINTING ANOMALOUS BRAIN PATTERNS IS CHILD'S PLAY FOR ONE ENDOWED WITH CYBERPSIONIC SCANNERS.>
<BUT AT THE VERY LEAST THIS SHOULD PROVIDE ME WITH AN OPPORTUNITY TO SEE HOW WELL MY ARSENAL PERFORMS IN A COMBAT SITUATION.>
<THIS ONE SCANS AS THE MOST POWERFUL OF THE GROUP. I'LL INCAPACITATE HER FIRST!>
OHHH!
ZPP
OFFWORLDERS! YOU MAY HAVE ELUDED THE ACCUSERS WITH YOUR FEEBLE DISGUISES BUT NOT KORATH THE PURSUER!
HE ZAPPED SERSI-- AND WE ALL REVERTED TO OUR UNIFORMS! I'VE GOT MY PHOTONIC SWORD BACK! JUST WISH THERE WAS MORE ROOM TO--
CRYS--!
ZPP
CRAVEN JACKAL! ATTACKING OUR WOMENFOLK--!

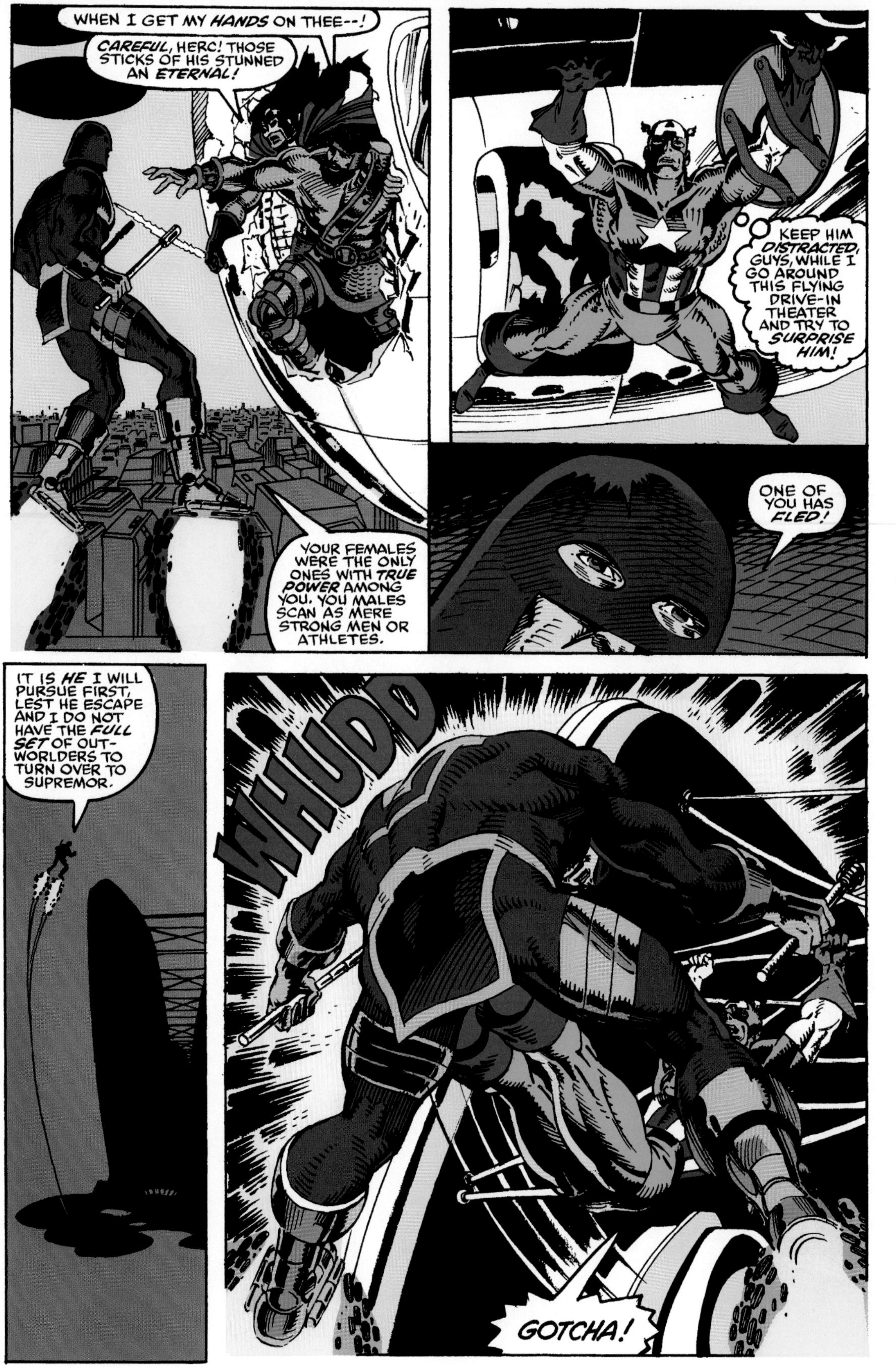

WHEN I GET MY HANDS ON THEE--!
CAREFUL, HERC! THOSE STICKS OF HIS STUNNED AN ETERNAL!
YOUR FEMALES WERE THE ONLY ONES WITH TRUE POWER AMONG YOU. YOU MALES SCAN AS MERE STRONG MEN OR ATHLETES.
KEEP HIM DISTRACTED, GUYS, WHILE I GO AROUND THIS FLYING DRIVE-IN THEATER AND TRY TO SURPRISE HIM!
ONE OF YOU HAS FLED!
IT IS HE I WILL PURSUE FIRST, LEST HE ESCAPE AND I DO NOT HAVE THE FULL SET OF OUT-WORLDERS TO TURN OVER TO SUPREMOR.
WHUDD
GOTCHA!

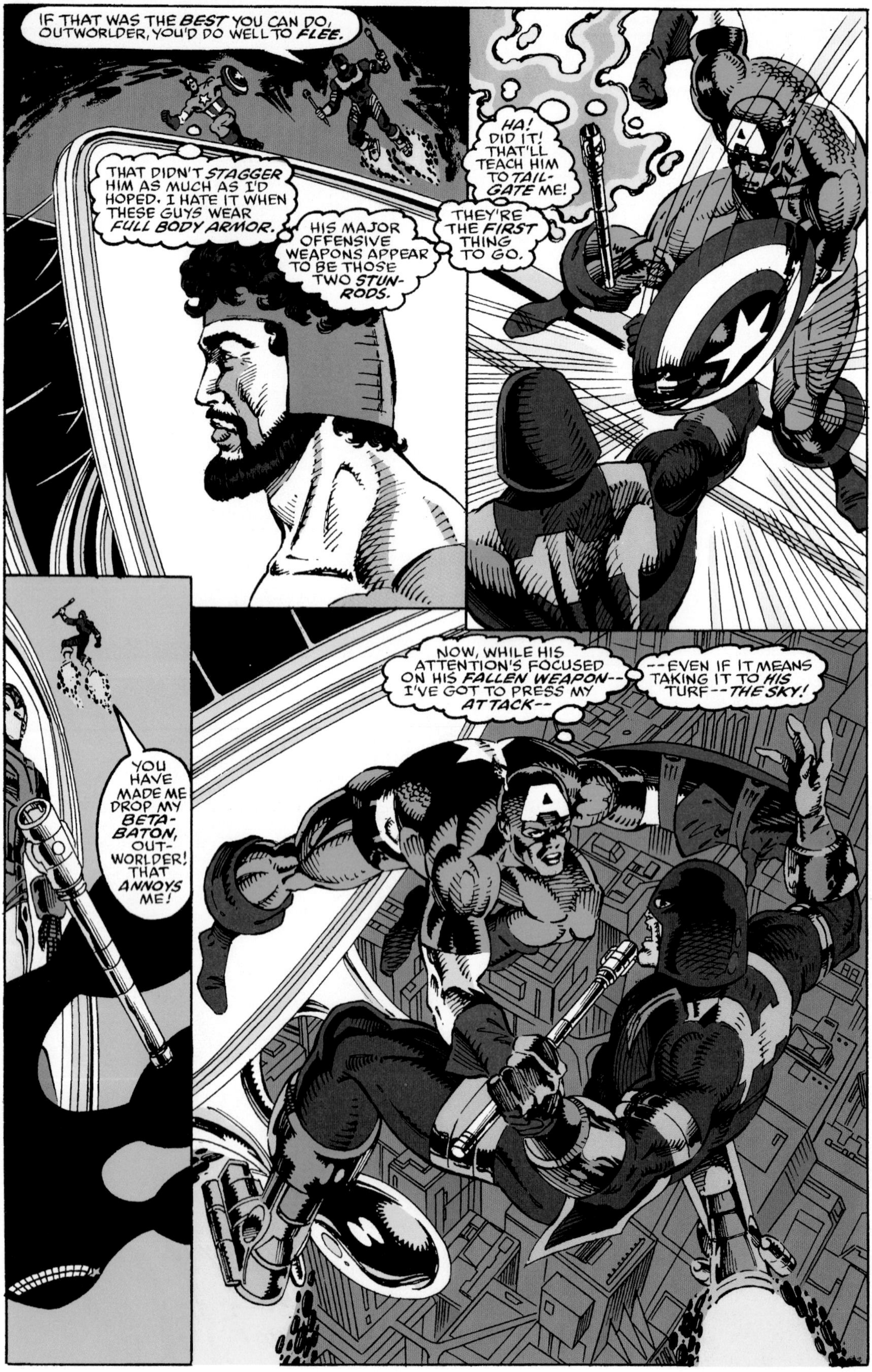
IF THAT WAS THE BEST YOU CAN DO, OUTWORLDER, YOU'D DO WELL TO FLEE.
THAT DIDN'T STAGGER HIM AS MUCH AS I'D HOPED. I HATE IT WHEN THESE GUYS WEAR FULL BODY ARMOR.
HIS MAJOR OFFENSIVE WEAPONS APPEAR TO BE THOSE TWO STUN-RODS.
THEY'RE THE FIRST THING TO GO.
HA! DID IT! THAT'LL TEACH HIM TO TAIL-GATE ME!
YOU HAVE MADE ME DROP MY BETA-BATON, OUT-WORLDER! THAT ANNOYS ME!
NOW, WHILE HIS ATTENTION'S FOCUSED ON HIS FALLEN WEAPON-- I'VE GOT TO PRESS MY ATTACK--
--EVEN IF IT MEANS TAKING IT TO HIS TURF--THE SKY!

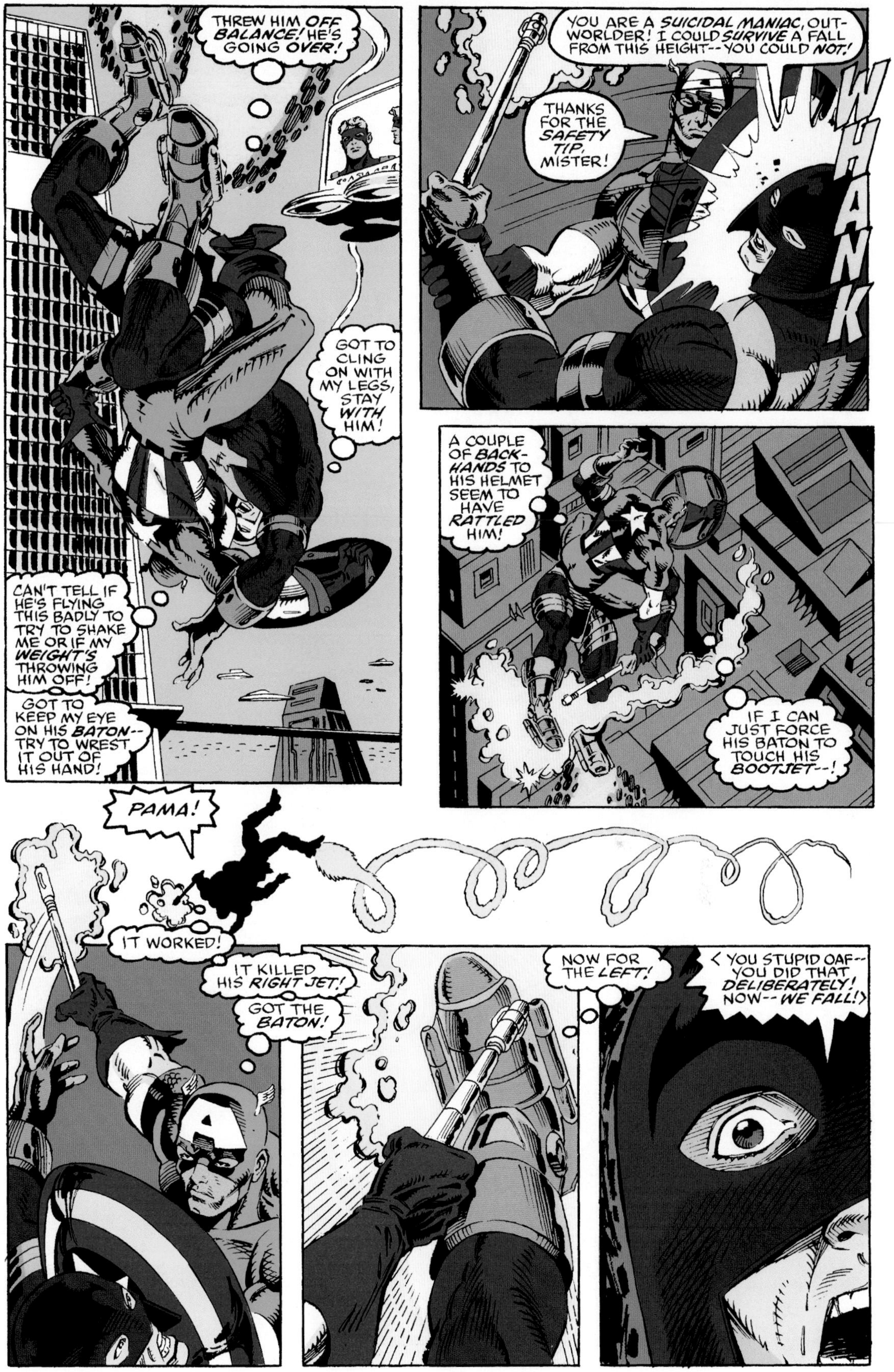

THREW HIM OFF BALANCE! HE'S GOING OVER!
GOT TO CLING ON WITH MY LEGS, STAY WITH HIM!
CAN'T TELL IF HE'S FLYING THIS BADLY TO TRY TO SHAKE ME OR IF MY WEIGHT'S THROWING HIM OFF!
GOT TO KEEP MY EYE ON HIS BATON-- TRY TO WREST IT OUT OF HIS HAND!
YOU ARE A SUICIDAL MANIAC, OUTWORLDER! I COULD SURVIVE A FALL FROM THIS HEIGHT--YOU COULD NOT!
THANKS FOR THE SAFETY TIP, MISTER!
WHANK
A COUPLE OF BACK-HANDS TO HIS HELMET SEEM TO HAVE RATTLED HIM!
IF I CAN JUST FORCE HIS BATON TO TOUCH HIS BOOTJET--!
PAMA!
IT WORKED!
IT KILLED HIS RIGHT JET!
GOT THE BATON!
NOW FOR THE LEFT!
< YOU STUPID OAF-- YOU DID THAT DELIBERATELY! NOW--WE FALL!>

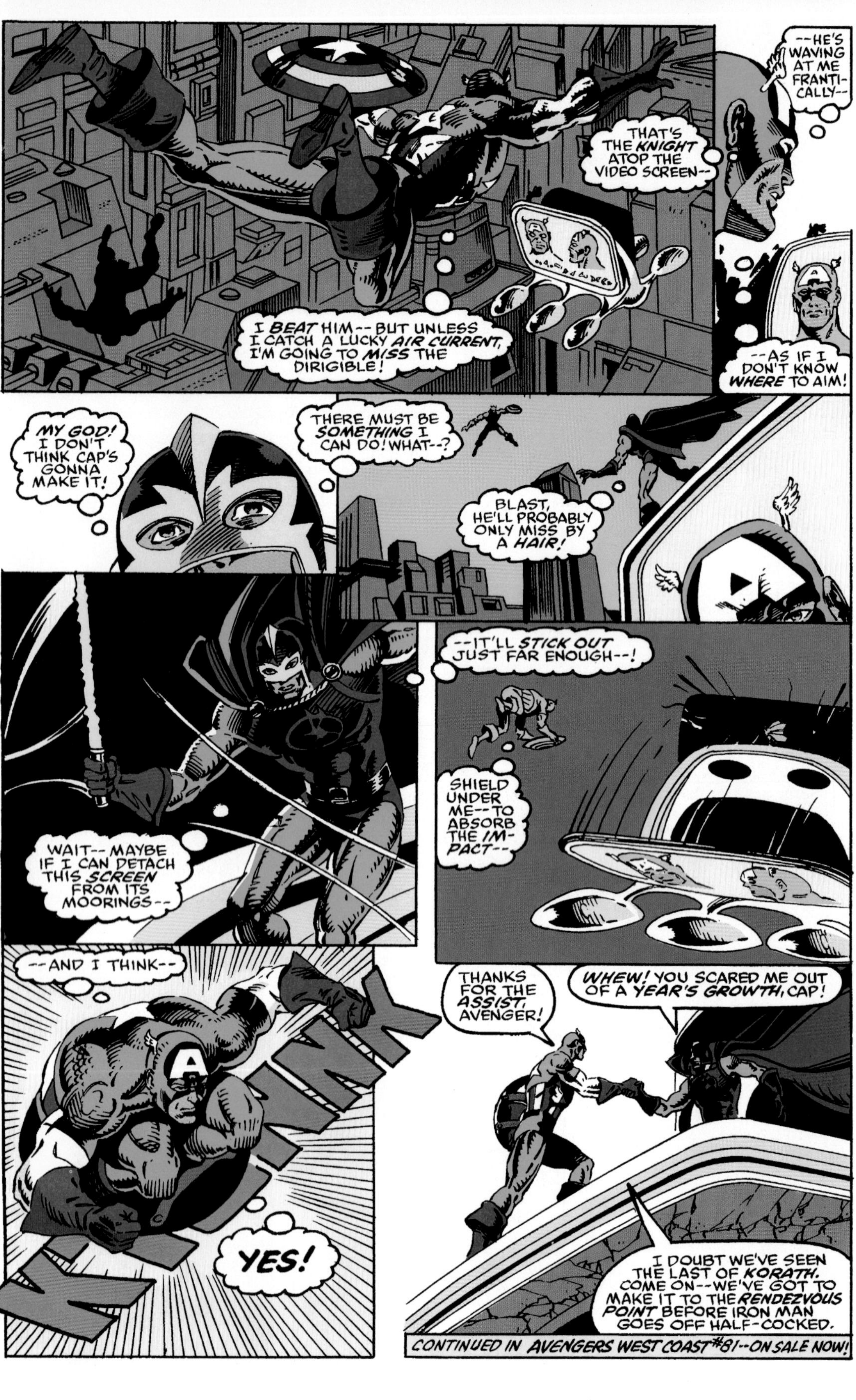

--HE'S WAVING AT ME FRANTICALLY--
THAT'S THE KNIGHT ATOP THE VIDEO SCREEN--
I BEAT HIM--BUT UNLESS I CATCH A LUCKY AIR CURRENT, I'M GOING TO MISS THE DIRIGIBLE!
--AS IF I DON'T KNOW WHERE TO AIM!
MY GOD! I DON'T THINK CAP'S GONNA MAKE IT!
THERE MUST BE SOMETHING I CAN DO! WHAT--?
BLAST, HE'LL PROBABLY ONLY MISS BY A HAIR!
WAIT--MAYBE IF I CAN DETACH THIS SCREEN FROM ITS MOORINGS--
--IT'LL STICK OUT JUST FAR ENOUGH--!
SHIELD UNDER ME--TO ABSORB THE IMPACT--
--AND I THINK--
YES!
THANKS FOR THE ASSIST, AVENGER!
WHEW! YOU SCARED ME OUT OF A YEAR'S GROWTH, CAP!
I DOUBT WE'VE SEEN THE LAST OF KORATH. COME ON--WE'VE GOT TO MAKE IT TO THE RENDEZVOUS POINT BEFORE IRON MAN GOES OFF HALF-COCKED.
CONTINUED IN AVENGERS WEST COAST #81--ON SALE NOW!

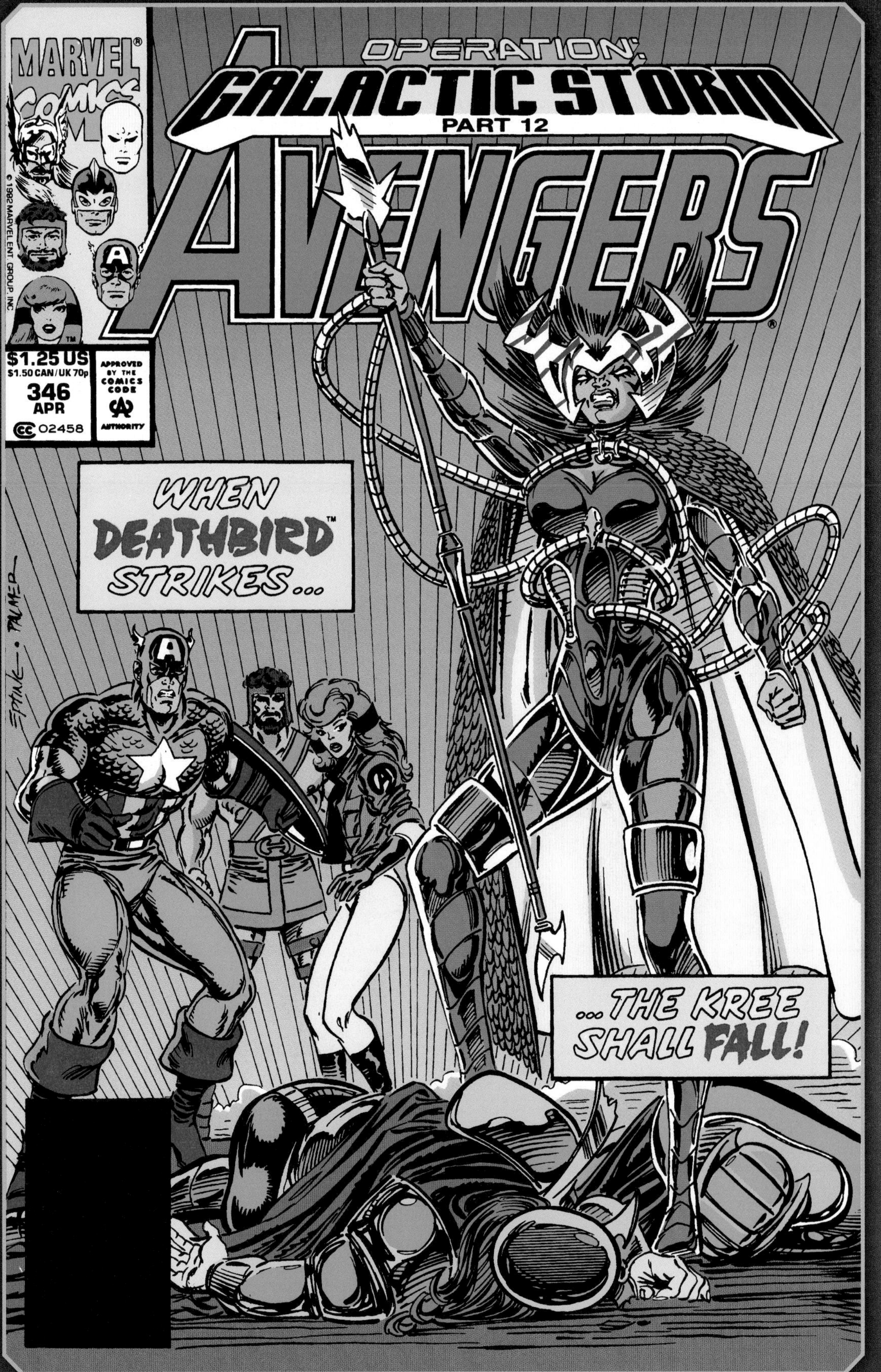
MARVEL COMICS
OPERATION: GALACTIC STORM
PART 12
AVENGERS
© 1992 MARVEL ENT. GROUP, INC.
$1.25 US
$1.50 CAN/UK 70p
346
APR
02458
APPROVED BY THE COMICS CODE AUTHORITY
WHEN DEATHBIRD™ STRIKES...
...THE KREE SHALL FALL!

Stan Lee PRESENTS:

OPERATION: GALACTIC STORM

PART 12

THE MIGHTY AVENGERS!

*TWO GALACTIC EMPIRES ARE AT WAR — THE MILITARISTIC **KREE** AND THE MATRIARCHAL **SHI'AR** — AND THE EARTH IS CAUGHT IN THE MIDDLE. ONE CADRE OF EARTH'S MIGHTIEST HEROES HAS JOURNEYED TO THE HEART OF THE KREE EMPIRE IN A DESPERATE ATTEMPT TO EASE TENSIONS. THEIR EFFORTS ARE ABOUT TO BECOME **MORE** DESPERATE. . .*

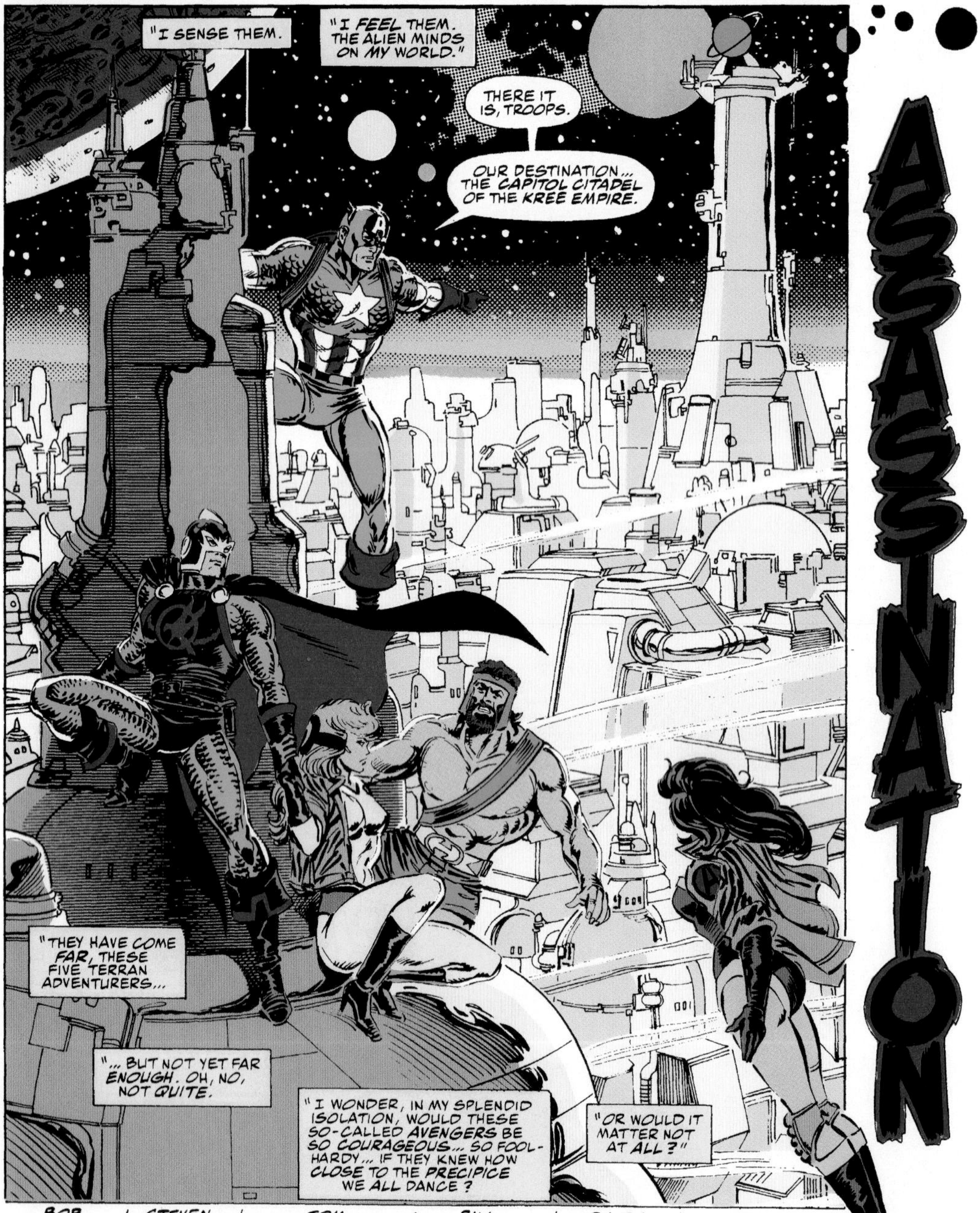
"I SENSE THEM.
"I FEEL THEM. THE ALIEN MINDS ON MY WORLD."
THERE IT IS, TROOPS.
OUR DESTINATION... THE CAPITOL CITADEL OF THE KREE EMPIRE.
"THEY HAVE COME FAR, THESE FIVE TERRAN ADVENTURERS...
"... BUT NOT YET FAR ENOUGH. OH, NO, NOT QUITE.
"I WONDER, IN MY SPLENDID ISOLATION, WOULD THESE SO-CALLED AVENGERS BE SO COURAGEOUS... SO FOOL-HARDY... IF THEY KNEW HOW CLOSE TO THE PRECIPICE WE ALL DANCE?
"OR WOULD IT MATTER NOT AT ALL?"
ASSASSINATION

BOB HARRAS WRITER / STEVEN EPTING PENCILER / TOM PALMER INKER/COLORIST / BILL OAKLEY LETTERER / RALPH MACCHIO EDITOR / TOM DEFALCO EDITOR IN CHIEF

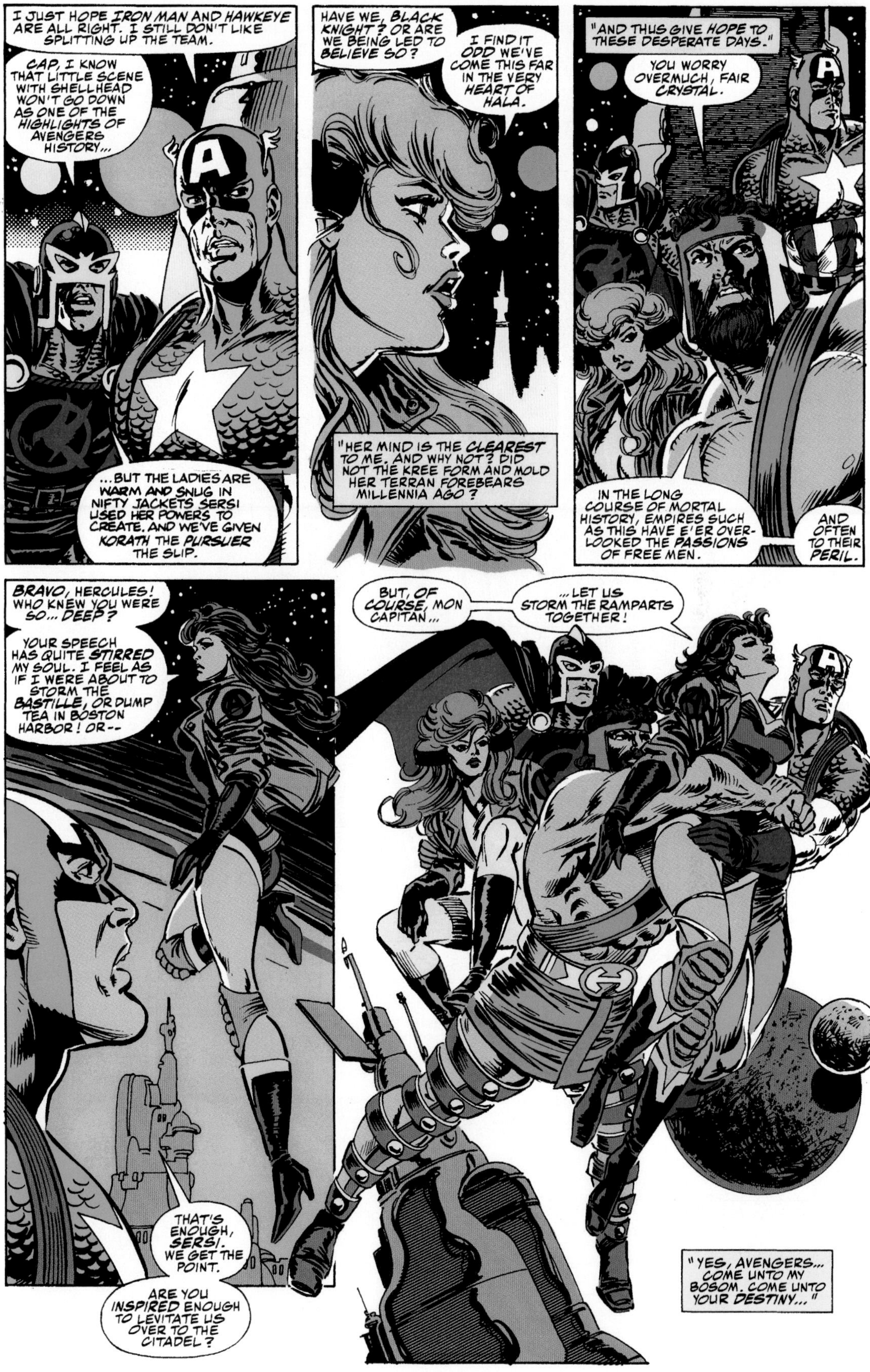
I JUST HOPE IRON MAN AND HAWKEYE ARE ALL RIGHT. I STILL DON'T LIKE SPLITTING UP THE TEAM.
CAP, I KNOW THAT LITTLE SCENE WITH SHELLHEAD WON'T GO DOWN AS ONE OF THE HIGHLIGHTS OF AVENGERS HISTORY...
...BUT THE LADIES ARE WARM AND SNUG IN NIFTY JACKETS SERSI USED HER POWERS TO CREATE. AND WE'VE GIVEN KORATH THE PURSUER THE SLIP.
HAVE WE, BLACK KNIGHT? OR ARE WE BEING LED TO BELIEVE SO?
I FIND IT ODD WE'VE COME THIS FAR IN THE VERY HEART OF HALA.
"HER MIND IS THE CLEAREST TO ME. AND WHY NOT? DID NOT THE KREE FORM AND MOLD HER TERRAN FOREBEARS MILLENNIA AGO?
"AND THUS GIVE HOPE TO THESE DESPERATE DAYS."
YOU WORRY OVERMUCH, FAIR CRYSTAL.
IN THE LONG COURSE OF MORTAL HISTORY, EMPIRES SUCH AS THIS HAVE E'ER OVERLOOKED THE PASSIONS OF FREE MEN.
AND OFTEN TO THEIR PERIL.
BRAVO, HERCULES! WHO KNEW YOU WERE SO... DEEP?
YOUR SPEECH HAS QUITE STIRRED MY SOUL. I FEEL AS IF I WERE ABOUT TO STORM THE BASTILLE, OR DUMP TEA IN BOSTON HARBOR! OR--
THAT'S ENOUGH, SERSI. WE GET THE POINT.
ARE YOU INSPIRED ENOUGH TO LEVITATE US OVER TO THE CITADEL?
BUT, OF COURSE, MON CAPITAN...
...LET US STORM THE RAMPARTS TOGETHER!
"YES, AVENGERS... COME UNTO MY BOSOM. COME UNTO YOUR DESTINY..."

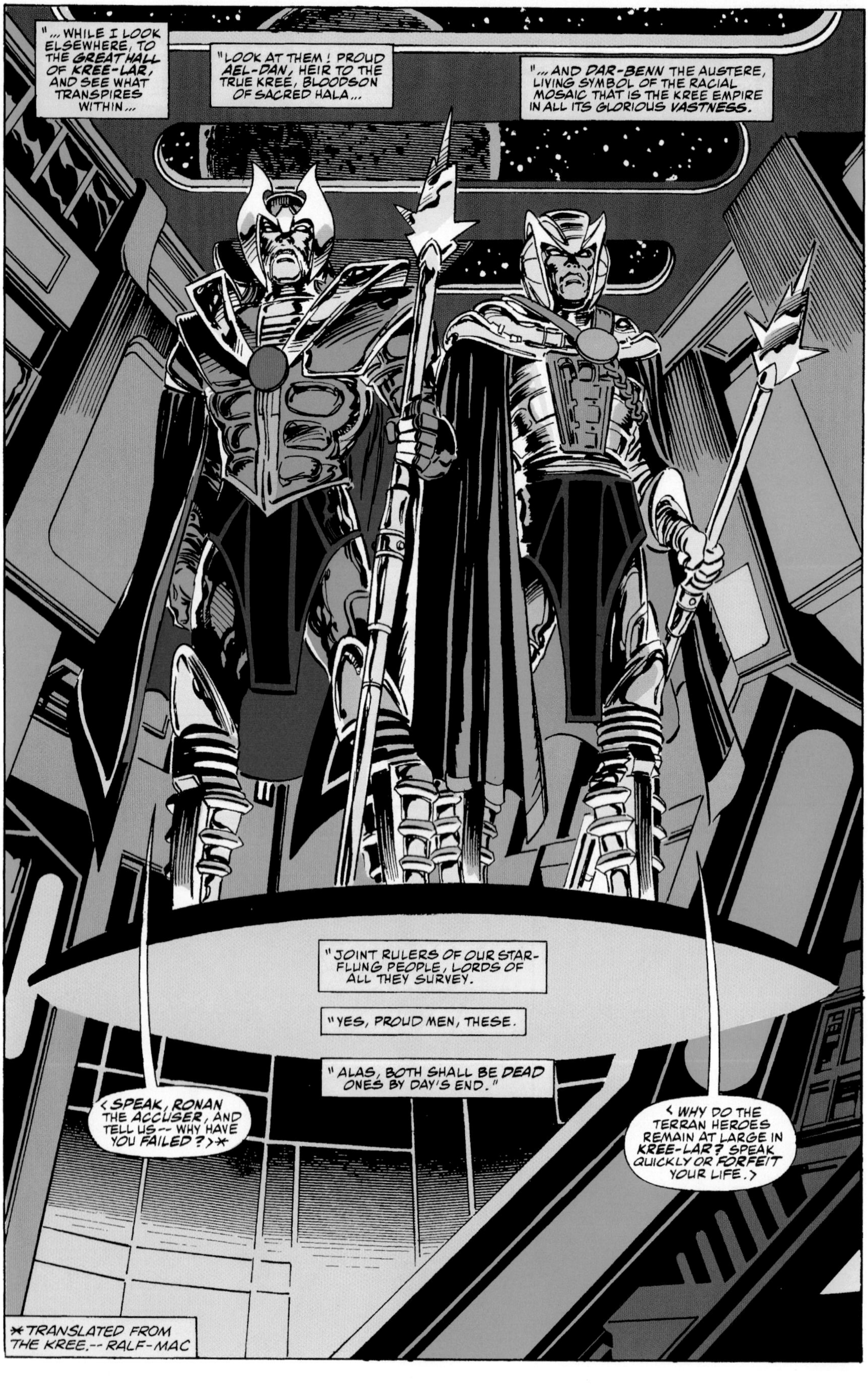
"... WHILE I LOOK ELSEWHERE, TO THE GREAT HALL OF KREE-LAR, AND SEE WHAT TRANSPIRES WITHIN...
"LOOK AT THEM! PROUD AEL-DAN, HEIR TO THE TRUE KREE, BLOODSON OF SACRED HALA...
"... AND DAR-BENN THE AUSTERE, LIVING SYMBOL OF THE RACIAL MOSAIC THAT IS THE KREE EMPIRE IN ALL ITS GLORIOUS VASTNESS.
"JOINT RULERS OF OUR STAR-FLUNG PEOPLE, LORDS OF ALL THEY SURVEY.
"YES, PROUD MEN, THESE.
"ALAS, BOTH SHALL BE DEAD ONES BY DAY'S END."
< SPEAK, RONAN THE ACCUSER, AND TELL US -- WHY HAVE YOU FAILED? >*
< WHY DO THE TERRAN HEROES REMAIN AT LARGE IN KREE-LAR? SPEAK QUICKLY OR FORFEIT YOUR LIFE. >
*TRANSLATED FROM THE KREE. -- RALF-MAC

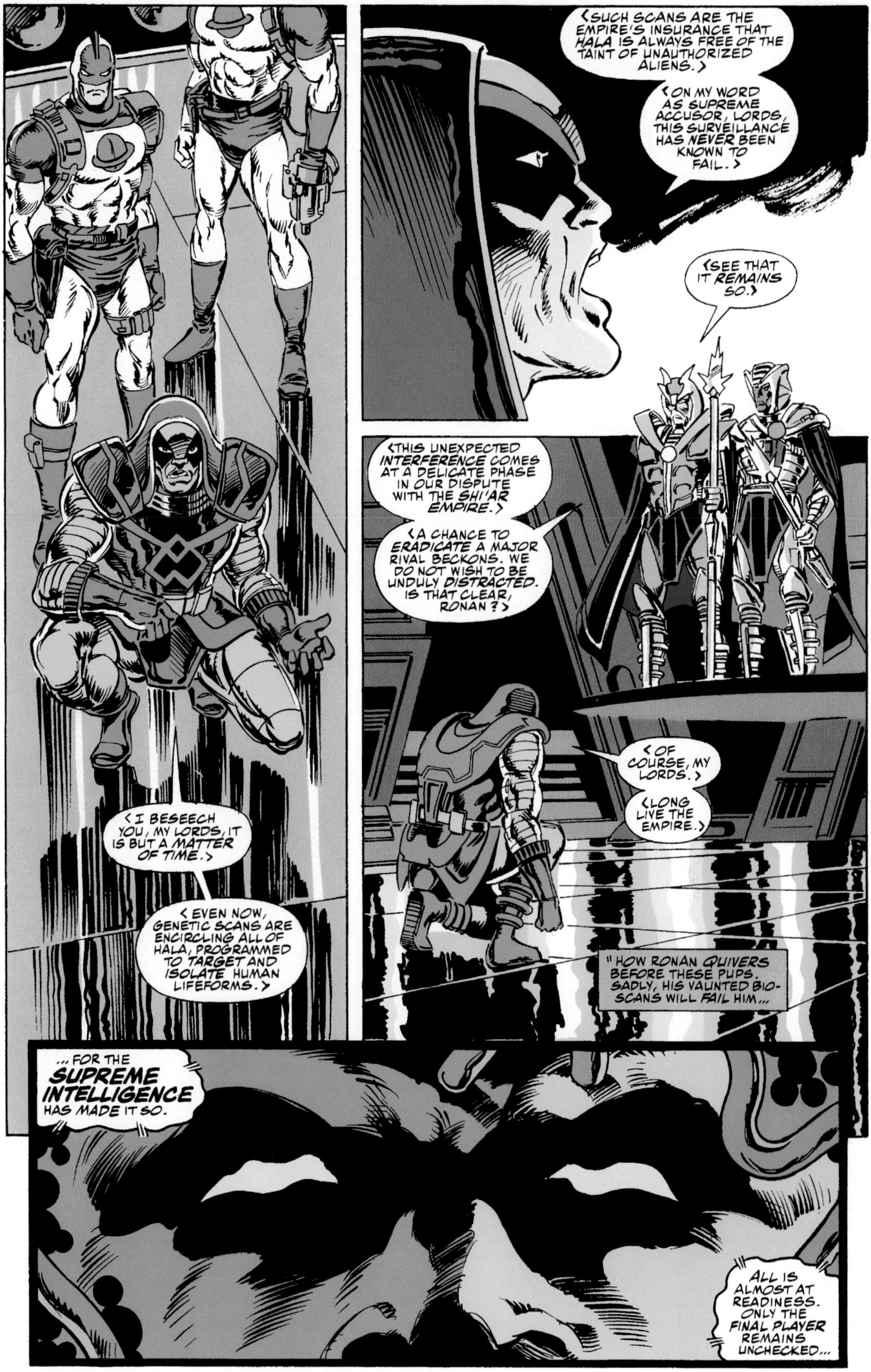

< I BESEECH YOU, MY LORDS, IT IS BUT A MATTER OF TIME. >
< EVEN NOW, GENETIC SCANS ARE ENCIRCLING ALL OF HALA, PROGRAMMED TO TARGET AND ISOLATE HUMAN LIFEFORMS. >
< SUCH SCANS ARE THE EMPIRE'S INSURANCE THAT HALA IS ALWAYS FREE OF THE TAINT OF UNAUTHORIZED ALIENS. >
< ON MY WORD AS SUPREME ACCUSOR, LORDS, THIS SURVEILLANCE HAS NEVER BEEN KNOWN TO FAIL. >
< SEE THAT IT REMAINS SO. >
< THIS UNEXPECTED INTERFERENCE COMES AT A DELICATE PHASE IN OUR DISPUTE WITH THE SHI'AR EMPIRE. >
< A CHANCE TO ERADICATE A MAJOR RIVAL BECKONS. WE DO NOT WISH TO BE UNDULY DISTRACTED. IS THAT CLEAR, RONAN? >
< OF COURSE, MY LORDS. >
< LONG LIVE THE EMPIRE. >
" HOW RONAN QUIVERS BEFORE THESE PUPS. SADLY, HIS VAUNTED BIO-SCANS WILL FAIL HIM...
... FOR THE SUPREME INTELLIGENCE HAS MADE IT SO.
ALL IS ALMOST AT READINESS. ONLY THE FINAL PLAYER REMAINS UNCHECKED...

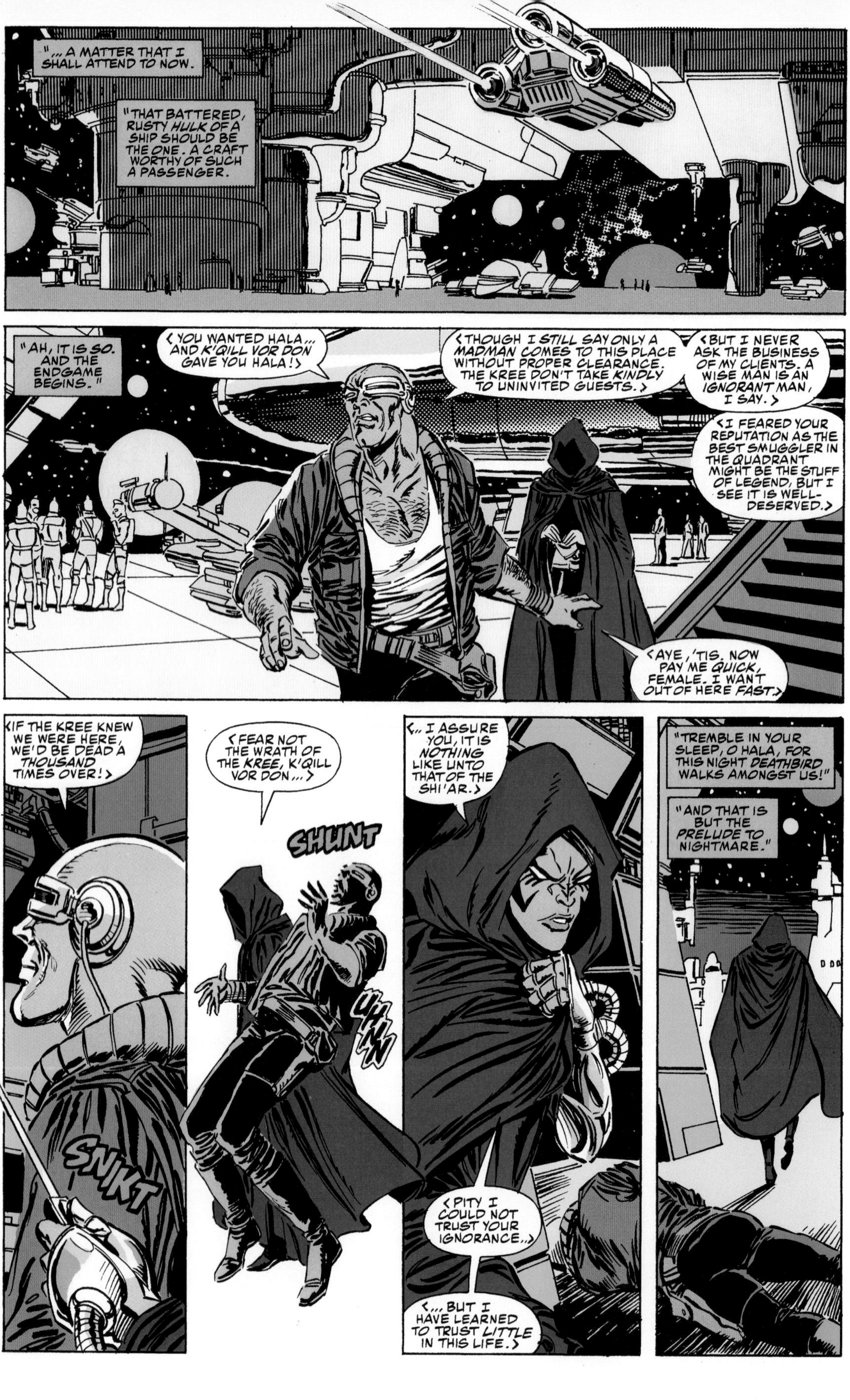
"... A MATTER THAT I SHALL ATTEND TO NOW.
"THAT BATTERED, RUSTY HULK OF A SHIP SHOULD BE THE ONE. A CRAFT WORTHY OF SUCH A PASSENGER.
"AH, IT IS SO. AND THE ENDGAME BEGINS."
<YOU WANTED HALA... AND K'QILL VOR DON GAVE YOU HALA!>
<THOUGH I STILL SAY ONLY A MADMAN COMES TO THIS PLACE WITHOUT PROPER CLEARANCE. THE KREE DON'T TAKE KINDLY TO UNINVITED GUESTS.>
<BUT I NEVER ASK THE BUSINESS OF MY CLIENTS. A WISE MAN IS AN IGNORANT MAN, I SAY.>
<I FEARED YOUR REPUTATION AS THE BEST SMUGGLER IN THE QUADRANT MIGHT BE THE STUFF OF LEGEND, BUT I SEE IT IS WELL-DESERVED.>
<AYE, 'TIS. NOW PAY ME QUICK, FEMALE. I WANT OUT OF HERE FAST.>
<IF THE KREE KNEW WE WERE HERE, WE'D BE DEAD A THOUSAND TIMES OVER!>
SNIKT
<FEAR NOT THE WRATH OF THE KREE, K'QILL VOR DON...>
SHUNT
UHHN
<... I ASSURE YOU, IT IS NOTHING LIKE UNTO THAT OF THE SHI'AR.>
<PITY I COULD NOT TRUST YOUR IGNORANCE...>
<... BUT I HAVE LEARNED TO TRUST LITTLE IN THIS LIFE.>
"TREMBLE IN YOUR SLEEP, O HALA, FOR THIS NIGHT DEATHBIRD WALKS AMONGST US!"
"AND THAT IS BUT THE PRELUDE TO NIGHTMARE."

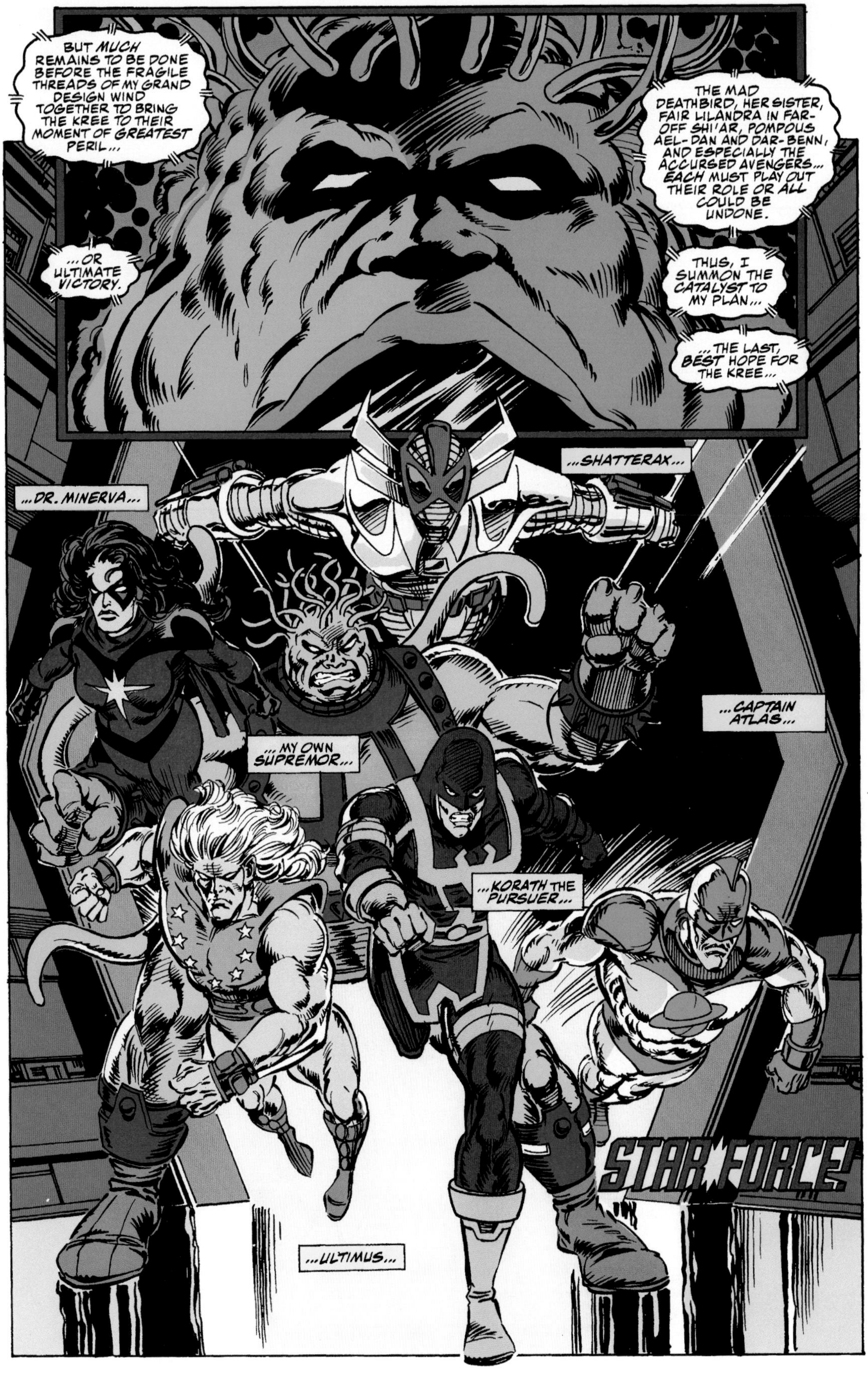

BUT MUCH REMAINS TO BE DONE BEFORE THE FRAGILE THREADS OF MY GRAND DESIGN WIND TOGETHER TO BRING THE KREE TO THEIR MOMENT OF GREATEST PERIL...
...OR ULTIMATE VICTORY.
THE MAD DEATHBIRD, HER SISTER, FAIR LILANDRA IN FAR-OFF SHI'AR, POMPOUS AEL-DAN AND DAR-BENN, AND ESPECIALLY THE ACCURSED AVENGERS... EACH MUST PLAY OUT THEIR ROLE OR ALL COULD BE UNDONE.
THUS, I SUMMON THE CATALYST TO MY PLAN...
...THE LAST, BEST HOPE FOR THE KREE...
...DR. MINERVA...
...SHATTERAX...
...MY OWN SUPREMOR...
...CAPTAIN ATLAS...
...KORATH THE PURSUER...
...ULTIMUS...
STAR FORCE!

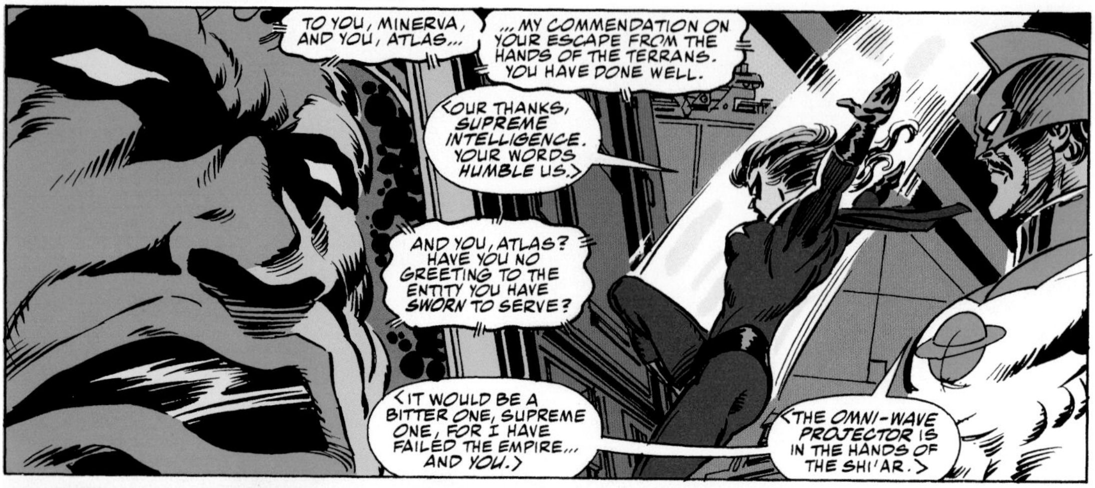
TO YOU, MINERVA, AND YOU, ATLAS...
...MY COMMENDATION ON YOUR ESCAPE FROM THE HANDS OF THE TERRANS. YOU HAVE DONE WELL.
<OUR THANKS, SUPREME INTELLIGENCE. YOUR WORDS HUMBLE US.>
AND YOU, ATLAS? HAVE YOU NO GREETING TO THE ENTITY YOU HAVE SWORN TO SERVE?
<IT WOULD BE A BITTER ONE, SUPREME ONE, FOR I HAVE FAILED THE EMPIRE... AND YOU.>
<THE OMNI-WAVE PROJECTOR IS IN THE HANDS OF THE SHI'AR.>

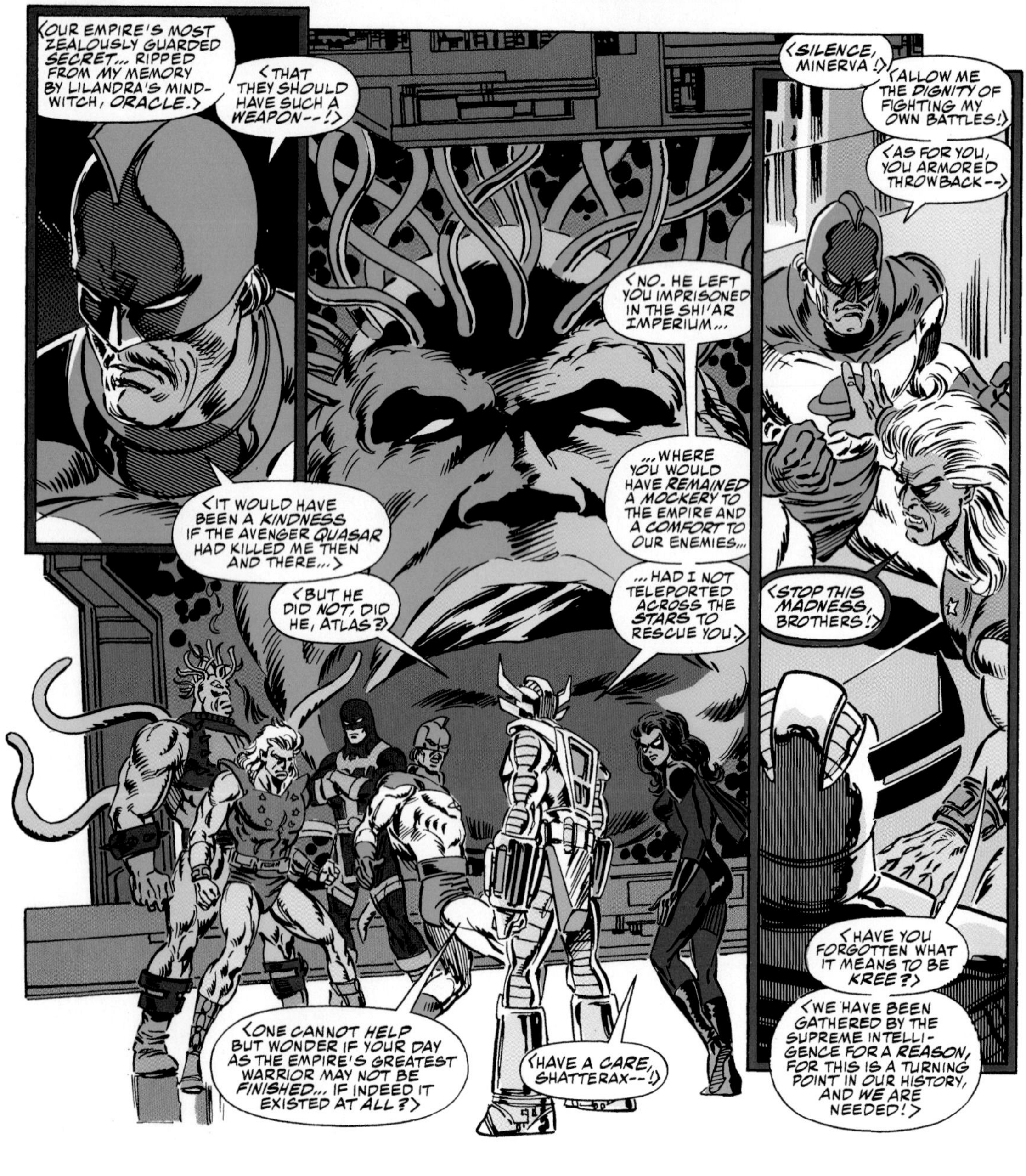
<OUR EMPIRE'S MOST ZEALOUSLY GUARDED SECRET... RIPPED FROM MY MEMORY BY LILANDRA'S MIND-WITCH, ORACLE.>
<THAT THEY SHOULD HAVE SUCH A WEAPON--!>
<IT WOULD HAVE BEEN A KINDNESS IF THE AVENGER QUASAR HAD KILLED ME THEN AND THERE...>
<BUT HE DID NOT, DID HE, ATLAS?>
<NO. HE LEFT YOU IMPRISONED IN THE SHI'AR IMPERIUM...
...WHERE YOU WOULD HAVE REMAINED A MOCKERY TO THE EMPIRE AND A COMFORT TO OUR ENEMIES...
...HAD I NOT TELEPORTED ACROSS THE STARS TO RESCUE YOU.>
<ONE CANNOT HELP BUT WONDER IF YOUR DAY AS THE EMPIRE'S GREATEST WARRIOR MAY NOT BE FINISHED... IF INDEED IT EXISTED AT ALL?>
<HAVE A CARE, SHATTERAX--!>
<SILENCE, MINERVA!>
<ALLOW ME THE DIGNITY OF FIGHTING MY OWN BATTLES!>
<AS FOR YOU, YOU ARMORED THROWBACK-->
<STOP THIS MADNESS, BROTHERS!>
<HAVE YOU FORGOTTEN WHAT IT MEANS TO BE KREE?>
<WE HAVE BEEN GATHERED BY THE SUPREME INTELLIGENCE FOR A REASON, FOR THIS IS A TURNING POINT IN OUR HISTORY, AND WE ARE NEEDED!>

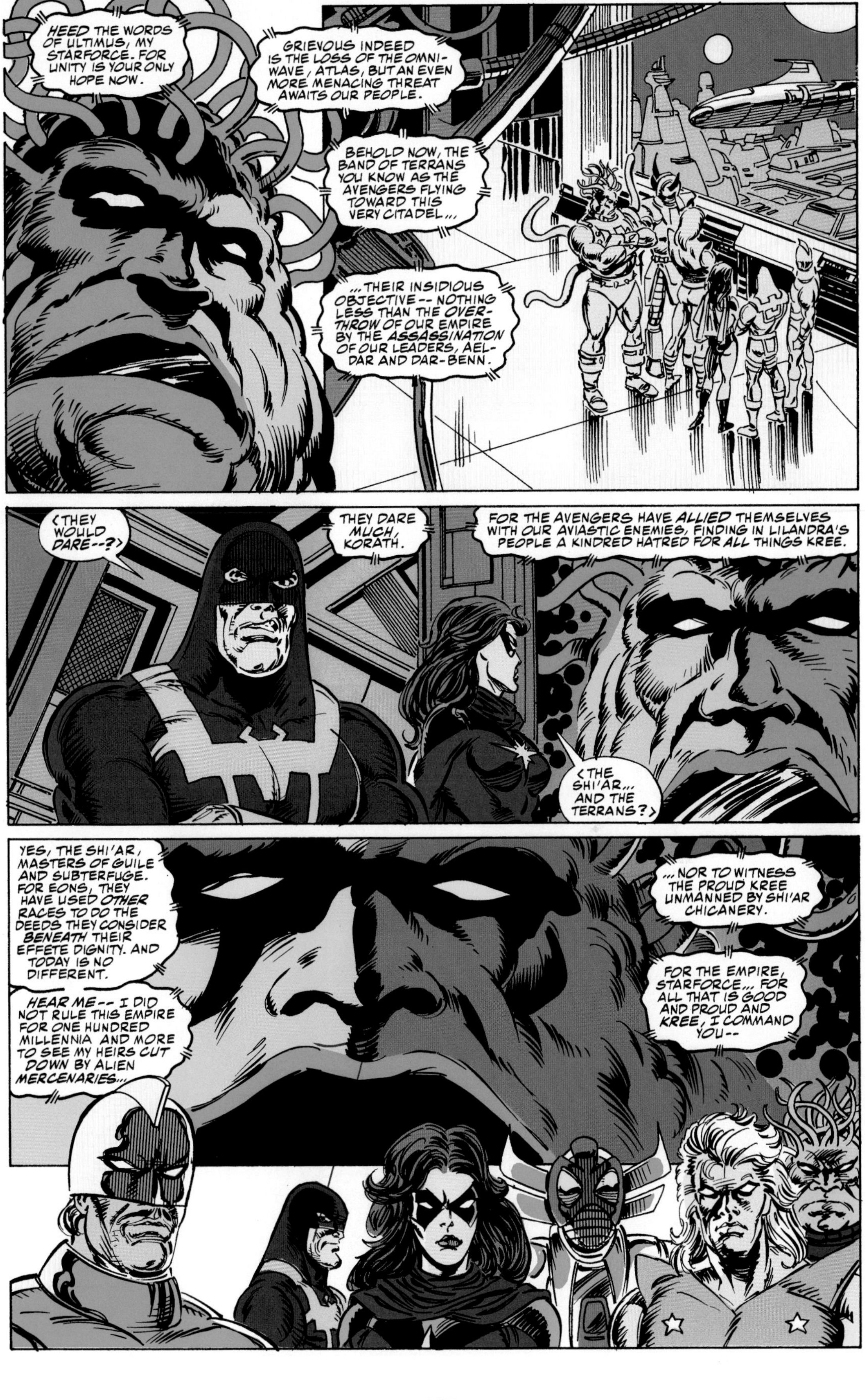
HEED THE WORDS OF ULTIMUS, MY STARFORCE. FOR UNITY IS YOUR ONLY HOPE NOW.
GRIEVOUS INDEED IS THE LOSS OF THE OMNI-WAVE, ATLAS, BUT AN EVEN MORE MENACING THREAT AWAITS OUR PEOPLE.
BEHOLD NOW, THE BAND OF TERRANS YOU KNOW AS THE AVENGERS FLYING TOWARD THIS VERY CITADEL...
...THEIR INSIDIOUS OBJECTIVE -- NOTHING LESS THAN THE OVERTHROW OF OUR EMPIRE BY THE ASSASSINATION OF OUR LEADERS, AELDAR AND DAR-BENN.
<THEY WOULD DARE--?>
THEY DARE MUCH, KORATH.
FOR THE AVENGERS HAVE ALLIED THEMSELVES WITH OUR AVIASTIC ENEMIES, FINDING IN LILANDRA'S PEOPLE A KINDRED HATRED FOR ALL THINGS KREE.
<THE SHI'AR... AND THE TERRANS?>
YES, THE SHI'AR, MASTERS OF GUILE AND SUBTERFUGE. FOR EONS, THEY HAVE USED OTHER RACES TO DO THE DEEDS THEY CONSIDER BENEATH THEIR EFFETE DIGNITY. AND TODAY IS NO DIFFERENT.
HEAR ME -- I DID NOT RULE THIS EMPIRE FOR ONE HUNDRED MILLENNIA AND MORE TO SEE MY HEIRS CUT DOWN BY ALIEN MERCENARIES...
...NOR TO WITNESS THE PROUD KREE UNMANNED BY SHI'AR CHICANERY.
FOR THE EMPIRE, STARFORCE... FOR ALL THAT IS GOOD AND PROUD AND KREE, I COMMAND YOU--

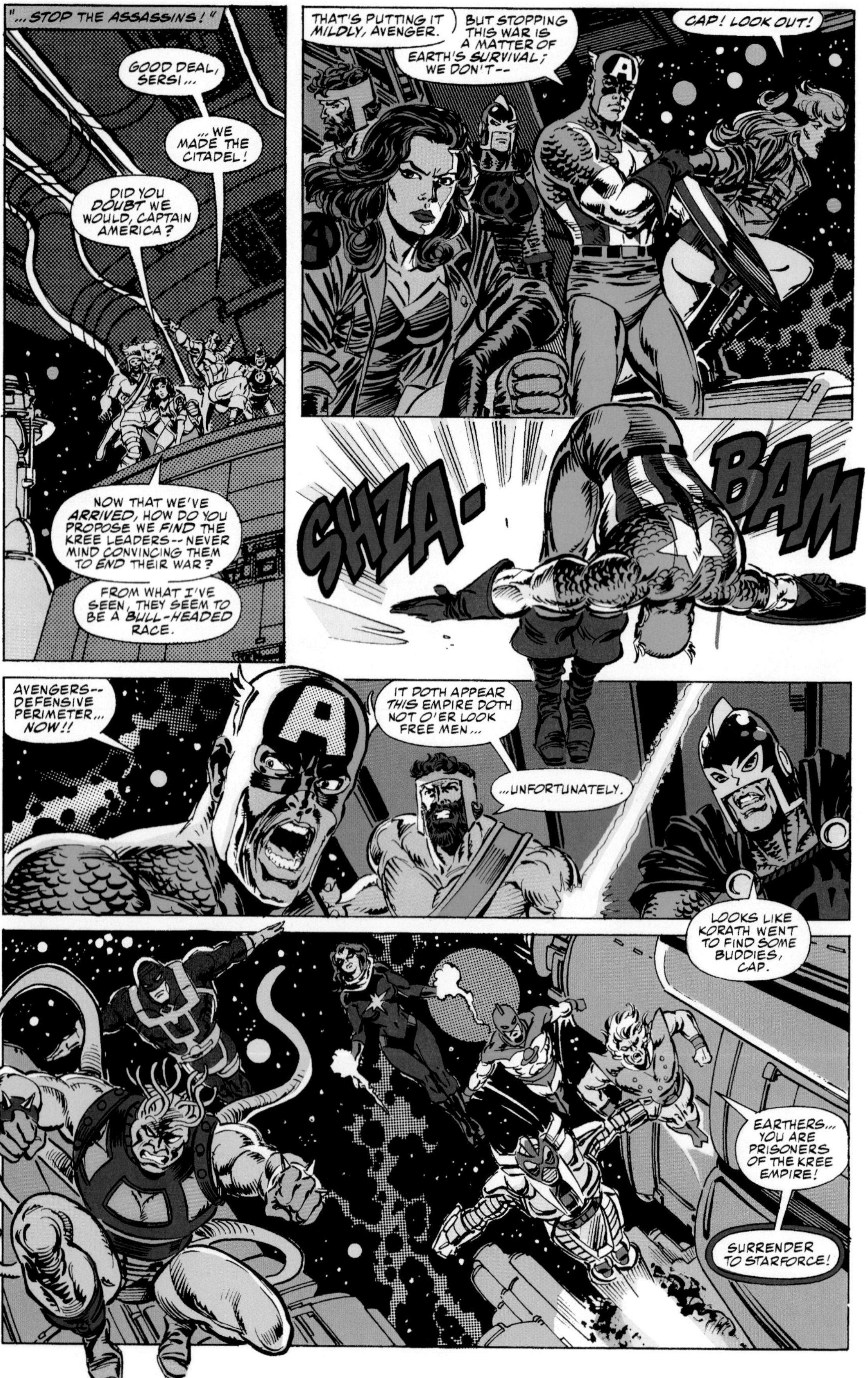
"...STOP THE ASSASSINS!"
GOOD DEAL, SERSI...
...WE MADE THE CITADEL!
DID YOU DOUBT WE WOULD, CAPTAIN AMERICA?
NOW THAT WE'VE ARRIVED, HOW DO YOU PROPOSE WE FIND THE KREE LEADERS--NEVER MIND CONVINCING THEM TO END THEIR WAR?
FROM WHAT I'VE SEEN, THEY SEEM TO BE A BULL-HEADED RACE.
THAT'S PUTTING IT MILDLY, AVENGER.
BUT STOPPING THIS WAR IS A MATTER OF EARTH'S SURVIVAL; WE DON'T--
CAP! LOOK OUT!
SHZA-
BAM
AVENGERS-- DEFENSIVE PERIMETER... NOW!!
IT DOTH APPEAR THIS EMPIRE DOTH NOT O'ER LOOK FREE MEN...
...UNFORTUNATELY.
LOOKS LIKE KORATH WENT TO FIND SOME BUDDIES, CAP.
EARTHERS... YOU ARE PRISONERS OF THE KREE EMPIRE!
SURRENDER TO STARFORCE!

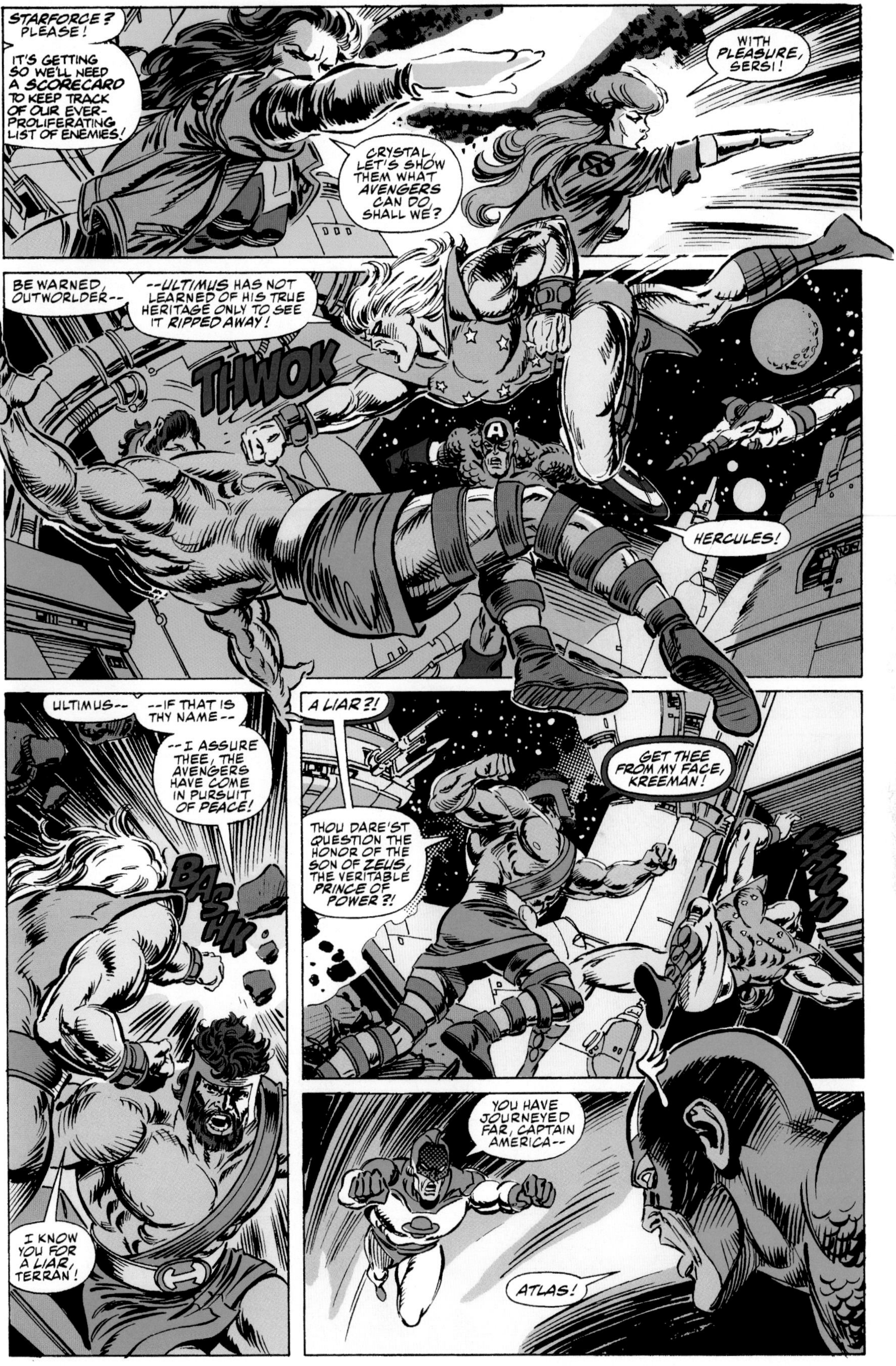

STARFORCE? PLEASE!
IT'S GETTING SO WE'LL NEED A SCORECARD TO KEEP TRACK OF OUR EVER-PROLIFERATING LIST OF ENEMIES!
CRYSTAL, LET'S SHOW THEM WHAT AVENGERS CAN DO, SHALL WE?
WITH PLEASURE, SERSI!
BE WARNED, OUTWORLDER--
--ULTIMUS HAS NOT LEARNED OF HIS TRUE HERITAGE ONLY TO SEE IT RIPPED AWAY!
THWOK
HERCULES!
ULTIMUS--
--IF THAT IS THY NAME--
--I ASSURE THEE, THE AVENGERS HAVE COME IN PURSUIT OF PEACE!
BASHK
I KNOW YOU FOR A LIAR, TERRAN!
A LIAR?!
THOU DARE'ST QUESTION THE HONOR OF THE SON OF ZEUS, THE VERITABLE PRINCE OF POWER?!
GET THEE FROM MY FACE, KREEMAN!
UHNN
YOU HAVE JOURNEYED FAR, CAPTAIN AMERICA--
ATLAS!

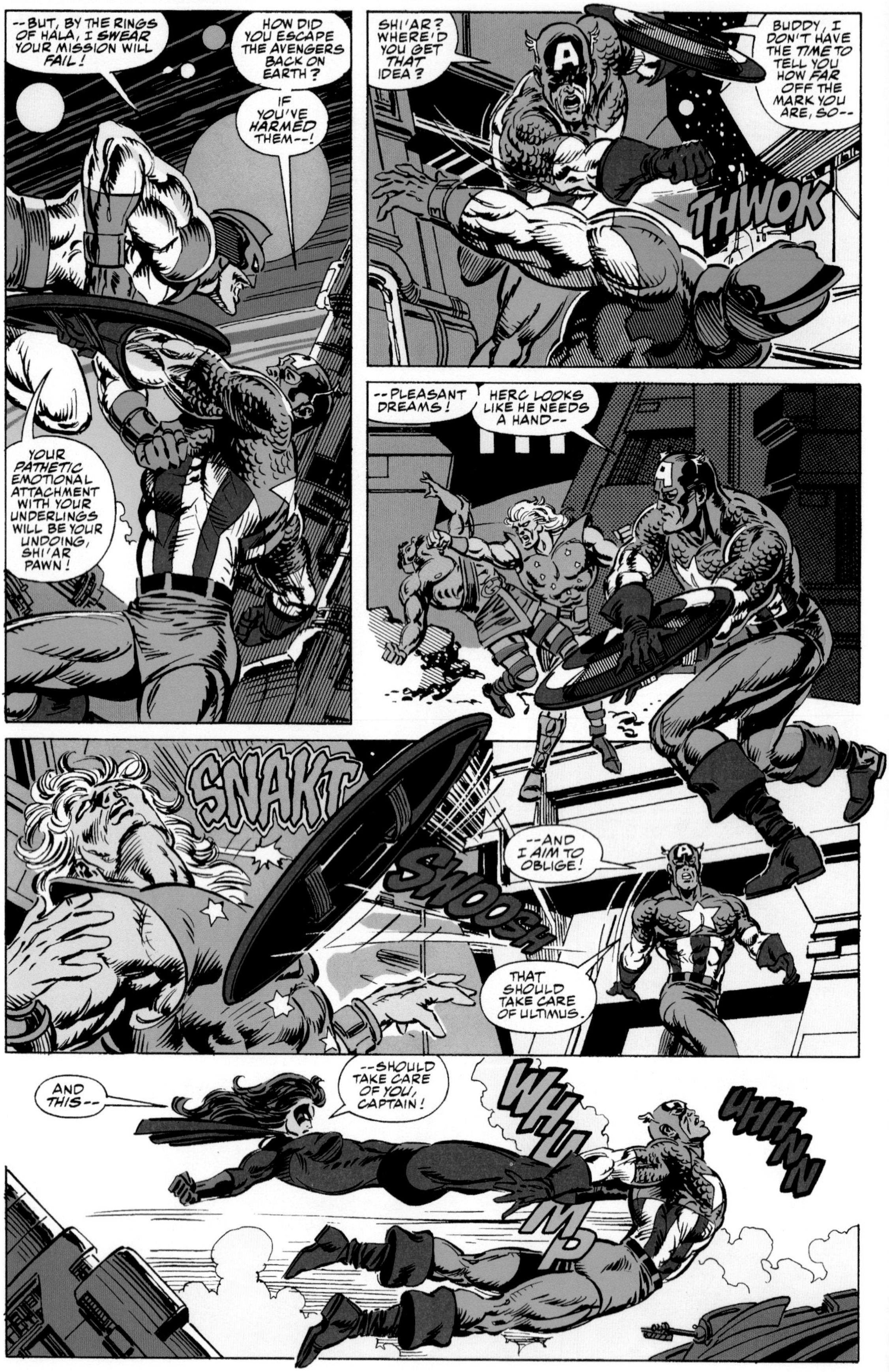
--BUT, BY THE RINGS OF HALA, I SWEAR YOUR MISSION WILL FAIL!
HOW DID YOU ESCAPE THE AVENGERS BACK ON EARTH?
IF YOU'VE HARMED THEM--!
YOUR PATHETIC EMOTIONAL ATTACHMENT WITH YOUR UNDERLINGS WILL BE YOUR UNDOING, SHI'AR PAWN!
SHI'AR? WHERE'D YOU GET THAT IDEA?
BUDDY, I DON'T HAVE THE TIME TO TELL YOU HOW FAR OFF THE MARK YOU ARE, SO--
THWOK
--PLEASANT DREAMS!
HERC LOOKS LIKE HE NEEDS A HAND--
SNAKT
SWOOSH
--AND I AIM TO OBLIGE!
THAT SHOULD TAKE CARE OF ULTIMUS.
AND THIS--
--SHOULD TAKE CARE OF YOU, CAPTAIN!
WHUMP
UHHNN

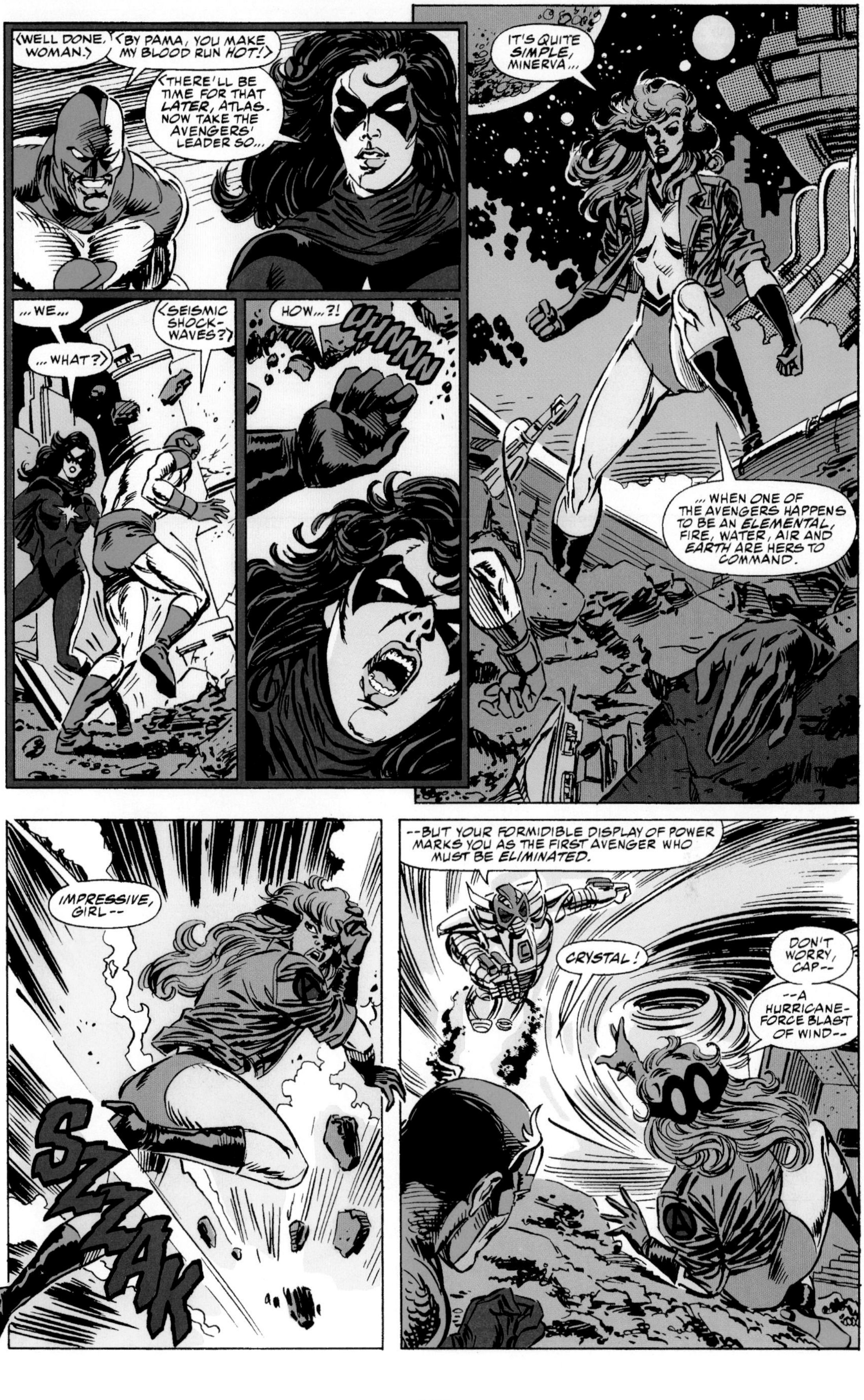

‹WELL DONE, WOMAN.›
‹BY PAMA, YOU MAKE MY BLOOD RUN HOT!›
‹THERE'LL BE TIME FOR THAT LATER, ATLAS. NOW TAKE THE AVENGERS' LEADER SO...
IT'S QUITE SIMPLE, MINERVA...
...WE...
...WHAT?›
‹SEISMIC SHOCK-WAVES?›
HOW...?!
UHNNN
...WHEN ONE OF THE AVENGERS HAPPENS TO BE AN ELEMENTAL, FIRE, WATER, AIR AND EARTH ARE HERS TO COMMAND.
IMPRESSIVE, GIRL--
SZZZAK
--BUT YOUR FORMIDIBLE DISPLAY OF POWER MARKS YOU AS THE FIRST AVENGER WHO MUST BE ELIMINATED.
CRYSTAL!
DON'T WORRY, CAP--
--A HURRICANE-FORCE BLAST OF WIND--

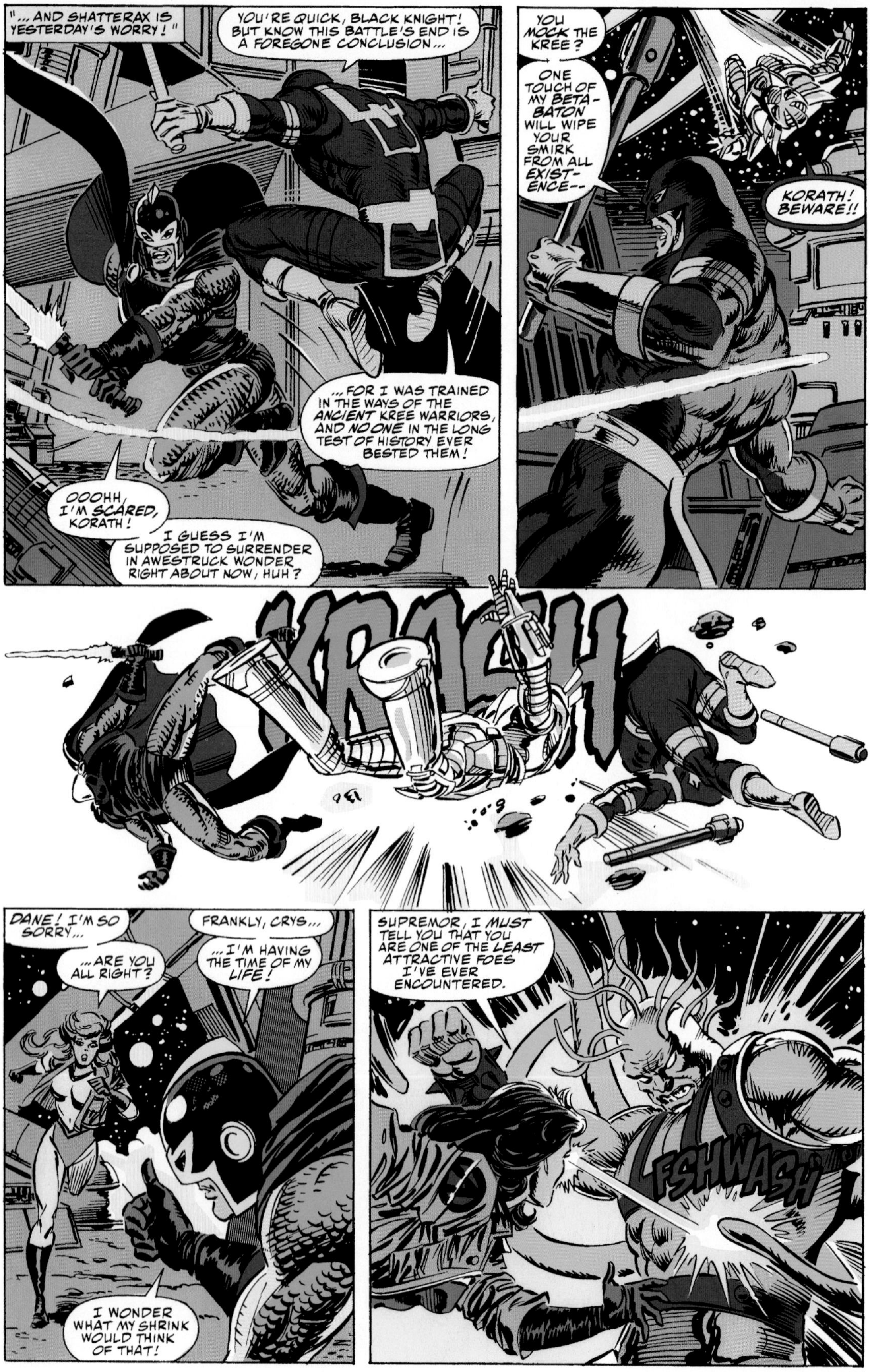
"...AND SHATTERAX IS YESTERDAY'S WORRY!"
YOU'RE QUICK, BLACK KNIGHT! BUT KNOW THIS BATTLE'S END IS A FOREGONE CONCLUSION...
...FOR I WAS TRAINED IN THE WAYS OF THE ANCIENT KREE WARRIORS, AND NO ONE IN THE LONG TEST OF HISTORY EVER BESTED THEM!
OOOHH, I'M SCARED, KORATH!
I GUESS I'M SUPPOSED TO SURRENDER IN AWESTRUCK WONDER RIGHT ABOUT NOW, HUH?
YOU MOCK THE KREE?
ONE TOUCH OF MY BETA-BATON WILL WIPE YOUR SMIRK FROM ALL EXIST-ENCE--
KORATH! BEWARE!!
KRASH
DANE! I'M SO SORRY...
...ARE YOU ALL RIGHT?
FRANKLY, CRYS...
...I'M HAVING THE TIME OF MY LIFE!
I WONDER WHAT MY SHRINK WOULD THINK OF THAT!
SUPREMOR, I MUST TELL YOU THAT YOU ARE ONE OF THE LEAST ATTRACTIVE FOES I'VE EVER ENCOUNTERED.
FSHWASH

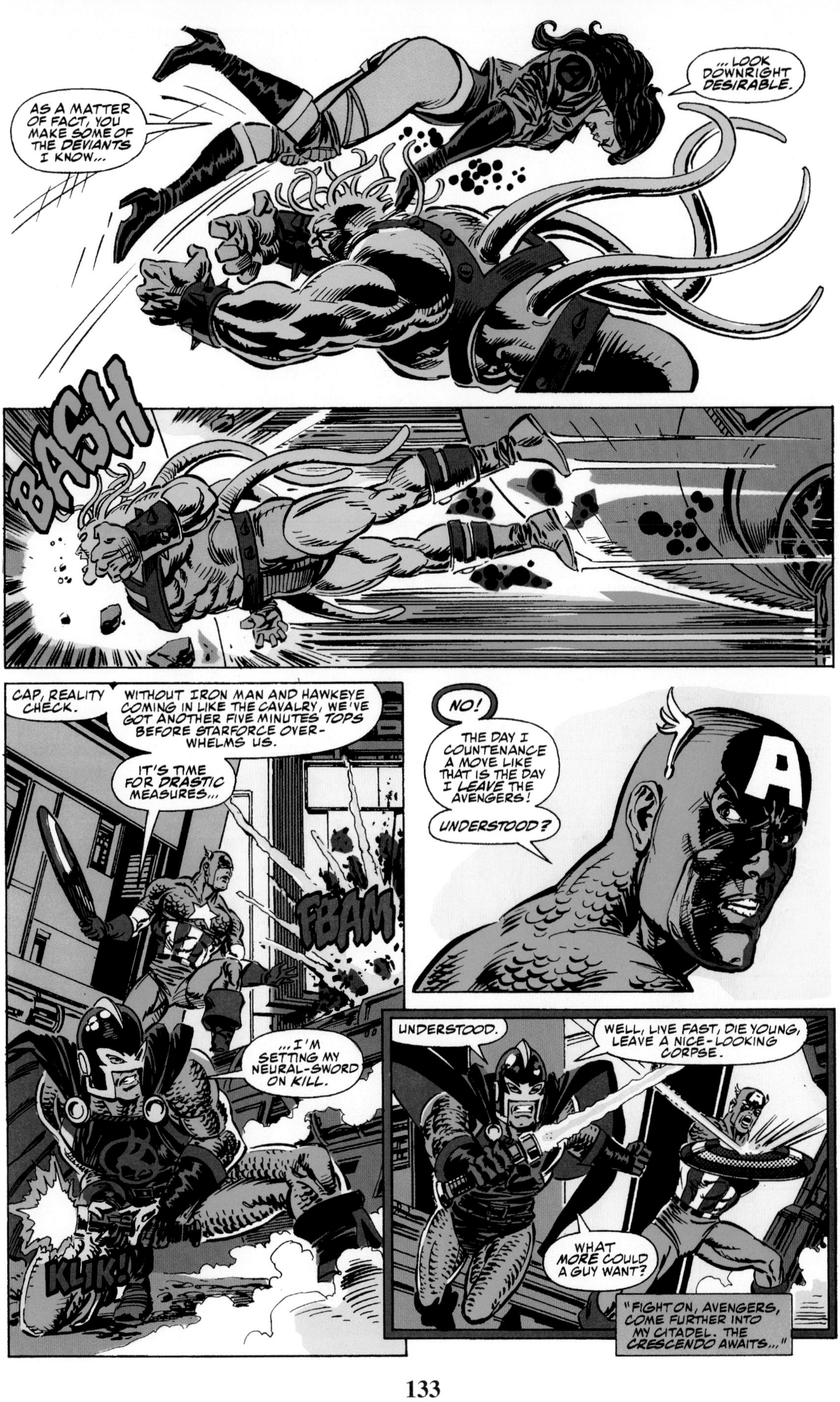
AS A MATTER OF FACT, YOU MAKE SOME OF THE DEVIANTS I KNOW...
...LOOK DOWNRIGHT DESIRABLE.
BASH
CAP, REALITY CHECK.
WITHOUT IRON MAN AND HAWKEYE COMING IN LIKE THE CAVALRY, WE'VE GOT ANOTHER FIVE MINUTES TOPS BEFORE STARFORCE OVERWHELMS US.
IT'S TIME FOR DRASTIC MEASURES...
FBAM
...I'M SETTING MY NEURAL-SWORD ON KILL.
KLIK!
NO!
THE DAY I COUNTENANCE A MOVE LIKE THAT IS THE DAY I LEAVE THE AVENGERS!
UNDERSTOOD?
UNDERSTOOD.
WELL, LIVE FAST, DIE YOUNG, LEAVE A NICE-LOOKING CORPSE.
WHAT MORE COULD A GUY WANT?
"FIGHT ON, AVENGERS, COME FURTHER INTO MY CITADEL. THE CRESCENDO AWAITS..."

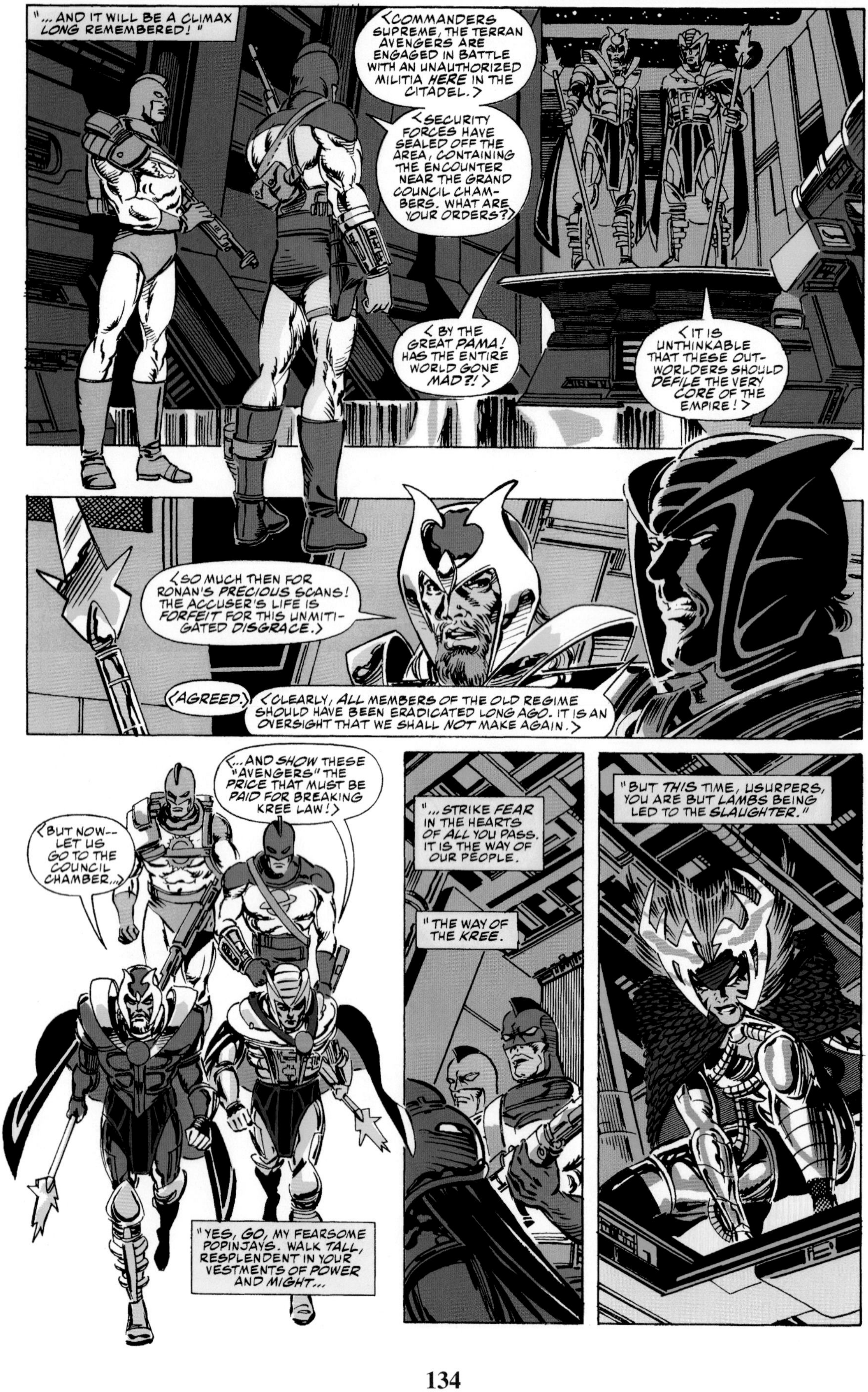
"... AND IT WILL BE A CLIMAX LONG REMEMBERED!"
<COMMANDERS SUPREME, THE TERRAN AVENGERS ARE ENGAGED IN BATTLE WITH AN UNAUTHORIZED MILITIA HERE IN THE CITADEL.>
<SECURITY FORCES HAVE SEALED OFF THE AREA, CONTAINING THE ENCOUNTER NEAR THE GRAND COUNCIL CHAMBERS. WHAT ARE YOUR ORDERS?>
<BY THE GREAT PAMA! HAS THE ENTIRE WORLD GONE MAD?!>
<IT IS UNTHINKABLE THAT THESE OUTWORLDERS SHOULD DEFILE THE VERY CORE OF THE EMPIRE!>
<SO MUCH THEN FOR RONAN'S PRECIOUS SCANS! THE ACCUSER'S LIFE IS FORFEIT FOR THIS UNMITIGATED DISGRACE.>
<AGREED.>
<CLEARLY, ALL MEMBERS OF THE OLD REGIME SHOULD HAVE BEEN ERADICATED LONG AGO. IT IS AN OVERSIGHT THAT WE SHALL NOT MAKE AGAIN.>
<BUT NOW-- LET US GO TO THE COUNCIL CHAMBER...
...AND SHOW THESE "AVENGERS" THE PRICE THAT MUST BE PAID FOR BREAKING KREE LAW!>
"YES, GO, MY FEARSOME POPINJAYS. WALK TALL, RESPLENDENT IN YOUR VESTMENTS OF POWER AND MIGHT...
"...STRIKE FEAR IN THE HEARTS OF ALL YOU PASS. IT IS THE WAY OF OUR PEOPLE.
"THE WAY OF THE KREE.
"BUT THIS TIME, USURPERS, YOU ARE BUT LAMBS BEING LED TO THE SLAUGHTER."

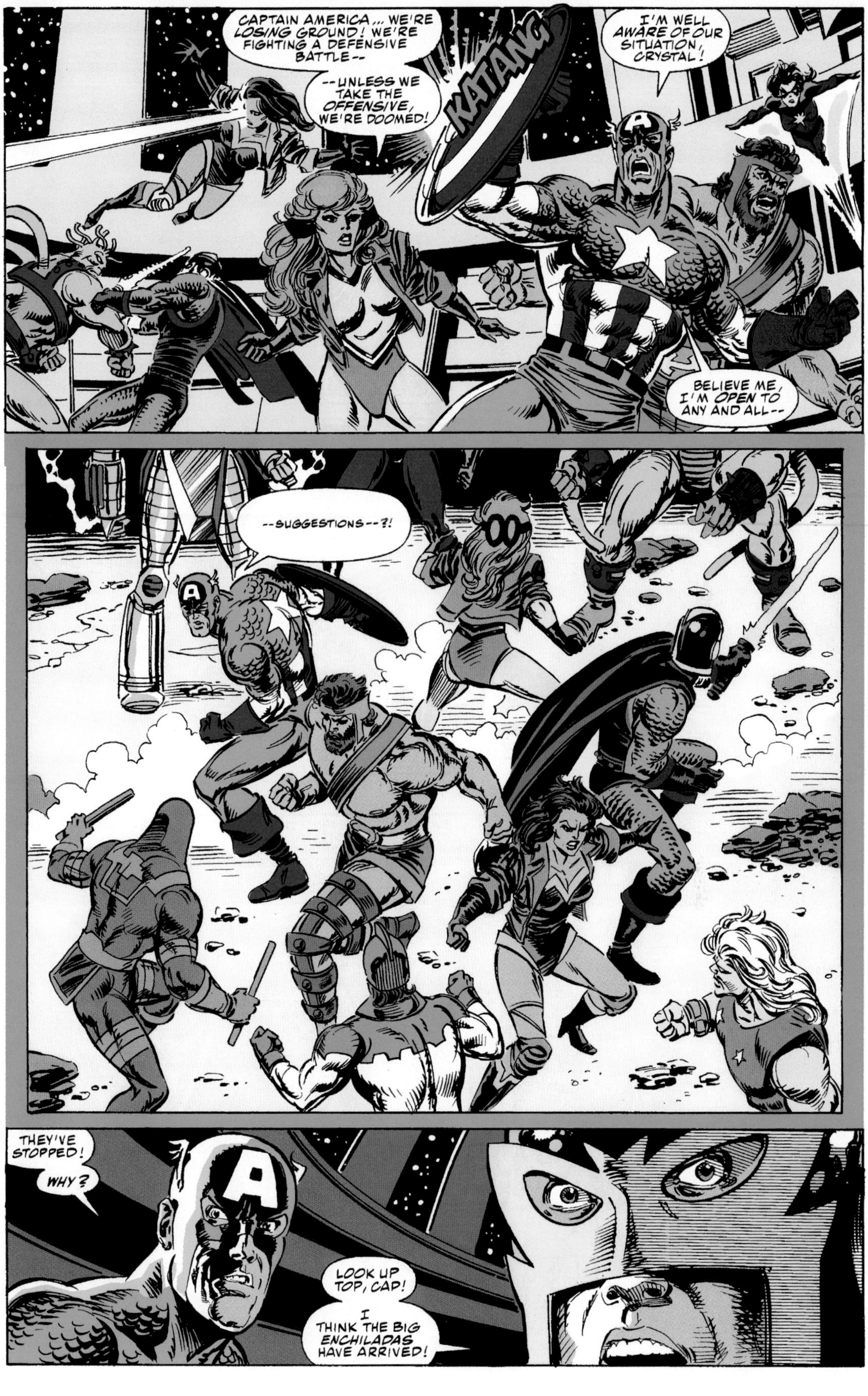
CAPTAIN AMERICA... WE'RE LOSING GROUND! WE'RE FIGHTING A DEFENSIVE BATTLE--
--UNLESS WE TAKE THE OFFENSIVE, WE'RE DOOMED!
KATANG
I'M WELL AWARE OF OUR SITUATION, CRYSTAL!
BELIEVE ME, I'M OPEN TO ANY AND ALL--
--SUGGESTIONS--?!
THEY'VE STOPPED!
WHY?
LOOK UP TOP, CAP!
I THINK THE BIG ENCHILADAS HAVE ARRIVED!

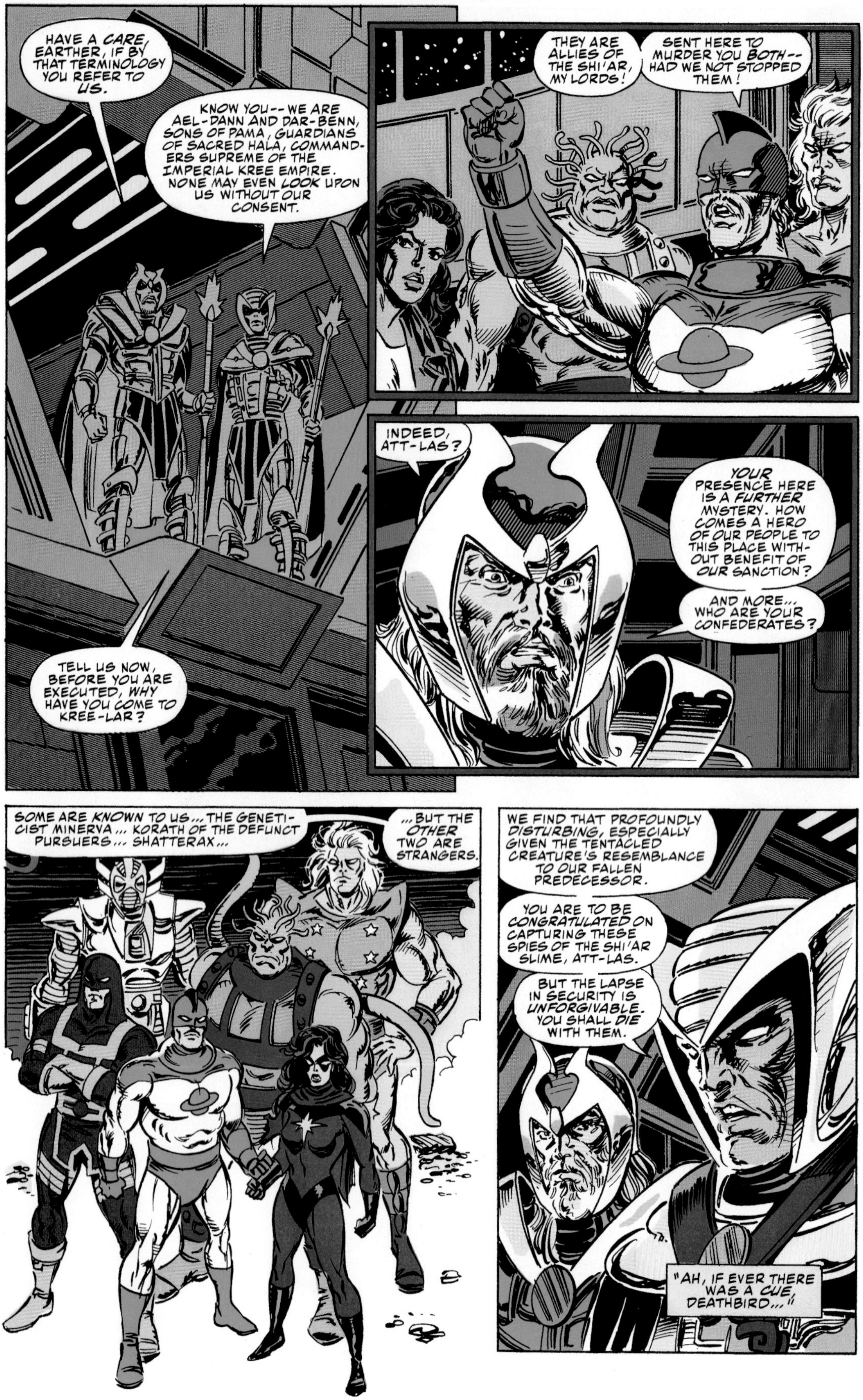

HAVE A *CARE*, EARTHER, IF BY THAT TERMINOLOGY YOU REFER TO *US*.
KNOW YOU--WE ARE AEL-DANN AND DAR-BENN, SONS OF PAMA, GUARDIANS OF SACRED HALA, COMMANDERS SUPREME OF THE IMPERIAL KREE EMPIRE. NONE MAY EVEN *LOOK* UPON US WITHOUT OUR CONSENT.
TELL US NOW, BEFORE YOU ARE EXECUTED, WHY HAVE YOU COME TO KREE-LAR?
THEY ARE ALLIES OF THE SHI'AR, MY LORDS!
SENT HERE TO MURDER YOU *BOTH*-- HAD WE NOT STOPPED THEM!
INDEED, ATT-LAS?
YOUR PRESENCE HERE IS A *FURTHER* MYSTERY. HOW COMES A HERO OF OUR PEOPLE TO THIS PLACE WITHOUT BENEFIT OF *OUR* SANCTION?
AND MORE... WHO ARE YOUR CONFEDERATES?
SOME ARE *KNOWN* TO US... THE GENETICIST MINERVA... KORATH OF THE DEFUNCT PURSUERS... SHATTERAX...
...BUT THE *OTHER* TWO ARE STRANGERS.
WE FIND THAT PROFOUNDLY *DISTURBING*, ESPECIALLY GIVEN THE TENTACLED CREATURE'S RESEMBLANCE TO OUR FALLEN PREDECESSOR.
YOU ARE TO BE *CONGRATULATED* ON CAPTURING THESE SPIES OF THE SHI'AR SLIME, ATT-LAS.
BUT THE LAPSE IN SECURITY IS *UNFORGIVABLE*. YOU SHALL *DIE* WITH THEM.
"AH, IF EVER THERE WAS A *CUE*, DEATHBIRD..."

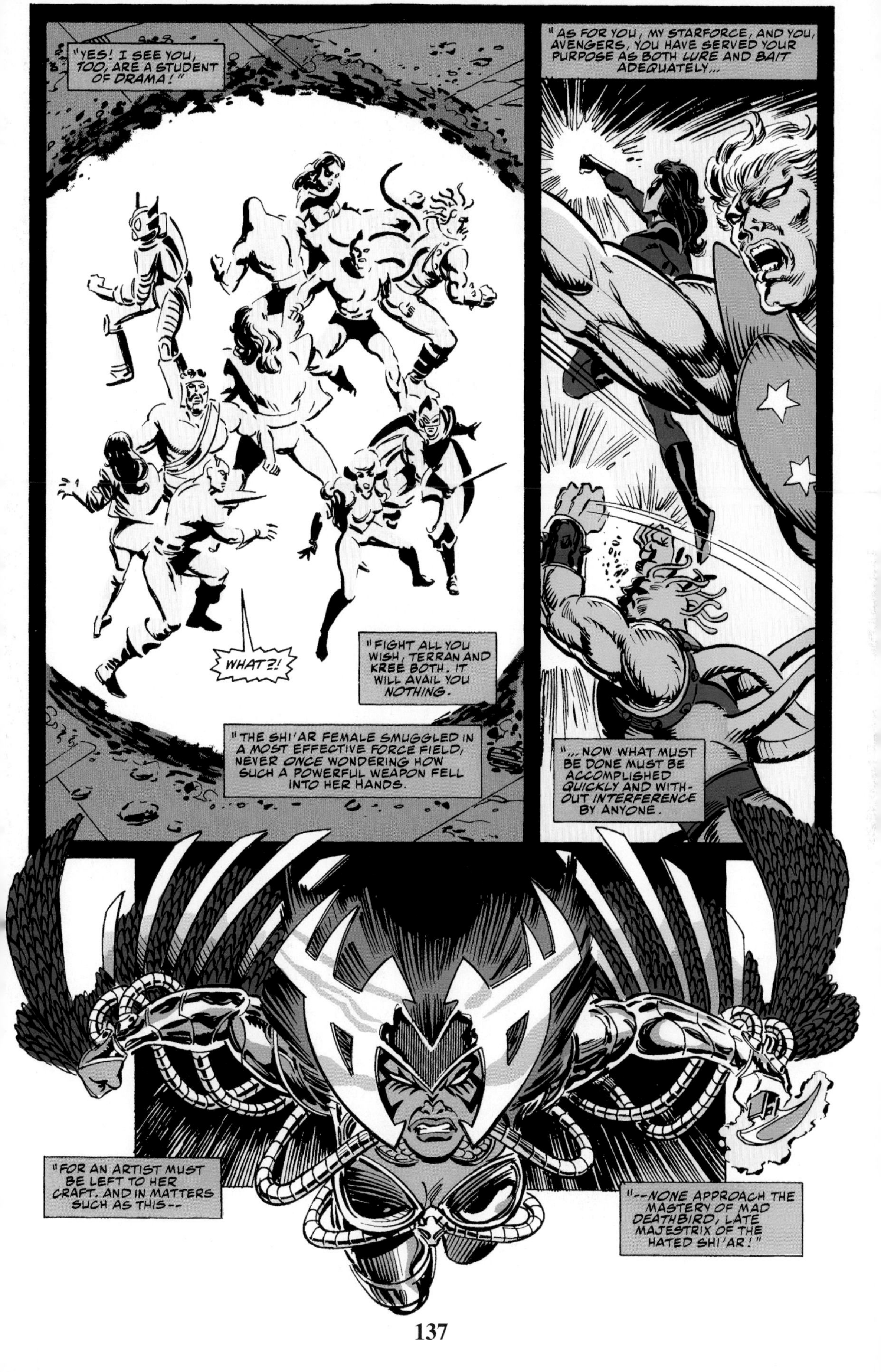
"YES! I SEE YOU, TOO, ARE A STUDENT OF DRAMA!"
"FIGHT ALL YOU WISH, TERRAN AND KREE BOTH. IT WILL AVAIL YOU NOTHING.
WHAT?!
"THE SHI'AR FEMALE SMUGGLED IN A MOST EFFECTIVE FORCE FIELD, NEVER ONCE WONDERING HOW SUCH A POWERFUL WEAPON FELL INTO HER HANDS.
"AS FOR YOU, MY STARFORCE, AND YOU, AVENGERS, YOU HAVE SERVED YOUR PURPOSE AS BOTH LURE AND BAIT ADEQUATELY...
"...NOW WHAT MUST BE DONE MUST BE ACCOMPLISHED QUICKLY AND WITHOUT INTERFERENCE BY ANYONE.
"FOR AN ARTIST MUST BE LEFT TO HER CRAFT. AND IN MATTERS SUCH AS THIS--
"--NONE APPROACH THE MASTERY OF MAD DEATHBIRD, LATE MAJESTRIX OF THE HATED SHI'AR!"

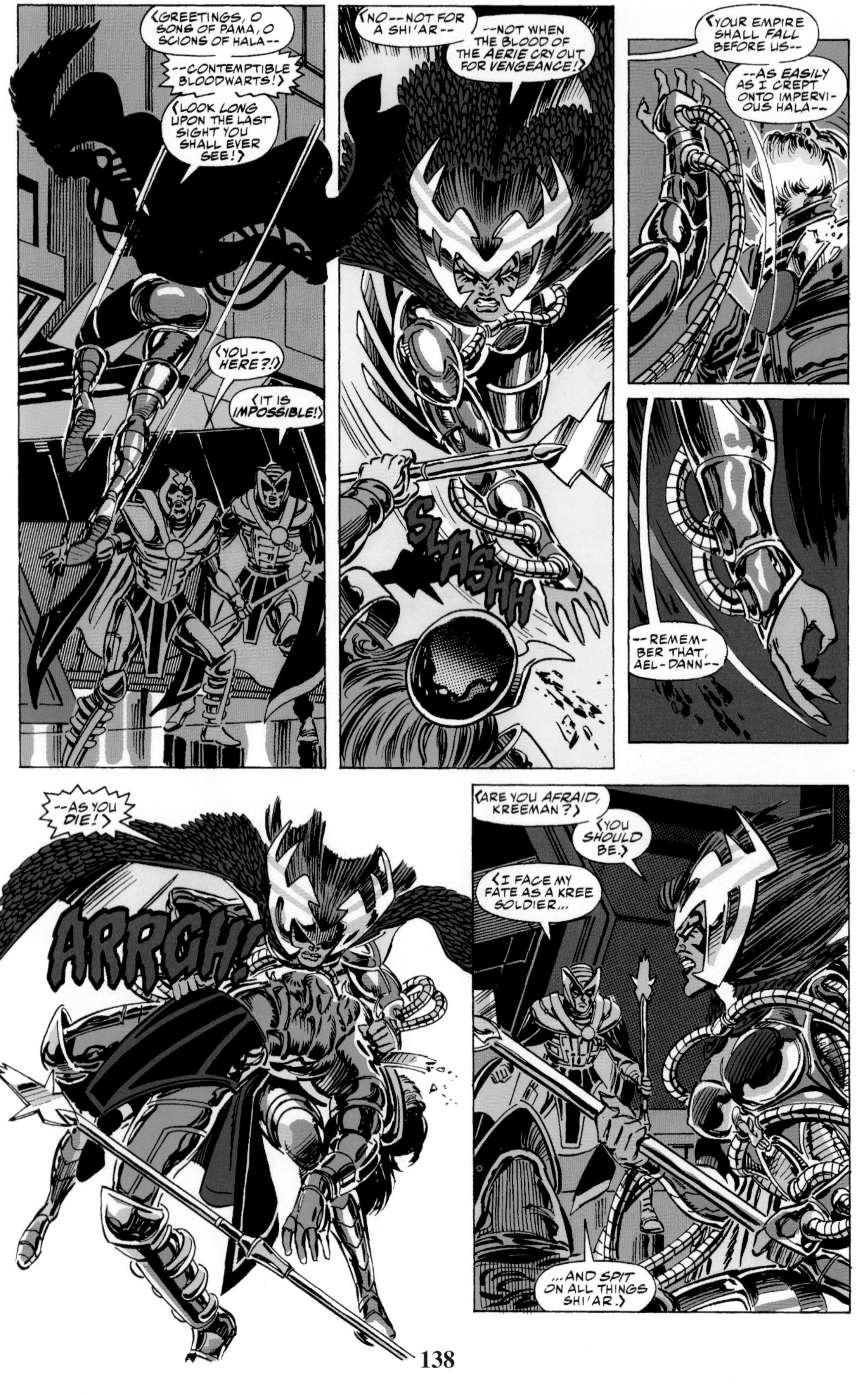
‹GREETINGS, O SONS OF PAMA, O SCIONS OF HALA--
--CONTEMPTIBLE BLOODWARTS!›
‹LOOK LONG UPON THE LAST SIGHT YOU SHALL EVER SEE!›
‹YOU-- HERE?!›
‹IT IS IMPOSSIBLE!›
‹NO--NOT FOR A SHI'AR--
--NOT WHEN THE BLOOD OF THE AERIE CRY OUT FOR VENGEANCE!›
SLASHH
‹YOUR EMPIRE SHALL FALL BEFORE US--
--AS EASILY AS I CREPT ONTO IMPERVIOUS HALA--
--REMEMBER THAT, AEL-DANN--
--AS YOU DIE!›
ARRGH!
‹ARE YOU AFRAID, KREEMAN?›
‹YOU SHOULD BE.›
‹I FACE MY FATE AS A KREE SOLDIER...
...AND SPIT ON ALL THINGS SHI'AR.›

‹HOW *TYPICALLY KREE*, THEN -- TO DIE WITH *EMPTY BOASTS* ON *TREMBLING LIPS!*›

ARRGH!

CHUNKT

‹*SO ENDS* YOUR 'GLORIOUS' *JOINT-REIGN*. GO NOW TO YOUR *AFTERLIFE*, IF YOU HAVE ONE --›

‹-- I *CARE NOT*.›

"IT IS *ACCOMPLISHED*. IN BUT A FEW BEATS OF A HEART... *EVERYTHING* HAS CHANGED."

SMASHH

"WHERE NOW, MY GENERALS, ARE THE *VANITIES* OF POWER AND STATION? WHAT *GOOD* DID THEY DO YOU?"

"NONE. YOUR *REACH* EXCEEDED YOUR *GRASP*, SONS OF PAMA..."

"...AND ALL THAT IS LEFT IS THE *QUINTESSENCE* OF *DUST*."

BY *AGON*...

A *DEMON*, METHINKS.

...WHO *IS* THAT *CREATURE*?

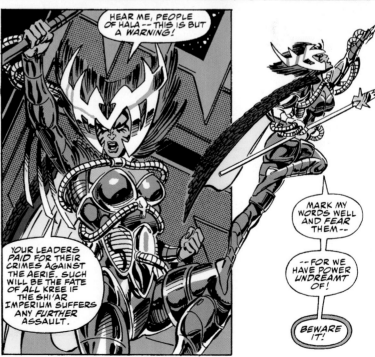

HEAR ME, PEOPLE OF *HALA* -- THIS IS BUT A *WARNING*!

YOUR LEADERS *PAID* FOR THEIR *CRIMES* AGAINST THE *AERIE*. SUCH WILL BE THE *FATE* OF ALL *KREE* IF THE *SHI'AR IMPERIUM* SUFFERS ANY *FURTHER* ASSAULT.

MARK MY WORDS WELL AND *FEAR* THEM --

-- FOR WE HAVE POWER *UNDREAMT* OF!

BEWARE IT!

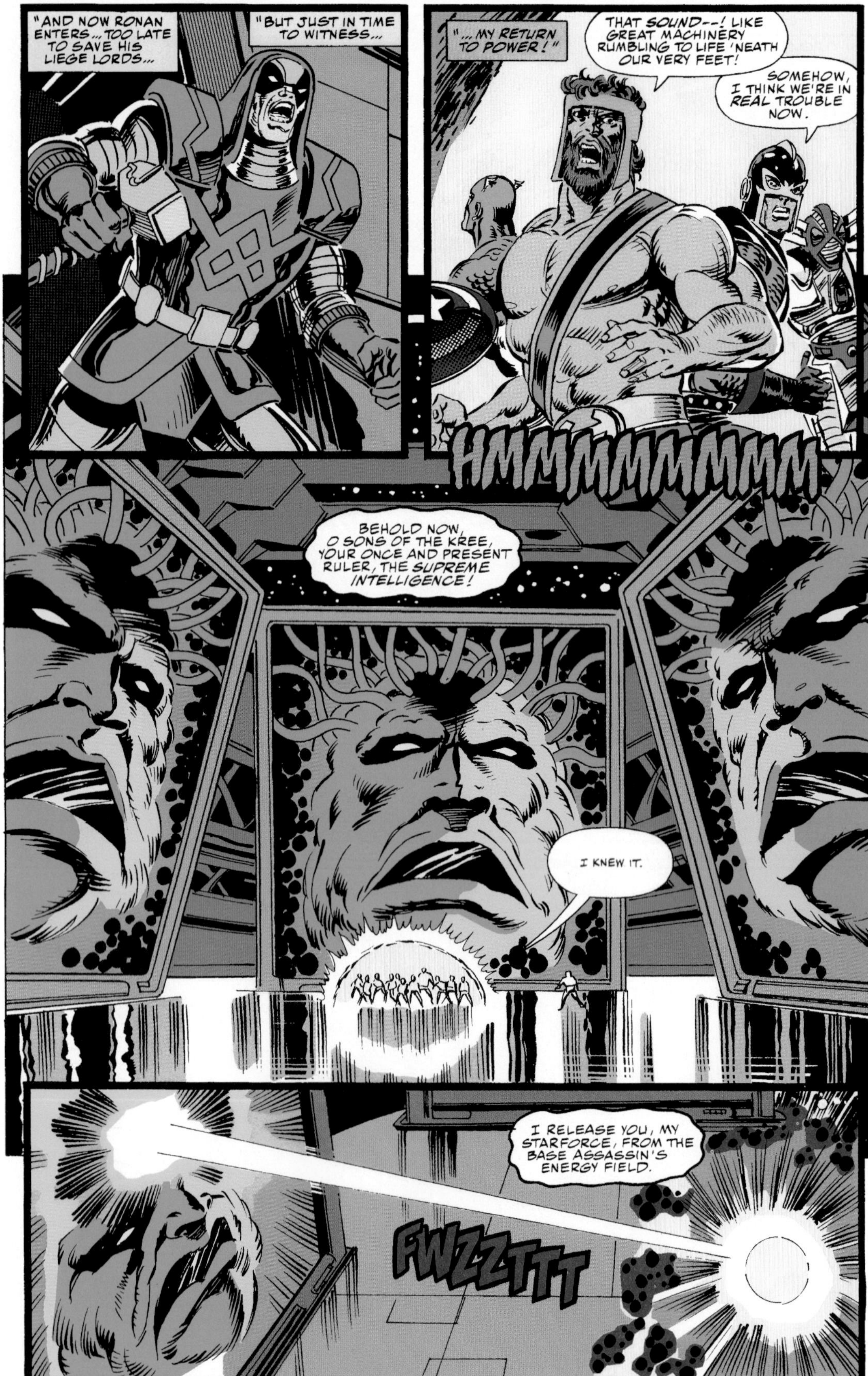
"AND NOW RONAN ENTERS... TOO LATE TO SAVE HIS LIEGE LORDS...
"BUT JUST IN TIME TO WITNESS...
"...MY RETURN TO POWER!"
THAT SOUND--! LIKE GREAT MACHINERY RUMBLING TO LIFE 'NEATH OUR VERY FEET!
SOMEHOW, I THINK WE'RE IN REAL TROUBLE NOW.
HMMMMMMMMM
BEHOLD NOW, O SONS OF THE KREE, YOUR ONCE AND PRESENT RULER, THE SUPREME INTELLIGENCE!
I KNEW IT.
I RELEASE YOU, MY STARFORCE, FROM THE BASE ASSASSIN'S ENERGY FIELD.
FWZZTTTT

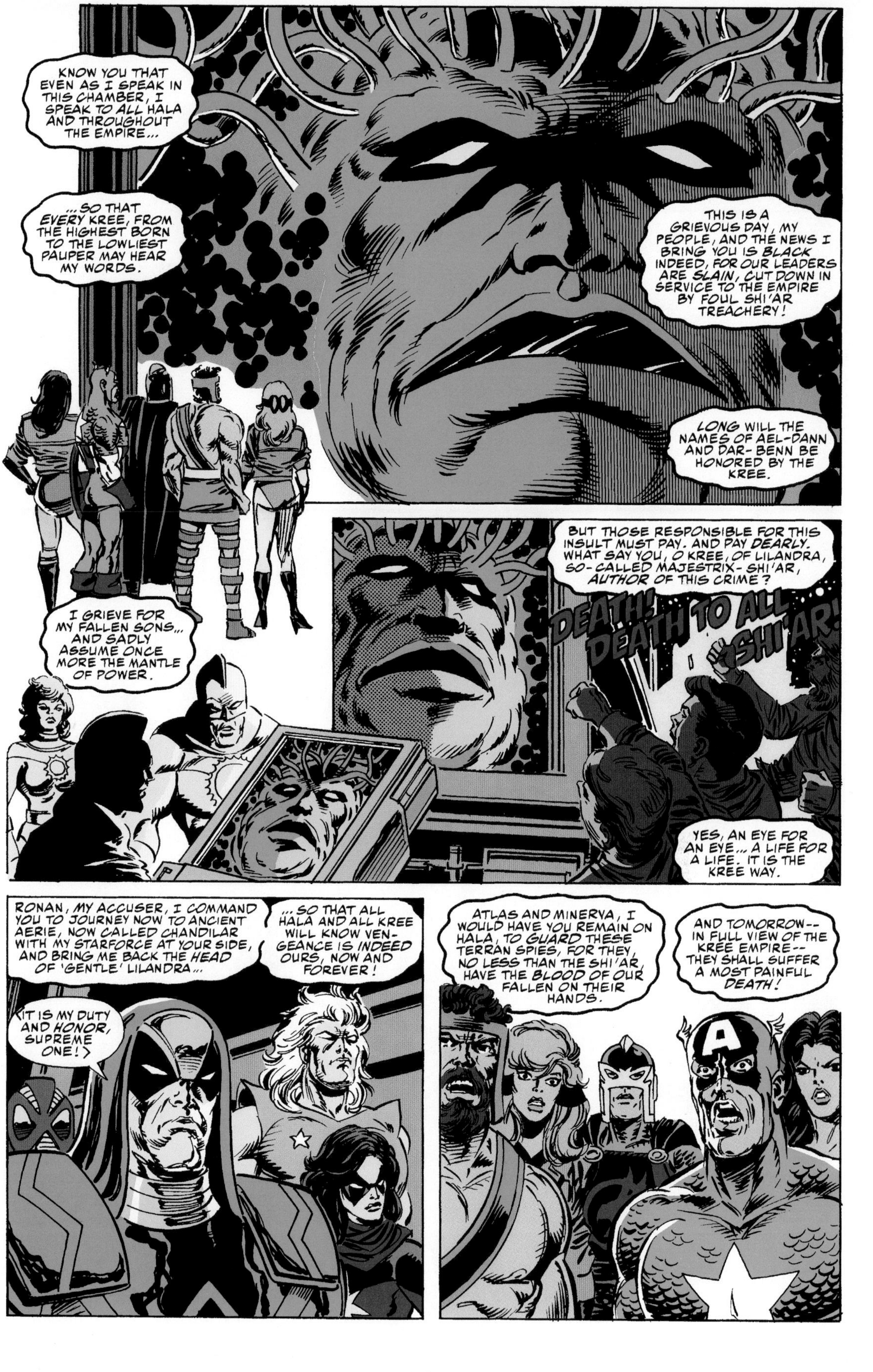

KNOW YOU THAT EVEN AS I SPEAK IN THIS CHAMBER, I SPEAK TO ALL HALA AND THROUGHOUT THE EMPIRE...
...SO THAT EVERY KREE, FROM THE HIGHEST BORN TO THE LOWLIEST PAUPER MAY HEAR MY WORDS.
THIS IS A GRIEVOUS DAY, MY PEOPLE, AND THE NEWS I BRING YOU IS BLACK INDEED, FOR OUR LEADERS ARE SLAIN, CUT DOWN IN SERVICE TO THE EMPIRE BY FOUL SHI'AR TREACHERY!
LONG WILL THE NAMES OF AEL-DANN AND DAR-BENN BE HONORED BY THE KREE.
BUT THOSE RESPONSIBLE FOR THIS INSULT MUST PAY. AND PAY DEARLY. WHAT SAY YOU, O KREE, OF LILANDRA, SO-CALLED MAJESTRIX-SHI'AR, AUTHOR OF THIS CRIME?
DEATH! DEATH TO ALL SHI'AR!
I GRIEVE FOR MY FALLEN SONS... AND SADLY ASSUME ONCE MORE THE MANTLE OF POWER.
YES, AN EYE FOR AN EYE... A LIFE FOR A LIFE. IT IS THE KREE WAY.
RONAN, MY ACCUSER, I COMMAND YOU TO JOURNEY NOW TO ANCIENT AERIE, NOW CALLED CHANDILAR WITH MY STARFORCE AT YOUR SIDE, AND BRING ME BACK THE HEAD OF 'GENTLE' LILANDRA...
...SO THAT ALL HALA AND ALL KREE WILL KNOW VENGEANCE IS INDEED OURS, NOW AND FOREVER!
<IT IS MY DUTY AND HONOR, SUPREME ONE!>
ATLAS AND MINERVA, I WOULD HAVE YOU REMAIN ON HALA, TO GUARD THESE TERRAN SPIES, FOR THEY, NO LESS THAN THE SHI'AR, HAVE THE BLOOD OF OUR FALLEN ON THEIR HANDS.
AND TOMORROW-- IN FULL VIEW OF THE KREE EMPIRE-- THEY SHALL SUFFER A MOST PAINFUL DEATH!

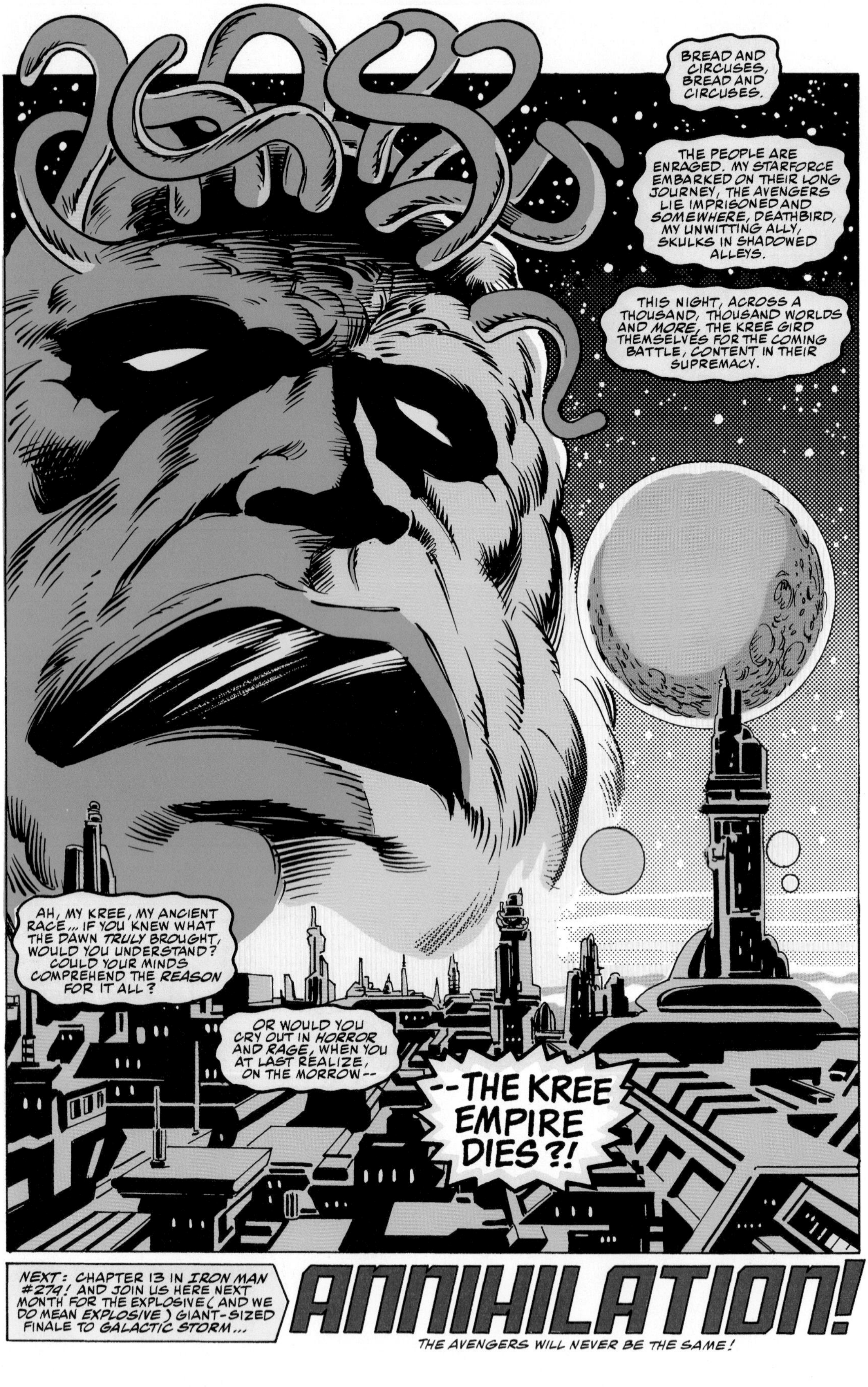
BREAD AND CIRCUSES, BREAD AND CIRCUSES.
THE PEOPLE ARE ENRAGED. MY STARFORCE EMBARKED ON THEIR LONG JOURNEY, THE AVENGERS LIE IMPRISONED AND SOMEWHERE, DEATHBIRD, MY UNWITTING ALLY, SKULKS IN SHADOWED ALLEYS.
THIS NIGHT, ACROSS A THOUSAND, THOUSAND WORLDS AND MORE, THE KREE GIRD THEMSELVES FOR THE COMING BATTLE, CONTENT IN THEIR SUPREMACY.
AH, MY KREE, MY ANCIENT RACE... IF YOU KNEW WHAT THE DAWN TRULY BROUGHT, WOULD YOU UNDERSTAND? COULD YOUR MINDS COMPREHEND THE REASON FOR IT ALL?
OR WOULD YOU CRY OUT IN HORROR AND RAGE, WHEN YOU AT LAST REALIZE, ON THE MORROW--
--THE KREE EMPIRE DIES?!
NEXT: CHAPTER 13 IN IRON MAN #279! AND JOIN US HERE NEXT MONTH FOR THE EXPLOSIVE (AND WE DO MEAN EXPLOSIVE) GIANT-SIZED FINALE TO GALACTIC STORM...
ANNIHILATION!
THE AVENGERS WILL NEVER BE THE SAME!

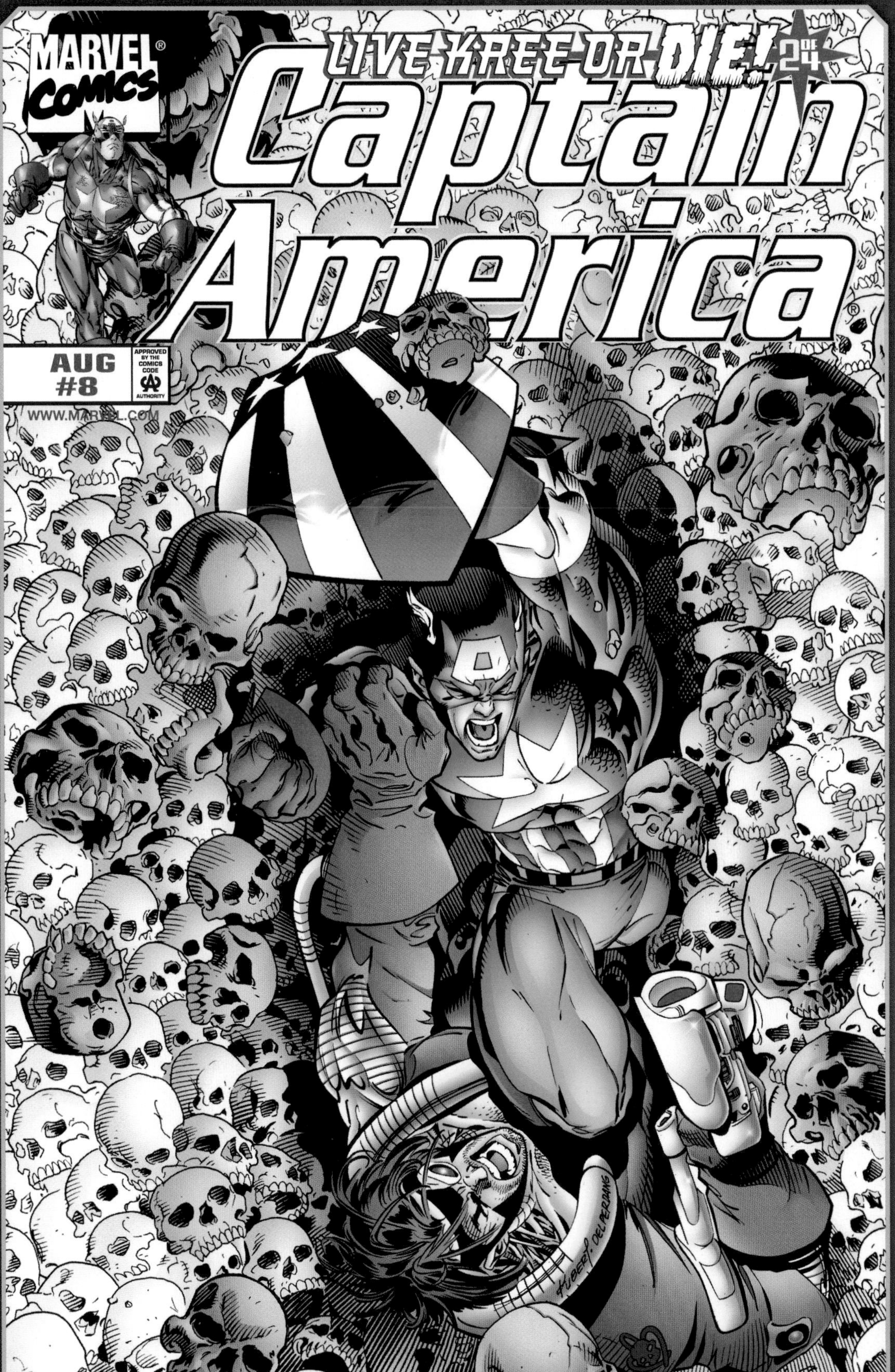
MARVEL COMICS
LIVE KREE OR DIE! 2 OF 4
Captain America
AUG #8
APPROVED BY THE COMICS CODE AUTHORITY
WWW.MARVEL.COM
WAID • KUBERT • DELPERDANG

THERE IS NO *HOPE* HERE.

DURING *WORLD WAR TWO,* THE NAZIS BROUGHT UNLUCKY INNOCENTS TO PRISON CAMPS FOR EXPERIMENTATION.

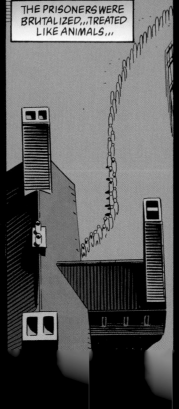

THE PRISONERS WERE BRUTALIZED...TREATED LIKE ANIMALS...

...AND, EVENTUALLY, HERDED INTO SEALED CHAMBERS...

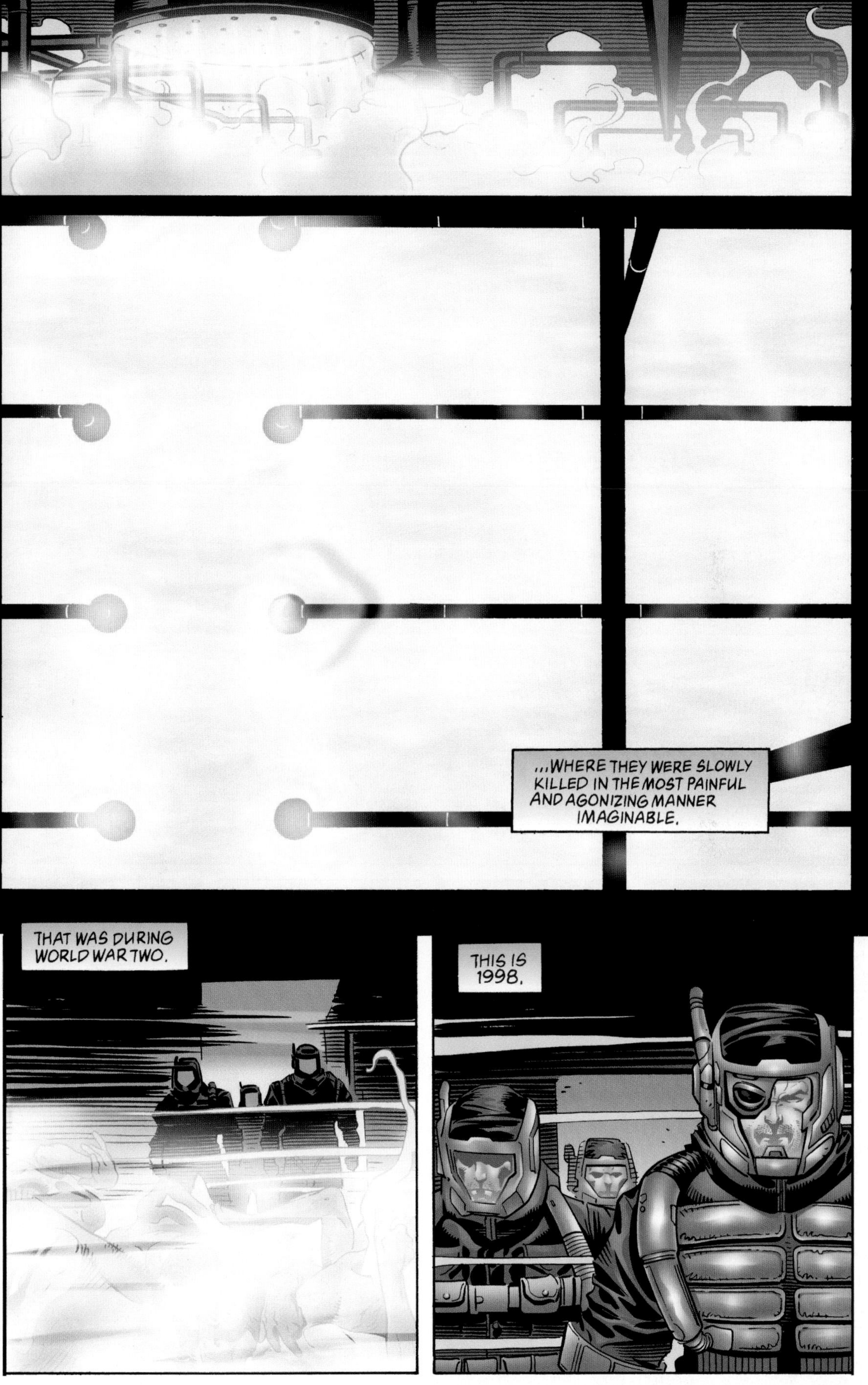
...WHERE THEY WERE SLOWLY KILLED IN THE MOST PAINFUL AND AGONIZING MANNER IMAGINABLE.
THAT WAS DURING WORLD WAR TWO.
THIS IS 1998.

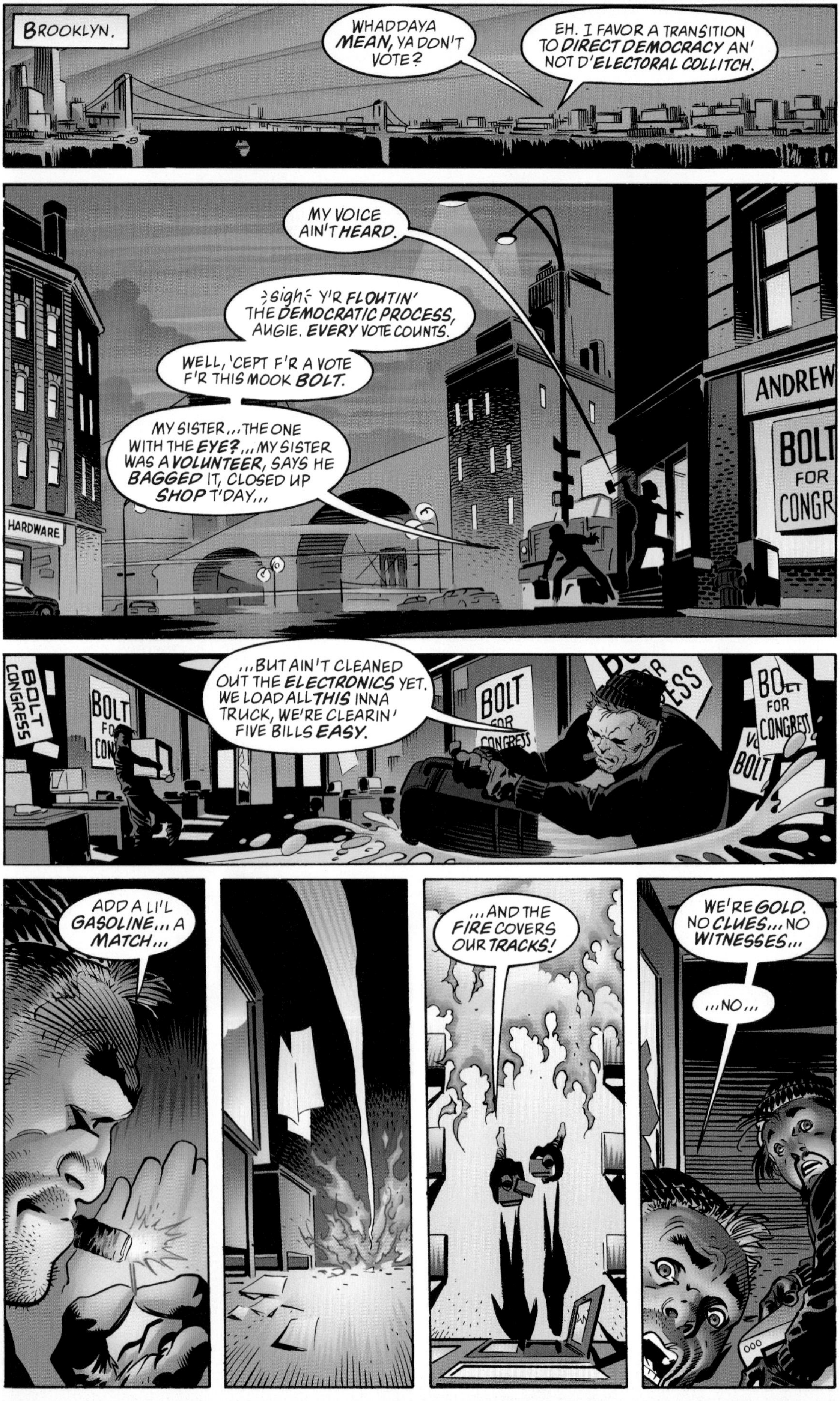
BROOKLYN.
WHADDAYA MEAN, YA DON'T VOTE?
EH. I FAVOR A TRANSITION TO DIRECT DEMOCRACY AN' NOT D'ELECTORAL COLLITCH.
MY VOICE AIN'T HEARD.
sigh Y'R FLOUTIN' THE DEMOCRATIC PROCESS, AUGIE. EVERY VOTE COUNTS.
WELL, 'CEPT F'R A VOTE F'R THIS MOOK BOLT.
MY SISTER... THE ONE WITH THE EYE?... MY SISTER WAS A VOLUNTEER, SAYS HE BAGGED IT, CLOSED UP SHOP T'DAY...
HARDWARE
ANDREW
BOLT FOR CONGR
...BUT AIN'T CLEANED OUT THE ELECTRONICS YET. WE LOAD ALL THIS INNA TRUCK, WE'RE CLEARIN' FIVE BILLS EASY.
BOLT CONGRESS
BOLT FOR CONGRESS
ADD A LI'L GASOLINE... A MATCH...
...AND THE FIRE COVERS OUR TRACKS!
WE'RE GOLD. NO CLUES... NO WITNESSES...
...NO...

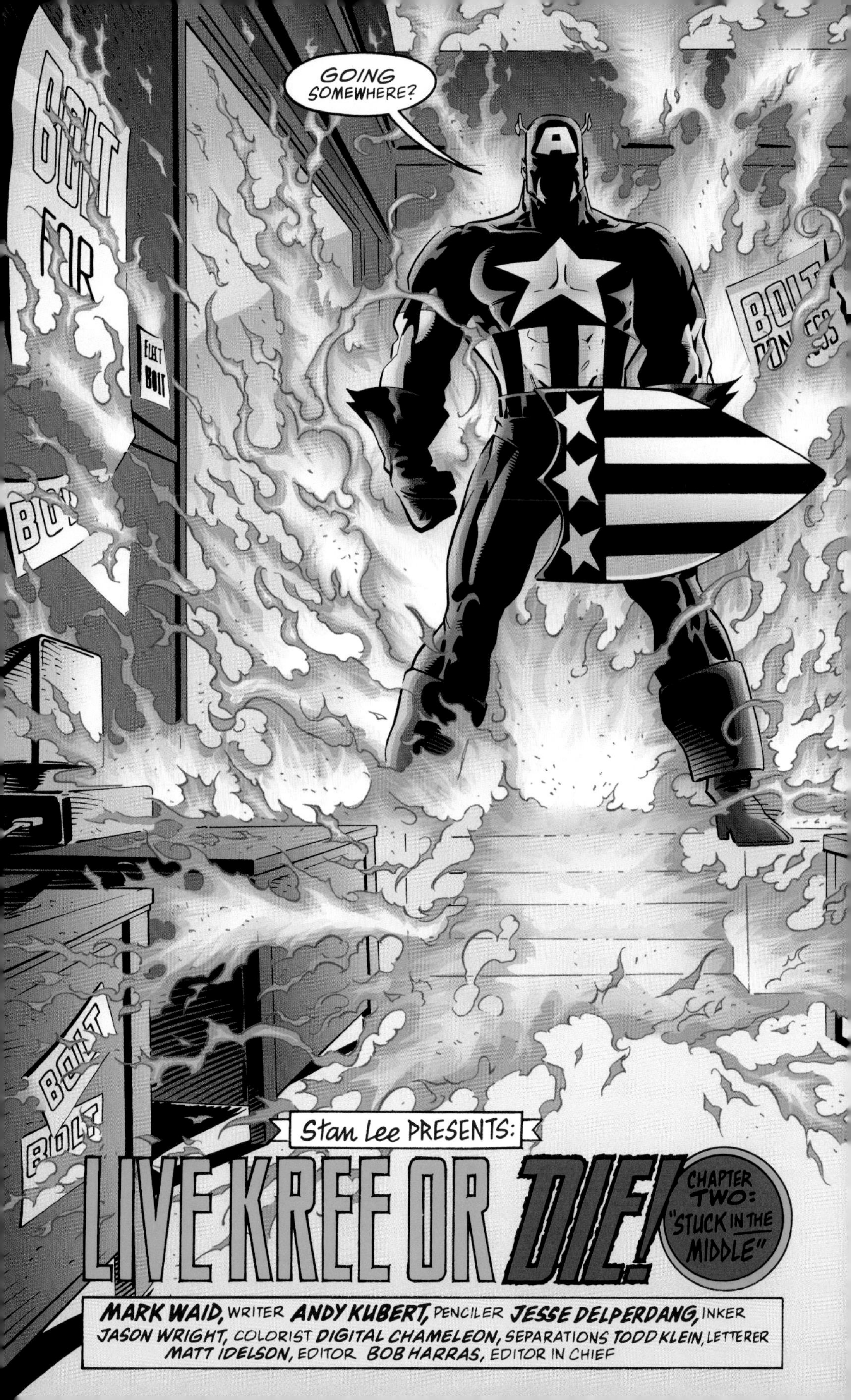
GOING SOMEWHERE?
BOLT FOR
ELECT BOLT
BOLT
BOLT
Stan Lee PRESENTS:
LIVE KREE OR DIE!
CHAPTER TWO: "STUCK IN THE MIDDLE"
MARK WAID, WRITER ANDY KUBERT, PENCILER JESSE DELPERDANG, INKER
JASON WRIGHT, COLORIST DIGITAL CHAMELEON, SEPARATIONS TODD KLEIN, LETTERER
MATT IDELSON, EDITOR BOB HARRAS, EDITOR IN CHIEF

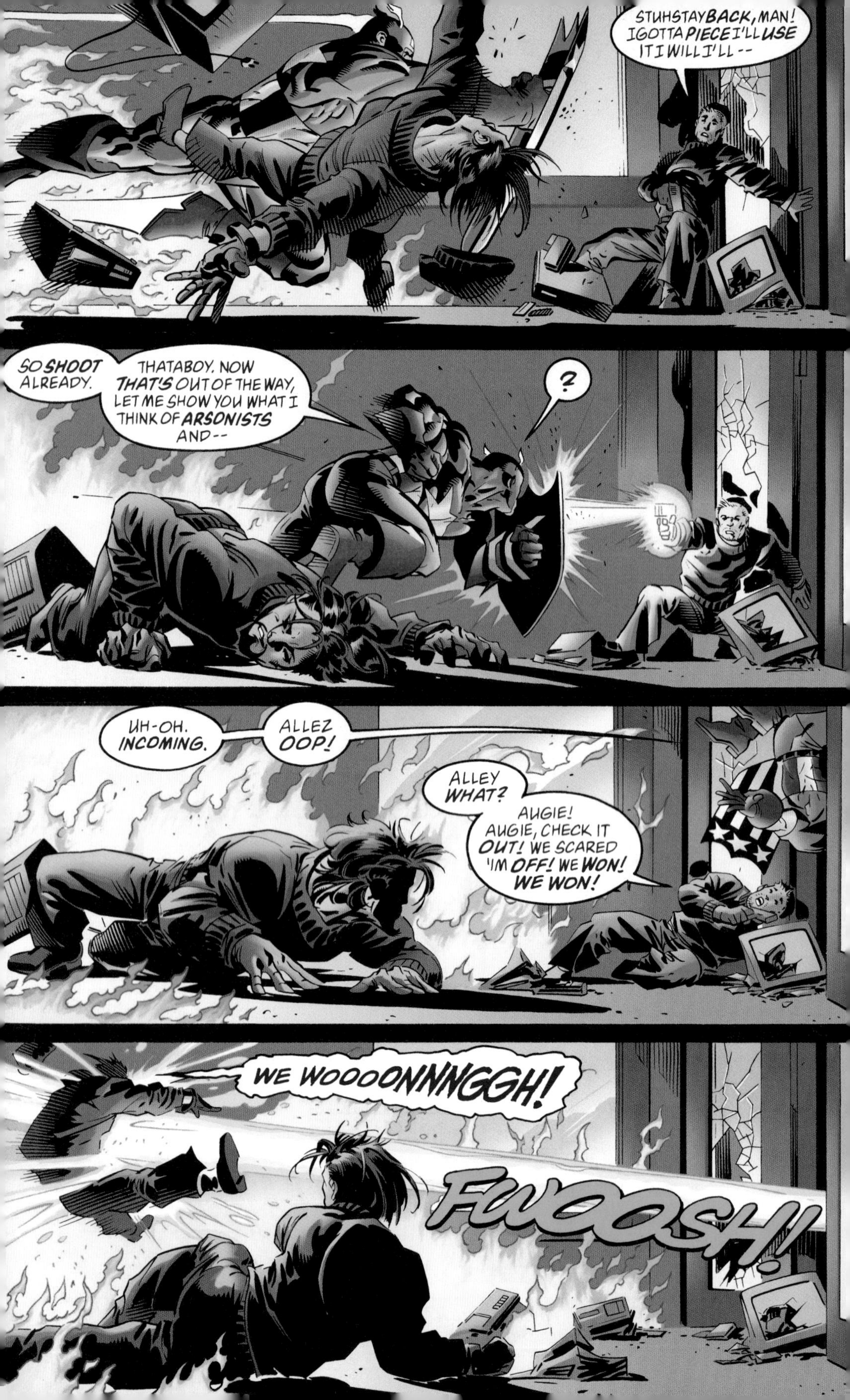
STUHSTAYBACK, MAN! IGOTTA PIECE I'LL USE IT I WILL I'LL --
SO SHOOT ALREADY.
THATABOY. NOW THAT'S OUT OF THE WAY, LET ME SHOW YOU WHAT I THINK OF ARSONISTS AND--
?
UH-OH. INCOMING.
ALLEZ OOP!
ALLEY WHAT?
AUGIE! AUGIE, CHECK IT OUT! WE SCARED 'IM OFF! WE WON! WE WON!
WE WOOOONNNGGH!
FWOOSH!!

--AND WE'RE *DONE!* SHOW'S *OVER,* FOLKS! FIRE'S *OUT!*

AND THE CULPRITS ARE BEHIND *BARS...* THANKS TO *YOU,* CAP. WHAT BRINGS YOU HERE?

I WAS LOOKING FOR *YOU,* FRANKLY, WHY WAS YOUR OFFICE *DESERTED?*

WHY GO *ON?* CONGRESS IS OUT OF *REACH* FOR *THIS* UNLUCKY COUNCILMAN, CAP. CAMPAIGN TOOK TOO BIG A *HIT* THE OTHER DAY.

I THOUGHT I WAS GETTING YOUR *ENDORSEMENT,* RIGHT?

TURNS OUT I GOT THE NOD FROM THE SKRULL *IMPERSONATING* YOU...AND THE MEDIA'S HAVING A *FIELD DAY* WITH THAT. I'M A *LAUGHING STOCK.**

THE *DAILY NEWS* HAS ALREADY MOCKED UP MY *POLL RESULTS* ON MARS.

AILY BUGL

Wednesday, June 17, 1998

Congressional Hopeful Endorsed by Cap Impos

*Issue 6. --Matt

I--I DON'T KNOW WHAT TO *SAY.* THIS IS *EXACTLY* THE KIND OF DAMAGE I WAS *AFRAID* HE'D CAUSE.

THE SKRULL USED MY REPUTATION TO SHATTER LIVES...AND I *CANNOT* HAVE THAT ON MY *CONSCIENCE...*

BREET

EXCUSE ME, BOLT. AVENGERS *ALERT.*

WARBIRD? WHAT'S *WRONG?*

PRIORITY RED, CAP! I NEED *HELP*-- FAST!

FULL SECURITY CLEARANCE AUTHORIZED

GERS

I'M UNDER **ALL-OUT ATTACK** BY A BAND OF **KREE SOLDIERS!**

THEY CALL THEMSELVES THE **LUNATIC LEGION!**

KREE--? LOCATION!

AN ABANDONED **MISSILE SILO** NEAR **CAPE CANAVERAL!**

GRAB A **QUINJET** AND TRACK MY **SIGNAL!** HURRY!

I'M ON IT! REINFORCEMENTS?

ALREADY CALLED IN! I CAN'T HOLD THE KREE OFF MUCH **LONGER, CAP!**

GET **MOVING!**

OVER AND **OUT!**

BOLT, I HAVE TO **GO--** BUT **LISTEN.** DON'T GIVE UP THE **CAMPAIGN,** NOT JUST **YET.**

I STILL CAN'T USE MY POSITION TO ENDORSE YOU AS A **CANDIDATE--**

--BUT I FEEL **RESPONSIBLE** FOR WHAT **HAPPENED.** MAYBE I CAN **HELP** YOU. I'LL BE IN **TOUCH.**

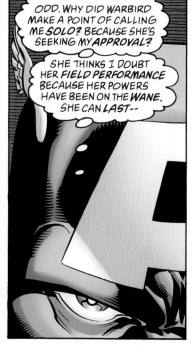

ODD. WHY DID WARBIRD MAKE A POINT OF CALLING ME **SOLO?** BECAUSE SHE'S SEEKING MY **APPROVAL?**

SHE THINKS I DOUBT HER **FIELD PERFORMANCE** BECAUSE HER POWERS HAVE BEEN ON THE **WANE.** SHE CAN **LAST--**

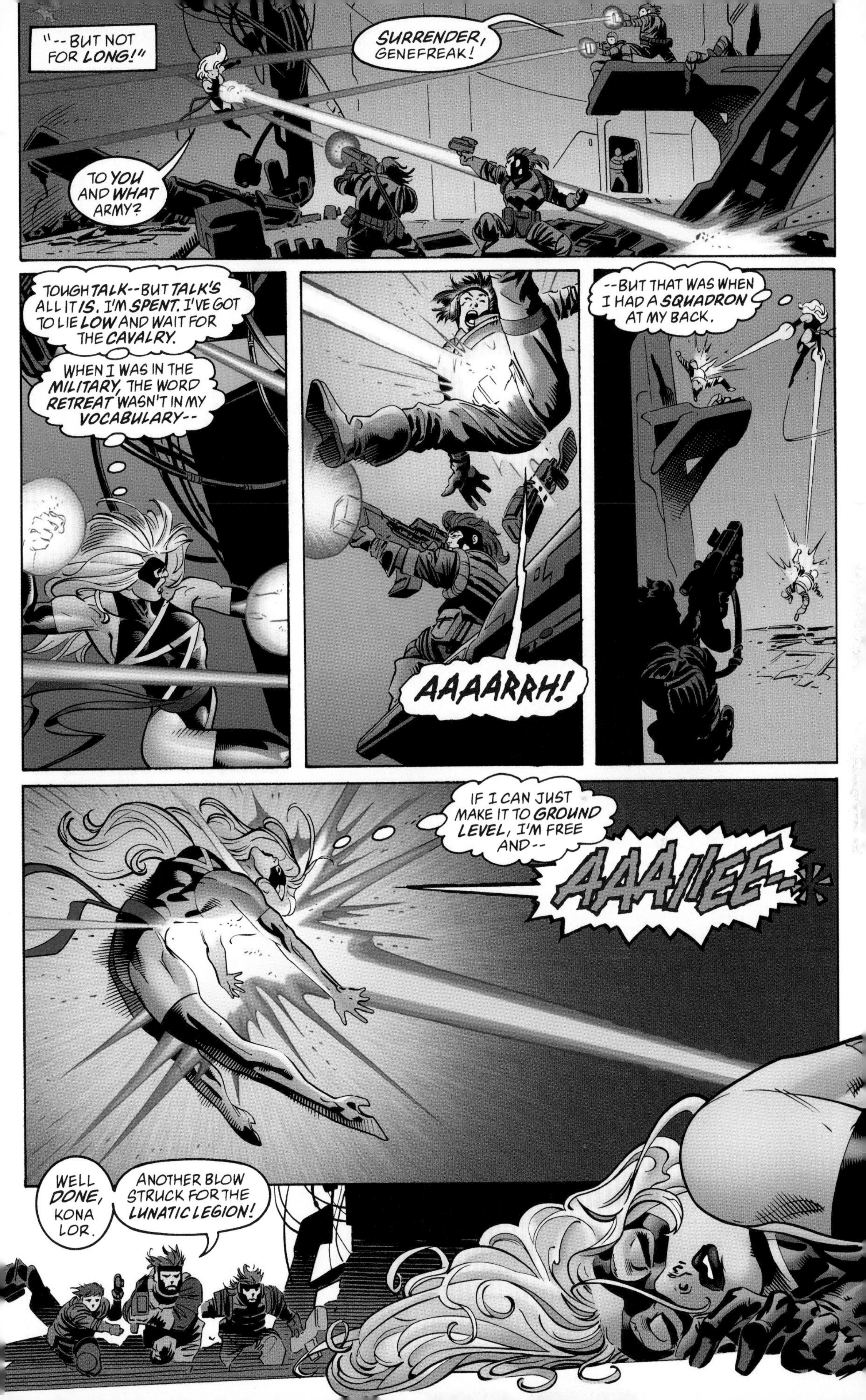
"--BUT NOT FOR LONG!"
SURRENDER, GENEFREAK!
TO YOU AND WHAT ARMY?
TOUGH TALK--BUT TALK'S ALL IT IS. I'M SPENT. I'VE GOT TO LIE LOW AND WAIT FOR THE CAVALRY.
WHEN I WAS IN THE MILITARY, THE WORD RETREAT WASN'T IN MY VOCABULARY--
AAAARRH!
--BUT THAT WAS WHEN I HAD A SQUADRON AT MY BACK.
IF I CAN JUST MAKE IT TO GROUND LEVEL, I'M FREE AND--
AAAIIEE--
WELL DONE, KONA LOR.
ANOTHER BLOW STRUCK FOR THE LUNATIC LEGION!

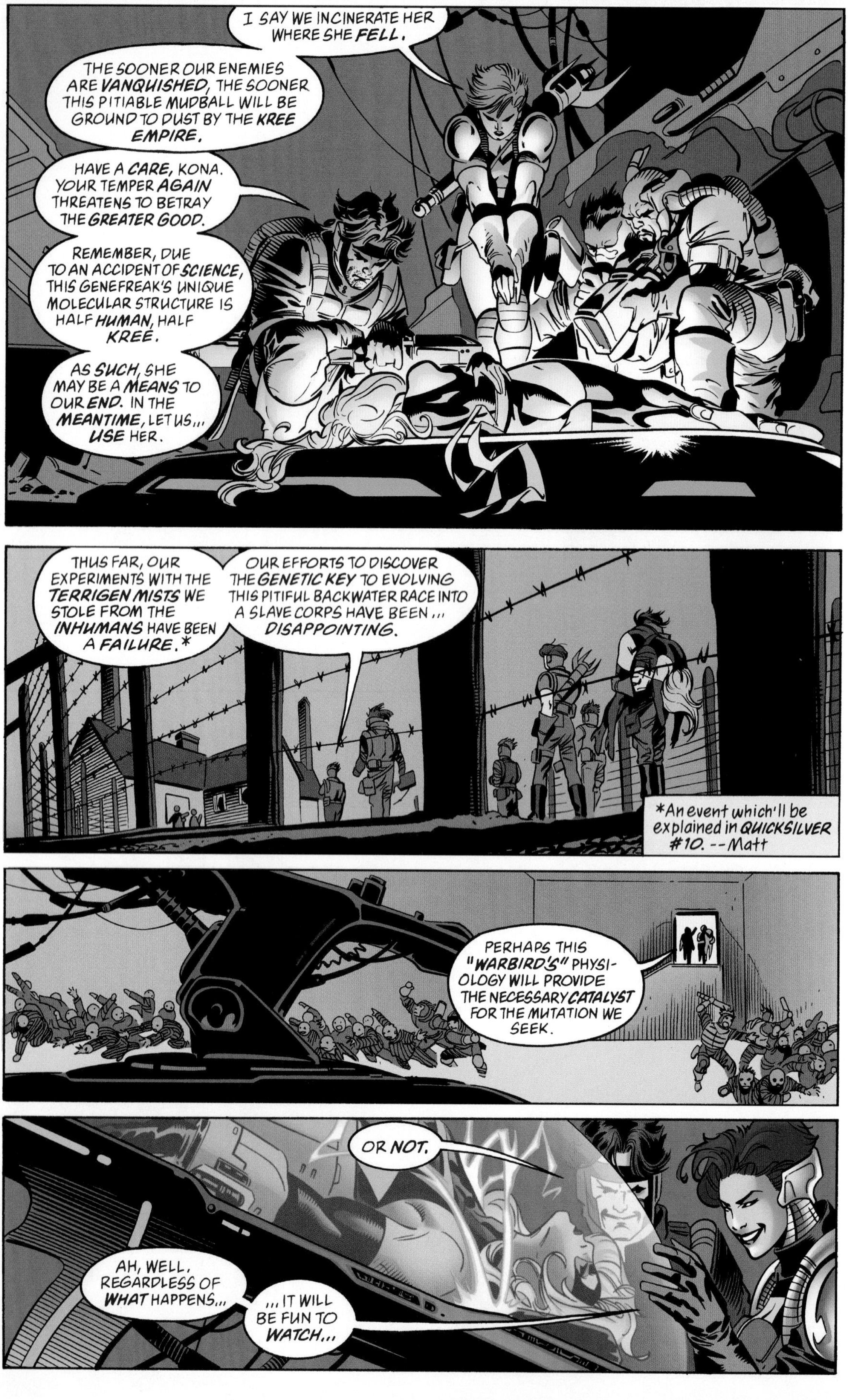

I SAY WE INCINERATE HER WHERE SHE FELL.
THE SOONER OUR ENEMIES ARE VANQUISHED, THE SOONER THIS PITIABLE MUDBALL WILL BE GROUND TO DUST BY THE KREE EMPIRE.
HAVE A CARE, KONA. YOUR TEMPER AGAIN THREATENS TO BETRAY THE GREATER GOOD.
REMEMBER, DUE TO AN ACCIDENT OF SCIENCE, THIS GENEFREAK'S UNIQUE MOLECULAR STRUCTURE IS HALF HUMAN, HALF KREE.
AS SUCH, SHE MAY BE A MEANS TO OUR END. IN THE MEANTIME, LET US... USE HER.
THUS FAR, OUR EXPERIMENTS WITH THE TERRIGEN MISTS WE STOLE FROM THE INHUMANS HAVE BEEN A FAILURE.*
OUR EFFORTS TO DISCOVER THE GENETIC KEY TO EVOLVING THIS PITIFUL BACKWATER RACE INTO A SLAVE CORPS HAVE BEEN... DISAPPOINTING.
*An event which'll be explained in QUICKSILVER #10. --Matt
PERHAPS THIS "WARBIRD'S" PHYSIOLOGY WILL PROVIDE THE NECESSARY CATALYST FOR THE MUTATION WE SEEK.
OR NOT.
AH, WELL, REGARDLESS OF WHAT HAPPENS...
...IT WILL BE FUN TO WATCH...

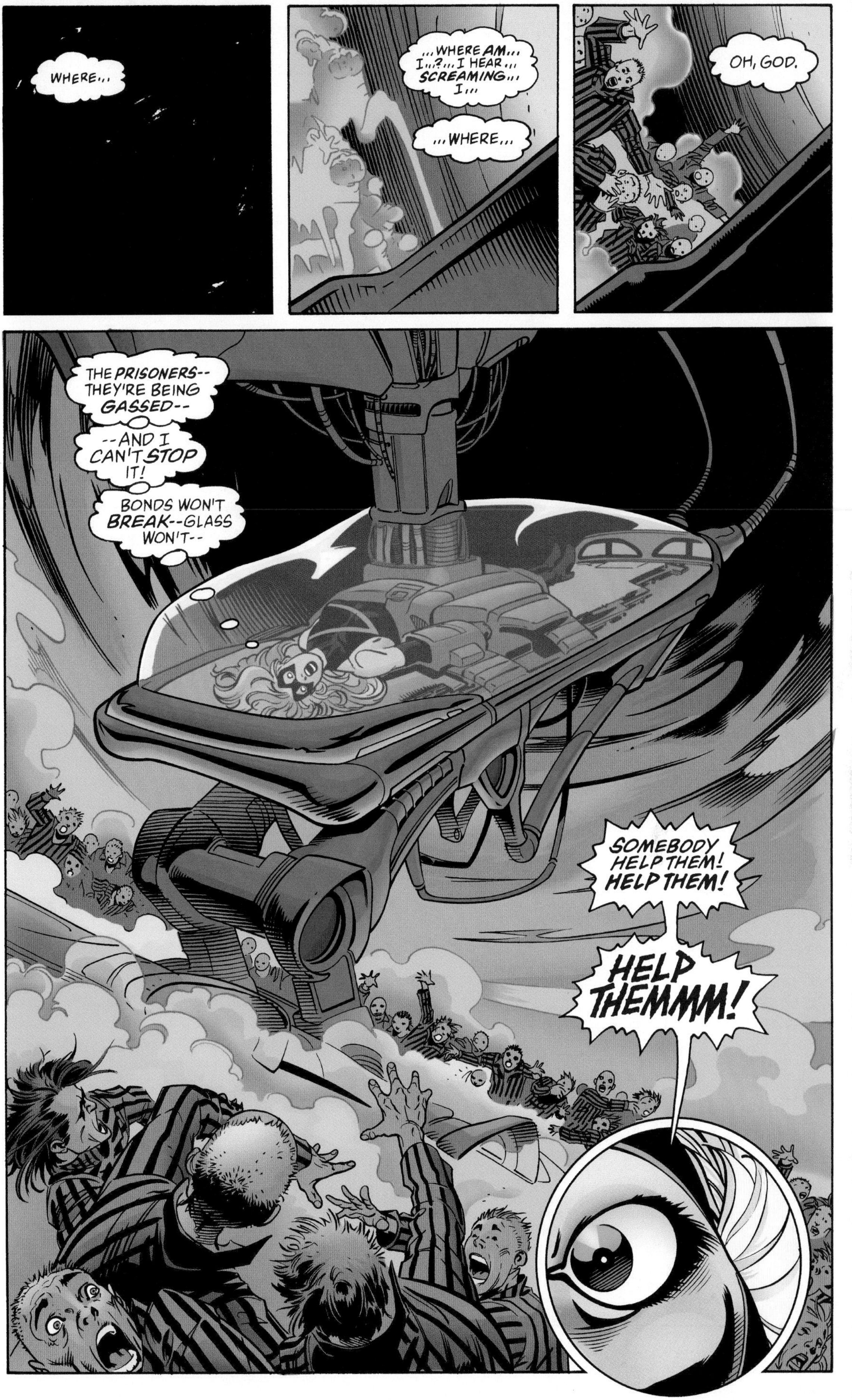
WHERE...
...WHERE AM I...?...I HEAR... SCREAMING... I...
...WHERE...
OH, GOD.
THE PRISONERS-- THEY'RE BEING GASSED--
--AND I CAN'T STOP IT!
BONDS WON'T BREAK--GLASS WON'T--
SOMEBODY HELP THEM! HELP THEM!
HELP THEMMM!

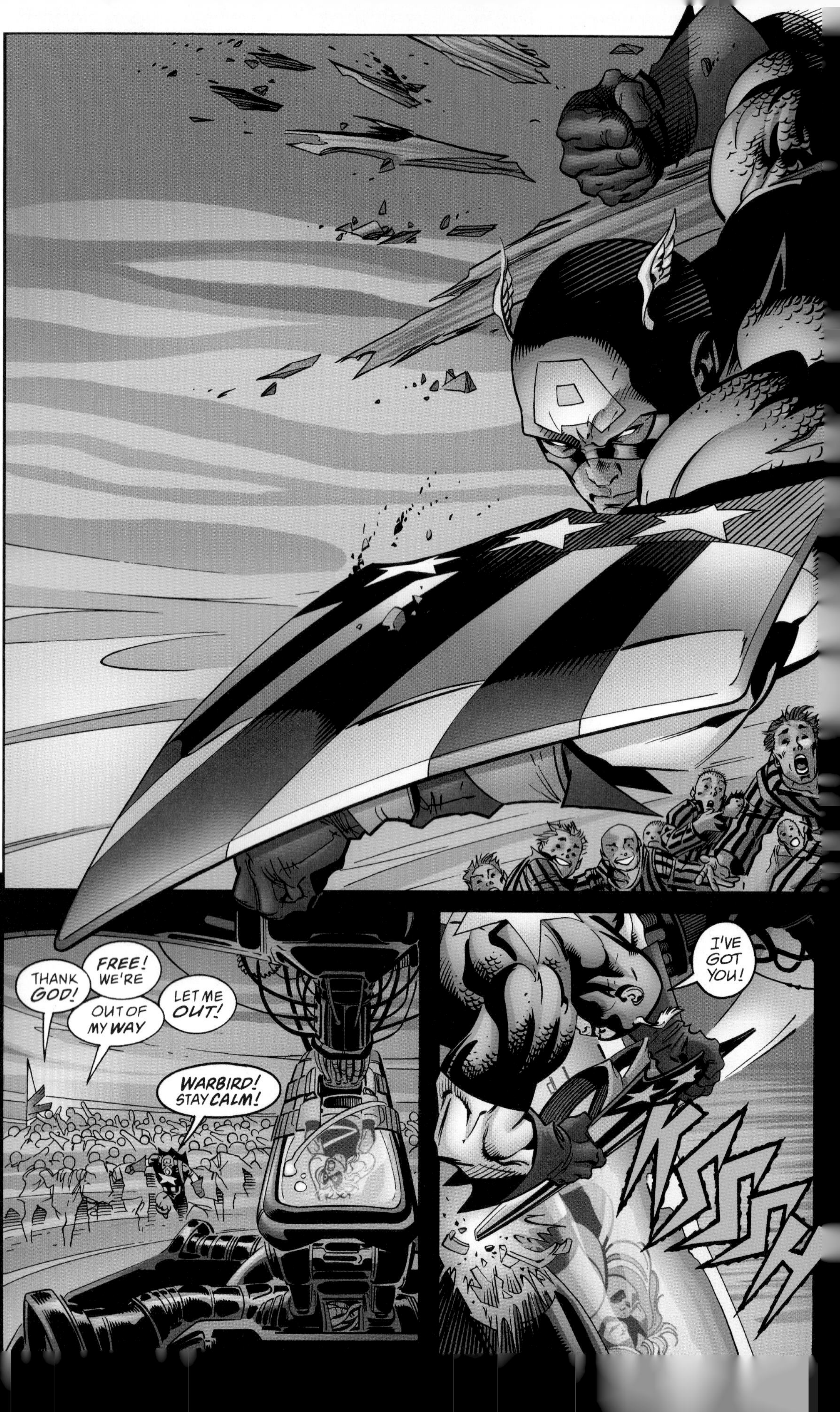

THANK GOD!
FREE! WE'RE
OUT OF MY WAY
LET ME OUT!
WARBIRD! STAY CALM!
I'VE GOT YOU!
KSSSH

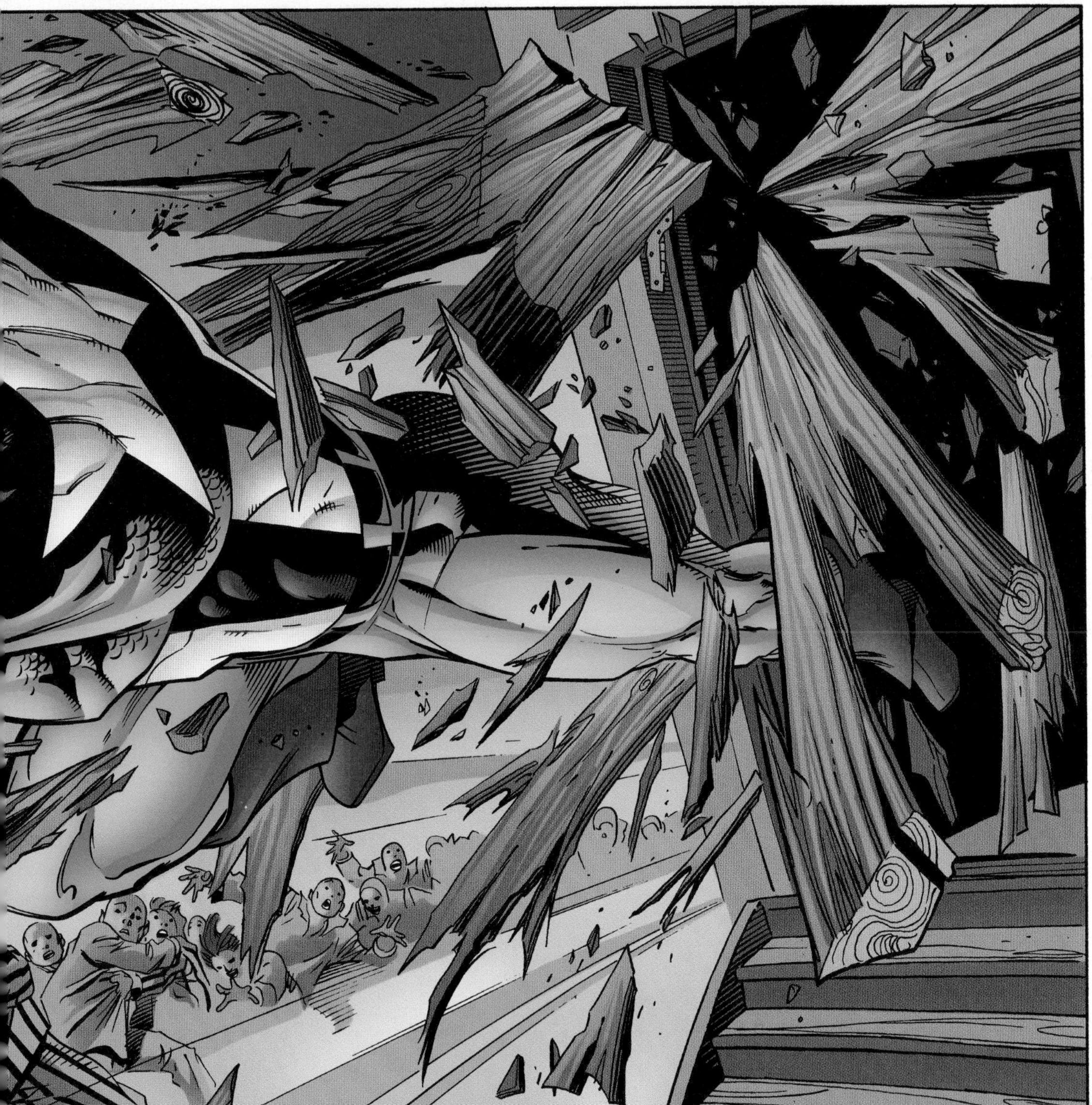
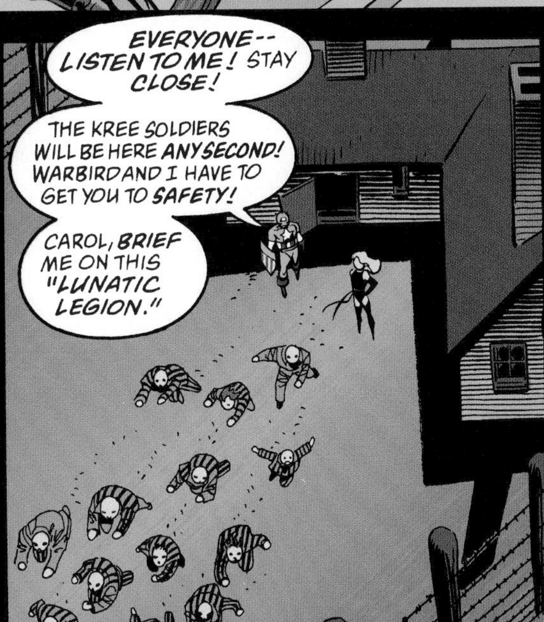
EVERYONE-- LISTEN TO ME! STAY CLOSE!
THE KREE SOLDIERS WILL BE HERE ANY SECOND! WARBIRD AND I HAVE TO GET YOU TO SAFETY!
CAROL, BRIEF ME ON THIS "LUNATIC LEGION."
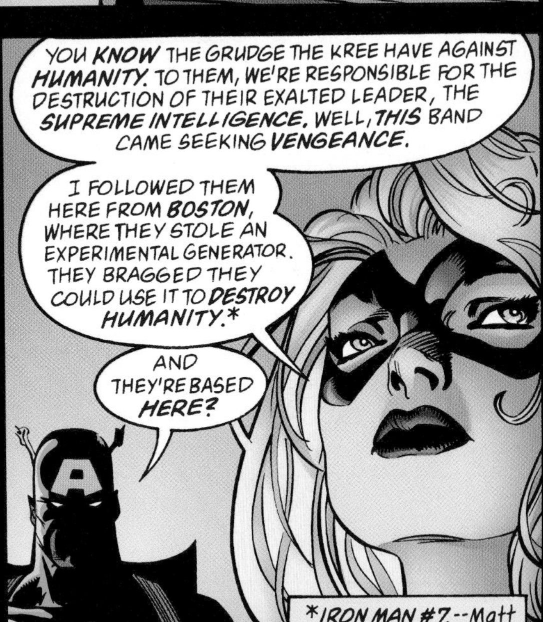
YOU KNOW THE GRUDGE THE KREE HAVE AGAINST HUMANITY. TO THEM, WE'RE RESPONSIBLE FOR THE DESTRUCTION OF THEIR EXALTED LEADER, THE SUPREME INTELLIGENCE. WELL, THIS BAND CAME SEEKING VENGEANCE.
I FOLLOWED THEM HERE FROM BOSTON, WHERE THEY STOLE AN EXPERIMENTAL GENERATOR. THEY BRAGGED THEY COULD USE IT TO DESTROY HUMANITY.*
AND THEY'RE BASED HERE?
*IRON MAN #7.--Matt

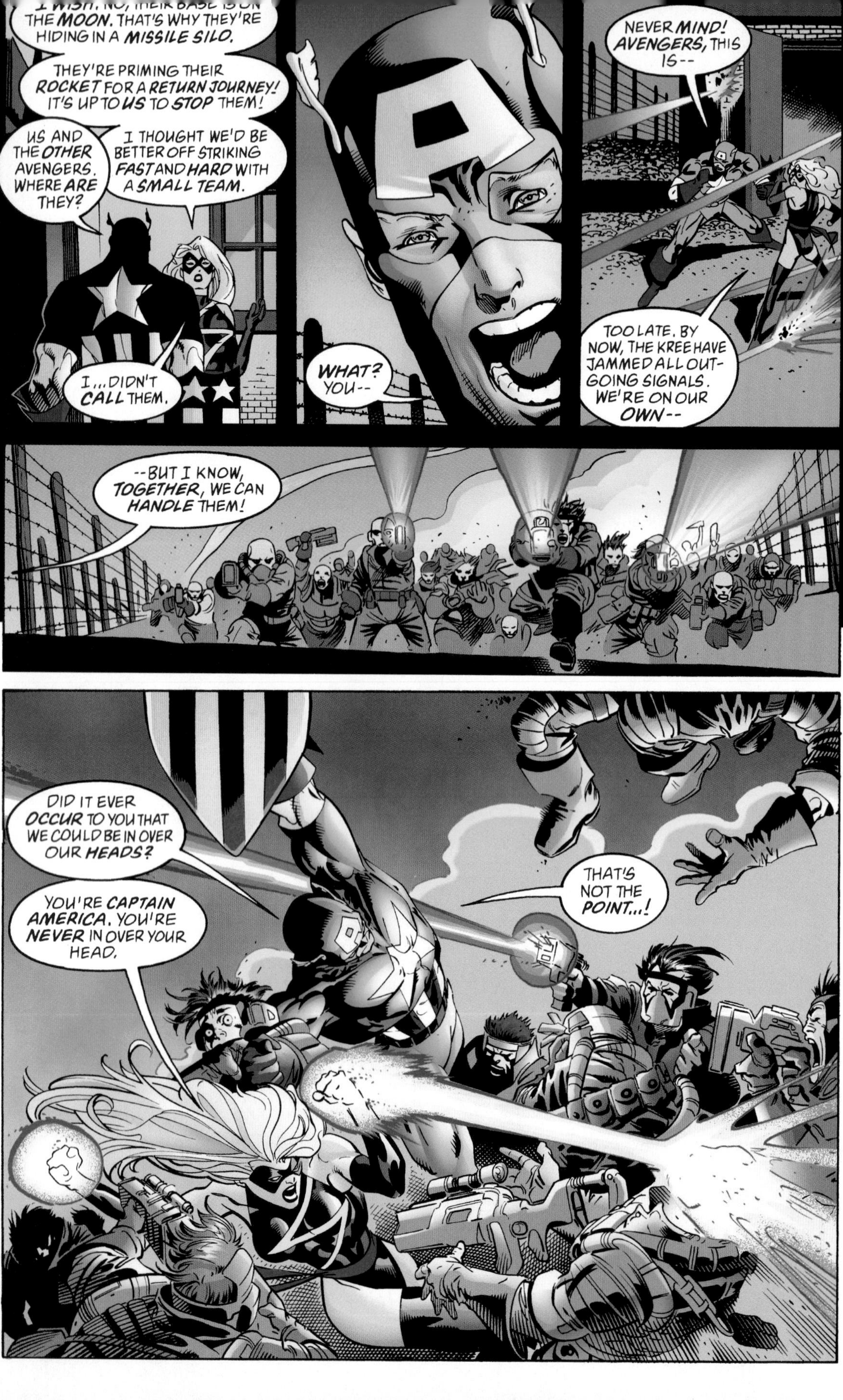
I WISH. NO, THEIR BASE IS ON THE MOON. THAT'S WHY THEY'RE HIDING IN A MISSILE SILO.
THEY'RE PRIMING THEIR ROCKET FOR A RETURN JOURNEY! IT'S UP TO US TO STOP THEM!
US AND THE OTHER AVENGERS. WHERE ARE THEY?
I THOUGHT WE'D BE BETTER OFF STRIKING FAST AND HARD WITH A SMALL TEAM.
I...DIDN'T CALL THEM.
WHAT? YOU--
NEVER MIND! AVENGERS, THIS IS--
TOO LATE. BY NOW, THE KREE HAVE JAMMED ALL OUT-GOING SIGNALS. WE'RE ON OUR OWN--
--BUT I KNOW, TOGETHER, WE CAN HANDLE THEM!
DID IT EVER OCCUR TO YOU THAT WE COULD BE IN OVER OUR HEADS?
YOU'RE CAPTAIN AMERICA. YOU'RE NEVER IN OVER YOUR HEAD.
THAT'S NOT THE POINT...!

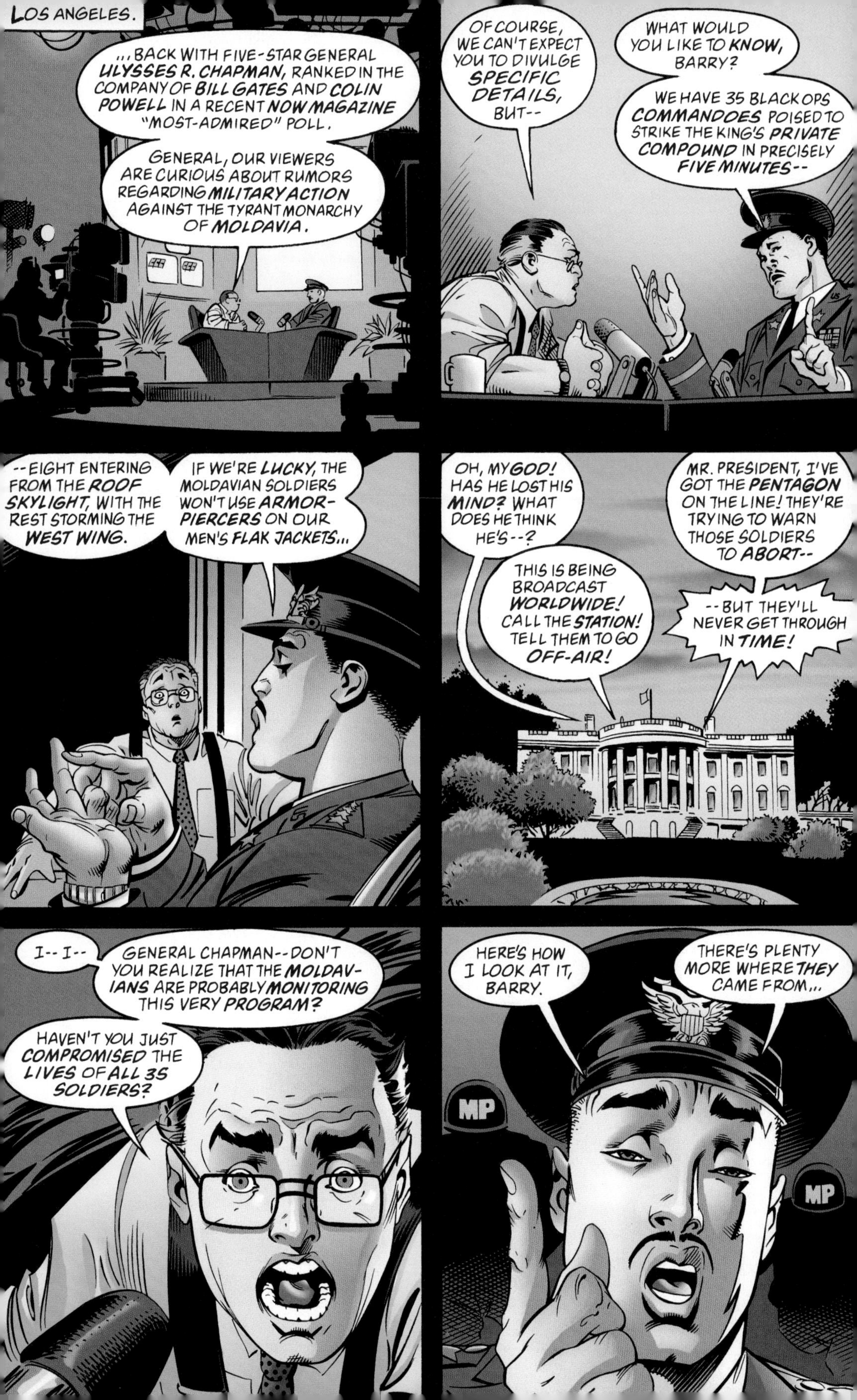
LOS ANGELES.
...BACK WITH FIVE-STAR GENERAL ULYSSES R. CHAPMAN, RANKED IN THE COMPANY OF BILL GATES AND COLIN POWELL IN A RECENT NOW MAGAZINE "MOST-ADMIRED" POLL.
GENERAL, OUR VIEWERS ARE CURIOUS ABOUT RUMORS REGARDING MILITARY ACTION AGAINST THE TYRANT MONARCHY OF MOLDAVIA.
OF COURSE, WE CAN'T EXPECT YOU TO DIVULGE SPECIFIC DETAILS, BUT--
WHAT WOULD YOU LIKE TO KNOW, BARRY?
WE HAVE 35 BLACK OPS COMMANDOES POISED TO STRIKE THE KING'S PRIVATE COMPOUND IN PRECISELY FIVE MINUTES--
--EIGHT ENTERING FROM THE ROOF SKYLIGHT, WITH THE REST STORMING THE WEST WING.
IF WE'RE LUCKY, THE MOLDAVIAN SOLDIERS WON'T USE ARMOR-PIERCERS ON OUR MEN'S FLAK JACKETS...
OH, MY GOD! HAS HE LOST HIS MIND? WHAT DOES HE THINK HE'S--?
THIS IS BEING BROADCAST WORLDWIDE! CALL THE STATION! TELL THEM TO GO OFF-AIR!
MR. PRESIDENT, I'VE GOT THE PENTAGON ON THE LINE! THEY'RE TRYING TO WARN THOSE SOLDIERS TO ABORT--
--BUT THEY'LL NEVER GET THROUGH IN TIME!
I-- I--
GENERAL CHAPMAN--DON'T YOU REALIZE THAT THE MOLDAVIANS ARE PROBABLY MONITORING THIS VERY PROGRAM?
HAVEN'T YOU JUST COMPROMISED THE LIVES OF ALL 35 SOLDIERS?
HERE'S HOW I LOOK AT IT, BARRY.
THERE'S PLENTY MORE WHERE THEY CAME FROM...
MP
MP

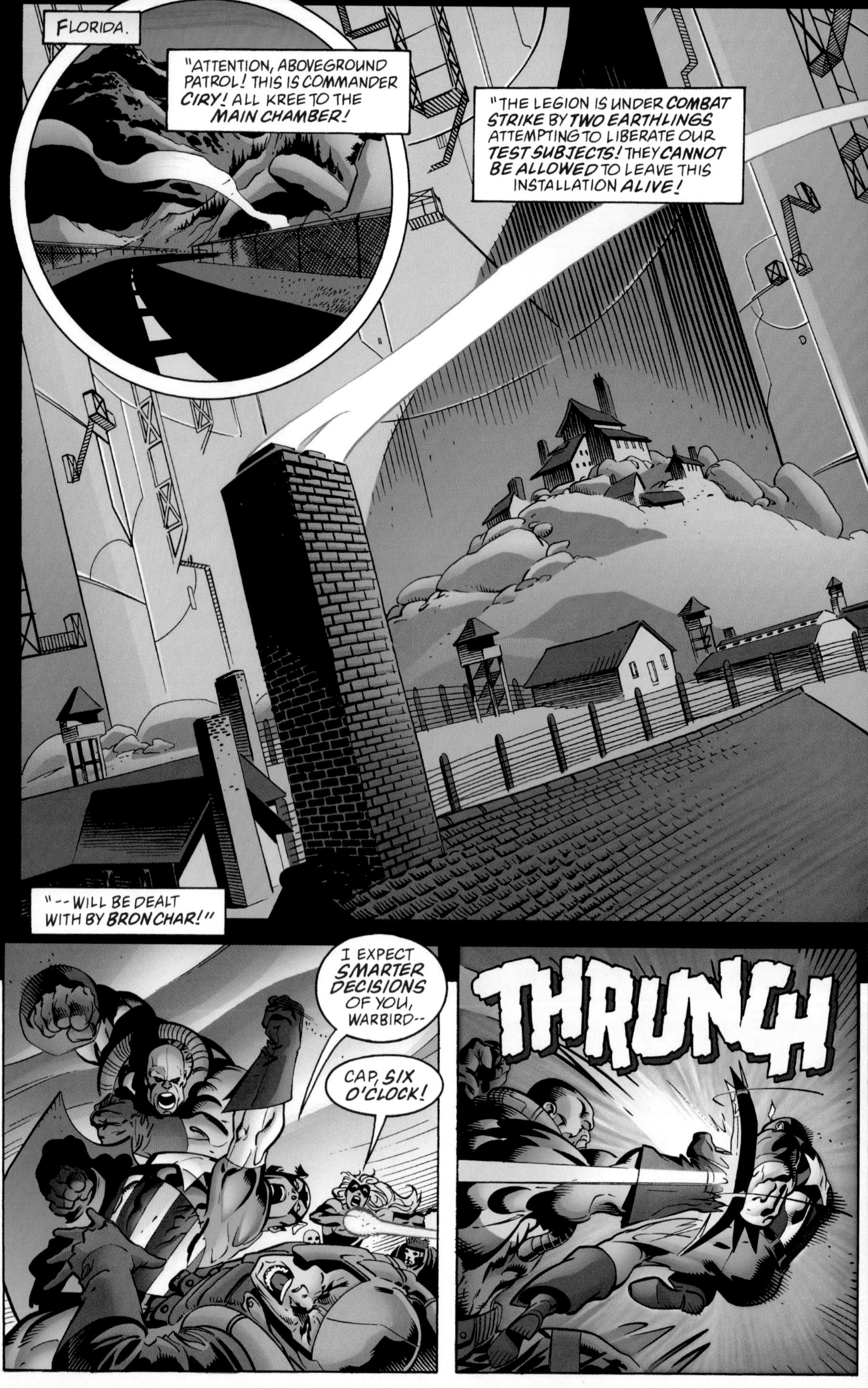
FLORIDA.
"ATTENTION, ABOVEGROUND PATROL! THIS IS COMMANDER CIRY! ALL KREE TO THE MAIN CHAMBER!
"THE LEGION IS UNDER COMBAT STRIKE BY TWO EARTHLINGS ATTEMPTING TO LIBERATE OUR TEST SUBJECTS! THEY CANNOT BE ALLOWED TO LEAVE THIS INSTALLATION ALIVE!
"--WILL BE DEALT WITH BY BRONCHAR!"
I EXPECT SMARTER DECISIONS OF YOU, WARBIRD--
CAP, SIX O'CLOCK!
THRUNCH

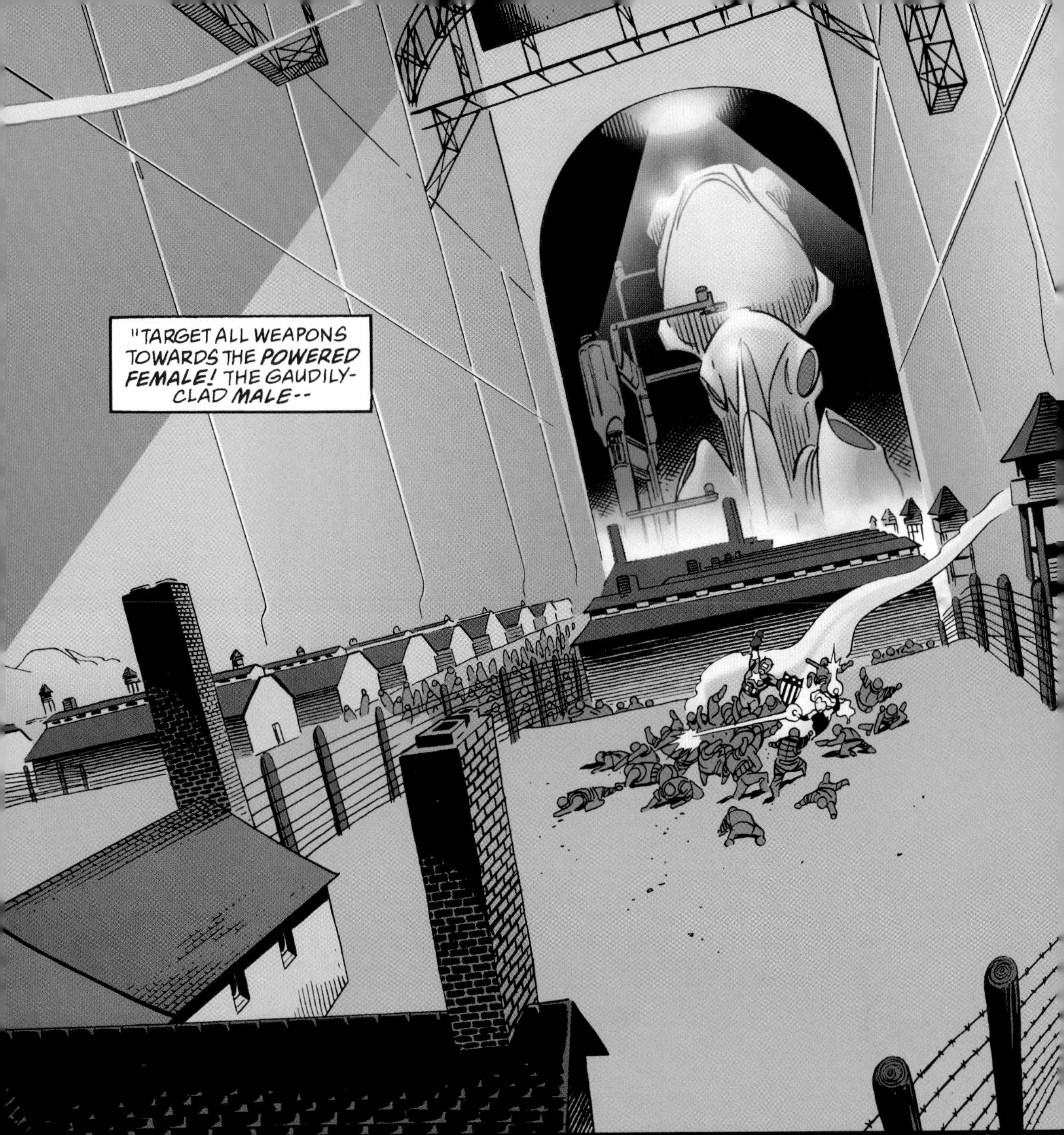
"TARGET ALL WEAPONS TOWARDS THE POWERED FEMALE! THE GAUDILY-CLAD MALE--

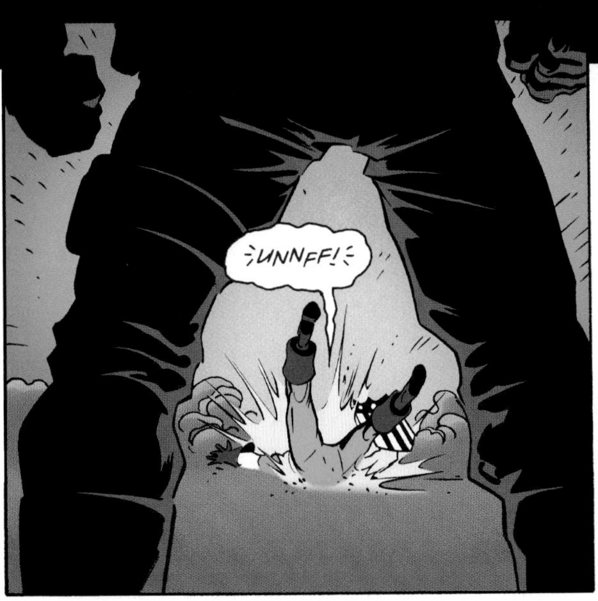
UNNFF!

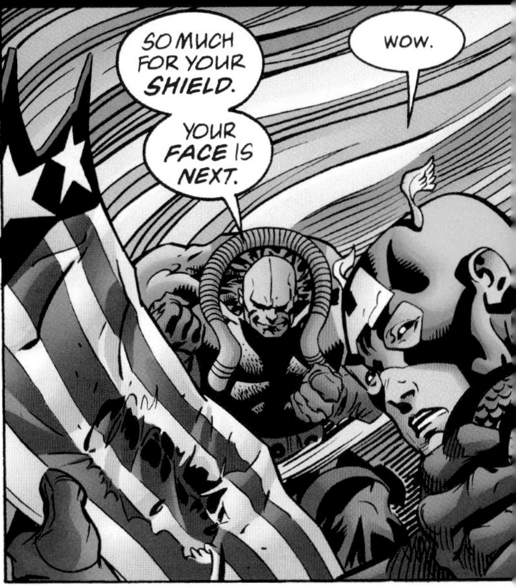
SO MUCH FOR YOUR SHIELD.
YOUR FACE IS NEXT.
WOW.

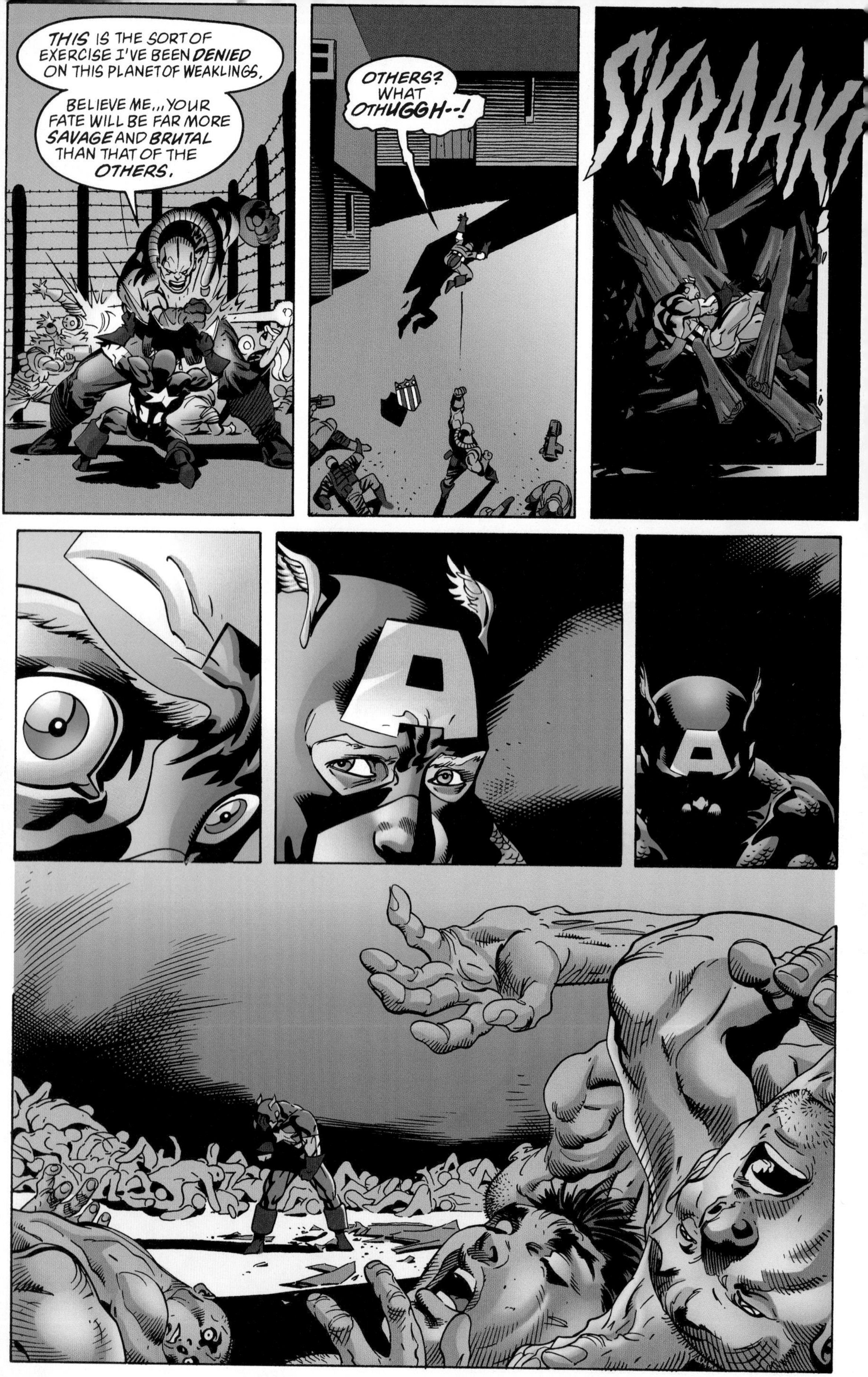
THIS IS THE SORT OF EXERCISE I'VE BEEN DENIED ON THIS PLANET OF WEAKLINGS.
BELIEVE ME... YOUR FATE WILL BE FAR MORE SAVAGE AND BRUTAL THAN THAT OF THE OTHERS.
OTHERS? WHAT OTHUGGH--!
SKRAAK!

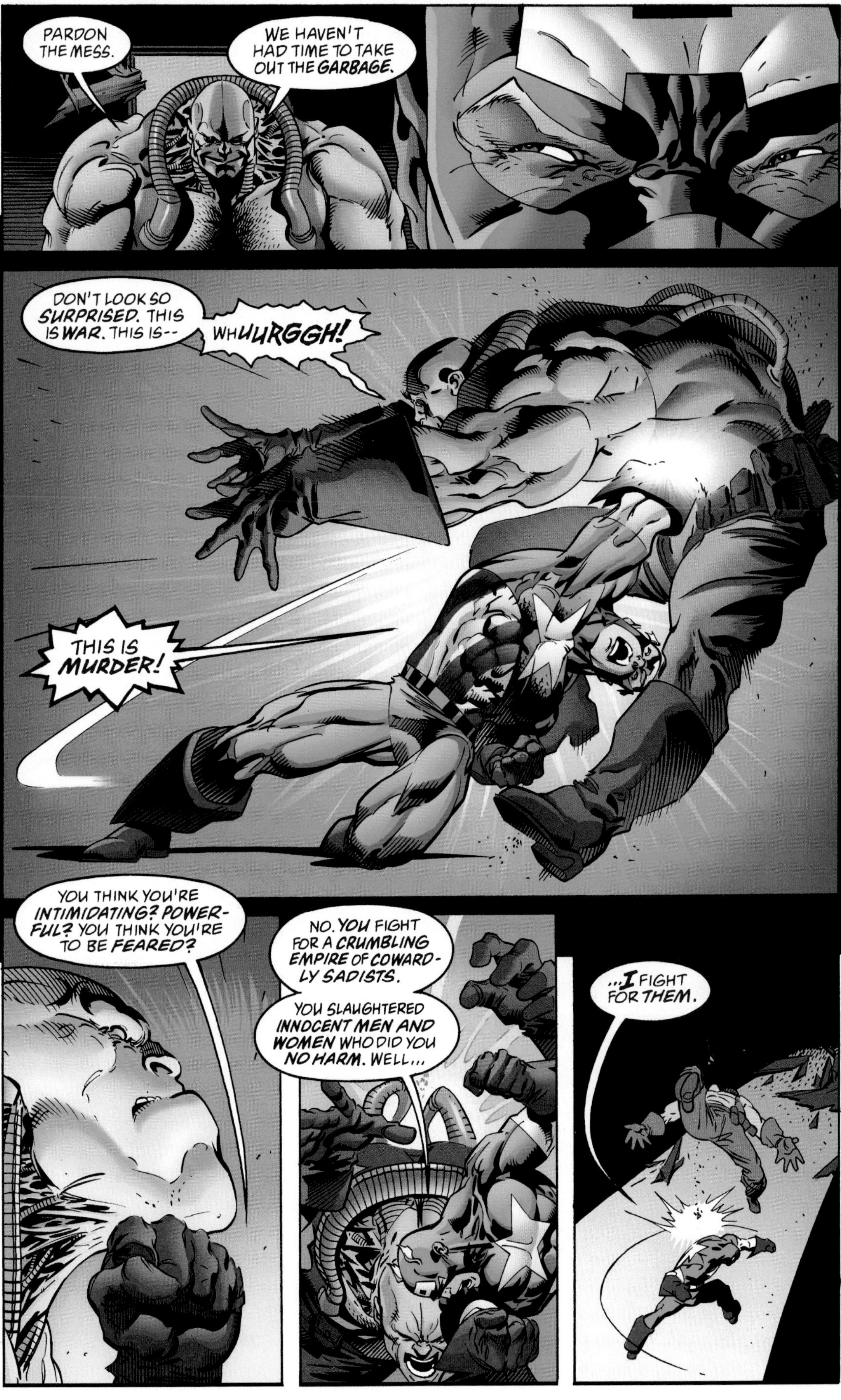

PARDON THE MESS.
WE HAVEN'T HAD TIME TO TAKE OUT THE GARBAGE.
DON'T LOOK SO SURPRISED. THIS IS WAR. THIS IS--
WHUURGGH!
THIS IS MURDER!
YOU THINK YOU'RE INTIMIDATING? POWER-FUL? YOU THINK YOU'RE TO BE FEARED?
NO. YOU FIGHT FOR A CRUMBLING EMPIRE OF COWARD-LY SADISTS.
YOU SLAUGHTERED INNOCENT MEN AND WOMEN WHO DID YOU NO HARM. WELL...
...I FIGHT FOR THEM.

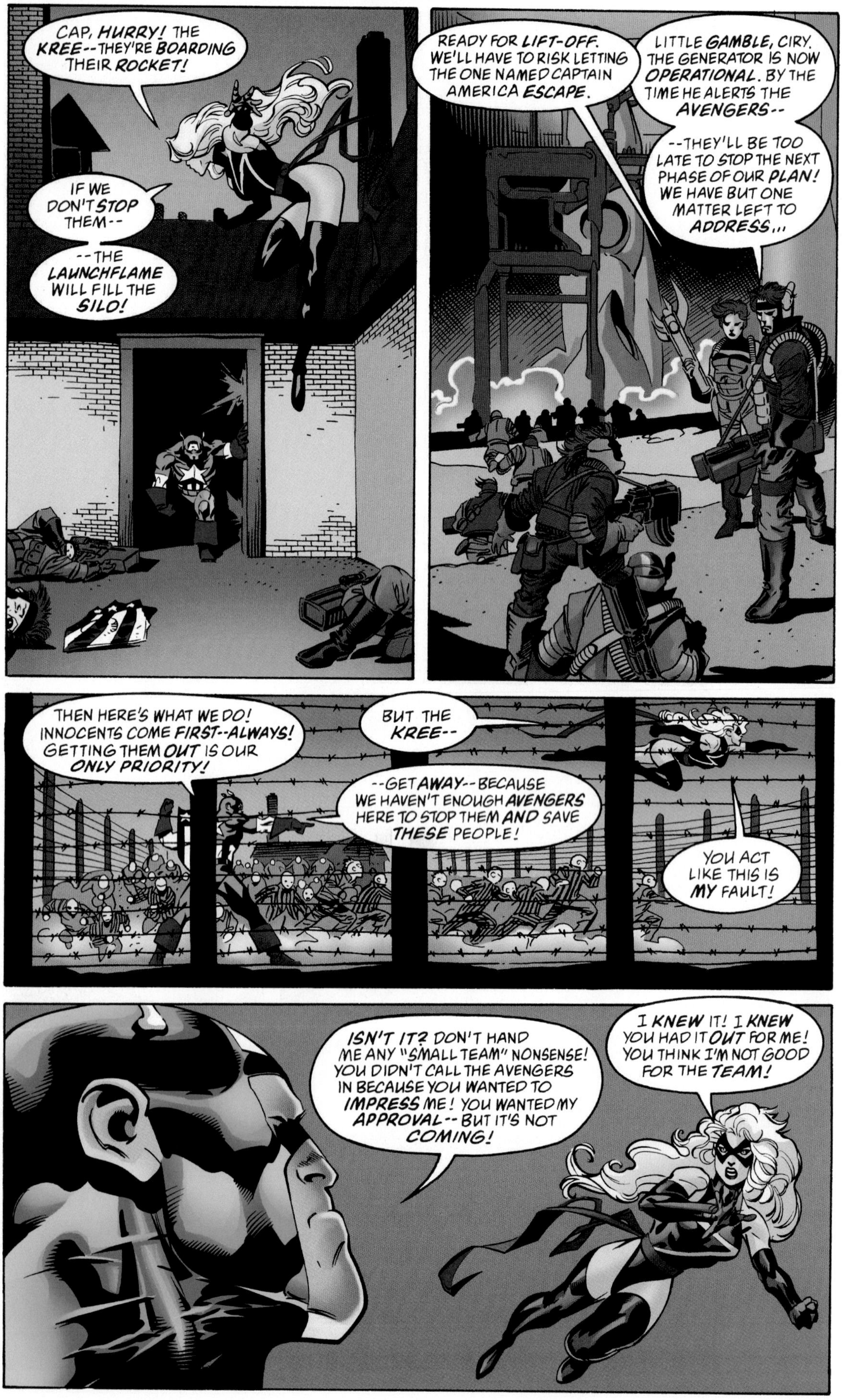
CAP, HURRY! THE KREE--THEY'RE BOARDING THEIR ROCKET!
IF WE DON'T STOP THEM--
--THE LAUNCHFLAME WILL FILL THE SILO!
READY FOR LIFT-OFF. WE'LL HAVE TO RISK LETTING THE ONE NAMED CAPTAIN AMERICA ESCAPE.
LITTLE GAMBLE, CIRY. THE GENERATOR IS NOW OPERATIONAL. BY THE TIME HE ALERTS THE AVENGERS--
--THEY'LL BE TOO LATE TO STOP THE NEXT PHASE OF OUR PLAN! WE HAVE BUT ONE MATTER LEFT TO ADDRESS...
THEN HERE'S WHAT WE DO! INNOCENTS COME FIRST--ALWAYS! GETTING THEM OUT IS OUR ONLY PRIORITY!
BUT THE KREE--
--GET AWAY--BECAUSE WE HAVEN'T ENOUGH AVENGERS HERE TO STOP THEM AND SAVE THESE PEOPLE!
YOU ACT LIKE THIS IS MY FAULT!
ISN'T IT? DON'T HAND ME ANY "SMALL TEAM" NONSENSE! YOU DIDN'T CALL THE AVENGERS IN BECAUSE YOU WANTED TO IMPRESS ME! YOU WANTED MY APPROVAL--BUT IT'S NOT COMING!
I KNEW IT! I KNEW YOU HAD IT OUT FOR ME! YOU THINK I'M NOT GOOD FOR THE TEAM!

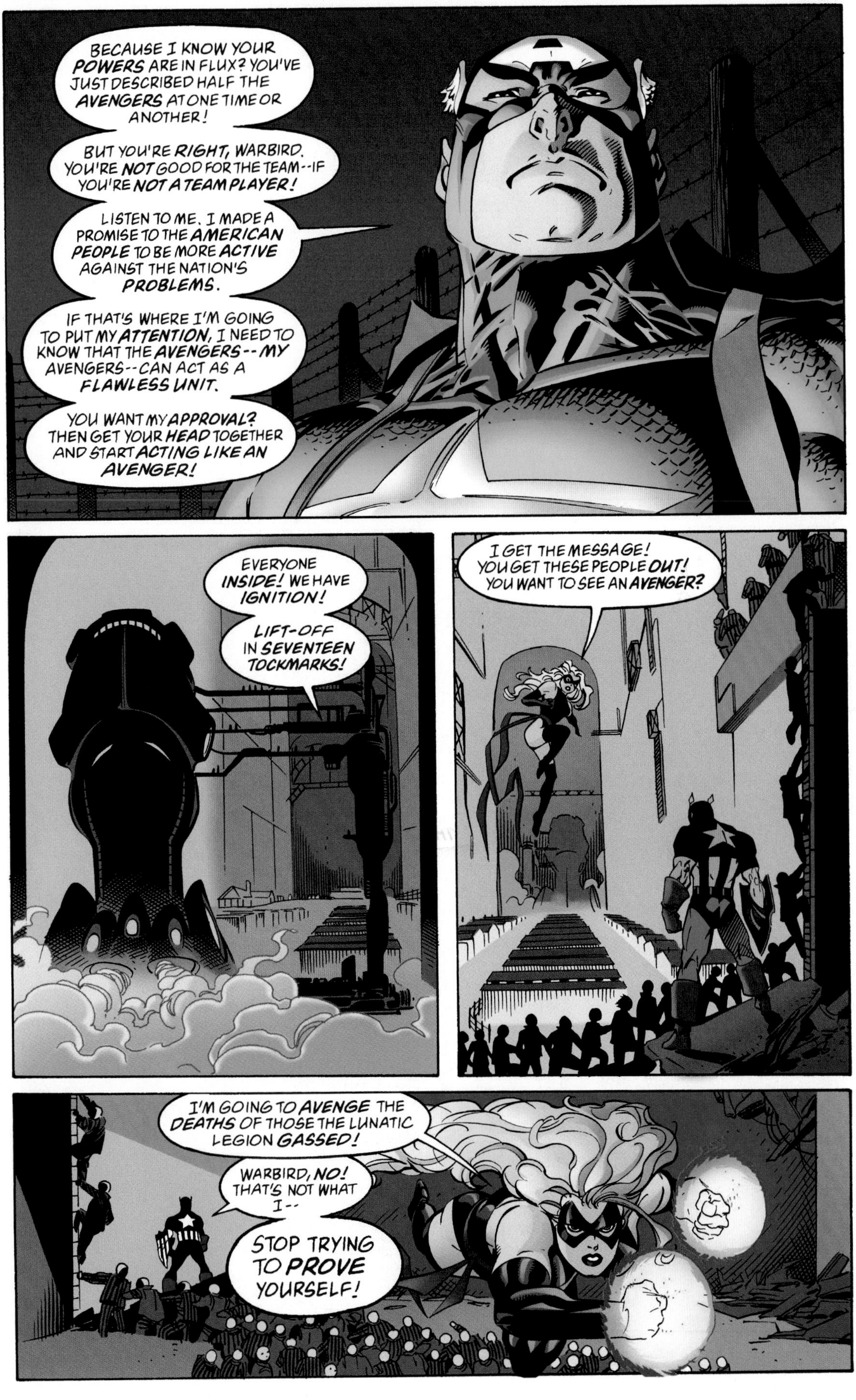
BECAUSE I KNOW YOUR POWERS ARE IN FLUX? YOU'VE JUST DESCRIBED HALF THE AVENGERS AT ONE TIME OR ANOTHER!
BUT YOU'RE RIGHT, WARBIRD. YOU'RE NOT GOOD FOR THE TEAM--IF YOU'RE NOT A TEAM PLAYER!
LISTEN TO ME. I MADE A PROMISE TO THE AMERICAN PEOPLE TO BE MORE ACTIVE AGAINST THE NATION'S PROBLEMS.
IF THAT'S WHERE I'M GOING TO PUT MY ATTENTION, I NEED TO KNOW THAT THE AVENGERS--MY AVENGERS--CAN ACT AS A FLAWLESS UNIT.
YOU WANT MY APPROVAL? THEN GET YOUR HEAD TOGETHER AND START ACTING LIKE AN AVENGER!
EVERYONE INSIDE! WE HAVE IGNITION!
LIFT-OFF IN SEVENTEEN TOCKMARKS!
I GET THE MESSAGE! YOU GET THESE PEOPLE OUT! YOU WANT TO SEE AN AVENGER?
I'M GOING TO AVENGE THE DEATHS OF THOSE THE LUNATIC LEGION GASSED!
WARBIRD, NO! THAT'S NOT WHAT I--
STOP TRYING TO PROVE YOURSELF!

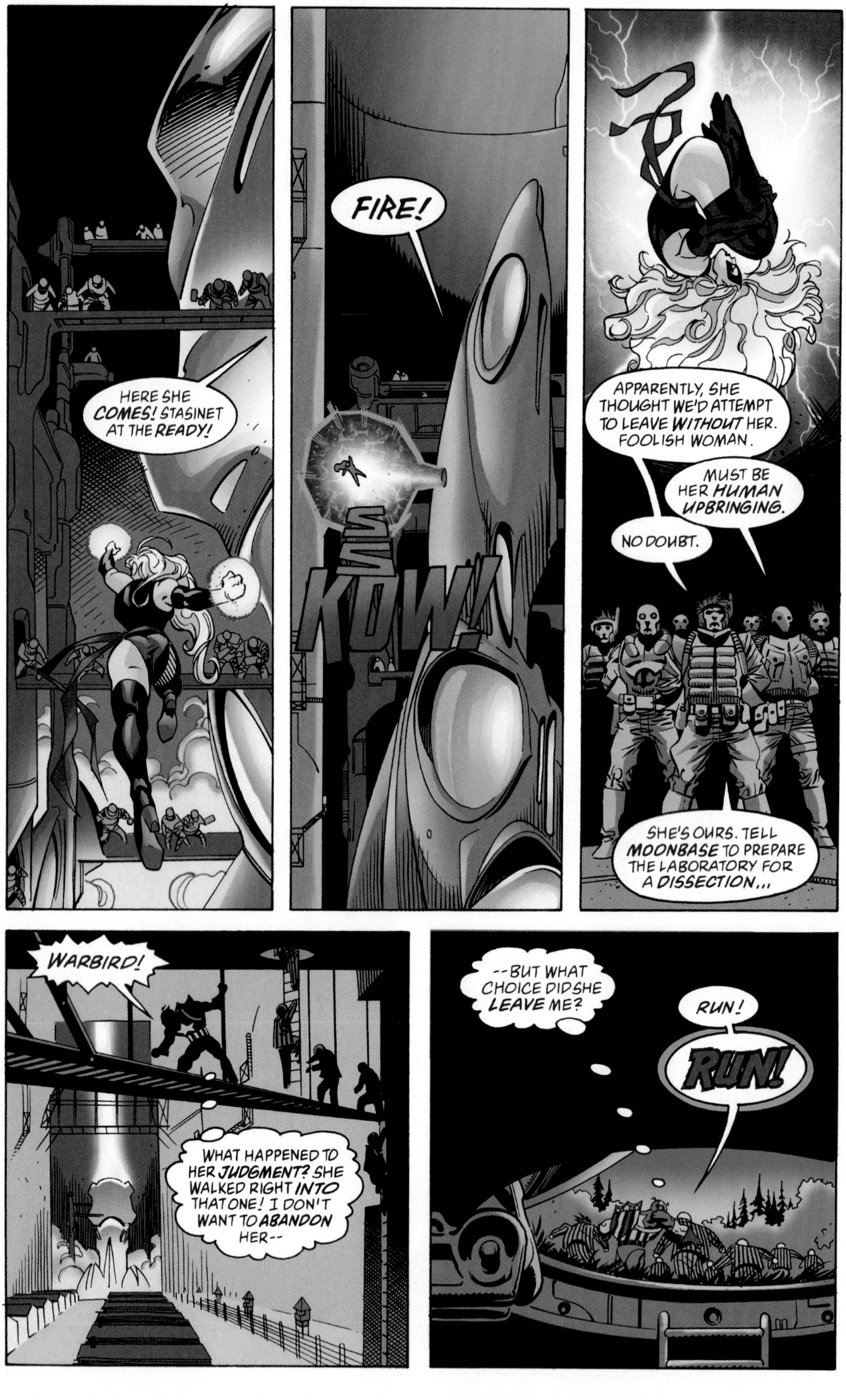
HERE SHE COMES! STASINET AT THE READY!
FIRE!
SSKOW!
APPARENTLY, SHE THOUGHT WE'D ATTEMPT TO LEAVE WITHOUT HER. FOOLISH WOMAN.
MUST BE HER HUMAN UPBRINGING.
NO DOUBT.
SHE'S OURS. TELL MOONBASE TO PREPARE THE LABORATORY FOR A DISSECTION...
WARBIRD!
WHAT HAPPENED TO HER JUDGMENT? SHE WALKED RIGHT INTO THAT ONE! I DON'T WANT TO ABANDON HER--
--BUT WHAT CHOICE DID SHE LEAVE ME?
RUN!
RUN!

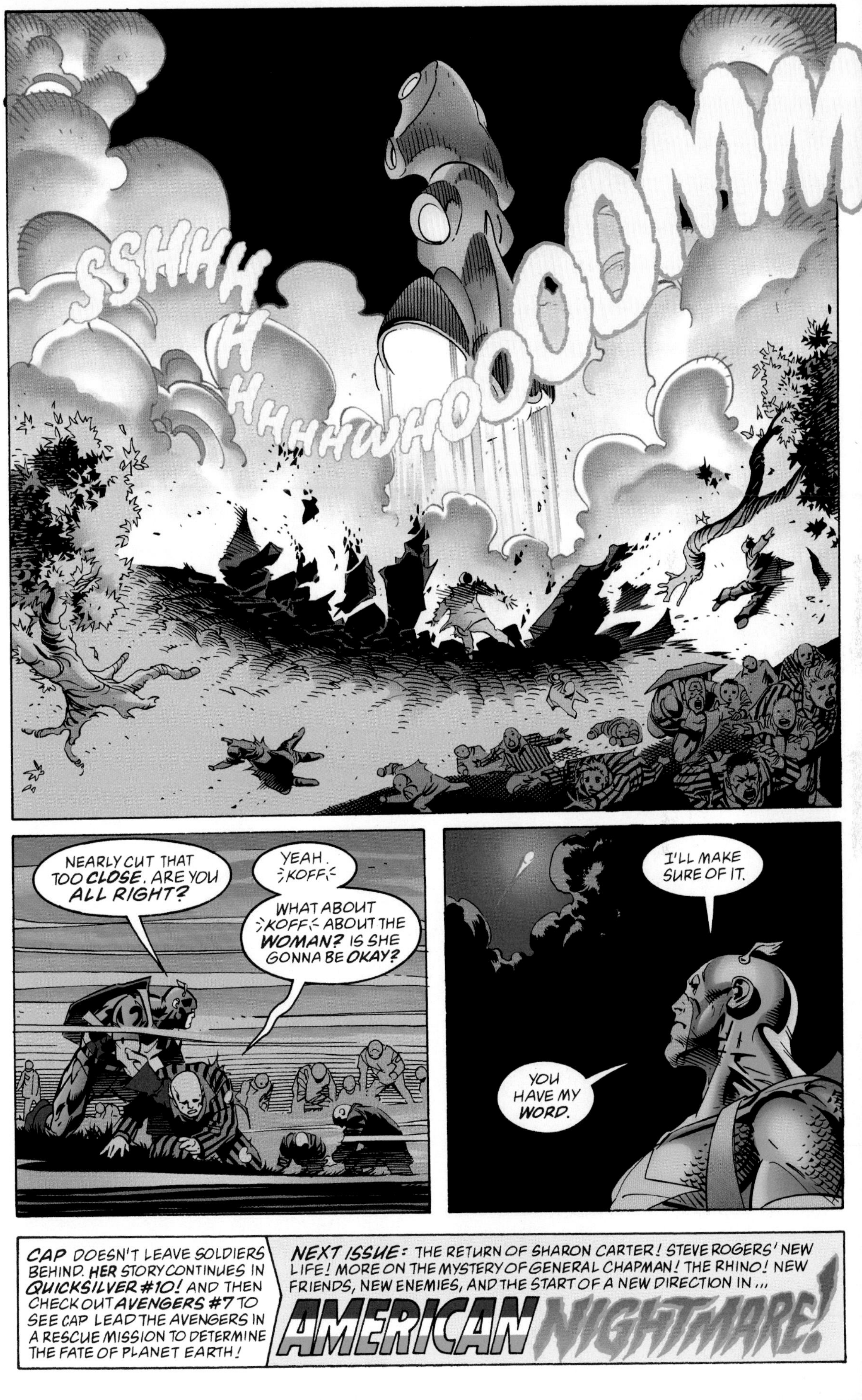
SSHHHH
H
HHHHWHOOOOOOMM
NEARLY CUT THAT TOO CLOSE. ARE YOU ALL RIGHT?
YEAH. KOFF
WHAT ABOUT KOFF ABOUT THE WOMAN? IS SHE GONNA BE OKAY?
I'LL MAKE SURE OF IT.
YOU HAVE MY WORD.
CAP DOESN'T LEAVE SOLDIERS BEHIND. HER STORY CONTINUES IN QUICKSILVER #10! AND THEN CHECK OUT AVENGERS #7 TO SEE CAP LEAD THE AVENGERS IN A RESCUE MISSION TO DETERMINE THE FATE OF PLANET EARTH!
NEXT ISSUE: THE RETURN OF SHARON CARTER! STEVE ROGERS' NEW LIFE! MORE ON THE MYSTERY OF GENERAL CHAPMAN! THE RHINO! NEW FRIENDS, NEW ENEMIES, AND THE START OF A NEW DIRECTION IN...
AMERICAN NIGHTMARE!

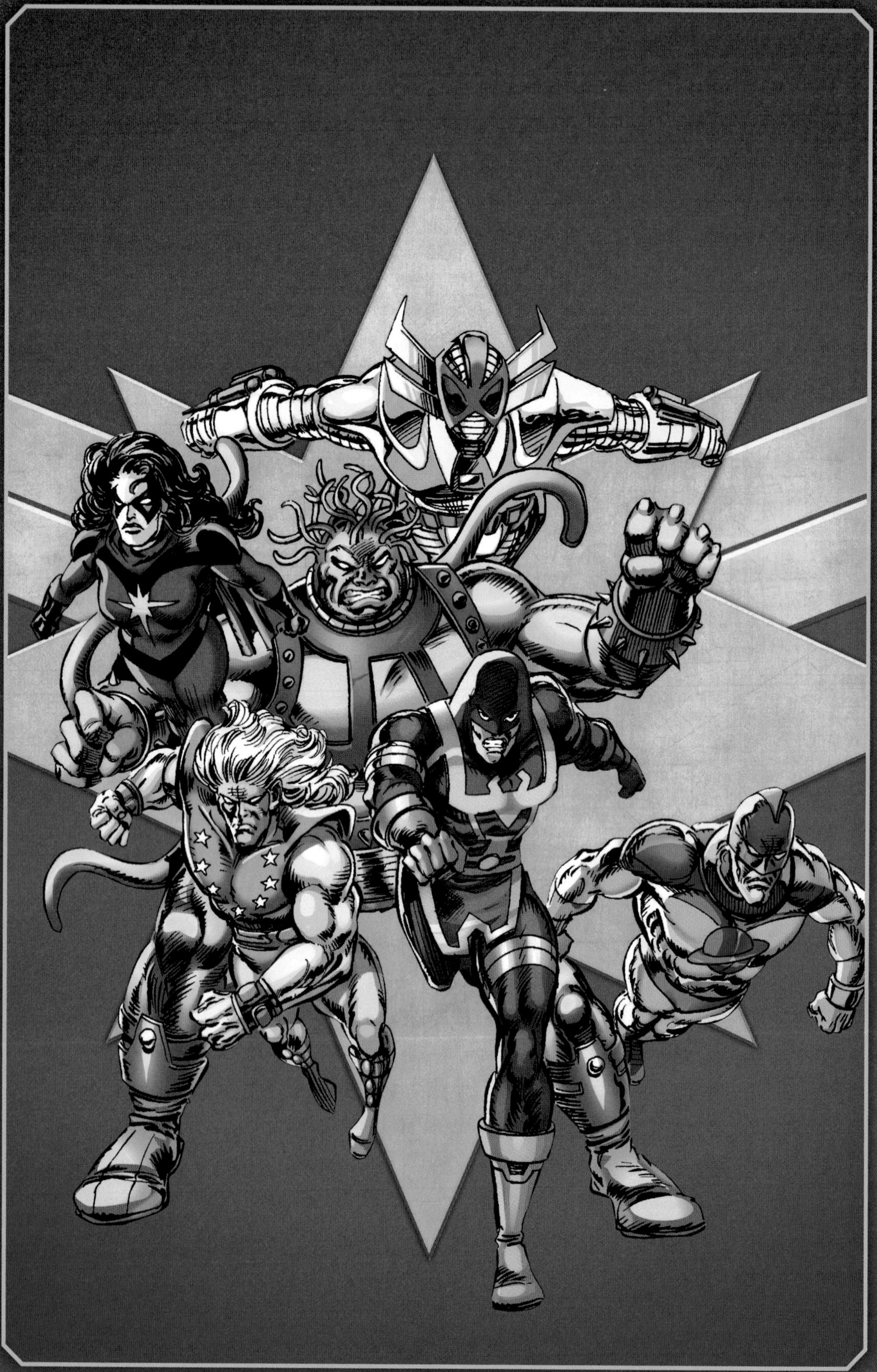

CAPTAIN MARVEL

HISTORY: Carol Danvers grew up the oldest child of three in a traditional Boston home, with a contractor father who believed in hard work. When he built their Cape Cod summer home, Carol insisted on working as hard as her younger brothers, trying to make herself the equal of both in her father's eyes. A voracious reader, she dreamed of becoming an astronaut and visiting distant planets; as a teen she even hitchhiked to watch a launch at Cape Canaveral. Her father, however, could not accept women as men's equals, and when financial troubles meant he could send only one child to college, he chose middle child Steve despite Carol's superior grades. Having been moved ahead in school as a child, Steve graduated a year before Carol and chose to enlist in the military at age 17 with his father's permission; at some point, Steve introduced Carol to one of her heroes, pioneering pilot Helen Cobb, the two bonded over a kindred adventurous spirit. When Steve was killed shortly thereafter, the tragedy initially brought the family closer together, Carol's father blamed himself for Steve's death and drank heavily, verbally taking his guilt out on Carol. Carol graduated from high school first in her class and took a summer sales job. A few months later, the day after she turned 18, Carol turned her back on her father and joined the Air Force, intending to get a college degree via the military while pursuing her love of flying.

Rising quickly to the top of her Air Force class, Carol became one of the Force's best fliers and was selected to pilot the new Stark S-73 stealth surveillance jet on its first mission. While taking holographic images of Afghanistan, the plane was shot down, presumably by insurgent Ghazi Rashid's men. Carol survived the crash with an open leg fracture, was captured and repeatedly tortured. After three days, she escaped, killing several of her captors; though Carol believed Rashid was among the slain, he survived. She also stole some of her captors' computer disks, which implied Rashid may have had CIA ties, before limping to a safe house. Air Force Special Operations Colonel Michael Jonathan Rossi debriefed her there. Impressed by Carol, he had her pilot status revoked and enlisted her into Special Operations. While undergoing months of physical rehabilitation for her injuries, Carol trained beside Rossi as a spy, and the pair investigated Rashid's CIA contact (code-named Vitamin). They tracked Vitamin to Berlin only to see his apartment bombed by freelance operative Rick Mason (the Agent), who then escaped. Unbeknownst to Carol, Rossi secretly was Vitamin, and was initially plotting to eventually recruit Carol as his CIA mole in Air Force Special Operations.

Carol became romantically involved with her now partner/mentor Rossi, whom she nicknamed "Ace" on their first Russian mission. Their mission record proved excellent, but their romance eventually faded. She later became friends with Canadian agent Logan (James Howlett, later Wolverine); they faced underworld ninjas in Madripoor, and Logan saved Carol's life when her cover was blown while investigating Jacques Preen, a dangerous Canadian arms dealer. Carol was later drawn into New York's Hellfire Club's plot to conceal the existence of mutants while privately exploiting them. After killing four agents who tried to murder her in her hotel room, Carol helped Logan protect Dr. Perry Edwards, who intended to expose the so-called "mutant hierarchy." Edwards died when the Hellfire Club's Victor Creed seemingly killed himself while detonating a bomb, hospitalizing Carol for a month. Following her recovery, she took her information on the underground mutants to up-and-coming Senator Robert Kelly, setting him on a path that would define his career.

Carol later teamed with the CIA's Colonel Nick Fury; posing as scientist Myron MacLain's secretary, she again encountered Logan, now an amnesiac, when he came to MacLain for Adamantium information. Carol and Fury witnessed a conflict involving Logan, a team of Hydra agents, operative Victor Creed (later Sabretooth) and Russian Natalia Shostakova (later the Black Widow/Natasha Romanoff). Fury soon sent Carol, pilot Ben Grimm (later the Fantastic Four's Thing) and Logan into Russia to investigate the top-secret Red Storm espionage project; shot down by Russians, Carol escaped capture, stole a plane, rescued Grimm and Logan (despite a dogfight with Shostakova), and completed the mission.

REAL NAME: Carol Susan Jane Danvers
ALIASES: Ms. Marvel, Warbird, Lady Marvel, Binary, "Ace," Cheeseburger; pseudonyms used have included Carol Daniels, Karolya Danilovska, Linda Danvers, Catherine Donovan, others.
IDENTITY: Publicly known
OCCUPATION: Adventurer; former licensed super hero, instructor in "Training Day" program, author, Department of Homeland Security chief of tactical operations, freelance writer, NASA security chief, Woman Magazine chief editor, US Air Force Special Operations intelligence agent, pilot, salesgirl (Note: Carol's intelligence work required her to claim to be working for several agencies, including the CIA, the Department of Defense, and the Defense Intelligence Agency. Though she did work with many of these agencies, she was a USAF employee.)
CITIZENSHIP: USA
PLACE OF BIRTH: Boston, Massachusetts
KNOWN RELATIVES: Joseph "Joe" Danvers (father, deceased), Marie Danvers (mother), Steven J. Danvers (brother, deceased), Joseph "Joe" Danvers, Jr. (brother), Benny (uncle)
GROUP AFFILIATION: Avengers; formerly Operation: Lightning Storm, Initiative, Queen's Vengeance, Starjammers
EDUCATION: Extensive military training, acquired BA while in military
FIRST APPEARANCE: (Danvers) Marvel Super-Heroes #13 (1967); (Ms. Marvel) Ms. Marvel #1 (1977); (Binary) Uncanny X-Men #164 (1982); (Warbird) Avengers #4 (1998); (Captain Marvel, Reality-58163) Secrets of the House of M (2005); (Captain Marvel, Reality-616) Avenging Spider-Man #9 (2012)

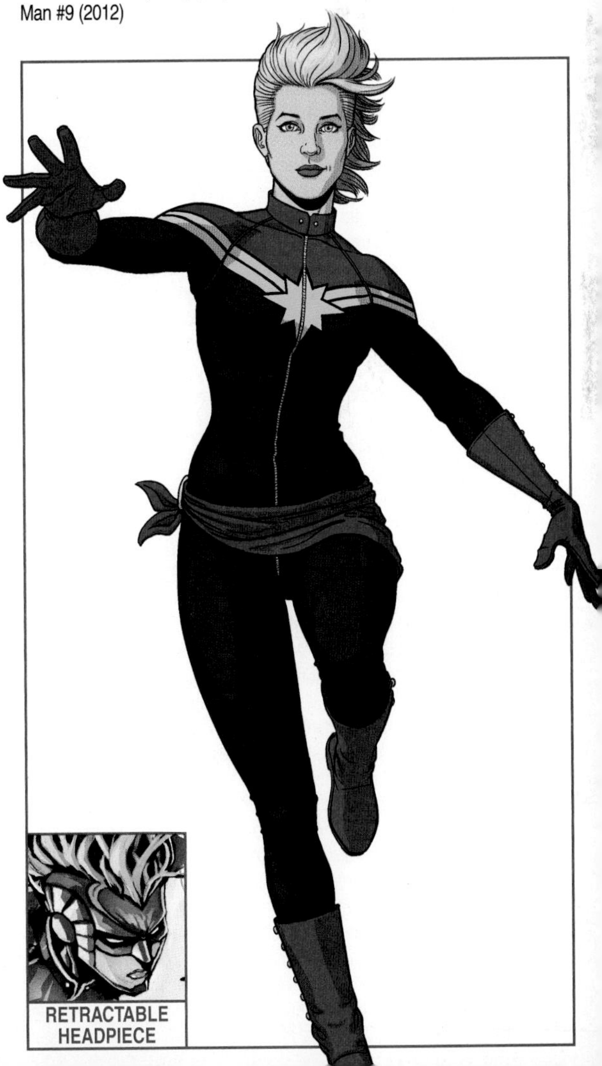

RETRACTABLE HEADPIECE

As all this was classified top secret, she and her fellows would later publicly pretend not to recognize each other.

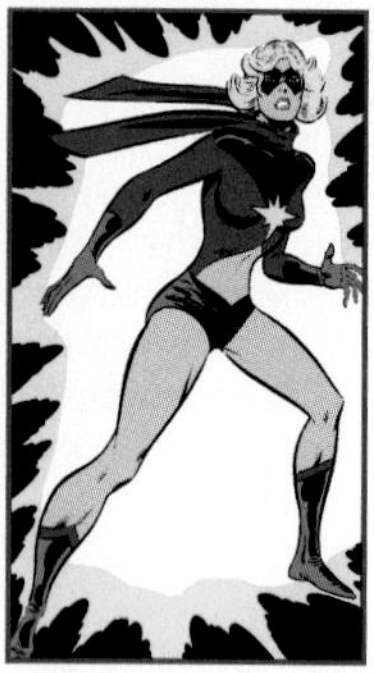

Art by Sal Buscema

When Carol was captured and held in Russia's Lubyanka prison, Rossi and Logan went rogue to break her out. Shortly thereafter, a position as head of security at NASA's Kennedy Space Center opened up, and Carol's old dreams of space led her to call in her markers as she exploited the many contacts she had made in NASA over the years to lobby for that job. NASA eventually requested her for the position and she resigned from the Air Force, bumping to full colonel at retirement. Now the youngest security captain in NASA's history, she became embroiled in the schemes of the interstellar Kree Empire. She was present when the robotic Kree Sentry 459 was transported to NASA for study, and got caught in the middle when Kree soldier Captain Mar-Vell battled it after it awoke. During her NASA stint she led an investigation into Mar-Vell's assumed alter ego, Dr. Lawson, which proved beneficial when the Super-Skrull (Kl'rt) briefly also impersonated Lawson and was exposed. On another occasion, Carol singlehandedly recovered a shuttle stolen by a Skrull agent and in doing so finally achieved her dream of traveling into space. In the coming months Carol would be kidnapped by the robotic Cyberex and then hospitalized when a villain-controlled Iron Man (Tony Stark) attacked the Center. Still concussed, Carol was kidnapped by Mar-Vell's enemy Yon-Rogg; while Mar-Vell fought Yon-Rogg, Carol was knocked into a damaged Kree Psyche-Magnitron, a powerful device that could turn imagination into reality. Carol's dreams of flight and her envy of Mar-Vell's powers led the machine to alter her genetically, effectively making her a half-Kree superhuman; however, this change was gradual, and Carol was unaware of it for months. After the Sentry reactivated and damaged the Center before departing in pursuit of the Avengers, Earth's premier superhuman team, Carol's continued inability to control superhuman incursions led to her removal. She was reassigned to a minor NASA facility near Chicago. After Nitro raided that base, Carol was demoted to a mere security guard and returned to Kennedy Space Center. Not long after another alien incursion, Carol learned of Rossi's reported death in a plane crash, unaware he had actually survived. In the aftermath of this loss and her plummeting career, Carol resigned from NASA.

Living off accumulated salary, Carol wrote an angry tell-all exposé of NASA, burning many bridges. The best-selling book briefly made Carol a celebrity, and she wrote for national magazines like Rolling Stone; however, she also developed a dual personality due to the Psyche-Magnitron's alterations. She would black out and become a Kree warrior, instantaneously donning a costume which the Psyche-Magnitron had created for her to ease her body's changes. These fugue-like blackouts seriously alarmed Carol, but didn't stop her from accepting a New York position as chief editor at the Daily Bugle's new Woman Magazine. In times of stress, she would continue to transform into her Kree alter ego, who soon took the name Ms. Marvel after Mar-Vell. She fought foes such as the Scorpion (Mac Gargan) and AIM (Advanced Idea Mechanics) before before Carol discovered the truth behind her dual identity while back at Kennedy on a story; the Psyche-Magnitron was destroyed during her battle there against the Destructor, and the explosion completed Carol's genetic change; the explosion apparently sent shards of the Magnitron through time and space, one of which was found by Helen Cobb, who used it to transform a plane into a time machine. Over the next few months Carol's fragmented mind slowly recovered, first pushed by the benevolent interference of the extradimensional Hecate, and when a Kree attack with the mind-altering Millennia Bloom device backfired, Carol's mind was completely healed. Meanwhile, she became one of New York's premier heroines, Woman Magazine profiling her while she worked with Spider-Man (Peter Parker), the Defenders, the Avengers and others, and became friendly with the Avengers' Wonder Man (Simon Williams). Abandoning her Mar-Vell-derived costume, she donned her own original costume and became a full-fledged Avenger, replacing an absent Scarlet Witch. Carol reveled in her new status, aiding the team against foes like Chthon, the Absorbing Man and the Grey Gargoyle (Paul Duval), and fitting in personally as well, even joining the Avengers' regular poker games; however, things began to grow bleak when Carol was fired from her editorial job due to her frequent disappearances. She rescued her astronaut friend Salia Petrie from the alien Faceless One, but Salia was severely traumatized. Carol's psychiatrist and close friend, Michael Barnett, was murdered by mutant shape-shifter Mystique, whose precognitive associate Destiny (Irene Adler) had warned her that Carol would hurt Mystique's foster-daughter Rogue (Anna Marie). Barnett's murder pulled Ms. Marvel into conflict with the Hellfire Club and Mystique's Brotherhood of Evil Mutants. Before she could track down Mystique, Carol's extradimensional admirer Marcus, the son of time-traveler Immortus, kidnapped Carol to timeless Limbo, wooed her with a "subtle boost" from mind-influencing devices, impregnated himself into her, and returned her to Earth with no memory of this. Finding herself seemingly impossibly pregnant, Carol came to term in less than two days, and she delivered the child, Marcus, who grew to adulthood in one day; however, Marcus continued to age quickly towards death. Still under the lingering mental influence of his devices, Carol told the Avengers she loved Marcus and accompanied him back to Limbo. Once there, his rapid aging unexpectedly continued and he soon died, leaving Carol trapped in Limbo. She eventually found her way home and, resenting the Avengers for not seeing through Marcus, gave up her Ms. Marvel identity and secretly settled down in San Francisco.

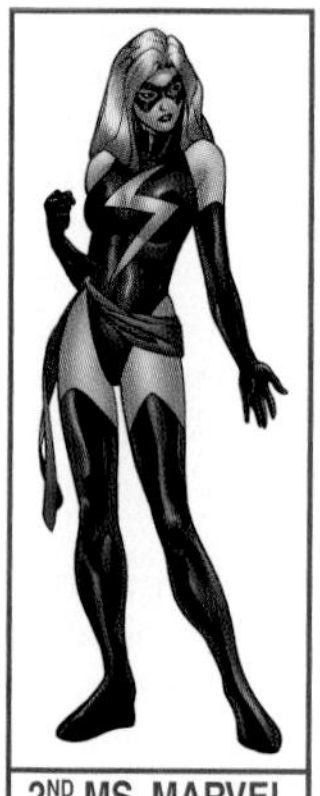

2ND MS. MARVEL OUTFIT

Art by Aaron Lopresti

Mystique continued plotting Carol's downfall, however, and Rogue decided to remove this thorn from her foster-mother's side, attacking Carol herself. Their fierce battle atop the Golden Gate Bridge ended when Rogue's absorption of Carol's powers, memories and emotions accidentally became permanent. Thrown from the bridge, Carol was rescued by Spider-Woman (Jessica Drew), who brought the powerless and near-amnesiac Carol to Professor Charles Xavier for treatment. He restored most of her memories, though her emotional ties to them remained lost. After a bitter confrontation with the Avengers, Carol remained with Xavier and his X-Men, working to restore her mind.Aiding the X-Men for weeks, Carol led them in infiltrating the Pentagon to delete their governmental records. She encountered Rogue and Mystique there for the first time since their attacks on her; while the X-Men defeated Rogue, Carol captured Mystique and turned her over to the authorities. Soon after, the alien Brood captured Carol and the X-Men. Fascinated by her genetic structure, they manipulated Carol's physiology up and down the evolutionary scale before Wolverine freed her. These manipulations transformed Carol into the energy-wielding Binary, and she helped defeat the Brood, destroying their homeworld and the outworld of Madrizar, and freeing the Brood's slave race, the Acanti. She returned home with the X-Men, but her childhood dreams of space travel beckoned. After learning of Mar-Vell's death by cancer and holding an emotionless farewell with her parents, she left the X-Men on bad terms upon learning they had allowed the troubled Rogue to join their group, Destiny's prediction coming true as Carol's stolen memories had come to torment her. After punching Rogue through their roof, Carol departed Earth and joined the space-faring Starjammers.

Alongside the Starjammers, Carol traveled with exiled Shi'ar ruler Lilandra Neramani and aided her when she and her embittered sister Deathbird (one of Ms. Marvel's early foes) fought to use the cosmic Phoenix Force's

power to increase their positions. When the Kree-Shi'ar War menaced Earth's sun, Carol nearly burned out her own powers in saving the sun and was hospitalized in Avengers Headquarters for weeks, during which time she made peace with her past as an Avenger. When Starjammer Raza was coerced by Kree into trying to kill the Avengers' Black Knight (Dane Whitman) for his actions during the war, Binary ended the conflict and falsely claimed Raza had been mind-controlled to protect him; afterward she decided to remain on Earth, feeling that she had been running from her problems. She moved into her parents' Beverly, Massachusetts home and began a semi-autobiographical science fiction novel titled "Binary." She also worked with Peter Corbeau of Starcore in orbital projects, as well as with other heroes. When the alien Skeletron pushed the Moon out of orbit, Binary was among those who opposed him, pursuing Skeletron to the Stranger's World alongside Quasar (Wendell Vaughn) and other heroes; wanting full-strength allies against Skeletron, the Stranger restored Carol's damaged psyche, briefly giving her full access to her lost memories and buried emotions, though they soon faded. When another alien plot destabilized the wormhole from which Carol drew her powers, she worked with the X-Men to restore it; weeks later, she realized this had failed when her Binary powers ceased replenishing themselves. Troubled by her apparently fading powers and memories of her short-lived emotional reconnection to her past, Carol began drinking heavily. When the disbanded Avengers re-formed while facing Morgan Le Fay, Carol rejoined the team as Warbird. Though her powers had stabilized at her old Ms. Marvel levels, she kept the loss of her Binary-level powers secret. Her drinking led to bad judgment calls against Kree enemies, and the Avengers called a special tribunal to investigate Warbird's actions. When it looked like Carol would be demoted to reserve status, she quit before a decision was reached. She moved to Seattle and resumed writing while her first novel successfully saw print; a contract for several others followed. Meanwhile, Avengers founder Iron Man had also relocated to Seattle, and the recovered alcoholic Stark tried to offer Carol guidance despite her resistance. She bottomed out when, during an alcoholic blackout, she threw Iron Man through the wing of a passenger jet. She and Iron Man saved the passengers, but Carol finally realized she had a problem and began attending AA meetings. She revealed her identity to governmental authorities and took responsibility for the crash; much to her surprise, the judge gave her a suspended sentence, demanding that she rejoin the Avengers and that they supervise her.

Back with the Avengers and sober, Carol thrived. She drew the standoffish Triathlon closer into the team, helped end the Shi'ar conversion of Earth into a "prison planet," led an Avengers contingent against a Deviant army in China, and led a mission to find the Master (Eshu) during Kang's invasion of Earth. On the latter mission she encountered Kang's son Marcus, a virtual duplicate of the Marcus who had once kidnapped her (as Kang is an alternate temporal counterpart to Immortus). Like his predecessor, this Marcus was smitten with Carol, who was in turn both intrigued and disturbed by him. Reluctantly accepting aid against the Master's forces from Marcus, Carol ultimately killed the Master in combat (Carol would later demand she be court-martialed for this "murder," eventually being declared innocent of wrongdoing). Carol played a key role in the destruction of Kang's orbital Damocles base, helping defeat Kang's invasion. The Avengers' seizure of the Master's technology made this victory possible, and Kang ultimately slew Marcus for disloyalty since he knew his son had secretly aided Carol against the Master. Later, after the Avengers helped contain the "Red Zone" disaster, the US president offered Carol a position as chief tactical officer for the Department of Homeland Security (DHS); she accepted, leaving the Avengers.

Carol recruited the Thunderbolts' Dallas Riordan to work with her at the DHS, but chafed at the deskwork and kept slipping into costume — she teamed with Wolverine and Captain America (Steve Rogers) against Rapture and Project Contingency (a renegade SHIELD anti-mutant operation), with the Thunderbolts against Fathom Five and Baron Strucker's Hydra forces, and with several heroes against Titannus. The Commission

on Superhuman Activities (CSA) cornered her into approving an assault by the Thunderbolts on the Avengers, and her discontent grew. Eventually, the mad Scarlet Witch altered Earth to create the mutant-ruled Reality-58163 ("House of M") where Carol, despite her non-mutant status, was that world's greatest hero as Captain Marvel. When the world was restored to normal, Carol retained her Captain Marvel memories, and decided she was wasting her time in a desk job. She resigned from the DHS, resolving to make herself into

BINARY

Art by Paul Smith

the hero she now knew she could be. Carol hired an agent, Sarah Day, to help with her public image, and readopted her Ms. Marvel name at Day's suggestion. Carol subsequently defeated a Brood army and the Brood-hunting Cru, aided the Avengers against the Collective, attended the birth of close friend Jessica Jones' baby, and served as the maid of honor at Jessica's wedding. She battled Warren Traveler, a dimension-lost foe from Reality-58163, and battled Titannus again, all while conducting TV interviews and maintaining a very public blog. When the Superhuman Registration Act passed, Carol became one of its strongest supporters and an early recruit of the government's new super-hero army, the Initiative. She and fellow Initiative agents apprehended anti-registration heroes like the Prowler (Hobie Brown), Shroud and fellow Avenger Arachne (Julia Carpenter), and trained would-be heroes like Araña, who regarded Carol as a surrogate mother.

Asked by Initiative founder Iron Man to lead a new government-backed Avengers group, Carol reluctantly agreed. She personally selected Wasp (Janet Van Dyne), Wonder Man and Ares for her team, and at Stark's request also included Black Widow, Sentry (Robert Reynolds) and Iron Man himself. The balance of power within the group between Carol and Iron Man was uneasy. He had recruited Sentry and later added Spider-Woman over Carol's objections, and often ignored her opinions. Still, the team performed well against the Mole Man, Ultron, an invasion of Venom-like symbiotes, Tiger Shark, and the BAD Girls, and even brought Dr. Doom (Victor von Doom) to trial for his terrorist activities. As a condition of accepting the Avengers leadership, Carol had demanded her own elite SHIELD strike force, known as Operation: Lightning Storm; she hoped to use this force to right what she saw as the world's wrongs, undertaking missions too quiet or too questionable for the Avengers. After initially using the strike force for personal reasons to try to mend fences with Arachne, Carol defeated AIM forces who had unleashed a genetic bomb in Indianapolis, Lightning Storm suffering serious casualties in the process. She began recruiting her core agents from the Initiative rather than SHIELD thereafter, working with Machine Man (X-51) and Sleepwalker to end the Puppet Master (Phillip Masters)'s slave ring and stop a Brood invasion. During this time, Carol also honored the Initiative's Ultragirl with a copy of her earlier Ms. Marvel costume, although administrators would later confiscate that from her. When a Skrull imposter impersonated her and her sometime boyfriend, William Wagner, the succeeding investigation resulted in the Skrulls blowing up Lightning Storm's minicarrier headquarters, killing many of Carol's support personnel as well as civilians on the ground. Suffering the aftermath of the Skrulls' actions, Lightning Storm has not yet been reconstituted.

On the personal front, Carol's romantic interest Wagner, possibly a Kree spy, was later apparently kidnapped by AIM and Carol had an ill-advised fling with Wonder Man. Amidst this, Carol believed she was failing at her mission to become a true hero and regretted her work with the Initiative and Lightning Storm resulted in betrayal of friends and operative deaths. The more responsibility Carol took on, the more she doubted her own abilities and looked back fondly on the times when she only relied on herself. She also learned that her parents and brother had relocated to the more agreeable climate of the Maine coast, but that her father was dying of lung cancer. Carol began losing control of her powers during a full-blown Skrull invasion of Earth, having apparently burned herself out while fighting the invaders. She aided friend Jessica Jones in recovering her baby (kidnapped by the Skrulls), and during that process she returned to Avengers Tower and found corrupt businessman Norman Osborn assuming control of the Avengers. Carol angrily quit rather than serve under him, and Osborn replaced Carol with a new Ms. Marvel: Moonstone (Karla Sofen). Carol joined a renegade Avengers team in opposing these "Dark Avengers," but her destabilizing power set led to her vowing to cut back on use of her powers; at some point during this time, Carol's father passed away.

not welcome on Earth. On Earth, Carol later adopted a new costume and claimed the Captain Marvel name, inspired by Mar-Vell's sacrifice. She inherited a vintage plane from Helen Cobb upon her death, which sent Carol through time; first, to World War II, where she fought alongside the Banshee Squad, a Women Air Force Service Pilot squad, against a platoon of Japanese pilots armed with Kree technology; to 1961, where she met Cobb, who joined her time-spanning journey; and to her own empowerment with the Psyche-Magnitron. During the latter adventure, Cobb usurped Carol's powers, challenging her to reach the plane first and return to the present; Carol succeeded, learning that Helen had apparently orchestrated the entire adventure to repair the damage she'd done to history by stealing the Psyche-Magnitron shard.

Art by Olivier Coipel

WARBIRD

Osborn saw Carol as a major threat, and decided to eliminate her. Investigating, he uncovered her early history with Ghazi Rashid and Michael Rossi, and recruited Rossi to treat Rashid with the Ascension serum, empowering Rashid. Rossi finally revealed his survival to Carol by summoning her and Rick Mason to a secret meeting at his own grave, where he told them that Rashid was still alive and in possession of a very powerful weapon. Eagerly grasping this link to what she regarded as a more successful time in her life, Carol agreed to help bring Rashid down. After trading with the information siphon known as Essential for a complete dossier on Osborn and confronting a new Captain Marvel (the Kree Noh-Varr, later called Protector), Carol faced down Ghazi in Hong Kong. Confronting the now super-powered Rashid and being reminded of her hate for him finally triggered an unlocking of Carol's lost emotions, but Carol's power use also further destabilized her. She defeated Rashid, but her powers overcharged and she explosively detonated over Hong Kong's Victoria Harbor, apparently disintegrating in a cosmic light explosion. Following Carol's seeming death, Rossi turned Ghazi over to Osborn, and Rick Mason swore to avenge her, apparently killing Rossi. As her dispersed energies coalesced, Carol returned in multiple forms, including one as Ms. Marvel and a civilian guise as successful writer Catherine Donovan, but her mental energies and physical substance eventually merged back into a complete Carol Danvers. As Ms. Marvel, Carol handed her would-be successor Moonstone a painful and humiliating defeat, sparing her life in the hopes it might motivate Sofen to change her ways. Later, happily reunited with Rick Mason, Carol exposed Mystique as the killer behind a murder spree supposedly committed by Mar-Vell.

Later, Carol assisted the Avengers when they defeated and discredited Osborn during his siege of Asgard, but was briefly possessed by the Venom symbiote when she separated it from its host, Mac Gargan (formerly the Scorpion). Carol rejoined the Avengers after their reorganization and became particularly close with Spider-Man. When the cosmic Phoenix Force went on a destructive journey through the universe, Carol and a contingent of Avengers left Earth to contain it. While pursuing the Force on Kree world Hala, Carol was affected by megalomaniacal Kree leader Minister Marvel's control of the Kree (via his son Marvel Mind's psychic powers) and was compelled to turn on her teammates alongside Captain Marvel (Mar-Vell), resurrected by the Minister and a portion of the Force. When the Phoenix Force approached Hala, Carol rejected Marvel Mind's influence and tried to absorb the Force, but Mar-Vell sacrificed his life to save Carol and Hala. Soon after, Carol was deeply upset by now-teammate Protector siding with the Kree against the Avengers, despite his later repentance, and told him he was

HEIGHT: 5'11" EYES: Blue
WEIGHT: 145 lbs. HAIR: Blonde

ABILITIES/ACCESSORIES: The Psyche-Magnitron transformed Carol into a peak human, athletically as fit as humanly possible, and also modified her DNA with Kree genes. It gave her the powers of flight, superhuman strength (sufficient to press 70 tons following subsequent genetic alterations) and greatly enhanced durability, as well as "seventh-sense" precognitive flashes and the ability to change into her costume instantaneously. Six months after her transformation, the Psyche-Magnitron produced a suit that enabled her to survive in space and was designed to ease her body's continuing transformation; however, this suit was eventually destroyed. After Carol lost her powers to Rogue, she maintained her "peak human" status though she lacked super-powers, save apparently the ability to change instantaneously into costume. Carol currently wears a costume made from Tony Stark-designed impervious fabric that features a retractable protective headpiece. As Binary, Carol channeled the energies of a white hole (also known as a wormhole) through her body to release any form of radiation or gravity. The white hole boosted her strength and endurance levels far beyond her old Ms. Marvel levels, and she could survive indefinitely in space. Losing access to the white hole didn't change her Binary powers, merely the level at which they function — she can still fly, can still project photonic energy blasts, and still possesses extreme strength and durability approximating her original Ms. Marvel levels. These powers are maintained by ambient energy absorbed from her environment, and as a result she can have negative effects on sensitive machinery and raises the temperature around her 2-3 degrees. She can temporarily augment her powers by absorbing energy forms, most notably electromagnetic radiation, plasma and sonics; however, unless she is prepared, her energy absorption is rarely instantaneous, so she draws only miniscule power from many energy attacks and can still be damaged by them. Without energy sources, Carol can no longer survive unaided in space. If she absorbs particularly high levels of energy, her old Binary energy corona may surround her hands, head or body. Carol is fluent in English, Russian and another unrevealed Earth language, as well as Kree and Shi'ar languages. She speaks passable Rajaki and has a limited vocabulary in many other languages, including Arabic. Carol is an accomplished pilot, having extensive experience with USAF planes as well as with Kree, Shi'ar and other alien starships. She has extensive training in military tactics, espionage, armed and unarmed combat, including numerous martial arts. Carol is an accomplished author and editor, is immensely strong-willed, able to endure incredible physical pain and is a recovering alcoholic.

POWER GRID	1	2	3	4	5	6	7
INTELLIGENCE							
STRENGTH							
SPEED							
DURABILITY							
ENERGY PROJECTION							
FIGHTING SKILLS							

HISTORY: Researching a way to advance the Kree, who were stuck in an evolutionary dead end according to their leader, the Supreme Intelligence, Kree geneticist Dr. Minerva theorized Captain Marvel (Mar-Vell)'s mutated genetic makeup could produce superior offspring. The Supreme Science Council (SSC) allowed her to travel on science cruiser *Ananim* to Earth to mate with Mar-Vell, but Mar-Vell went on a mission to the planet Gramos. Fearing he would never return, she abducted Rick Jones, whose previous atomic connection to Mar-Vell had left him with similar chromosomes, which Minerva intended to extract. Mar-Vell returned and saved Jones, rejecting Minerva even though he sympathized with her. When Minerva refused to abandon her mission, SSC leader Phae-Dor knocked her unconscious and remotely controlled her ship. Mar-Vell crashed the vessel during combat with a Phae-Dorr-controlled energy construct and hid Minerva from authorities before bringing her to a farm in Sullivan County, Texas, to live with other Kree refugees while Minerva started genetic research on humanity.

When Minerva learned of Mar-Vell's death from cancer, she despaired but soon discovered the Psyche-Magnitron device and mutated herself to become the savior Mar-Vell refused to be. She contacted the Kree Empire, who sent Captain Atlas (Att-Lass) to retrieve her, and Minerva fell in love with him and mutated him to make him her ideal mate. Before leaving Earth, they saw footage of Quasar (Wendell Vaughn), and Atlas recognized the Quantum Bands as the legendary Power-Bands of Rinn. Posing as humans working for the Xenotech corporation, they hired AIM (Advanced Idea Mechanics) to steal the Quantum Bands. When AIM failed, they abducted Quasar while he slept. On Atlas' light cruiser *Ramatam*, Minerva tried to remove Quasar's hands with lasers to retrieve the Quantum Bands, but Quasar subconsciously activated the bands to defend himself and, upon awakening, fought Atlas and Minerva; Atlas accidentally blew a hole in the ship's hull and was sucked into space. Fearing her year-long work ruined, Minerva begged Quasar to help her rescue Atlas. He did, and both Kree promised never to return to Earth's solar system.

During the Kree/Shi'ar War, Minerva supported the Supreme Intelligence's plan to jump-start Kree evolution by detonating a Nega-Bomb in the Kree Empire. To help power the bomb, she and Atlas stole Mar-Vell's Nega-Bands from his grave on Titan, but Quasar and Wonder Man (Simon Williams) caught them respectively. Shrunk by Dr. Henry Pym and imprisoned at Avengers Compound alongside Shi'ar Imperial Guardsmen, they were soon freed by other Guardsmen, including the Chameleoid known as Shapeshifter, who knocked Minerva out and impersonated her to trick Atlas into stealing the Nega-Bands for the Shi'ar. Minerva somehow escaped and joined the Supreme Intelligence's

REAL NAME: Minn-Erva
ALIASES: None
IDENTITY: Known to authorities
OCCUPATION: Agent of Kree Empire, geneticist
CITIZENSHIP: Kree-Lar, Kree Empire
PLACE OF BIRTH: Edelix, Kree-Lar
KNOWN RELATIVES: None
GROUP AFFILIATION: Starforce
EDUCATION: Graduated in bio-genetics at Kree Science Academy in Vartanos, Kree-Lar
FIRST APPEARANCE: Captain Marvel #50 (1977)

Starforce to protect Kree rulers Ael-Dann and Dar-Benn from the Avengers only to become trapped under an energy shield and witness Shi'ar Empress Lilandra Neramani's sister Deathbird slay both rulers. Starforce caught the Avengers, and Minerva and Atlas guarded them until the Nega-Bomb detonated and further mutated Minerva and Atlas, who were among the relatively few survivors on Kree-Lar. When Captain America (Steve Rogers) confronted Minerva about her involvement with the Intelligence's plan, Atlas claimed to have activated a self-destruct mechanism in his battle-suit to commit suicide but actually teleported himself and Minerva to a nearby planet, where they planned to parent a race of Super-Kree. When the Silver Surfer (Norrin Radd) found them, they feared he was sent to capture them, but when they realized this was not the case they convinced him they wanted to live peacefully in exile, leaving him oblivious to their plans. Soon after, Kosmosian criminals connected Goliath (Erik Josten) to those previously altered by Pym Particles, including Minerva and Atlas, and sent them after Pym, whom the Kosmosians blamed for everybody's ongoing size alterations. Minerva and Atlas returned to Kosmos after failing to capture Goliath (Bill Foster) and were apparently stranded on Kosmos when Pym severed the Kosmosians' connection to Earth.

HEIGHT: 5'9"   **EYES:** Blue
WEIGHT: 136 lbs.   **HAIR:** Black

ABILITIES/ACCESSORIES: Superhumanly strong (lifting 10 tons) and durable, Dr. Minerva can fly at subsonic speed by manipulating gravitons. Her enhanced perception allows her to home in on individuals and energy signatures on a planet-wide radius. A gifted bio-geneticist knowledgeable in genetic engineering and procreation, she occasionally uses glove-mounted energy blasters and can operate sophisticated Kree technology and spaceships.

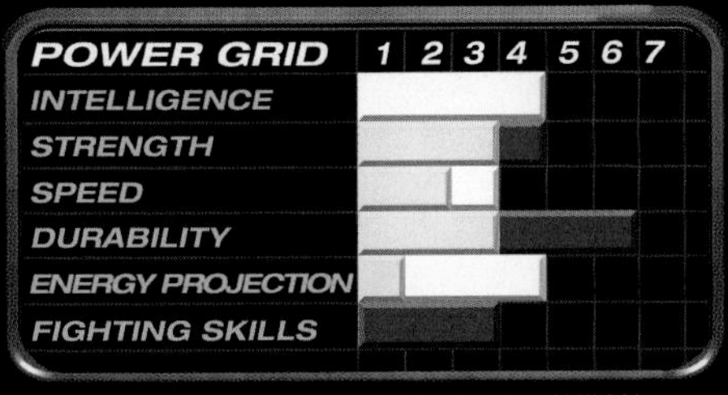

POWER GRID	1	2	3	4	5	6	7
INTELLIGENCE							
STRENGTH							
SPEED							
DURABILITY							
ENERGY PROJECTION							
FIGHTING SKILLS							

YELLOW BARS INDICATE PRE-MUTATION

1st COSTUME

1st STARFORCE COSTUME

Art by Dalibor Talajić with Al Milgrom & Steve Epting (insets)

KORATH THE PURSUER

REAL NAME: Korath-Thak
ALIASES: None
IDENTITY: Publicly known in Kree and Shi'ar empires
OCCUPATION: Phalanx select, warrior, cyber-geneticist; factory foreman
CITIZENSHIP: Kree Empire
PLACE OF BIRTH: Unrevealed location in Kree Empire
KNOWN RELATIVES: None
GROUP AFFILIATION: Phalanx; formerly Starforce, Supreme Science Council
EDUCATION: Unrevealed
FIRST APPEARANCE: Inhumans #11 (1977); (identified; as Pursuer) Quasar #32 (1992)

HISTORY: After the Inhuman Royal family destroyed a Kree space station, the Kree's Supreme Science Council elected to use cyber-geneticist Korath-Thak's Pursuer project to eliminate the Inhumans. They created a solidified holographic template that tracked the Inhumans, then condensed it into a malleable energy-mass state for transmission to Earth's New York City; but instead of encountering stone or metal first to absorb that material's properties to enhance its strength, the template hit a cockroach and used that material instead. The hybrid Pursuer fought the Inhumans and immobilized them until the Inhumans' dissident Kree ally Falzon sprayed an industrial strength pesticide in the Pursuer's face, dropping it. It awoke in police custody and escaped, resuming its hunt for the Inhumans. Sometime later the Pursuer was recalled from Earth by its creators, its ultimate fate unrevealed.

UNTRANSFORMED COCKROACH

PURSUER HYBRID

Korath-Thak spent the next few years making the Pursuer process more cost-effective, but new Kree leaders, Generals Ael-Dan and Dar-Benn, decided that the project would not be viable quickly enough and terminated it. A bitter Korath-Thak was transferred to a munitions plant, where he re-created another template and bonded it to himself. The Supreme Intelligence had Korath the Pursuer join his new Starforce on Kree homeworld Hala, where he attacked a group of Avengers before being defeated by Captain America. Recovering, Korath and Starforce again attacked the Avengers, overwhelming them. However, both teams were powerless to stop the royal Shi'ar renegade Deathbird while she killed Ael-Dan and Dar-Benn. The Supreme Intelligence sent Starforce to kill Shi'ar Majestrix Lilandra in retaliation, but they were defeated by the Shi'ar Imperial Guard and a second Avengers team. When all sides learned their mutual enemies, the Skrulls, had tricked them into the war, Lilandra freed Starforce member Ultimus to inform the Supreme Intelligence of the plot and kept Korath and the others as collateral, but the Kree Empire fell before that plan succeeded. Lilandra sentenced Starforce to serve as personal guard to the new Kree Viceroy, Deathbird. In that role, they chased off Quasar (Wendell Vaughn) when he came to help rebuild the planet, and helped put down a prisoner revolt when outlaw Admiral Galen-Kor broke out of prison, and aided the alien Deviant Blackwulf (Lucian) against his father, Tantalus. When the Shi'ar occupation ended, Starforce, branded as defectors, was forced into exile. Korath eventually settled on Kree fringeworld Godthab Omega. When the exiled Ronan the Accuser made his way to the Kree colony, Korath gained his aid against assassin Gamora and her Graces, who were trying to take their land. While Ronan took the fight to Gamora, Korath learned of Negative Zone ruler Annihilus' invasion. Korath convinced Ronan to abandon his battle against Gamora and help evacuate the planet from the advancing force. After the Armistice ending the war was signed, Korath went on a covert mission to locate the High Evolutionary, who was secretly creating genetically perfect Kree for the Supreme Intelligence, but fell prey to the robot Ultron and his new Phalanx allies. Transformed into the first Phalanx Selects, Korath and his allies Shatterax and Xemnu failed to capture the just-awakened Adam Warlock. They reported this failure to Ultron, who slew Korath as an example.

HEIGHT: 6'   **EYES:** Blue
WEIGHT: 290 lbs.   **HAIR:** Bald

ABILITIES/ACCESSORIES: The Pursuer template had greater strength (lifting 1 ton), reflexes, and durability than that of an average Kree, sensors to track anomalous genetic/energy patterns from miles away, and could recover from exposure to poisonous gases. The template transformed on contact any available organic and inorganic materials into parts of its body. It carried a scepter that rearranged matter to create tentacles and hands from asphalt and a brick building, transparent globes from air, and could fire energy blasts. The American cockroach (Periplaneta Americana) absorbed into the template could go 1 month without water, 2-3 months without food, and eat any organic substance it found. It is unclear if the bug's abilities carried over into the combined Pursuer form.

Korath's strength, durability, and reflexes were greater than the average Kree's, presumably close to the template's levels. He carried two "beta batons" that could stun or kill opponents either on contact or by firing energy blasts, and flew using jet boots. Korath had some combat training, but limited real combat experience. He was also a leading researcher in Kree genetics and cybernetic systems.

POWER GRID	1	2	3	4	5	6	7
INTELLIGENCE							
STRENGTH							
SPEED							
DURABILITY							
ENERGY PROJECTION							
FIGHTING SKILLS							

Art by Jorge Lucas with Keith Pollard (insets)

KNOWN MEMBERS: Ael-Dan, Ahmbar (Amber Watkins), Ajes'ha, Arides (Shatterstar), Arjai-Ush, Att-Lass, Av-Rom, Bas-For, Bav-Tek, Bel-Dann, Bheton, Boko, Bron-Char, Bronek, Bun-Dall, Cha-Mount, Ciry, Clar-Roc, Dandre, Dan-Forr, Dantella, Dar-Benn, Dal, Dea-Sea, Devros, Dor-Art, Dwi-Zann, Dylon-Cir, Eine, En-Vad, Ept-Rass, Fahr, Falzon, Fer-Porr, Galen-Kor, Hal-Konn, Hav-Ak, Hez-Tarr, Hon-Sann, Jac'oyaa, Jella, Jenna, Jordann, Kaer-Linn, Kalum-Lo, Kam-Lorr, Kar-Sagg, Kay-Sade, Keeyah, Klaer, Klynn, Kni-Konn, Kona-Lor, Korath-Thak (Korath the Pursuer), Ko-Rel, Lar-Ka, "Leigh," Levan, Lon-Lorr, Mac-Ronn, Malakii, Mar-Vell (Captain Marvel), Maston-Dar, Minn-Erva, M-Nell (Commando), Mon-Tog, Morag, Murius, Muz-Kott, Om-Fad, Nenora, Nep'perr, Nera, Nos-Verr, Pap-Tonn, Phae-Dor, Phaht, Por-Bat, Primus, Ran-Deff, Ra-Venn, Rojett, Ronan, Sallen-Bei, Sals-Bek, Saria, Sar-Torr, Shatterax, Shym'r Sr., Shym'r Jr., Sig-Rass, Singhre/Shen-Garh, Sintaris, Son-Dar, Sro-Himm, Staak, Sta-Ramm, Star-Lyn, Stug-Bar, Talla-Ron, Tallun, Tara, Tar-Rell, Tar-Vash, Tarnok-Kol, Tellis, Teress, Tir-Zarr, Tokk, Tol-Nok, Tohn-Bil, Trigor, Tunis-Var, Tus-Katt, Tzu-Zana (Suzy Sherman, Ultragirl), Ultimus, Una, Una-Rogg, Uni, Visog, Vron-Ikka, Yon-Rogg, Zak-Del (Wraith), Zamsed, Zarek, Zenna, Zen-Pram, Zey-Rogg, Zyro, others

KNOWN HYBRIDS: Teddy Altman/Dorrek VIII (Hulkling), Candidie, Hav-Rogg, Genis-Vell (Photon), Phyla-Vell (Quasar), others

BASE OF OPERATIONS: Hala, Pama system, Greater Magellanic Cloud Galaxy

FIRST APPEARANCE: (Mentioned) Fantastic Four #64 (1967), (full) Fantastic Four #65 (1967)

TRAITS: Kree bodies are denser and more durable than those of normal humans, making them about twice as strong, though Pink (aka White) Kree have a greater range of differences in these areas than Blue Kree do. They also have duplicates of several internal organs. While the average Kree is the same height as an average human, a significant percentage of Kree are far taller. The Kree's native environment has a much higher gravity and higher nitrogen-to-oxygen air content as compared to Earth's native environment, and the Kree originally could not survive in high-oxygen environments without special breathing devices and potions. Some Kree women can psychically manipulate the desires of men, with one in 100,000 of these women able to drain another's life force completely. In recent years, such Kree girls were forced to undergo surgical procedures to eradicate this ability completely, with techno-organic "bloodhounds" used to hunt down any female who reached adulthood with her psychic abilities intact.

Kree who were artificially evolved by the Forever Crystal — formerly called the Ruul — can adapt to survive in any hostile environment by changing form, though the exact shape taken during the initial shape-changing is determined by the individual's exact genetic makeup, not by conscious choice. The "Ruul" Kree can have several different forms adapted for separate tasks, including but not limited to, a warrior form, a super-intelligent "scientist" form, and separate forms for surviving in outer space, underwater, methane atmospheres, and solar surfaces. Virtually all of the early Ruul Kree were grey with lumpy foreheads and tentacles in place of hair, though later they changed to a blue coloration and mostly non-lumpy appearances. Since then almost all Kree, whether originally Pink or Blue, returned to their former pre-Ruul appearances (with some Pink Kree evidently turning to a blue color), though whether the cause is a refinement of their new shape-changing abilities or artificial has yet to be revealed. It has also been stated that all newly evolved Kree women have their psychic manipulation powers permanently removed at the genetic level, though whether this is true, or if some women secretly retain their powers remains to be seen.

Though 98% of the Kree population was wiped out when the Shi'ar's Nega-Bomb exploded in their galaxy, they have since rebuilt their numbers far faster than expected through unrevealed means, possibly via mass cloning and artificially aging the resultant children.

HISTORY: The Kree are one of two native races on the planet Hala in the Pama system of the Greater Magellanic Cloud galaxy, the other race being the plant-like Cotati. By some accounts the Kree are one of the many biped races spawned from the ancient Xorri race. In their distant past, the Celestials experimented on the ancient Kree as they did ancient humans millennia later. This experimentation produced the sub-races of Kree Eternals — all but extinct in the modern era — and Kree Deviants, whose ultimate fate remains unrevealed. The aggressive hunter-gatherer Blue Kree tribes allegedly considered all plants beneath their notice and ignored the Cotati, while the Cotati considered the Kree too frenetic for their quieter natures and left the Kree alone. About a million years ago, in the first year of recorded Kree history, a delegation of pacifist Skrulls arrived to advance the primitive natives to a point where they could join the Skrull Empire as trade partners. The Skrull Emperor Dorrek I proposed a test to decide which of Hala's races would be advanced as citizens of the Skrull Empire and which would not: Two groups of seventeen would be left on separate barren worlds for one year with "rudimentary" Skrull technology to create something of worth. The telepathic Cotati, sensing no deceit, accepted quickly; the distrustful Kree tribesmen debated for a day before their leader Morag accepted. The Cotati were taken to one barren moon while the Kree were taken to Earth's barren moon, where an artificial environment was created for them (the place later called the Blue Area of the Moon). The Stone Age tribesmen, using knowledge learned while en route, created an advanced city. The returning Skrulls were impressed, but were more impressed by the garden the Cotati had created on their moon. Enraged at his people being left behind by the Skrull Empire, Morag had his men slaughter every Cotati they could find. When the horrified Skrull Emperor forever banished Hala from the empire, he and his men were killed as well. Morag then led his Kree to master the Skrulls' technology, eventually creating an armada of spaceships to carve out their own interstellar empire and attack the homeworld of the Skrulls, formally igniting the Kree-Skrull War.

PRIESTS OF PAMA WITH THE COTATI

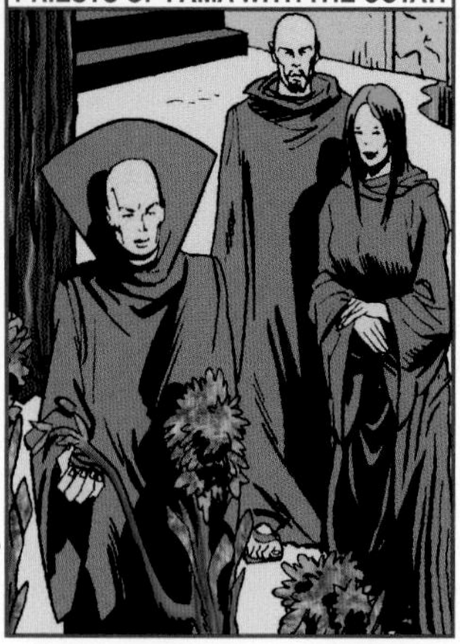

Art by Sal Buscema

In the early centuries of the empire, a pacifist Kree sect developed and was forced underground in Hala's slums. They secretly developed their martial and meditative skills for decades, until the Kree year 4760, when they were contacted by descendants of the murdered Cotati who had survived unnoticed by their killers. The telepathic plants had concentrated on developing their minds at the expense of their mobility, and found themselves forever rooted to the same place. They formed an alliance with the Kree sect, the more mobile Kree taking care of the Cotati's needs while the Cotati shared secrets of the mind. The sect became the Priests of Pama, concealing the existence of the Cotati while the Priests were ridiculed by mainstream Kree society.

Over the centuries, the Kree became renowned for their battle prowess, convinced that fighting wars made them stronger and better than seeking peace did. They created Kree-Lar, a planetwide city on Hala seemingly devoid of all non-Kree life. They made their empire's capital on a planet in the Turunal system also called Kree-Lar, while Hala became a sacred planet. They designated the planet Cyllandra as the main historical library of their people. The Kree Empire was ruled as a military dictatorship, originally by various aristocratic military clans (including one named after its founder, the warrior Fiyero) elected to the post of supreme ruler, before the organic computer construct Supreme Intelligence (SI), repository of all the greatest Kree scientific and military minds that have been downloaded into it, officially took over rulership of the Empire 253 years after it went on-line in Kree Year 4791 (circa 990,497 BC). The SI was aided by its administrators in Kree-Lar, member world governors, the Supreme Science Council, a vast standing army, highly trained paired assassins called Evolvers, and the Accusers, enforcers of Kree law. The Kree developed Plan Atavus to devolve any planet they deemed a future threat to the Empire. Kree engineer Bronek created robotic Sentries to guard their weapons depots, and to keep selected worlds under surveillance. Over time the Kree invented many weapons and devices like their main communication power source, the Omni-Wave Projector; some inventions, like the organic-destroying robotic Null-Trons, and the genetic-enhancer Psyche-Magnitron device, were later outlawed.

Interbreeding with the "aliens" they encountered while empire building created a second hybrid race of Kree with pink skin, which eventually outnumbered the "pure" blue race. The Blue Kree managed to remain the upper class in Kree society by creating a strict apartheid system that persisted into the modern era. Some Pink Kree rebelled against this subjection over the millennia, with one known band of rebels and their families forever exiled to the mining planet Daccara for their unrevealed crimes. Occasionally a "throwback" Blue Kree is born into a Pink family, but the precise social status of these Kree as compared to trueborn Blue Kree is unrevealed. A rare "Black" Kree race exists, but their origins are unrevealed. At an unrevealed point in time a small fleet of generation ships passed into a space warp and emerged in the so-called Exoteric Latitude, where the ships' populations fell prey to the tiny soul parasites, the Exolon. The affected Kree turned a pale white, gaining extra strength, a regenerative healing factor, immortality, and the ability to summon the Exolon to swarm and expose "the soul of a living being," driving fear into many of those who saw it. However, these Kree lost all conscious memory of their former identities and pursuits except when experiencing pain, leaving the so-called Nameless Kree to spend their now endless lives doing nothing but savagely maiming each other and themselves just to remember who they once were.

When the Priests of Pama were exiled by the SI on a trumped-up assault charge and imprisoned on a barren world far from the Cotati, the Cotati telepathically lured the ionic-powered alien Star-Stalker to the prison planet, confident their Kree allies would be able to discover for themselves how to successfully defeat it. The Priests informed the SI of the Star-Stalker's existence and offered to defend the Empire by sending two Priests to every imperial world to stand watch against the Stalker's return. Though it doubted the creature truly existed, the SI agreed, demanding four Priests to remain on Hala as its personal guard. The Priests secretly took one Cotati per Priest with them to establish garden temples on each world known to the Kree, including Saturn's moon Titan, and Earth.

A stone of great power and unrevealed origin was discovered on Kree-Lar; when it was split in two, the resultant energy release killed thousands. Revealed to control the forces of Chaos and Order, the two halves were dubbed Ke-Thia (Alpha) and Vi-Ska (Omega) respectively. Scientists from other space-faring races brought their stones of power (including the future Bloodgem, part of which was later worn by Ulysses Bloodstone) to Kree-Lar, and formed the Lifestone Tree to advance the evolutionary traits of all living things in the universe. The gems accessed the Hellfire Helix, which was used as a conduit for otherdimensional energies that were funneled through Ke-Thia and Vi-Ska to create smaller power stones. The stones manifested facets of the elements (air, water, fire, earth), spirits (life, death, anima), creation, entropy, and gravity. The stones were used to transform eight individuals from different races, including the Kree woman Ajes'ha (using the future Moongem, aka Moonstone) into the Chosen Eight of Fate (aka the Guardians of the Galaxy). The Eight kept the galactic peace for 200 years until they disbanded. When the peace collapsed, the stones were moved from Kree-Lar in a failed attempt to keep pirates from stealing them; during the attack the warp drive of the stones' ship imploded, breaking and scattering the gems all over the galaxy. Some of the stones seeded the Earth system, eventually giving rise to the adventurers Moonstone, Ulysses Bloodstone, Dr. Spectrum, the Sphinx, Man-Wolf, and many others.

Over the millennia the Kree secretly kept a close eye on Earth, originally because the Sol system was near a natural space-warp access used by the Skrulls. When a band of exiled Earth Eternals raided the Kree weapons depot on Uranus, the investigating Kree slew all but one, whom they vivisected to learn he was human in origin. Intrigued, the Kree scientists conducted their own experiments on humanity, creating the sub-race later called Inhumans for use as future spies against the Kree's various interstellar foes, then left their new subjects to refine their genetic abilities over the next few centuries. The Kree left robotic Sentries on Earth to guard their hidden bases and monitor the Inhumans' progress, and set up Plan Atavus in case humans ever became a threat to the Empire.

In modern times, the Kree's militaristic society calcified into oppressive regimentation: The two races were strictly segregated in both civilian and military societies, seldom mingling even in battle. Eugenic philosophies informed most social activities, with state military academies doing the majority of child-raising. Kree society allowed little in the way of public dissent and social mobility, especially for Pink Kree, considered "half-breeds" by some "full bred" Blue Kree. Dissenters were often arrested for showing the slightest distrust towards their leaders. Occasionally, political and religious dissidents found limited freedom on distant colony worlds or deep space starships. Cold dedication to honor, duty, and battle was considered the highest of virtues, with torture and revenge almost an art form, while emotions like love, friendship, and mercy were considered base and unnatural, a "virus of the spirit" to be cauterized at all costs. While the Cotati's survival was now publicly known, identified Cotati worshipers were often put to death for sedition. The SI was all but worshiped as a god,

CLASSIC KREE MILITIA UNIFORMS

PRIVATE

LIEUTENANT

CAPTAIN

MAJOR

COLONEL

GENERAL

Art by Keith Pollard

with many private shrines built to it. The Universal Church of Truth won permission to build their temples throughout the Kree Empire due to the battle prowess of their Black Knight cadre. When Earth's Fantastic Four defeated both Sentry 459 and Accuser-Prime Ronan, the SI sent the starship Helion to Earth to conduct a feasibility study for a future invasion. Military hero Captain Mar-Vell was sent undercover to study humanity's defenses, but he grew to love the Earth instead and defected, eventually becoming Earth's protector as Captain Marvel. The Supreme Science Council sent agents to conscript the Inhumans into the Kree army, but the Inhuman Royal Family defeated them each time. A new skirmish in the ancient Kree-Skrull War began when Ronan the Accuser overthrew and imprisoned the SI over what he considered the SI's too-liberal policies encouraging Kree marriages with non-Kree, and the increased social acceptance of the resulting progeny. The Super-Skrull (Kl'rt) kidnapped Mar-Vell and brought him to the Skrull homeworld, Tarnax IV, to force him to build an Omni-Wave Projector as an ultimate death ray. Both Kree and Skrull armies were stopped cold when the SI unleashed fellow prisoner Rick Jones' latent psychic powers (the Destiny Force) to freeze every soldier in their tracks, allowing the SI to depose Ronan. Later, Captain Marvel and Inhuman King Black Bolt stopped the Council from starting the dreaded War of Three Galaxies — the Greater Magellanic Cloud, Andromeda, and Milky Way galaxies — by revealing the main instigator for the war as a disguised Skrull agent, who intended to direct the Kree into a Skrull trap. Meanwhile, Earth became a secret refuge for dissident Kree, with some expatriates settling in Raven's Perch, New Jersey, some members of the Free Kree Liberation Army basing themselves in the London music scene, and a sect settling in Brea, California, to watch over Tzu-Zana (later Ultragirl), a girl prophesized as the Universal Unifier, destined to remake all Kree races equal in a new golden age of Kreekind.

When the Skrulls lost Empress R'Kill to Galactus, and later their shape-changing powers due to the machinations of the would-be Emperor Zabyk, they feared that the Kree would sweep over them like a vengeful tide, so one of the remaining would-be rulers, Kylor, decided to preemptively attack the Kree before they learned of the Skrull's lost shape-changing abilities, re-igniting the war once more. The Supreme Intelligence tried to absorb the Silver Surfer into his collective mind when the Surfer tried to keep Earth and his native Zenn-La out of this latest conflict, but the Surfer escaped, driving the SI temporarily insane in the process. The new Supreme Leader, Nenora (actually Skrull

RUUL (ORIGINAL APPEARANCE)

Art by John Romita Jr.

Agent K6@, who had killed and replaced the real Nenora), led the Kree to many impressive victories until the Surfer and acting Skrull Empress S'Byll were tipped off by the Cotati to Nenora's true nature. S'Byll and the Surfer sneaked onto Hala, where they confronted Nenora and publicly restored her shape-shifting power, stunning the Kree, who agreed to a temporary truce. Schemes of both the Cotati and another Skrull posing as the Elder of the Universe called Contemplator placed hapless alien Clumsy Foulup in charge of the Kree until a plot by Generals Ael-Dan and Dar-Benn killed him, leaving them joint rulers of the Empire.

The now-recovered SI conceived a monstrous plan to prod the Kree out of their so-called evolutionary dead end. It secretly implanted the idea of creating a Nega-Bomb large enough to destroy an interstellar empire in the minds of the rival Shi'ar Imperium rulers, and mentally intensified the prejudices of the ruling Kree, Shi'ar, and Skrull leaders to the point of inciting war. Shi'ar Majestrix Lilandra and Kree rulers Ael-Dann and Dar-Benn were manipulated into a race to gather the necessary pieces to build the bomb. The Shi'ar ultimately acquired the energy core of a Psyche-Magnitron, the now-deceased Captain Marvel's Nega-Bands, and the secret of the Omni-Wave Projector, then delivered the finished bomb to Skrull soldiers to deploy in the center of the Kree's galaxy. Despite the best efforts of Earth's Avengers (dragged into the war because two of the bomb's components were in the Sol system) the bomb exploded, killing 98% of the Kree population and many other subject races as well. The SI secretly smuggled its mind to a nearby mercenary spaceship while manipulating the Avenger Black Knight (Dane Whitman) into killing its original body. Lilandra's sister, Deathbird, became Viceroy of the Kree territories, ruling with an iron hand and aided by the indentured Kree super-team, Starforce. Many rebel groups sprang up, with some, like the Kree Consolidated Peace Battalion, fighting to return the military back to power, while others, like the Kree Resistance Front, sought to create a society free from both the Shi'ar and the old ways. A few Kree, such as Ronan, pretended to serve Shi'ar interests while secretly undermining them, while the pirate band Starjammers (Corsair, Raza, Ch'od, Hepzibah, Keeyah) smuggled several groups of refugees to the anarchist Clench world Standing Still. Several Kree officers banded together under Admiral Galen-Kor to unleash a much smaller Nega-Bomb on Earth, but the Avengers' Sersi stopped the bomb before it did much damage. However, a later attack by the Starstealth Cadre on the Avengers' Vision and Wonder Man (Simon Williams) did succeed in temporarily killing Wonder Man, who they blamed along with the Vision for actually setting off the bomb. A ragtag armada of Kree refugees led by General Maston-Dar came to the Inhuman city of Attilan (then located in the Blue Area of the Moon) to beg asylum, but were ultimately refused when Maston-Dar's attempt to keep the then-deposed Black Bolt from objecting backfired.

After tricking Rick Jones into restoring its full powers, the Supreme Intelligence contacted Galen-Kor and his band to rescue it from its hiding place in the New York City sewers. Renaming themselves the Lunatic Legion, Galen-Kor's forces sought to turn the Earth's population into neo-Kree slaves using an Omni-Wave Projector modified with the Inhumans' mutating Terrigen Mists, not realizing that this plan went against the SI's ultimate plans for humans. The SI secretly aided the Avengers against the Legion, who

RUUL, LATER APPEARANCE

Art by Scott Kolins

were absorbed into the Projector and seemingly killed when it exploded. While aiding the time traveler Kang and a cross-time group of Avengers against Immortus, the SI gained possession of the time-warping Forever Crystal, secretly using it to accelerate the evolution of the now-mutable Kree into what they would have eventually become centuries later. Taking the fake name "Ruul," the super-evolved Kree convinced the Intergalactic Council to turn Earth into a prison planet for the worst interstellar criminals, in a bid to keep Earth's heroes busy while Ronan absorbed the essence of Ego the Living Planet into himself. Ronan almost succeeded before Quasar (Wendell Vaughn) diverted Ego's essence into himself instead. The Kree then concentrated on reconstructing their lost empire, and evolving those of their number who were initially out of range of the Crystal's transformation wave, with some becoming members of the Nu-Elite ruling class, with Fiyero House (long since degenerated into a merchant house) once more the new rulers of the Empire.

To solidify their regained status and enact political reforms they believed were necessary, the Fiyero leaders secretly bribed Rigellian Tana Nile to falsely accuse Ronan of plotting to give Skrull Baroness S'bak control over several Kree borderworlds, exiling the former Accuser and eliminating a major obstacle to their plans. When the SI protested, the Fiyeros disabled it by quietly giving it a lobotomy, fearing the public reaction if they killed it outright. When invading Negative Zone ruler Annihilus' army reached Kree space, the Fiyeros publicly allied with surviving Nova Centurion Richard Rider's United Front to fight the invaders, but secretly contracted with one of Annihilus' Seekers, Ravenous, to not significantly oppose Annihilus due to the Fiyeros' belief that they couldn't win against him, and sent the Kree army into battle without an overall battle strategy to guide their actions. The Fiyeros placed their family members in key strategic military positions to ensure that the lack of plan was enforced, leading to massive casualties in the military. When UF ally Ronan confronted the Fiyero representatives stationed on the front over their lack of strategy, the Fiyeros arrogantly disregarded his advice and threatened to pull out of the alliance. They then tried to arrest Ronan, who angrily killed them instead. When an attack by Annihilus' Centurions (the Negative Zone's rough equivalent to the Shi'ar Imperial Guard) and an enslaved Galactus broke the United Front for good, Ronan and new UF allies Super-Skrull and the robotic Praxagora went to Hala to free the Kree from Fiyero leadership, and discovered them under the protection of Ravenous and the Centurions. Angered by this betrayal of Kree interests, Ronan attacked and delivered his judgment against Ravenous by breaking his head open. The Centurions then teleported to their ships and left the Fiyero leaders to their fate. Shocked when the Kree soldiers present defected to Ronan's side, the Fiyeros tried to excuse their actions to Ronan, claiming that their agreement with Annihilus was the only way to save the Empire, but Ronan was not moved by the argument and executed them.

After granting the SI a mercy killing, Ronan found himself publicly proclaimed the new leader of the Empire. When Ravenous' ships began firing on Hala from orbit, Ronan led the military counterattack by launching several city blocks of Kree-Lar city at the fleet, then had the soldiers occupying the buildings emerge en masse to blast away at the exposed ships, driving the fleet from Hala. After being forced to sign a treaty ceding the entirety of the Skrull Empire and parts of the Kree Empire (including capital planet Kree-Lar) to a now-recovered Ravenous in order to buy time to rebuild the Kree, Emperor Ronan allied with the Galadorian

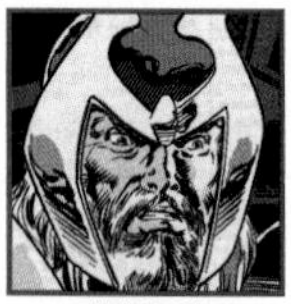

AEL-DAN
Kree leader (deceased)
Silver Surfer #53 (1991)

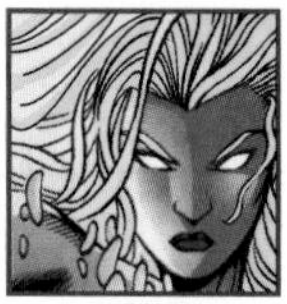

AJES'HA
Chosen Eight of Fate
Thunderbolts Annual 2000

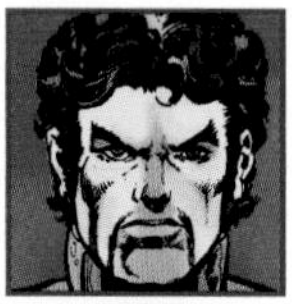

ARIDES
(Shatterstar)
Super-Kree Agent
Inhumans #3 (1975)

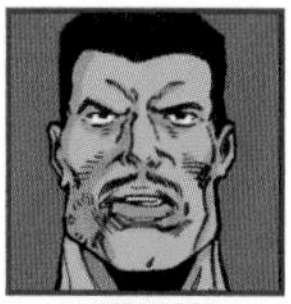

ATT-LASS (CAPTAIN ATLAS)
Captain, Kree Military;
Starforce
Quasar #9 (1990)

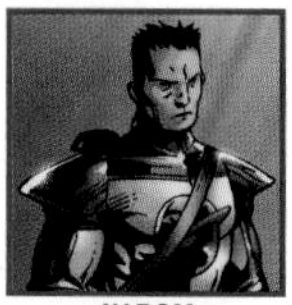

AV-ROM
Captain, Kree Military
Young Avengers #10 (2006)

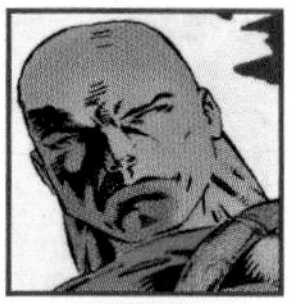

BAV-TEK
Kree Resistance Front
Captain Marvel #4 (1996)

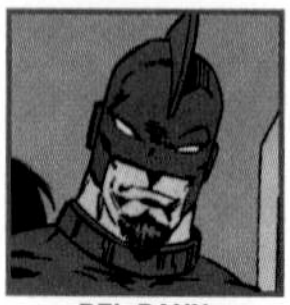

BEL-DANN
General, Kree Military;
member, Kree Consolidated Peace Battalion
X-Men #137 (1976)

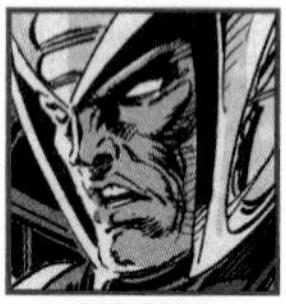

DAR-BENN
Kree leader (deceased)
Silver Surfer #53 (1991)

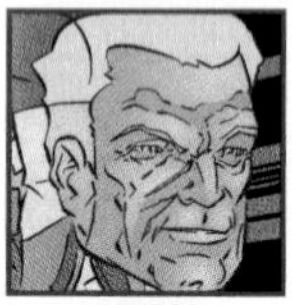

DEVROS
Grand Admiral, Kree Military;
so-called 'Brood King'
(deceased)
Untold Tales of Captain Marvel #2 (1997)

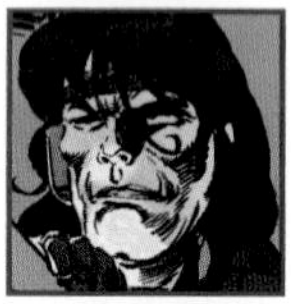

DYLON-CIR
Kree Military Lieutenant;
Lunatic Legion
Avengers #364 (1993)

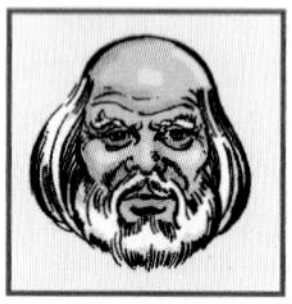

FALZON
Scientist
Inhumans #3 (1975)

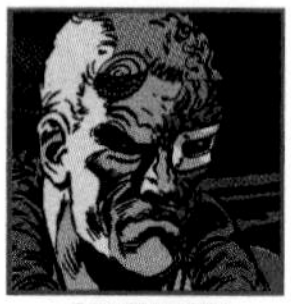

GALEN-KOR
Admiral, Kree Military;
leader of Lunatic Legion
(deceased)
Avengers #350 (1992)

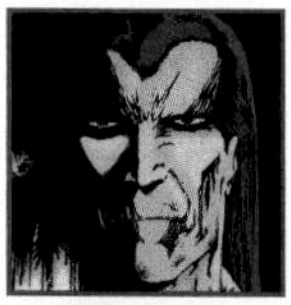

KALUM-LO
Major, Kree Military;
leader of the Starstealth
Force Works #1 (1994)

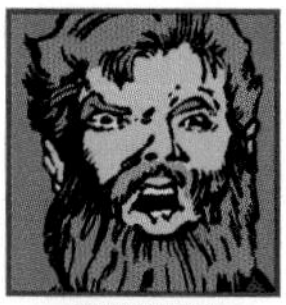

KAR-SAGG
Cyber-geneticist
Silver Surfer #29 (1989)

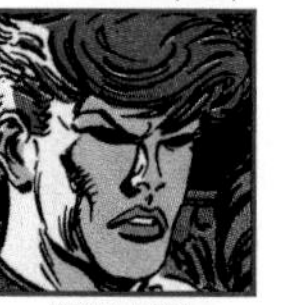

KONA-LOR
Lieutenant, Kree Military;
Lunatic Legion
Avengers #364 (1993)

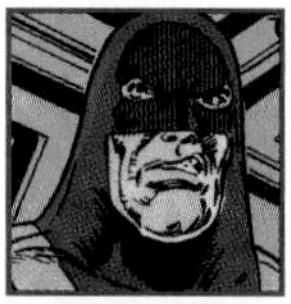

KORATH-THAK
(Korath the Pursuer)
Cyber-geneticist,
member of Starforce
Quasar #32 (1992)

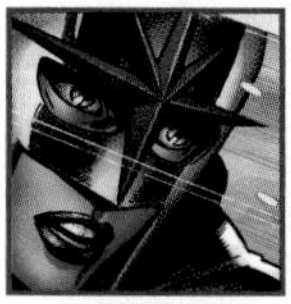

KO-REL
Military medic, Nova Centurion 0001
(deceased)
Nova #4 (2007)

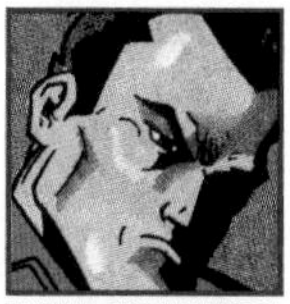

M-NELL (COMMANDO)
Kree Military Captain;
Shi'ar Imperial Guard
Imperial Guard #1 (1997)

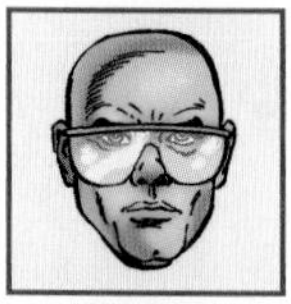

MAC-RONN
Medic
Captain Marvel #47 (1976)

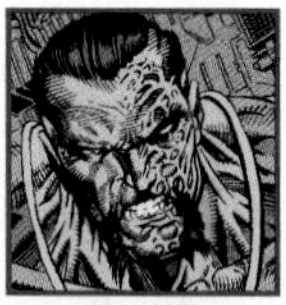

MALAKII
Aeronautics designer;
Kree Resistance Front leader
X-Men Unlimited #5 (1994)

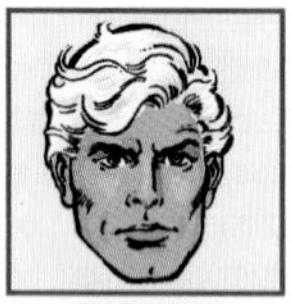

MAR-VELL
Captain, Kree Military
(deceased)
Marvel Super-Heroes #12 (1968)

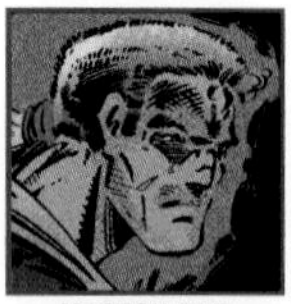

MASTON-DAR
General, Kree Military
Inhumans:
The Great Refuge #1 (1995)

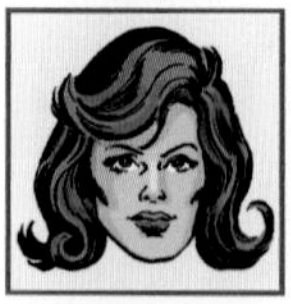

MINN-ERVA
(Dr. Minerva)
Geneticist, Starforce
Captain Marvel #49 (1977)

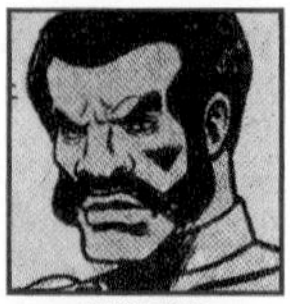

MON-TOG
Major, Kree Military;
Stationmaster,
Kree Space Station Web
Inhumans #10 (1977)

Spaceknights to use their Restitution Program's A-ware software as part of the Kree war-net to help build up their military defenses again. During special military advisor Peter Quill's (Star-Lord) demonstration of the new defenses, he and Ronan learned that the cybernetic Spaceknights had been taken over by Terran robot Ultron and the techno-organic Phalanx, who used the Kree's war-net to take control of hundreds of Sentries and fused them into their Babel Spire. Phasing the entire Kree galaxy out of sync with the rest of the universe, the Phalanx began to assimilate all inside of it to either their cause of perfect machine/organic unions (the Phalanx Selects) or as food. While various resistance groups using low-tech weapons and devices sprang up to fight the Phalanx invasion, others who worshipped the Phalanx sprang up as well, giving themselves the name "Kree-Lanx" to show their support.

Fitted with assimilation devices to make him a Select, Ronan was forced to aid the Phalanx in their conquest of the Kree until he discovered the Phalanx had captured the corpse of the SI and intended to reactivate it to use the resulting psychic echo to brainwash all the Kree to the Phalanx cause. When Ronan learned the alternative to the brainwashing was the Phalanx phasing the entire galaxy into oblivion, killing all trapped within, he finally submitted to the assimilation devices and became a Select to save his people from that fate. An assault team led by the nameless Kree Wraith (formerly Zak-Del) instead freed the SI and used the psychic echo to kill all Phalanx within range, Ronan found himself spared death due to his leadership abilities being needed by the remaining Kree to defeat the Phalanx. With the aid of Wraith, Super-Skrull, Praxagora, and resistance leader Ra-Venn, Ronan traveled to the planet Kree-Lar to access the hidden cache of Sentries there to use them to cleanse Hala's surface of

all life to rid the Kree homeworld of the invaders. Using the Wraith's Exolon swarms to Phalanx-proof the Sentries and Praxagora's ability to take over other mechanical devices, Ronan launched the Sentries towards Hala, only to have Ultron's consciousness take over Praxagora's body, knocking out Wraith and deactivating his Exolon swarms. Taking control of the Sentries and setting Praxagora up to self-destruct before leaving, Ultron used the Sentries to create a gigantic body for himself and began to rampage through downtown Kree-Lar before a recovered Wraith used his Exolon swarm to trap Ultron's consciousness in that body so Quasar (Phyla-Vell) and Adam Warlock could kill it. The Phalanx now dormant minus Ultron's leadership, and the Kree galaxy now back in phase with the rest of the universe, the Kree have concentrated on once more rebuilding their numbers and strength, though looming interstellar political troubles, including an alliance with the Inhumans, may severely test their society once again.

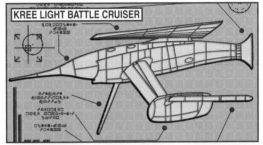
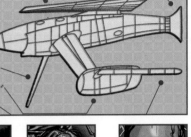

KREE LIGHT BATTLE CRUISER

Art by Eliot R. Brown

MORAG
Ancient Kree tribal leader (deceased)
Avengers #133 (1976)

NENORA
Supreme Leader, killed and replaced by Skrull Agent K6@
Silver Surfer #6 (1987)

PHAE-DOR
Head, Supreme Science Council
Inhumans #3 (1975)

PRIMUS
Leader, Underground Militia
Imperial Guard #1 (1997)

RA-VENN
Phalanx resistance leader
Annihilation: Wraith #1 (2007)

SALLEN-BEI
Keeper of Memory, planet Cyllandra (presumed deceased)
Avengers Strikefile #1 (1994)

SRO-HIMM
Admiral, Kree Military; Lunatic Legion member
Captain Marvel #37 (1975)

STAAK THE EVOLVER
Member, the Evolvers (top-ranked assassins)
Thing: Freakshow #3 (2002)

STUG-BAR
Bo'sun, Kree Military; the Starstealth
Force Works #1 (1994)

SUPREME INTELLIGENCE
Cyberorganic Ruler
Fanatstic Four #65 (1967)

TALLA-RON
First Officer to Galen-Kor, Kree Military; Lunatic Legion
Avengers #365 (1993)

TAR-RELLL
Primary Espionage Unit Captain
Silver Surfer #5 (1987)

TAR-VASH
Commander, Kree Military
Defenders #8 (2001)

TARNOK-KOL
Major, Kree Military
Inhumans: The Great Refuge #1 (1995)

TSU-ZANA
(Suzy Sherman, Ultragirl) Fashion model, super hero
Ultragirl #1 (1996)

ULTIMUS
Kree Eternal, Starforce
Wonder Man #7 (1992)

UNA
Medic, Kree Military (deceased)
Marvel Super-Heroes #12 (1968)

UNA-ROGG
Criminal exile
Captain Marvel #12 (2000)

VRON-IKKA
Major, Kree Military; espionage agent
Avengers Spotlight #25 (1989)

WRAITH
Nameless Kree, formerly Zak-Del
Annihilation: Conquest Prologue #1 (2007)

YON-ROGG
Colonel, Kree Military (deceased)
Marvel Super-Heroes #12 (1968)

ZAREK
Former Kree Imperial Minister; Lunatic Legion leader
Marvel Super-Heroes #12 (1967)

ZEN-PRAM
Kree Military Colonel (deceased)
Untold Tales of Captain Marvel #1 (1997)

ZEY-ROGG
Kree Consolidated Peace Battalion leader
Captain Marvel #2 (1996)

REAL NAME: Yon-Rogg
ALIASES: None
IDENTITY: Publicly known
OCCUPATION: Terrorist; former Kree military colonel
CITIZENSHIP: Kree Empire
PLACE OF BIRTH: Planet Hala, Greater Magellanic Cloud galaxy
KNOWN RELATIVES: Una-Rogg (daughter), Zey-Rogg (son), Hav-Rogg (grandson)
GROUP AFFILIATION: None; formerly Kree military
EDUCATION: Kree Imperial Academy
FIRST APPEARANCE: Marvel Super-Heroes #12 (1967); (Magnitron) Avengers Assemble #16 (2013)

WITH CONSTRUCTS

Art by Matteo Buffagni

HISTORY: Yon-Rogg used his Kree military rank and bribes to falsify documents stating his daughter had undergone psychic surgery routinely performed on Kree females to curb their psychic powers. As a colonel, Yon-Rogg led a mission alongside his unrequited love, the medic Una, with Captain Mar-Vell to retrieve Grand Admiral Devros from a planet held by the insectoid alien Brood. Fighting past Shi'ar and Skrull ships, the Kree crew were captured and implanted with Brood eggs. Mar-Vell, Yon-Rogg and Una survived the implantation, and Una modified a Kree Omni-Wave projector to purge the eggs. Yon-Rogg took credit for the mission and was assigned to Earth to investigate Kree Sentry robot #459's destruction by the Fantastic Four, and assess Earth's threat level. Despising Mar-Vell, partly because of Una and Mar-Vell's blossoming romance, Yon-Rogg sent him to engage Earth forces alone, despite contrary regulations, and forcibly bonded a wrist monitor to Mar-Vell to document his movements. Yon-Rogg reactivated Sentry #459 at Kennedy Space Center to fight Mar-Vell, only the first of several attempts to eliminate and discredit Mar-Vell. Suspecting Mar-Vell of growing sympathy for humans, Yon-Rogg contacted Ronan, head of the Kree Accuser Corps, to judge Mar-Vell for un-Kree activity, but Ronan's decision was neutral. In Earth orbit, Yon-Rogg sought to hide evidence of his spaceship by obliterating suspicious Kennedy security chief Carol Danvers, but Mar-Vell saved her. Yon-Rogg attacked a stray Aakon spaceship and their later vengeful attack left Una dead. Cast adrift by Yon-Rogg in deep space, Mar-Vell eventually returned to Hala, where the Supreme Intelligence augmented his powers. Mar-Vell soon after became trapped in the antimatter Negative Zone.

On Earth, the Supreme Intelligence influenced Rick Jones to don the

Kree Nega-Bands, which led to Mar-Vell and Jones sharing time between their universe and the Negative Zone. Yon-Rogg uncovered the outlawed Kree Psyche-Magnitron device, which could instantly generate any Kree science or weaponry. He kidnapped Danvers, Mar-Vell's new paramour, to trap Mar-Vell, and attempted to kill Rick Jones to strand Mar-Vell in the Negative Zone. But Mar-Vell returned to confront Yon-Rogg, who merged with the Psyche-Magnitron to form a Kree Mandroid to attack. Its blasts damaged the device and injured Danvers. Mar-Vell saved Danvers when the Psyche-Magnitron exploded, but Yon-Rogg was seemingly killed in the explosion, the blast scattering him across time and space; the blast also empowered Danvers, imbuing her with Kree physiology with a small third brain lobe; she became Ms. Marvel and later Captain Marvel. Yon-Rogg's two children blamed Mar-Vell (who had died from cancer) for their father's seeming death and later targeted Mar-Vell's son, Genis-Vell. Later, Yon-Rogg slowly re-formed his body through sheer force of will, and having gained the Psyche-Magnitron's power of weapon generation, each recovered fragment of the device increased his powers. The tiny piece of shrapnel from the Psyche-Magnitron inside Captain Marvel (Danvers)'s head enabled Yon-Rogg to access her memories, but also caused a lesion to grow on her third brain lobe and affected her powers; further use of her Kree-based powers threatened her brain. To humiliate Danvers, Yon-Rogg generated constructs of her past opponents, such as dinosaurs, the super-powered Grapplers wrestlers, Brood and Deathbird (Cal'syee Neramani). Aided by fellow Avengers, Danvers defeated them, while Yon-Rogg stole a shard of the device Danvers had located and hidden. Seeking extraction, Yon-Rogg contacted the Kree capital, Kree-Lar, and offered Danvers and Earth, but was dismissed as outdated and irrelevant. Yon-Rogg used the shard to transform into Magnitron and activated Kree Sentries to create a giant circuit to remake Earth as a second Hala. Magnitron eventually cannibalized his constructs to further amplify his energy and forge a new Kree-Lar city over New York. He generated Kree Mandroids to stop the Avengers while he tried to use the final fragment in Danvers' head to complete the circuit, but Danvers flew up beyond Earth's atmosphere where her brain hemorrhaged, severing the link with the circuit. This caused Magnitron's weaponry and constructs to deactivate. Apparently powerless, Magnitron was taken into custody. Danvers' brain eventually healed, but much of her memory was lost.

KREE UNIFORM

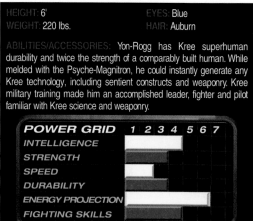

HEIGHT: 6'
WEIGHT: 220 lbs.
EYES: Blue
HAIR: Auburn

ABILITIES/ACCESSORIES: Yon-Rogg has Kree superhuman durability and twice the strength of a comparably built human. While melded with the Psyche-Magnitron, he could instantly generate any Kree technology, including sentient constructs and weaponry. Kree military training made him an accomplished leader, fighter and pilot familiar with Kree science and weaponry.

POWER GRID	1	2	3	4	5	6	7
INTELLIGENCE							
STRENGTH							
SPEED							
DURABILITY							
ENERGY PROJECTION							
FIGHTING SKILLS							

RONAN THE ACCUSER

REAL NAME: Ronan
ALIASES: Prime Accuser, Imperial Accuser, Ronan the Free, Ronan the Accused
IDENTITY: No dual identity
OCCUPATION: Supreme Public Accuser; former emperor, exile
CITIZENSHIP: Kree Empire
PLACE OF BIRTH: Planet Hala, Pama system, Greater Magellanic Cloud galaxy
KNOWN RELATIVES: Crystal (wife), Luna Amaquelin (stepdaughter), Quelin (father-in-law), Ambur (mother-in-law), Medusa (sister-in-law), Black Bolt (brother-in-law), extended family through marriage
GROUP AFFILIATION: Accuser Corps; formerly the United Front, Starforce
EDUCATION: Completed unspecified education program
FIRST APPEARANCE: Fantastic Four #65 (1967)

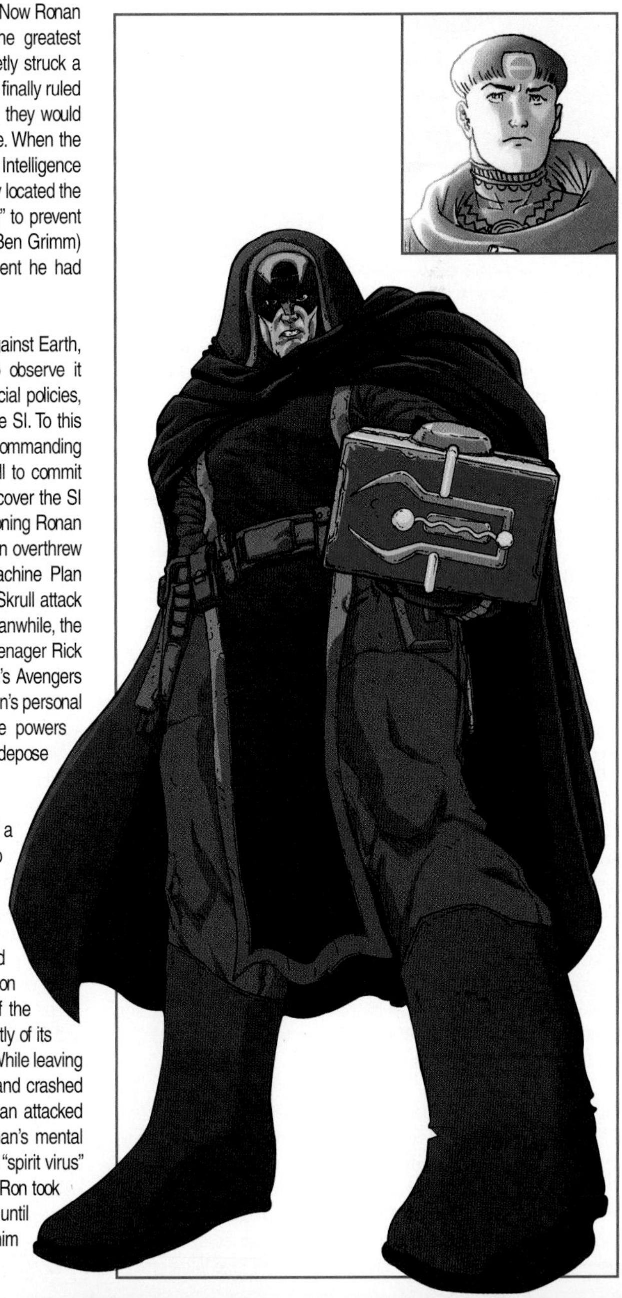

HISTORY: Born over 100 years ago into a proud old aristocratic family, Ronan was accepted into the interstellar Kree Empire's Accuser Corps upon completion of his education, becoming a living weapon of justice. Accuser Ronan strictly enforced the severe Kree penal codes on the Empire's many worlds, and on other worlds where the Kree had placed observation bases or had merely visited. He rose rapidly in the ranks by apprehending many alleged traitors, holding several planetary governorships, and leading many imperialistic and punitive military police actions, in addition to his usual duties as judge, jury and executioner of any criminals brought to his attention. At a later point during these years Ronan pursued a relationship with Una-Rogg, biracial younger daughter of a prominent non-aristocratic family. The relationship ended badly for unrevealed reasons, with the two still bitter over it years later.

After winning a major battle on the Skrullian border, Ronan was promoted to Supreme Public Accuser, third highest post in the Empire (only the Supreme Intelligence and Imperial Minister ranked above it). Now Ronan the Accuser, he personally only performed missions of the greatest importance to the Empire. Through intermediaries, he secretly struck a deal with Earth's Inhuman Prince Maximus that when Ronan finally ruled the Empire, and when Maximus finally ruled the Inhumans, they would ally, with the Inhumans ruling Earth as viceroys for the Kree. When the Fantastic Four defeated the Kree Sentry #459, the Supreme Intelligence sent Ronan to Earth to punish them personally. Ronan quickly located the Four and teleported them inside his "cone of impenetrability" to prevent outside interference from other hostile humans. The Thing (Ben Grimm) eventually forced Ronan to take the brunt of the punishment he had intended for the FF.

Humiliated, Ronan intended to launch a full-scale reprisal against Earth, but the Supreme Intelligence sent the starship Helion to observe it instead. Already disgruntled with the Intelligence's liberal racial policies, Ronan teamed with Imperial Minister Zarek to overthrow the SI. To this end they manipulated a love triangle among the Helion's commanding officers to try to force celebrated war hero Captain Mar-Vell to commit treason so they could frame him for their crimes, only to discover the SI had manipulated them all for its own ends, ultimately imprisoning Ronan and Zarek for their insurrection. Freed by his followers, Ronan overthrew the Supreme Intelligence and activated the de-evolver machine Plan Atavus on Earth, only to have his revenge interrupted by a Skrull attack on Kree territories, renewing the ancient Kree-Skrull War. Meanwhile, the SI secretly manipulated a Kree soldier into taking human teenager Rick Jones prisoner. Ronan recognized Jones as an ally of Earth's Avengers and locked him in a cell to rethink his refusal to become Ronan's personal slave. The SI then stimulated Jones' latent Destiny Force powers to freeze both Kree and Skrull armies in their tracks and depose Ronan, whom the SI placed under its psionic control.

When Mar-Vell and Jones came to Hala to warn the SI of a Kree plot against it, the SI forced Ronan to fight the two to further its own plans for Mar-Vell. Ronan resisted the SI's control until his mind snapped. Insane, he somehow left Hala to rampage on hated Earth, only to be captured by an unknown party, contained in a restraint-cube, and placed in custody of Kree doctors Tara and Mac-Ron, who were on a separate mission to retrieve and cleanse Sentry #459 of the "virus of the spirit" they believed caused it to act independently of its programming, and which they also believed infected Ronan. While leaving Earth, the Kree's spacecraft was hit by a SHIELD missile and crashed in rural Texas, damaging the restraint-cube. Escaping, Ronan attacked Mar-Vell, who had been alerted by the two doctors of Ronan's mental deterioration. Ronan killed Tara and battled Mar-Vell until the "spirit virus" destroyed his mind, leaving Ronan in an infantile state. Mac-Ron took care of him on a Texas ranch, where Ronan slowly recovered until the SI suddenly remade his mind in its own image and sent him

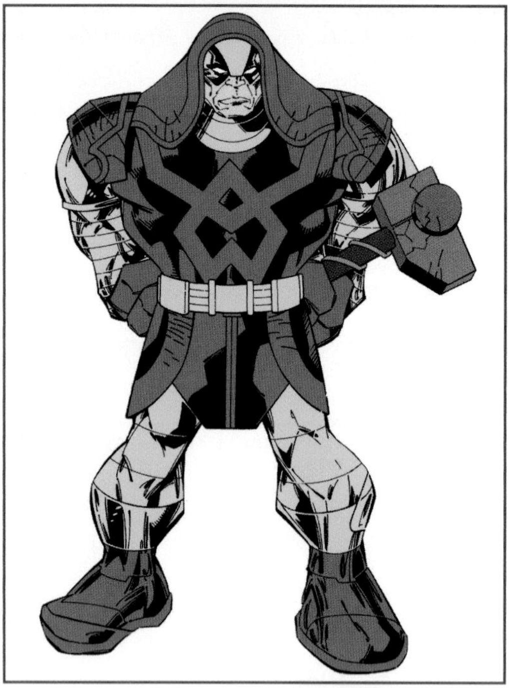
Art by Salvador Larroca

to retrieve Ms. Marvel (Carol Danvers) for its own secretive ends.

Ronan continued as Public Accuser, serving the Supreme Intelligence and later the various claimants for Kree leadership after an encounter with the Silver Surfer (Norrin Radd) left the SI mentally incapacitated. Under the orders of Supreme Leader Nenora (secretly replaced by Skrull agent K6@), Ronan confronted the Surfer over his destruction of several Kree worlds and military ships, not realizing at the time that the true culprit was a Skrull, Bartak, who was impersonating the Surfer to further the plans of one of the five main claimants to the Skrull throne. Ronan later confronted the real Silver Surfer over the planet Zenn-La (the Surfer's native world) to prove to the inhabitants that their protector couldn't defend them against the Kree's military might, but the Surfer defeated Ronan, and chased off the Kree armada with the aid of the Surfer's unwanted allies, the Skrull armada. Sometime after Nenora's true nature was exposed, a secretly recovered SI manipulated then-current Kree co-leaders Ael-Dann and Zar-Benn into renewing the Kree-Shi'ar conflict, dragging the Avengers into it as well. Ronan was unable to prevent the Shi'ar Deathbird from killing the joint leaders, though he did capture the Avengers who were present at the time. The SI sent Ronan and its superteam Starforce (Korath the Pursuer, Ultimus, Shatterax & Supremor) to Chandilar to kill Majestrix Lilandra in retaliation, but the combined efforts of her Imperial Guard and a second group of Avengers took them prisoner. When one of Lilandra's advisors was exposed as a Skrull agent, she set Ultimus free to inform the SI while keeping Ronan and the other Starforce members hostage. After the Shi'ar's Nega-Bomb destroyed the Kree Empire, a disaster secretly engineered by the SI as a means of jumpstarting long-stagnant Kree genetic evolution, the Shi'ar took over the Kree's territory and Starforce was conscripted as the new Viceroy of Deathbird's guards. Though he initially escaped, Ronan was soon recaptured, pretending to aid Shi'ar interests while plotting their downfall.

During a mission involving deported Kree criminals, Ronan captured the FF's Invisible Woman (Sue Richards) and forced her to help break into the Watcher Uatu's lunar home to steal the Universal Power Core of a Psyche-Magnetron unit; though the FF and Iron Man (Tony Stark) forced him to leave without the device, Ronan recorded the device's designs for later re-creation. After using the Inhumans in an unsuccessful attempt to assassinate Lilandra, Ronan became one of the first Kree to be evolved by the SI's use of the time-warping Forever Crystal into the adaptable "Ruul." Initially concealing their Kree identity, the Ruul convinced the Intergalactic Council to take action against Earth as a danger to galactic peace. The Council turned the planet into a penal institution under Ronan's control, not realizing until too late that Ronan was part of the SI's plot to use Ego the Living Planet to devour Earth and siphon its power into itself and all Kree within range. The plan was ultimately foiled when Quasar (Wendell Vaughn) absorbed Ego into himself, though the Ruul still managed to retake much of the Kree Empire's former territory in a series of simultaneous surprise attacks. Ronan once more became Supreme Public Accuser under the Supreme Intelligence's rule, transforming those Kree initially unaffected by the Forever Crystal into "Ruul."

A cadre of so-called Nu-Elite Kree, the House of Fiyero, subsequently took over rulership of the Kree Empire. To consolidate their power, one House member bribed Rigellian dissident Tana Nile into falsely accusing Ronan of colluding with Skrull Baron S'Bak to overthrow Fiyero House and allowing parts of the Kree Empire to be placed under S'Bak's control. Exiled from the Empire he had faithfully served, Ronan traced Nile to the backwater planet Godthab Omega, where he was reunited with his old friend Korath, also exiled from the Empire for aiding the Shi'ar years earlier. Ronan was secretly influenced by unhinged world-shaper Glorian into a battle with the super-assassin Gamora, so Glorian could use the energy from their battle to reshape the planet into a paradise to spite his former mentor, the Shaper of Worlds. Pushed to the seldom-reached upper limits of his powers, Ronan exulted in the combat until his urge to clear his name overcame his battle lust and he left the fight to find Glorian in the spaceport town Abyss. Ronan and Korath arrived just as Negative Zone ruler Annihilus' Annihilation Wave hit the planet. Ronan and Gamora joined forces to fight the invading alien insectoids and to confront Glorian, who was catatonic after the forced undoing of his "masterpiece" world. Finally confronting Nile on her deathbed, Ronan confirmed the Fiyeros' treachery but was unable to learn which Fiyero had bribed her before she died.

Ronan joined other cosmic-powered beings in the United Front alliance against Annihilus, becoming a trusted advisor of UF leader Nova (Richard Rider), only known survivor of the Xandarian Nova Corps. House Fiyero sent the Kree army to aid the UF, but unknown to the UF leadership, the Fiyeros had secretly lobotomized the Supreme Intelligence to secure their rule, and made a deal with Annihilus to not seriously oppose his army in return for trade arrangements in his new order. Representatives of the Fiyeros tried unsuccessfully to get Nova to hand Ronan over to their justice; they then tried to kill Ronan, who killed them instead. Distressed by the Kree's army deliberate lack of a battle plan and the inexplicable silence of the SI, Ronan tried to convince Nova to lend him some troops to overthrow House Fiyero, but they were interrupted by the arrival of Negative Zone robot Praxagora, who had brought the seemingly dead body of Super-Skrull (Kl'rt) with her to the front line. Shortly thereafter, the UF was attacked by Annihilus' head Seeker, Ravenous, and Annihilus' elite guard, the Centurions. Energies from a battle between Ronan, Ravenous and Galactus' former herald Firelord somehow revitalized Super-Skrull, who joined with the UF just long enough to help them escape Annihilus' newest super-weapon, which drew destructive energies from an imprisoned Galactus. With the United Front officially broken, Ronan grudgingly accepted Super-Skrull and Praxagora's aid in his quest to overthrow House Fiyero. On Hala, Ronan discovered the Fiyeros' deal with Annihilus, and once more faced Ravenous and the Centurions, with Ronan breaking his universal weapon on Ravenous' head before the Centurions teleported back to their ships. Ronan executed the Fiyero leaders before seeking out the SI. Learning that the SI's condition was irreversible, Ronan sadly granted it a mercy kill before formally taking the leadership of the Kree Empire, dealing a recovered Ravenous a crushing defeat by launching sections of Kree-Lar city filled with soldiers at Ravenous' fleet and using them to drive Ravenous from Hala's skies.

After Annihilus' death at the hands of Nova, Ronan reluctantly signed an armistice treaty with Ravenous, ceding much of the Kree Empire (including former capital planet Kree-Lar) to him in order to buy time to rebuild the depleted Kree ranks; however, when former UF ally Peter Quill (aka Star-Lord) rebuilt the Kree's warnet using Galadorian Spaceknight software, he unwittingly gave the techno-organic Phalanx the means to conquer the Kree Empire within hours. Led by Terran robot Ultron, the Phalanx sealed off Kree space by building a modified Babel Spire and phasing the Kree galaxy out of sync with the rest of the universe while they converted everyone within to low level Phalanx, with the "expendables" further processed into food, and a few joining their elite Select ranks. Outfitted with Phalanx converter technology, Ronan resisted assimilation even while obeying Phalanx orders to learn the secrets of a Nameless Kree whom he dubbed the Wraith (the former Zak-Del), whose alien parasitic swarm, the Exolon, could strike deadly fear into the Phalanx themselves. When a horrified Ronan learned the Phalanx intended to use the SI's corpse as a weapon to send a psychic order to the Kree to willingly assimilate with them, and that the Phalanx were willing to phase the Kree's galaxy to oblivion if the Kree continued to refuse, Ronan unhappily surrendered, becoming a Select. When Wraith instead used the SI's powers to augment his own Exolon fear powers to slay every Phalanx within range, Ronan found himself the only one spared. Humiliated by his surrender, Ronan tried to get Wraith to kill him, but Wraith told him that the Kree needed Ronan's leadership more than he needed to purge his humiliation by dying. Recovering, Ronan led a strike team made up of Wraith, Super-Skrull, Praxagora and resistance leader Ra-Venn to Kree-Lar, where he intended to activate a cache of 15,000 Kree Sentries hidden in an underground bunker to destroy Hala and free the Kree of Phalanx infection. Restraining Ravenous to keep him out of their way, Ronan had Wraith coat the Sentries with his Exolon parasites to keep them from being infected by the Phalanx, then had Praxagora put them under her direct control. Arriving on Hala, Ronan ordered the purge to continue despite the presence of Nova and several other cosmic-powered warriors fighting Ultron; however, Ultron took over Praxagora's body and used it to take over the Sentries before setting Praxagora to self-destruct and leaving. Surviving the resultant explosion via Super-Skrull's force fields, Ronan, Ra-Venn and Wraith were horrified to find Ultron had used the Sentries to create a gigantic body for himself. Seeing the cosmic warrior Adam Warlock empower Quasar (Phyla-Vell) to destroy Ultron, Ronan had Wraith use his Exolons to trap Ultron in his gigantic body to keep him from transferring his mind into anther host body when Quasar struck the killing blow.

After the Kree galaxy was re-synchronized with the rest of the universe, Ronan, once more the emperor, resumed the task of rebuilding the Empire. He allowed the outlawed ancient Priests of Pama religious order to openly operate in the Empire to help the needy with their medical and food supplies. He forged an alliance with Negative Zone ruler Blastaar to support his rule of that dimension and keep it from invading the positive universe anytime soon. Ronan had the Babel Spire rebuilt to use its shield to protect the weakened Empire from space-based enemies. He also rooted out Skrull agents sent to Hala to prevent the Kree from interfering with the Skrull invasion of Earth. Contacted by Inhuman Queen Medusa for aid in freeing her husband Black Bolt from the same group of Skrulls, Ronan agreed to a new alliance between their peoples, his price being that Medusa's sister Crystal would become his wife. Medusa agreed, and Ronan lent his resources to help locate Black Bolt. Once freed from his captivity, Black Bolt decided it was time for the Inhumans to take a more proactive role in the universe to protect themselves, starting with the Kree race, which created them thousands of years ago, and challenged Ronan for his throne. Seeing a chance for the Kree's genetic revival in the Inhumans' rule, Ronan allowed Black Bolt to take his throne in exchange for the Inhumans using their mutation-inducing Terrigen Mists to uplift the Kree once more and give his then-moribund race a new lease on life; however, during Ronan's wedding ceremony the Shi'ar Majestrator Vulcan (Gabriel Summers) ordered the Shi'ar Imperial Guard to slaughter the guests as a first step to conquering the Kree Empire. Seriously injured in the resultant battle, Ronan was forced to watch the war between Vulcan and Black Bolt from his hospital bed with his new wife Crystal keeping him updated on events, though news of the Uplift program's apparent failures may dampen his spirits.

| HEIGHT: 7'5" | EYES: Blue |
| WEIGHT: 480 lbs. | HAIR: Bald (formerly brown) |

ABILITIES/ACCESSORIES: A virtually indestructible cyborg, Ronan has superhuman strength (lifting 10 tons without armor or roughly 60 tons with armor), though he seldom uses his strength in battle, preferring to use his universal weapon instead. Ronan can fire various beams from his eyes, including electromagnetic pulses and intensifier rays. As a "Ruul" Kree, Ronan can adapt his body to survive any hostile environment, though he has not shown that ability for some time. His armor can generate electrical shocks and cryogenically freeze a selected subject. Ronan's main weapon (roughly translated into English as "cosmi-rod" or universal weapon) can tap cosmic energy at the mental command of its wielder for various effects: Creating highly impenetrable "cones," auras of negativism to render himself invisible to both sight and mechanical sensors, matter rearrangement and transmutation, creating wind vortexes, generating temporal displacement bubbles and hard vacuums, and discharging energy blasts, among other feats. If his cosmi-rod is somehow destroyed, he can instantaneously recreate it from components stored in his armor. The cosmi-rod can teleport its wielder through space, though its maximum jump distance is unknown. For a time it was used to funnel the energies that forcibly evolved the Kree; it is unknown if it still has access to those energies. As Supreme Public Accuser, Ronan wielded the Universal Weapon, a more powerful version of his current cosmi-rod. Ronan also carries several devices to aid his missions, such as the deadly alien parasitical "mannequin," and a device able to create localized "black hole" fields. He carries a blaster whose range is unknown. It is presumed he can somehow remove his armor to resume his original appearance.

POWER GRID	1	2	3	4	5	6	7
INTELLIGENCE							
STRENGTH							
SPEED							
DURABILITY							
ENERGY PROJECTION							
FIGHTING SKILLS							

'RONAN IS A TELEPORTER

FORMER MEMBERS: Captain Atlas (Att-Lass), Deathbird (Cal'syee Neramani), Dr. Minerva (Minn-Erva), Korath the Pursuer (Korath-Thak), Ronan the Accuser, Shatterax, Supremor, Ultimus
BASE OF OPERATIONS: Hala, Pama System, Greater Magellanic Cloud Galaxy
FIRST APPEARANCE: Avengers #346 (1992)

HISTORY: As the extraterrestrial Kree Empire waged an interstellar war against the Shi'ar, deposed Kree ruler the Supreme Intelligence conspired to reclaim the Empire, and began gathering superhuman Kree to serve him as the Starforce. To facilitate recruitment, the Supreme Intelligence activated the Supremor, an android fashioned after his own appearance which he had employed in the past for physical combat. Supremor's first recruits included the amnesiac Ultimus, imprisoned on Earth by the Deviant Tantalus for centuries, who had no memory of his origins but learned from Supremor that he was the last known surviving Kree Eternal; Shatterax, first of a new class of techno-warriors who had already helped defend the Kree against the Avengers; Korath, one of the scientists behind the cybernetic Pursuer warriors who turned the experiment upon himself when the project was abandoned by the Kree government; and the scientist Dr. Minerva and her lover, the soldier Captain Atlas, who together tried to steal the Nega Bands of Captain Mar-Vell but lost them to the Shi'ar.

The Avengers came to the Kree homeworld Hala to seek a diplomatic solution to the war because Earth's solar system had become embroiled in the conflict by the close proximity of a stargate which allowed passage between the two empires. While on Hala, the Avengers were present at the murder of Kree rulers General Ael-Dan and General Dar-Benn by Shi'ar assassin Deathbird. The Supreme Intelligence reclaimed leadership of the Empire (having secretly facilitated Deathbird's mission), and installed Starforce as an official Kree army. Starforce arrested the Avengers and Deathbird. Ronan, most prominent of the Kree judges called Accusers, was added to Starforce's ranks, and accompanied Korath, Shatterax, Supremor and Ultimus to Shi'ar space to assassinate the Shi'ar ruler Lilandra; however, another team of Avengers were in negotiations with the Shi'ar, and they helped the Shi'ar Imperial Guard defeat Starforce.

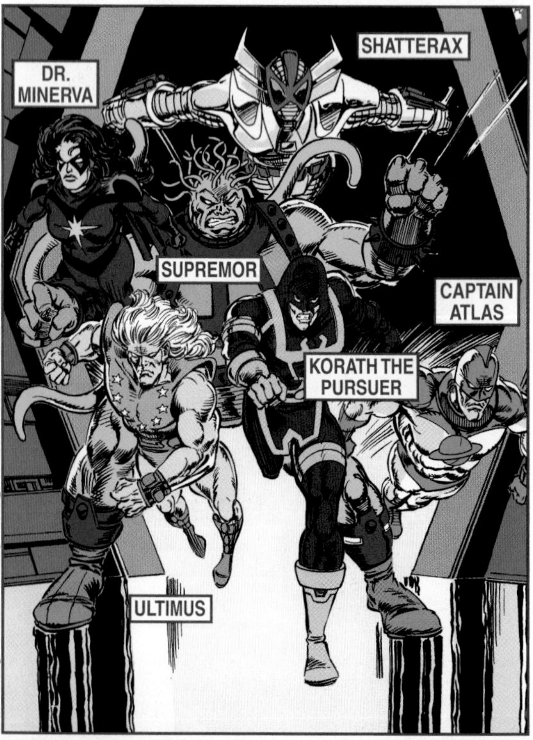
SHATTERAX
DR. MINERVA
SUPREMOR
CAPTAIN ATLAS
KORATH THE PURSUER
ULTIMUS

Art by Steve Epting

The Shi'ar had prepared a Nega-Bomb using the captured Nega Bands in an attempt to wipe out the Kree. Lilandra also intended to execute all of Starforce, but the Avengers pleaded for their lives, and when Lilandra found that longtime Kree enemies the Skrulls had infiltrated her council, she called off the executions in honor of Starforce's members. She was also persuaded to recall the Nega-Bomb, but Skrulls serving the Supreme Intelligence commandeered the weapon and detonated it in Kree space, decimating the population as part of the Supreme Intelligence's attempt at jump-starting Kree evolution. The Supreme Intelligence was seemingly killed by the Avengers in the aftermath, but he escaped thanks to his allies. Dr. Minerva and Captain Atlas seemingly committed suicide, but actually went into hiding, intending to fulfill the Supreme Intelligence's ambitions by bearing children that would benefit from their irradiation by the Nega-Bomb. Lilandra claimed Kree territory in the name of the Shi'ar, and named Deathbird her viceroy on Hala, assigning Korath, Shatterax and Ultimus as counterparts to the Imperial Guard. Ronan quit Starforce, and the Supremor was imprisoned.

When the Avengers member Quasar (Wendell Vaughn) came to Hala to offer assistance to the survivors, Deathbird and Starforce attacked him and rejected his overtures. Unable to convince them he was an ally, Quasar departed. Later, the rogue Kree admiral Galen-Kor initiated a breakout on Hala, recruiting escapees for his personal army. The Silver Surfer (Norrin Radd) aided Starforce in attempting to recapture the prisoners, but Galen-Kor and his forces escaped.

When Ultimus' old foe Tantalus rampaged through Kree space on his way to reclaiming his homeworld Armechadon, Starforce encountered Tantalus' enemies from Earth, the Underground Legion. Learning that Tantalus had escaped confinement on Earth, Ultimus insisted on Starforce aiding the Underground Legion, and they joined the battle against Tantalus on Armechadon, which ultimately resulted in Tantalus' death at the hands of his own son, Blackwulf (Pelops). Deathbird later returned to Shi'ar space to aid against the Phalanx, abandoning her post as viceroy. After the Kree regained their autonomy, the members of Starforce were branded traitors by the new ruling regimes and forced into exile. Many of them, including Korath, settled on the Kree fringeworld Godthab Omega, where sympathizers on various hubworlds kept them informed of current events in the Empire. While on Godthab Omega, several former Starforce members allegedly committed suicide over their fate; if true then which members did so remain unrevealed. Korath aided an exiled Ronan against agents of the worldshaper Glorian, only to later fall under the influence of the Ultron-influenced Phalanx as one of the Select, who alongside former Starforce member Shatterax failed to capture reborn mystic Adam Warlock. Ultron killed Korath to teach the other Selects that he would not tolerate such failures in the future.

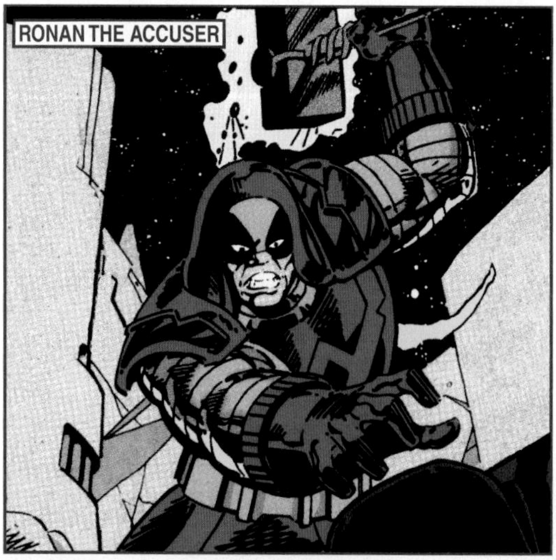
RONAN THE ACCUSER

Art by Paul Ryan

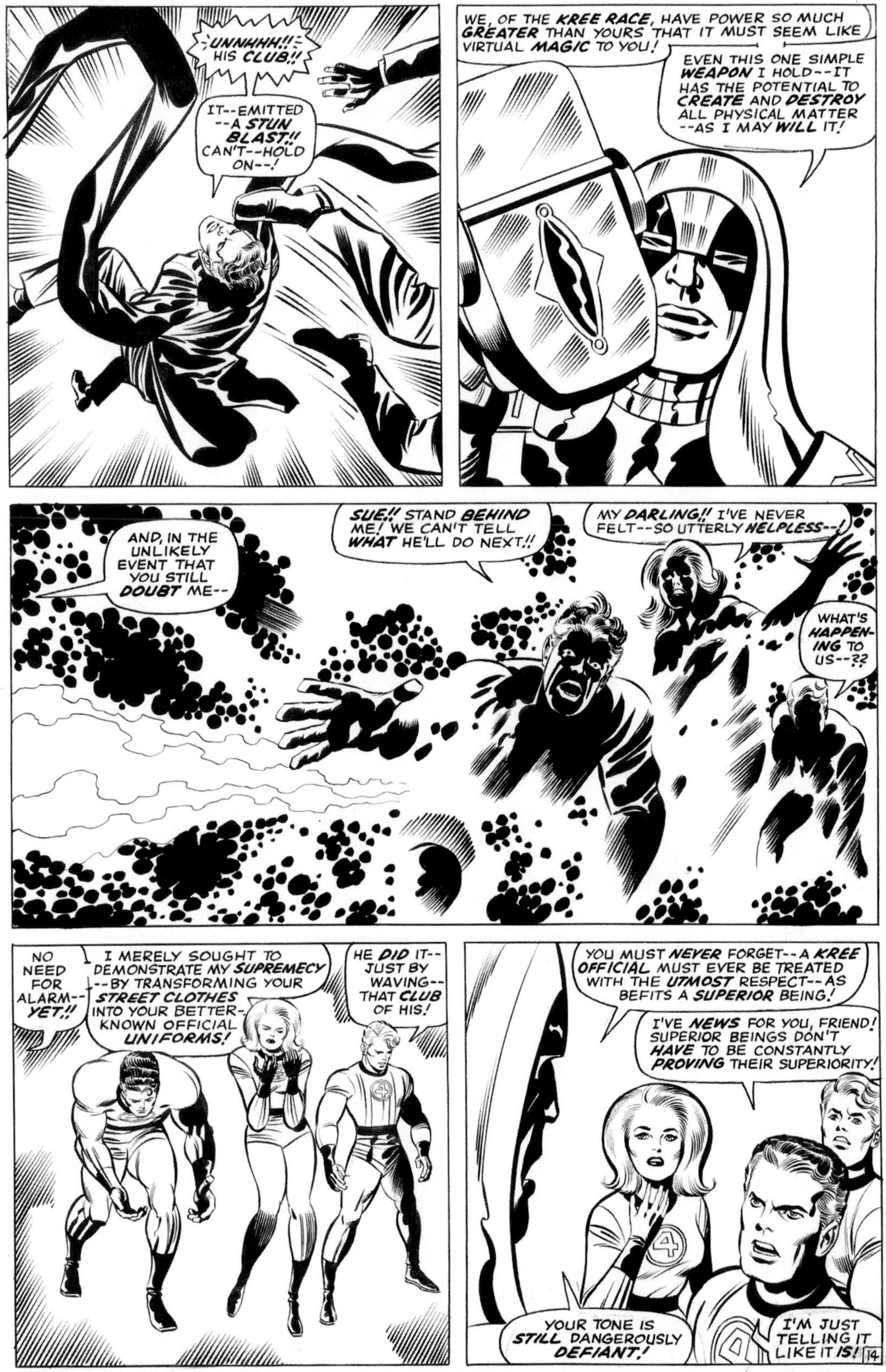
UNNHHH!! HIS CLUB!!
IT--EMITTED --A STUN BLAST!! CAN'T--HOLD ON--!
WE, OF THE KREE RACE, HAVE POWER SO MUCH GREATER THAN YOURS THAT IT MUST SEEM LIKE VIRTUAL MAGIC TO YOU!
EVEN THIS ONE SIMPLE WEAPON I HOLD--IT HAS THE POTENTIAL TO CREATE AND DESTROY ALL PHYSICAL MATTER --AS I MAY WILL IT!
AND, IN THE UNLIKELY EVENT THAT YOU STILL DOUBT ME--
SUE!! STAND BEHIND ME! WE CAN'T TELL WHAT HE'LL DO NEXT!!
MY DARLING!! I'VE NEVER FELT--SO UTTERLY HELPLESS--!
WHAT'S HAPPENING TO US--??
NO NEED FOR ALARM--YET!!
I MERELY SOUGHT TO DEMONSTRATE MY SUPREMECY --BY TRANSFORMING YOUR STREET CLOTHES INTO YOUR BETTER-KNOWN OFFICIAL UNIFORMS!
HE DID IT--JUST BY WAVING--THAT CLUB OF HIS!
YOU MUST NEVER FORGET--A KREE OFFICIAL MUST EVER BE TREATED WITH THE UTMOST RESPECT--AS BEFITS A SUPERIOR BEING!
I'VE NEWS FOR YOU, FRIEND! SUPERIOR BEINGS DON'T HAVE TO BE CONSTANTLY PROVING THEIR SUPERIORITY!
YOUR TONE IS STILL DANGEROUSLY DEFIANT!
I'M JUST TELLING IT LIKE IT IS!
14

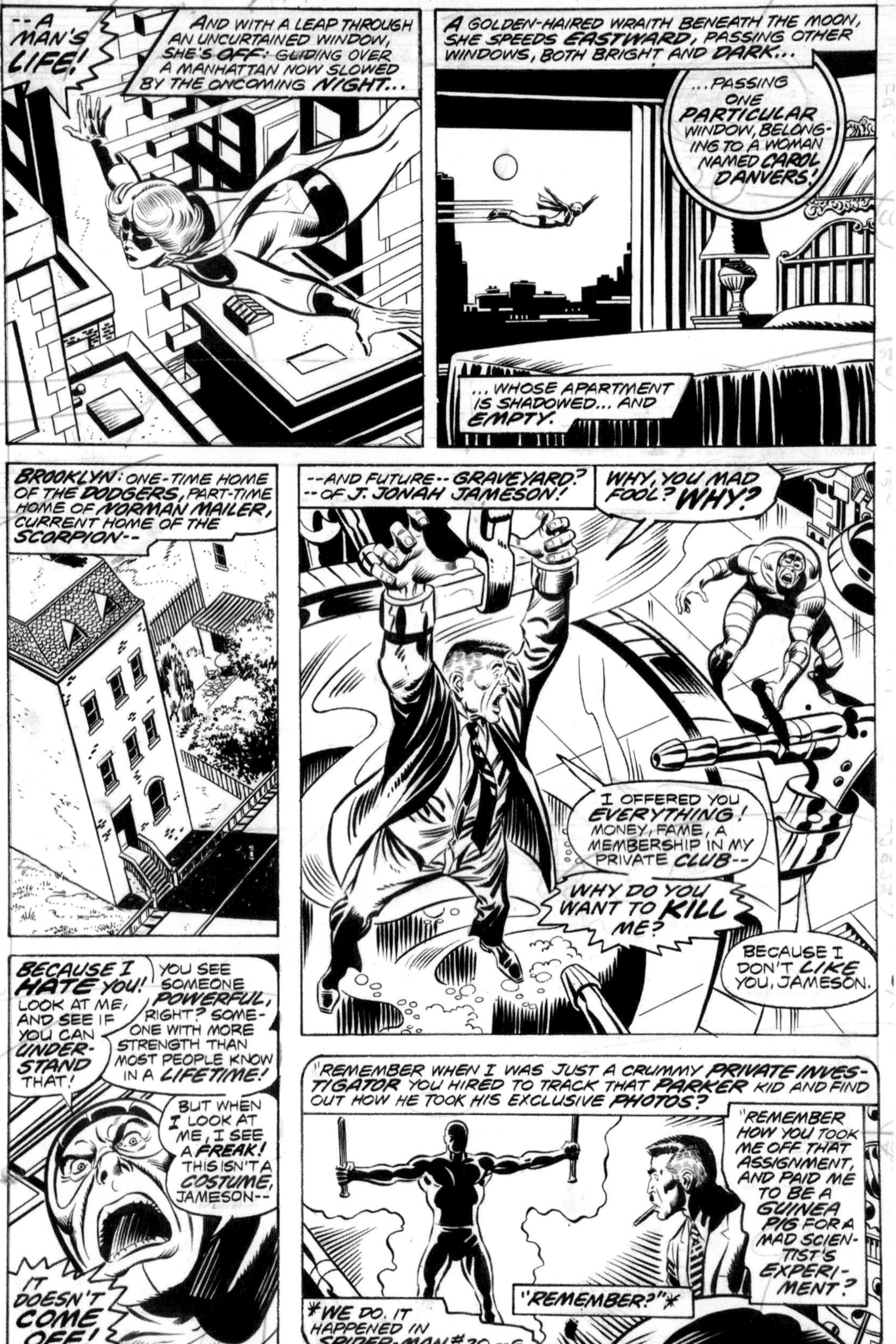
--A MAN'S LIFE!
AND WITH A LEAP THROUGH AN UNCURTAINED WINDOW, SHE'S OFF: GLIDING OVER A MANHATTAN NOW SLOWED BY THE ONCOMING NIGHT...
A GOLDEN-HAIRED WRAITH BENEATH THE MOON, SHE SPEEDS EASTWARD, PASSING OTHER WINDOWS, BOTH BRIGHT AND DARK...
...PASSING ONE PARTICULAR WINDOW, BELONGING TO A WOMAN NAMED CAROL DANVERS!
...WHOSE APARTMENT IS SHADOWED... AND EMPTY.
BROOKLYN: ONE-TIME HOME OF THE DODGERS, PART-TIME HOME OF NORMAN MAILER, CURRENT HOME OF THE SCORPION--
--AND FUTURE--GRAVEYARD? --OF J. JONAH JAMESON!
WHY, YOU MAD FOOL? WHY?
I OFFERED YOU EVERYTHING! MONEY, FAME, A MEMBERSHIP IN MY PRIVATE CLUB--
WHY DO YOU WANT TO KILL ME?
BECAUSE I DON'T LIKE YOU, JAMESON.
BECAUSE I HATE YOU! LOOK AT ME, AND SEE IF YOU CAN UNDERSTAND THAT!
YOU SEE SOMEONE POWERFUL, RIGHT? SOMEONE WITH MORE STRENGTH THAN MOST PEOPLE KNOW IN A LIFETIME!
BUT WHEN I LOOK AT ME, I SEE A FREAK! THIS ISN'T A COSTUME, JAMESON--
IT DOESN'T COME OFF!
"REMEMBER WHEN I WAS JUST A CRUMMY PRIVATE INVESTIGATOR YOU HIRED TO TRACK THAT PARKER KID AND FIND OUT HOW HE TOOK HIS EXCLUSIVE PHOTOS?
"REMEMBER HOW YOU TOOK ME OFF THAT ASSIGNMENT, AND PAID ME TO BE A GUINEA PIG FOR A MAD SCIENTIST'S EXPERIMENT?
"REMEMBER?"*
*WE DO. IT HAPPENED IN SPIDER-MAN #20. --G.

CONTINUED AFTER NEXT PAGE